W9-BIO-914

**Fourth Edition**

# RETAIL BUYING

**JAY DIAMOND,** Professor
*Department of Marketing, Retailing, and Fashion*
*Nassau Community College*

**GERALD PINTEL,** Professor Emeritus
*Nassau Community College*

REGENTS/PRENTICE HALL, Englewood Cliffs, New Jersey 07632

*Library of Congress Cataloging-in-Publication Data*
Diamond, Jay.
Retail buying / Jay Diamond, Gerald Pintel. — 4th ed.
p. cm.
Includes index.
ISBN 0-13-755497-4
1. Purchasing. I. Pintel, Gerald. II. Title.
HF5437.D46 1993
658.7'2'—dc20 92-24266
CIP

Editorial/production supervision and
interior design: **Janet M. DiBlasi**
Cover design: **Mike Fender**
Manufacturing buyer: **Ed O'Dougherty**
Prepress buyer: **Ilene Levy**
Acquisition editor: **Elizabeth Sugg**

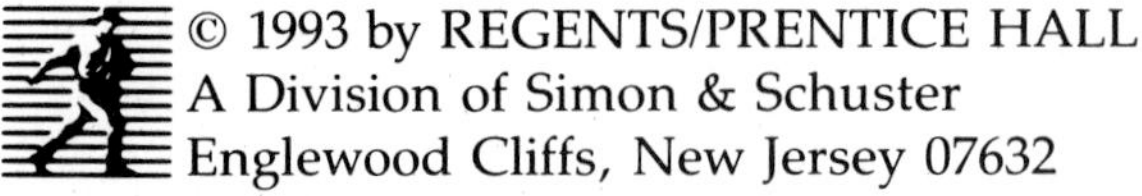


Printed in the United States of America
10 9 8 7 6 5 4 3 2 1

ISBN 0-13-755497-4

Prentice-Hall International (UK) Limited, *London*
Prentice-Hall of Australia Pty. Limited, *Sydney*
Prentice-Hall Canada Inc., *Toronto*
Prentice-Hall Hispanoamericana, S.A., *Mexico*
Prentice-Hall of India Private Limited, *New Delhi*
Prentice-Hall of Japan, Inc., *Tokyo*
Simon & Schuster Asia Pte. Ltd., *Singapore*
Editora Prentice-Hall do Brasil, Ltda., *Rio de Janeiro*

# CONTENTS

# PREFACE

As retailing heads toward the twentieth century, more and more competition is facing those in the business, and different techniques for reaching the customer, other than in-store purchasing, are becoming increasingly popular. One major factor that has contributed to these buying changes involves the significant number of women who have entered the workplace. Where females once spent many hours satisfying merchandise needs for themselves and family members in stores, the life-style change that accompanies women's new status as wage earners has resulted in fewer hours available for traditional shopping. With this significant change, store buyers have been called upon to make adjustments in their buying plans, and others have been recruited to concentrate on this new market segment, the working woman, by planning purchases for other types of retail "formats."

A new chapter, Buying for Catalogs and Home Buying Networks, has been added to the fourth edition of *Retail Buying*. It examines how catalogs and cable television operations work, and how their buyers' duties and responsibilities differ from their traditional store counterparts.

While most of the theoretical and practical concepts have been retained from earlier editions, many other changes have taken place in the retail buyer's arena. Some major retailers have closed their doors, and some of the resident buying offices either have terminated their operations or have joined forces with others to make a greater impact in the field. Each of the changes has been carefully addressed and presented in the text.

A major new feature to this edition has been the addition of "Focuses" that concentrate on specific retail operations, and their uniqueness in terms of buying, and other organizations and how they impact on the merchandise acquisition. Each story is labeled "A Retail Buying Focus" and features such organizations as The Spiegel Catalog, the QVC Network, The Sawgrass Mills, The Men's Fashion Association, The Limited, The New York Prêt, Macy's, and others. Exploration of each segment helps the reader to understand better retailing's actual approach to buying and serving the customer's needs.

Much of the illustrative artwork has been replaced with up-to-date photographs and drawings, and a significant number of additional pieces have been included.

Like the editions that have preceded this one, *Retail Buying*, fourth edition, includes Learning Objectives, Key Points in the chapter, Review Questions, and Case Problems.

Accompanying the text is a teacher's manual with solutions to the review questions and case problems and sample examinations.

# Section I

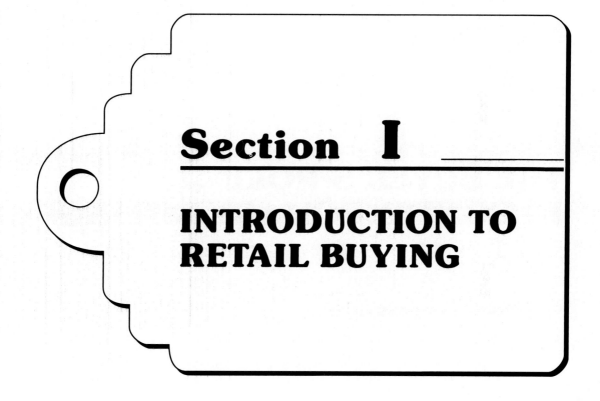

## INTRODUCTION TO RETAIL BUYING

# Chapter 1

# THE BUYER'S ROLE IN CONTEMPORARY BUYING

## LEARNING OBJECTIVES

*Upon completion of this chapter, the student should be able to:*

1. Explain the buyer's role in the following organizations: centrally managed chain, department store with branches, independent store, and franchised outlet.
2. List, define, and discuss six of a buyer's duties.
3. Discuss the importance to a buyer of maintaining a good working relationship with five of a store's other divisions.
4. List five necessary personal qualifications for a buying career and discuss the importance of each.

## INTRODUCTION

Self-satisfaction can be realized under many circumstances. An actor greeted by tumultuous applause after a successful opening night performance feels a moment of self-satisfaction. Athletes who have shattered previous world records and businesspeople who have masterminded profitable industrial deals must have felt this sense of accomplishment. Perhaps those with limited knowledge and understanding of retailing will argue when we compare this kind of elation to that which retail buyers feel when an item they have selected whisks out of the store and the customers clamor for more. Only if you have actually been a retail store buyer can you equate the feeling to other satisfactions.

Most retailers agree that the fate of their companies lies in the hands of their buyers. It is true that few retail operations could successfully function without the proper management of all activities, but without the appropriate merchandise there would be very little for executives to manage. In this chapter attention will focus on the role of the store buyer in contemporary retailing and the personal qualifications one must possess to attain such a position.

## THE BUYER'S ROLE

The notion of many that a buyer is an individual whose responsibility is limited to the selection of "exquisite and tasteful" merchandise is completely erroneous. How glamorous such a career would be! On the contrary, today's experienced buyer is a multitalented individual whose responsibilities run from managing a department to instructing a salesperson and all the decision-making processes that fall between the two.

Before exploring the various activities that usually fall within the buyer's domain, a simple definition of buying is offered, along with the factors that delineate the buyer's actual responsibilities.

*Retail buying involves the purchase of consumer goods from manufacturers and wholesalers for the express purpose of reselling them to the consumer.*

Aside from merchandise selection, the buyer in today's retail organization is very much concerned with the actual cost involved in the distribution of the goods. Retailers develop statistical information that enables the buyer to ascertain the real costs of merchandise so that a realistic retail price can be determined. Cost consciousness demands consideration of such factors as shrinkage (due to both internal and external theft), advertising costs, delivery expenses, warehousing requirements, and departmental payrolls.

The concept that the buyer is an independent entity is erroneous. No matter how important the role the buyer plays, he or she is an integral part of a merchandising team and an even larger group of managerial personnel who perform a multitude of functions. Those functions the buyer performs vary from company to company. Not every store has the same requirements. The buyer's activities are determined by a number of important factors.

## Factors That Determine the Scope of the Buyer's Activities

### *Company Organizational Structure*

In actual practice it is virtually impossible to classify accurately retail operations according to organizational structure because wide variety makes definition impossible. There are basically three major categories under which retailers operate their businesses: the single independent unit typical of the small retailer, the large department and specialty stores with branches, and the chain organizations, which generally function under a system of central management. Since these various arrangements dictate somewhat different assignment for their buyers, separate chapters will be devoted to exploring and explaining their significance. For the purpose of introduction and clarification, the three structures, and how buyers are affected in each, are presented briefly now.

**Central management of chains.** When a retail organization has several units (sometimes the numbers run into the thousands) and elects to manage these units from a central point, it is technically operating under the central management structure. This practice is becoming increasingly more popular. Under such a system, buyers as well as other managerial executives function from central headquarters or offices. The buyer, who is our major concern in this book, has little if any store contact, but rather confines his or her activities to purchasing. Management of salespeople, scheduling, inventory control, and so forth are the responsibilities of the store managers. Companies such as Sears, J. C. Penney, Merry-Go-Round, Contempo Casuals, featured in Fig. 1-1, each with an enormous number of units, operate in this fashion.

**Department and specialty stores with branches.** The traditional practice, still in use, of department stores is to operate in a manner such that buyers are responsible not only for the purchase of merchandise for the parent and branch stores but also for the management of their department's selling floors. These buyers have the main store as their base operation but regularly visit branches. Under this form of organization, the buyer's responsibilities include activities that central purchasers do not perform. These buyers are responsible for the sales their departments produce and the personnel expenses of the department, as well as actual purchasing.

In many of these organizations the buyer still has authority over sales personnel, but there is considerable movement toward separating buying and selling activities. With this system, buyers relinquish the responsibility for selling. The selling function is placed under the authority of the store management di-

**FIGURE 1-1.** Contempo Casuals, division of Neiman-Marcus, operates units in malls throughout the United States. *Courtesy:* Space Design International.

vision, with the department manager in charge of specific sales staffs. A disadvantage of this arrangement is the possible interruption of customer feedback via sales personnel. Since the buyer is no longer the salespeoples' boss, there might not be the continuity of information flow generated through the more traditional practice of buyer and sales personnel in the same division. There is also the difficulty of assigning the responsibility for poor volume. Is it the fault of the goods, or the salespeople? If the buyer is responsible for buying and selling, the responsibility is the buyer's, no matter which area is at fault.

**Independent stores.** Although retailing is big business today, thousands of entrepreneurs across the nation successfully operate individual stores. Their importance to retailing becomes more obvious as we realize how many independent resident buying offices (businesses organized to aid small retailers) are in operation. Unlike buyers engaged in chain and department store purchasing, the small store buyer has a multitude of responsibilities. Lacking the assistance and specialization available to the previously mentioned buyers, the independent purchaser is often the store's owner or manager. Duties such as purchasing, selling, promotion planning, and customer servicing are commonplace for this buyer. You need only walk down your town's main street to see the number of stores that are independently organized. They sell such products as men's wear, toys, groceries, furniture, shoes, and jewelry.

**Franchised operations.** Before one can comprehend the buyer's role in a franchise company, an understanding of franchising is imperative. As defined by the Small Business Administration, "A franchise contract is a legal agreement to conduct a given business in accordance with prescribed operating methods, financing systems, territorial domains, and commission fees." Under such an arrangement the franchisees frequently receive their merchandise from the franchiser. Sometimes the franchisees must purchase minimum amounts, sell at prescribed prices, and the like. Buyers for franchised organizations have no "store" responsibility. Their function is to provide merchandise for the franchisees. Store management is left to each franchisee.

Until recently, franchising was predominant only in the fast-food business. Today, clothing franchises such a Paraphernalia and 5-7-9 are gaining in importance. With this the case, there will be growing need for franchising buyers.

**Licensed stores.** Some retail operations are licensed. They operate under conditions that are similar to those found in franchising in that they are controlled somewhat by the licensors. The major difference between franchising and licensing involves the initial investment. Where franchisers require "start-up" fees for the privilege of joining the company, licensors do not require any "initiation" investment. Buyers are required to purchase their goods from the licensor. The largest fashion licensor in the world is Benetton with more than 800 licenses in the United States and many more in other countries.

### *Dollar Volume*

It is perhaps best to compare the buyer for a large department with his or her counterpart in a small organization whose volume is considerably lower. The large purchaser spends the most time in the pursuit and purchase of merchandise necessary to satisfy customers. The small-volume buyer, not equally preoccupied with purchasing, may find that the job calls for closer and more careful attention to the management of salespeople. Higher volume also provides the buyer with an assistant (sometimes more than one) to take care of duties and responsibilities otherwise left to the buyer.

### *Merchandise Classification*

By the very nature of the goods they purchase, buyers of fashion merchandise are called on to perform functions that other buyers do not. Since the fashion world is always changing, the buyers must be in constant touch with their customers as well as salespeople to educate and impress on them what's in fashion. The term fashion doesn't apply only to ready-to-wear or clothing, but to home furnishings, luggage, accessories, and so forth. Thus this buyer might

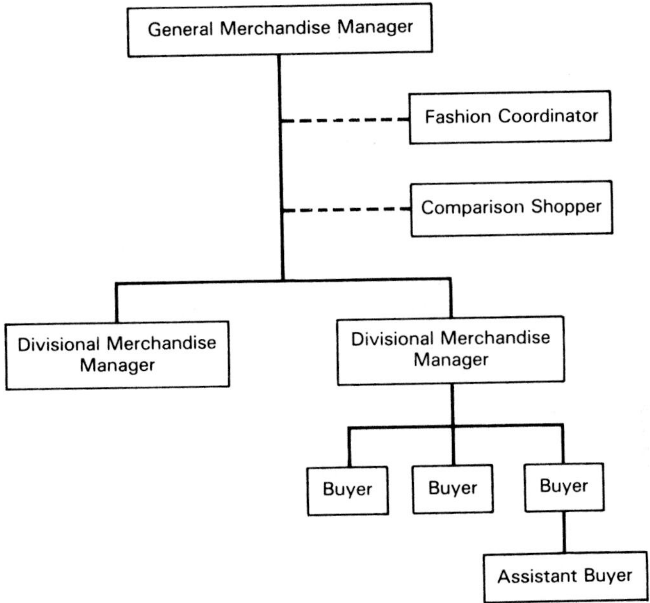


**FIGURE 1-2.**

have the responsibility of fashion show production to enlighten customers, as well as training sessions to teach sales personnel the proper coordination of contemporary fashion. Buyers of groceries, on the other hand, do not have to perform such activities.

### *Staff Personnel*

Most retail operations are structured as line and staff organizations. Figure 1-2 shows a simplified example of the merchandising division in a line and staff organization.

Under such an arrangement, the line people (decision-making individuals) are assisted by staff people (advisory specialists who provide information and assistance to the line). In companies with staff personnel, various activities are performed by them to help line executives in their decision making. In Figure 1-2 there is a fashion coordinator, sometimes called a fashion director, and a comparison shopper. The former is a specialist in fashion show production, color forecasting, and so forth. The latter provides comparative information on other retailers in the areas of prices, display, advertising, promotions, merchandise, and store activity. Companies that employ such people provide buyers with information and assistance they otherwise would have to get by themselves. In Figure 1-2 the general merchandise manager supervises the staff people, but they provide service for everyone in the division.

### Location of Retail Outlets

The retail organization that has a significant number of branches and units geographically distant from the parent store or home office finds that it is virtually impossible for the buyer to engage in effective "floor management." Under such conditions, the buyer's role centers on actual purchasing, pricing, policy making, and promotion rather than overseeing and managing the selling floors. In companies where units are located close to one another, the buyer is often called on to perform "in-store" activities at all nearby outlets.

## Duties and Responsibilities of Retail Buyers

The store buyer's daily routine includes a considerable number of diverse activities. Unlike the buyer at the resident buying office (to be discussed fully in a later chapter), a buyer who works directly for retail organizations has direct responsibility for all the merchandise he or she purchases. Not only does he or she perform duties within the merchandising division, but his or her activities may well cross with those of other divisions in the store, such as publicity and sales management. Later in the chapter we will explore the relationships with the company's other divisions.

It should be understood that the following duties and responsibilities may not be performed by every professional purchaser. As noted earlier, several factors serve to define buyer involvement, such as organizational structure and location and number of branches.

### Merchandise Selection

Of primary importance to the company is the acquisition of merchandise that will appeal to the tastes and needs of its clientele. Charged with this enormously important responsibility, the buyer spends the majority of time in this role. Not only must buyers choose the merchandise with the greatest potential for resale, but they must pay careful attention to the "buying mix," or the elements of buying. Knowing what to buy, in what quantities the purchase should be made, from which vendors to acquire the merchandise, and at what precise time purchasing should take place constitutes the buying mix. These elements are of such paramount importance to the buyer's success that a separate chapter will be presented on each. In Figure 1-3 a model in a runway fashion show wears a garment which the buyer considers for his or her store.

### Product Development

Many of today's buyers have taken on a new role. In addition to the merchandise they acquire from manufacturer or designer collections, the advent of "private labels" has turned some into product developers. Not only must they spend exhaustive periods scanning domestic and foreign markets for goods that will suit their customer's needs, but they may be called upon to furnish styles that would be for their company's exclusive marketing. This is not to say that the

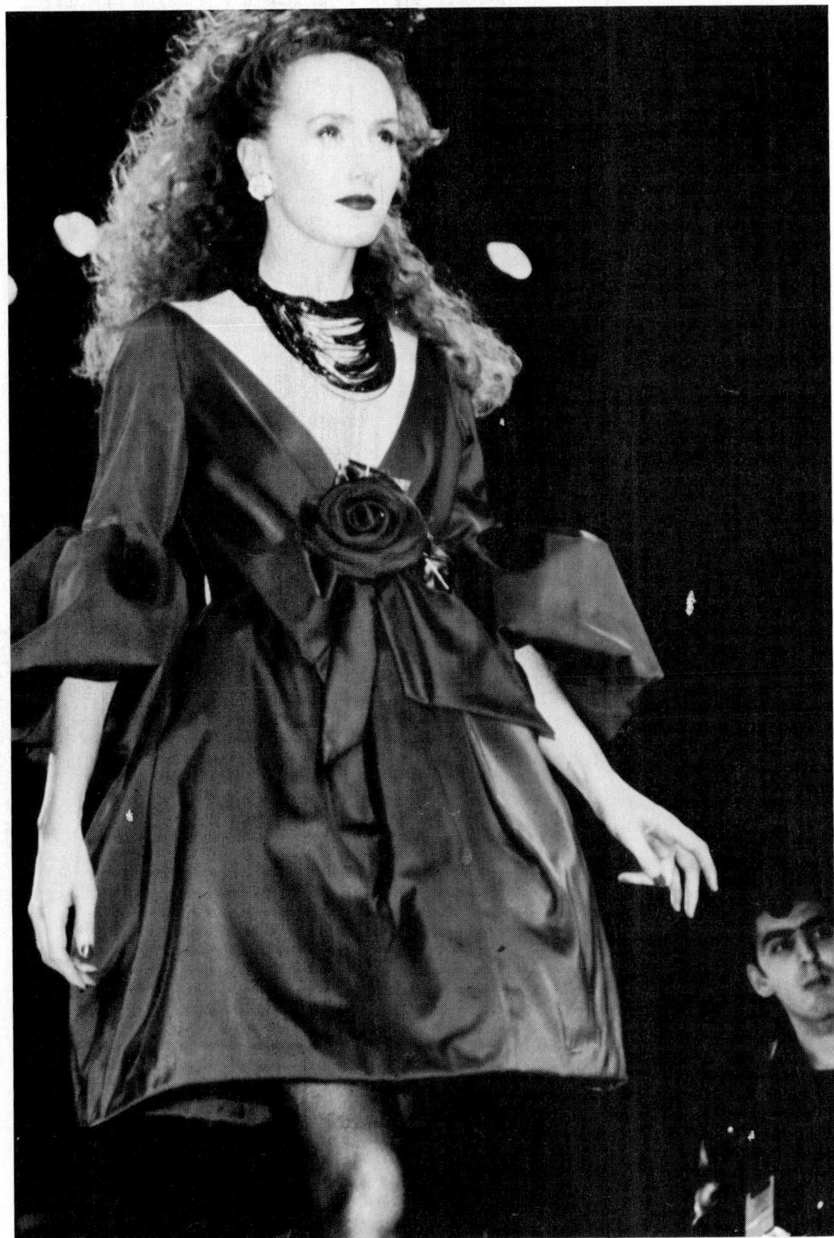

**FIGURE 1-3.** Runway fashion shows help buyers make their selections. *Courtesy:* Chicago Apparel Center.

buyers need the skills required to be designers, but they must be able to make suggestions for items that would be salable under the store's label.

Private label programs have become so important to many of today's retailers, with the buyers' involvement becoming commonplace, that a separate chapter will explore the subject.

### *Extensive Travel*

Regional markets have always been the mainstay for merchandise acquisition. Whether its New York's renowned Garment Center, the Dallas Merchandise Mart, or Chicago's Apparel Center, buyers regularly visit these places to shop the lines and write their orders. Traditionally, many buyers chose to utilize the market closest to their store's location so that they could easily attend to their in-house responsibilities. Attendance at other wholesale centers was usually relegated to "market week" visits. Buyers at the Chicago Apparel Center are featured in Figure 1-4.

Today, the nature of and demands of buying have changed. Whether it is fashion apparel, accessories, home furnishings, or food, the markets have spread all over the world. To assess the available product lines properly, buyers

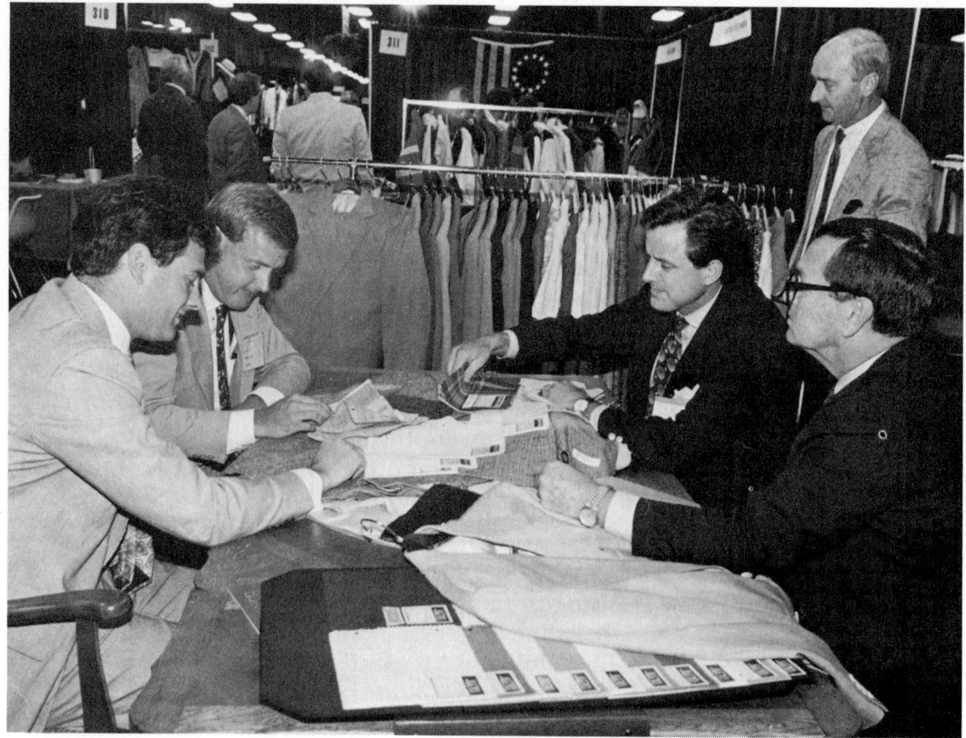

**FIGURE 1-4.** The Chicago Apparel Center is a regional market that buyers visit to procure merchandise. *Courtesy:* Chicago Apparel Center.

no longer stay close to home but travel all over the world. It might be Hong Kong for silks, Italy and France for designer collections, London for fashion forward styling, or Spain for leathers.

Chapters 11 and 12 fully examine the international nature of merchandise procurement and the demands it places on buyers.

### *Advertising*

Large retailers have advertising staffs and independent advertising agency assistance to carry out their advertising campaigns. Small retailers make use of media experts, agencies, and freelancers to plan their promotions. Although it is quite obvious that the buyer does not have the expertise to parallel these specialists in the technical aspects of promotional campaigns, he or she nonetheless has a significant responsibility in this area.

Who is better qualified than the buyer to select the merchandise from the department to be advertised? He or she knows the particular merchandise lines better than any other store employee. In actual practice, then, initiation of an advertising request begins with the buyer. The copy of the ad in Figure 1-5 clearly indicates the importance of the store buyers' role.

The meaningful role the buyer plays in this area will be discussed in Chapter 16.

### *Merchandise Pricing*

Although pricing policies are usually established by top management and administered by the merchandise managers (the buyers' superiors), the store buyer must price merchandise so that it will maximize the department's profits. Rarely do retail organizations set rigid pricing policies that prevent the buyer from exercising responsibility to determine prices. A buyer sometimes instinctively feels that a particular item merits an additional dollar of sales price and prices it higher than normal. Often competitive forces dictate a lower selling price. Whatever the reasons may be, and they are numerous, the buyer's knowledge of merchandise and market conditions dictates his or her responsibility for merchandise pricing. So great are the alternatives to be considered before pricing an item that this too demands further study later, in Chapter 14.

### *Management of the Sales Force*

Examination of what is commonly known as the Mazur plan, a four-function organization plan developed some 70 years ago and still the basis for many department store organizations, indicates that the buyer has direct responsibility for sales staff as well as the stock people who serve the department. Figure 1-6 shows a portion of the Mazur four-function organization plan—the merchandising division—and how it relates the buyer to sales and stock personnel. Of course, where buying and selling activities have been separated, the buyer relinquishes this responsibility.

"I've always wanted one!"

Entertainment was serious business for Mary Elitch. That's why a gift from Neiman Marcus would have tickled her fancy. We've always believed shopping should be fun, so our buyers seek out the most intriguing and inventive merchandise from exclusive sources throughout the world. The result is a delightful sense of discovery in every area of our Cherry Creek store, from hand-knitted sweaters in Sport Shop to hand-painted furniture in The Galleries to handcrafted jewelry in the Precious Jewels Salon. It's as much fun as—well, an amusement park! Denver's very own Neiman Marcus: Give it a whirl.

Neiman Marcus

Neiman Marcus opens Friday, August 17, at Cherry Creek.

3030 East First Avenue, Denver, (303) 329-2600

FIGURE 1-5. Advertisement of store opening stresses buyer's role in merchandise acquisition. *Courtesy:* Neiman Marcus.

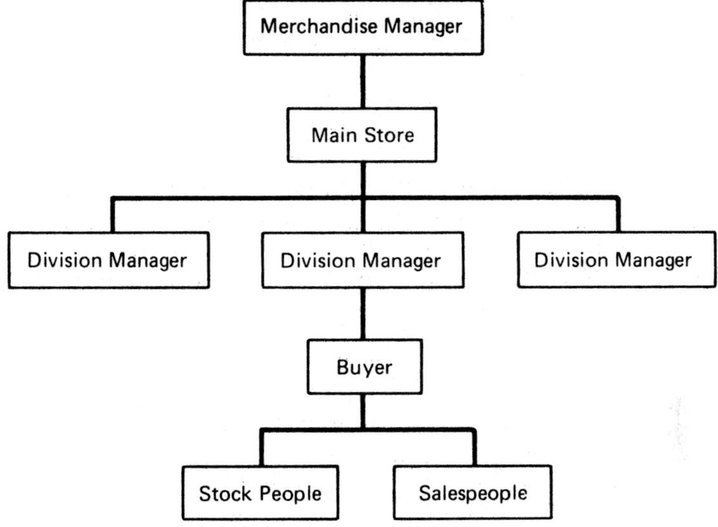


**FIGURE 1-6.**

Under this structure, buyers have complete responsibility for the salespeople. They instruct and counsel them on new merchandise, appropriate selling techniques, trends in customer needs and desires, unusual merchandise construction and assembly, caring for the goods, and a host of other merchandise-related information. Similarly, stock people are motivated to arrange merchandise carefully in reserve areas and on the selling floor.

Who else but the buyer is so capable of offering assistance on merchandise information to salespeople? There probably isn't another individual in the organization with comparable capabilities in this area. There is, however, a very important factor that has prompted retail organizations to rearrange their structures and reassign the sales and stock people to other supervisory personnel. That factor is expansion! Chains have grown so enormously that their geographic coverage often spreads to both coastlines. Department stores have done the same thing (although they are not as spread out as the chains) through the opening of branch stores. Even smaller retail outlets have opened second and third units to enlarge their operations. The expansion has mandated that buyers spend significantly more time attending to the elements of buying and less time on the selling floor.

Few people would argue that the salesperson is not an excellent source of buyer information, but the time it takes the buyer to purchase properly for a department takes away from duties such as sales management. In contemporary retailing, more and more salespeople (and stock people) are being supervised by store managers, department managers, and sometimes section managers. It should be understood, however, that many department stores, particularly in parent stores, continue to make buyers responsible for the management of salespeople. Today, with the marvel of the computer and its complement of informational reports, the buyer—previously fed information from the sales staff—is being serviced, to some extent at least, by the machine.

### *Management of the Department*

The management responsibilities of contemporary buyers cut across many areas. No longer are professional purchasers paid solely for their "merchandising resourcefulness." Today many buyers are held responsible for the overall management of their departments. This is particularly true of department and specialty store buyers, who operate within the framework of the Mazur plan, in which department management is the buyer's responsibility.

Among the various departmental management functions performed by buyers are the selection, motivation, and evaluation of the people under their supervision; control of the dollars expended for the department's operation; analysis of the costs involved in selling merchandise; budgeting; setting of standards for the department; and formulation of departmental schedules and procedures.

### *Setting a Schedule*

From the preceding discussion it must be clear that an unlimited number of tasks face the buyer. Some are routine, some are performed only periodically, some must be done each day, and others often come as a surprise. To carry out these multifaceted functions properly, buyers must carefully organize their own time.

Probably the most important factor in this area is the formulation of a workable schedule. In this sense, the word *workable* is of the utmost importance. Sometimes we overschedule ourselves, only to find that frustration and disappointment due to poor scheduling prevent the completion of our responsibilities. Experience or trial and error are perhaps best in setting schedules. Naturally, after years of scheduling oneself, tasks can be rather routinely completed without strict adherence to a written schedule. This experience may come after many trials and errors. The buyer must begin somewhere and gradually refine the tasks to be performed and the time each takes for completion. Among the various factors to be considered in self-scheduling are the following:

1. The number of hours in the buyer's workweek; this can only be approximated. (Wait until you are a buyer, and you'll understand!)
2. The number of people within your realm of supervision, such as assistant buyers, department managers, and salespeople, and how much time must be spent with each in regular meetings.
3. The responsibility, if any, to the selling floor.
4. The scope of your department, that is, the number of items carried and vendors represented.

5. The dollar volume of the department.
6. The geographic location of your wholesale markets; this is extremely important today, when many buyers travel to foreign lands for merchandise.
7. The relationship with other management personnel.
8. The responsibilities other than merchandise selection, as discussed earlier in the chapter.

Having considered these factors, the buyer must arrange a schedule on a priority basis, leaving some "breathing time" for the unexpected.

No matter how complete the list of buyers' duties and responsibilities, invariably some points are overlooked. With each buyer and within each organizational structure, there will undoubtedly be others worthy of mention. However, "complete" lists are never really complete. Certainly the expertise and knowledge of many retailers will demand more duties and responsibilities of their buyers than we have thus far discussed.

In the remainder of this book, many of the problems that confront retail buyers will be carefully explored.

## *COMPUTER UTILIZATION*

When the computer arrived on the retail scene, it had a profound effect on most buyers: It terrified them. From all they had heard, computers were enormously complicated devices for which they were completely untrained and probably untrainable. Typically, after having access to the machines for a year or two, most buyers don't know how they were able to function without them. The answer lies in the fact that the sophisticated electronic theory involved does not concern the buyers. As far as they are concerned, the only effect the machines have is to give them the same reports they were laboriously doing by hand, or should have been doing by hand, or wished they were able to do by hand. For the buyer, the computer is nothing more than a means for gathering information and compiling reports that provide a remarkably detailed, accurate, and up-to-date picture of what has happened in the department, and a somewhat less accurate forecast of what is likely to happen in the future. The speed and frequency of the reports far outdistance similar hand-compiled information. This vastly improves the buyer's competence by taking much of the guesswork out of decision-making functions.

One of the most sophisticated software computer packages is called Retail Express. It is an information system that is used with IBM or IBM-compatible computers. It gives the buyer invaluable information concerning purchase orders, receiving and checking of inventory, ticketing of garments, changes in prices, physical inventory taking, sales audits, open-to-buy, and merchandise planning. Those chapters that address the elements of buying will illustrate how the Retail Express program, and others, are used by the buyer.

Today's college graduates must be computer literate to engage successfully in retail buying. While the operation of specific systems can be learned on the job, basic comprehension prior to entering the field could be a plus when applying for the job.

It should be understood that even the smallest retail operations are utilizing computers for merchandise planning and procurement. Those desirous of participating at that level of retailing should also be aware that there, too, the computer is a fact of life.

## The Buyer's Relationship with Management Personnel

Having complete responsibility for the purchasing function does not separate the buyer from the store organization. How poorly the buyer would function in a vacuum! The buyer is responsible to and for many individuals in his or her own division. The buyer functions not only within a division or specialty, but also within a total organizational structure that encompasses other divisions that embrace the entire retailing spectrum. For a retail operation to be successful in terms of customer satisfaction and profits, all the divisions of the company must complement each other. The buyer is only one part of the business and must develop meaningful relationships with management personnel.

### *The Merchandising Division*

Refer back to Figure 1-2. You immediately come on the buyer's supervisor, the merchandise manager. In the illustration there are actually two levels of merchandise manager, the general and divisional. Although he or she is not nearly as involved in everyday actual purchasing, as the buyer, the general merchandise manager nonetheless is the guiding force in merchandising decision making. He advises the buyer in such areas as pricing (and repricing), style trends, market activity, promotional techniques, private brand utilization, report analysis, and research. The divisional merchandise manager is involved with the same responsibilities but restricts his activities to one division. For example, the men's wear divisional merchandise manager is responsible only for men's wear offerings and men's wear buyers. For their relationship to be productive, the buyer must be willing to heed the advice of both levels of managers. Working with them will enable the buyer to obtain valuable information such as what the other store buyers are experiencing, information that is sometimes difficult to come by. Since most merchandise managers have achieved their positions only after having been successful buyers, the buyer is wise to accept and use there suggestions.

Knowledgeable buyers are often heard extolling the talents of their assistants. If properly used, the assistant buyer can simplify the task and improve the success of the buyer. As the title implies, the buyer's subordinate assists in every way conceivable. A buyer who is secure and doesn't fear that the assistant will take over finds that a good relationship is rewarding. A seasoned, confident buyer knows how to delegate responsibility to an assistant. Although the job may be spelled out in the personnel department's job description file, the duties performed by the assistant are decided by the buyer. Thus the job may vary enormously within different departments of the same organization.

Though it is obvious that positive relationships must be developed and maintained by the buyer and the division managers, it is the interaction between merchandise manager and buyer and between buyer and assistant buyer that is of paramount importance for success.

### *Other Divisions*

No matter what the type of retail organization or its structural arrangement, the buyer comes into contact with management personnel from other divisions. For the buyer to achieve success, he or she must provide as well as receive cooperation from other store executives.

In companies where buyers operate from a main store and thus generally have overall responsibility for their departments, they must have a good relationship with the following management personnel.

**The advertising manager.** This person is responsible for all the forms of advertising the buyer needs to "prospect" for customers. Without cooperation from advertising, the job is hard to complete.

**The visual merchandising manager.** This person is responsible for interior as well as window installations. The expert buyer makes considerable use of this manager's talents. It is not just accidental that an exciting display helps the buyer turn a good seller into a winner.

**The human resources manager.** The experienced buyer can usually avoid guesswork in employee selection by taking the advice of the human resources or personnel department. Equipped to screen and recommend candidates for subordinate jobs such as assistant buyer, the department can simplify the buyer's role in proper staff selection.

**The receiving manager.** How disastrous it would be to have a stop in the flow of goods from the receiving department to the selling floor! Buyers who understand the receiver's problems and can work in conjunction with the receiving room can guarantee a steadier flow of merchandise. Good buyers seek out the receiving manager and develop a relationship that will help avoid dangerous in-store merchandise delays.

**The store manager.** This title represents different functions in different companies. The store manager usually has full responsibility for workrooms, security, delivery, and so forth. Although not every buyer has equal need for the store manager's attention, much of the department's proper functioning is dependent on him. For example, jewelry and fur buyers, by the very nature of their goods, require expert protection and security precautions. Furniture buyers must rely on delivery, adhering to customer requests concerning the specified day and time. And the men's suit buyer must work closely with the workrooms that provide customer fittings and alterations.

**The credit manager.** Most stores have credit policies, but it is still necessary for departments that sell expensive merchandise to work closely with the credit manager. Buyers of high-ticket goods such as carpets, furniture, and appliances must work closely with the credit department to facilitate the store's policies and the customer's needs concerning credit, because the size of the purchase and the time needed for payment are considerably greater than with other merchandise.

One needs to work for only a day in almost any retail store to appreciate the impact of charge accounts and credit purchases. Buyers are becoming more aware of the need to understand the store's credit policies.

A good buyer learns to make use of and assist in the development of relationships with other store executives. Remembering that the success of the organization can be assured only when all the divisions cooperate and complement one another, the buyer will do well to foster these relationships.

## Personal Qualifications for a Buying Career

Through careful analysis of the many tasks and duties performed by buyers, it is apparent that buying demands the efforts of unique and multitalented individuals. Long gone are the days when the stock clerk came up through the ranks and was finally made a buyer. The leadership, counseling, management, and decision making demanded of today's buyer require various skills, qualities, and professional training.

After a substantial number of interviews with buyers, merchandise managers, and personnel executives concerning their thoughts on buyer qualifications, the following qualities were found to be most important.

### *Education*

A college education is considered a must for a buying career. Looking at the responsibilities faced by buyers, one sees that it is virtually impossible to acquire these abilities without formal education. Retailers desire the best college-trained personnel they can find. Generally those sought after have majored in retail business management, fashion merchandising, marketing, or some other closely related business program. Considered essential by retailers are courses in merchandising, mathematics, marketing, salesmanship, and personnel management. Although the business-oriented student is preferred, retailers do consider liberal arts graduates who show the desire and potential for retailing careers as candidates for buying positions. Whether the individual is a business graduate or not, a working knowledge of the mathematics of retailing is essential. Quantitative analysis is an everyday necessity in the buyer's job. There must be thorough comprehension of profit and loss statements, markup and markdown principles, open-to-buy calculation, and so forth.

The question of whether the associate degree is sufficient or the bachelor's degree is absolutely necessary hasn't been resolved among retailers. Many prefer a four-year degree, but few have turned away the superior two-year graduate. Some companies will hire two-year students and pay their tuition for advanced college attendance.

### Enthusiasm

Many interviewers have passed over students with above-average college credentials to select the less distinguished but more enthusiastic individual. Enthusiasm is often infectious. The buyer's enthusiasm can help motivate assistant buyers and sales personnel. The excitement generated by the enthusiastic buyer may finally find its way to customers. If one thinks about enthusiastic friends or acquaintances, it might be easier to understand the value of such an intangible quality.

### Analytical Excellence

Buyers are always involved in decision-making situations. Should I choose red or black? Will customers be willing to pay the price? Where should the merchandise be displayed for maximum exposure? Will there be sufficient interest in a product to warrant additional reorders? Which form of advertising will bring the greatest response and thus maximize profits? The buyer is constantly analyzing and making judgments that will affect the department. The analytical mind can measure and evaluate situations and trends necessary for sound decision making.

### Ability to Articulate

Buyers, by the very nature of their job, are continuously exposed to people. They must trade in a knowledgeable and meaningful manner with vendors, delegate responsibility to assistants, train and advise salespeople, and confer with merchandise managers. If they can successfully articulate their feelings to the many individuals and groups they face, the job will be performed better. The ability to present one's ideas clearly to another is not easily achieved by many people. Buyers with this invaluable quality often find themselves coming away with the best possible deal. The ability to communicate in writing is more important than ever before. With vendors all over the world and branch stores scattered over great distances, oral communication is often insufficient. More and more written communication is being used to disseminate information.

### *Product Knowledge*

It is virtually impossible to be an expert on all the merchandise available to consumers. It is essential, however, that the buyer be fully aware of the goods it is his or her responsibility to purchase. Product knowledge is available through college courses, trade journals, visits to plants and factories, letters to companies, and discussions with vendors' representatives and merchandise managers. Potential buyers of soft goods (clothing) should have a complete understanding of sizes, styles, materials, color coordination, construction, fit, and the like. Buyers of hard goods (appliances, furniture) should be familiar with appropriate technical terms, materials, mechanical operations, warranties, and so forth. Similarly, food purchasers must be aware of the characteristics peculiar to their goods. Although some stores often call on assistants to transfer from one area to another, it is unlikely that the new job can be satisfactorily accomplished without additional product expertise. In order to maximize profits for their departments, buyers must have considerable knowledge of the products for which they are responsible.

### *Objective Reasoning*

Students often feel it is impossible to separate their personal feelings from the job to be performed. How unfortunate it would be for the buyer to select only what he or she likes personally! Buyers must be objective in their selections, convinced only by their consumers. Without objectivity, inventories can be filled with merchandise customers do not want.

### *Dedication*

While other workweeks seem to decrease, the buyer continues to work long, irregular hours. To face the challenge of meeting customer demand, the buyer must be dedicated to job and company. At peak periods such as Christmas and Easter, professional purchasers work endless days and weeks. Many buyers work well into the night at the beginning of a season or when opening a new unit. Only those with sincere dedication and love for the job can make successful careers as retail buyers.

### *Leadership*

Being able to supervise and direct subordinates is a characteristic needed not only by buyers, but by all management personnel. However, leadership in the buyer's realm of responsibility takes on another dimension. That is, the buyer must fearlessly make decisions about new, untried merchandise. He or she should be a leader and not wait to follow the rest of the pack. It is particularly important in fashion merchandising for buyers to take the lead on innovative merchandise. Once convinced of a feel for the goods, the buyer should take the initiative. Ultimately, if the work is carefully planned and executed, the buyer will be considered a leader by both staff and customers.

### *Appearance*

Possessing all the qualities noted thus far is not enough for success unless the individual has the proper appearance. The buyer is the store's representative and must project an image compatible with the store's. Proper dress and grooming immediately give an edge to the buyer's credibility in dealing with customers and vendors. At a time when many college students have resorted to "individualism" as it relates to appearance, it is important to understand that retail companies will not approve. Conformity to a store's projected image is a must for buyers.

### *Flexibility*

Buyers are constantly faced with new items on which they have to make decisions. There is always a new fashion, a new toy, a new appliance, and the buyer must decide whether to go into it heavily, lightly, or not at all. Nobody expects the buyer to be right on every occasion, but if an error has been made, the buyer is expected to recognize it quickly and make the appropriate adjustment. This can often be difficult, since it can involve the purchase of an item the buyer considers overpriced, or one that simply doesn't appeal to his or her taste. The point is this: If the item is what the customer wants the buyer must supply it, and quickly. Rigidity almost always guarantees failure.

In addition to flexibility to meet necessary changes in merchandise being offered, buyers must be ready to meet the challenge of nonmerchandising changes over which they have no control. Many of these changes occur slowly. Middle-class neighborhoods may gradually become slums. In some urban areas, slums are being replaced by middle- and even upper-class housing. Buyers must be alert to alter their offerings to meet the requirements of a changing clientele. Other external changes occur rapidly. These may be technological advances, new competition in the area, or governmental action. Whatever the reason for the changes, the buyer must be alert to them so that the proper adjustment can be made as quickly as possible.

## *CAREER OPPORTUNITIES*

Unlike many fields where changes in the economy curtail the need for workers or phase out existing jobs, the retailer's need for expert, professional buying continues. With the amount of competition generated by chain and department store expansion, the number of buying positions has increased. The future seems very bright.

It should be understood that rarely do college graduates enter retailing as buyers. They must first prove themselves as executive trainees or assistant buyers. The outlook seems excellent for college graduates to become buyers in retail organizations and resident buying offices. Since we live in such a rapidly changing society, it is virtually impossible to pinpoint the buyer's salary. However, there are some general guidelines worthy of mention:

1. Store buyers currently earn anywhere from $35,000 to $150,000 (and sometimes more).
2. Resident buyers generally are paid less than store buyers and earn from $25,000 to $60,000 (there are exceptions).
3. Buyers with in-store responsibilities often earn more than buyers for large chains who do not have store responsibility.

Although many industries have discriminated against women, retailing has long been offering equal opportunity employment. Women's salaries are commensurate with men's, and the number of women buyers in companies sometimes exceeds that of men buyers.

Since retailing is not confined to specific geographic areas as many fields are, buyers can work in just about any part of the country. In fact, those desirous of resident buying positions could even consider working abroad, since many offices have branches in foreign countries.

After an initial period as an assistant (the average time is four to seven years), the qualified individual can become a buyer at a salary better than that available in other fields for the same period of training. Buyers are paid their worth and need not sit and wait for carefully spelled out salary increases, as is commonplace in many industries.

## *EVALUATION OF BUYERS*

Although buyers are highly paid, their salaries are based strictly on the performance of their departments. They are judged on profitability and total volume. It is commonplace in the industry for buyers who do not perform satisfactorily to be relieved of their jobs.

Specifically, buyers are evaluated on the basis of the following criteria.

**Sales.** Sales volume is expected to increase according to reasonable goals that have been established. Sales results are figured not only in terms of dollars, but also in units of goods sold. Most major retailers evaluate effectiveness by sales per square foot. That is, each department must generate a specific annual dollar amount according to the square footage allocated. It is reported that Macy's, New York, has one of the higher square-foot sales ratios, at $450 per square foot. Most department stores achieve sales from $100 to $150 per square foot, and off-price merchants or discounters realize high numbers. For example, Marshall's gets more than $200 per square foot, and T. H. Mandy reports $350 per square foot.

**Inventory.** A careful inspection of inventory figures will reveal such indicators of buyer effectiveness as merchandise turnover or stockturn (the number of times in a period the average amount of stock on hand is sold), how much merchandise has been left from one season or period to be carried to the next, and the merchandise shortages for the department.

**Margin results.** Such factors as initial markup (the difference between the original cost and the selling price), maintained markup (actual selling price less any reductions), and the department's profit (after expenses have been charged) are just some of the margin considerations on which buyers are judged.

## ACTION FOR THE SMALL STORE BUYER

This country is dotted with thousands of small stores. In a significant number of the operations, the owners play many different roles. They often sell, arrange employee schedules, create displays, prepare advertisements, and bear the responsibility for purchasing merchandise. Unlike their large store counterparts, who often enjoy the assistance of others with purchasing decisions, small store buyers usually have sole responsibility for buying and all the decision making necessary for effective purchasing. Even when it is not the owner who is assigned the buying task, the employee who functions as the buyer generally assumes other roles.

To compete with the major retailers, the small store buyer must learn to improve his or her ability to purchase efficiently. There are numerous ways to achieve "buyer assistance" without having to hire another employee. Many of these aids will be fully developed in the body of this text, but at this point it is worth underscoring the point that the small store buyer need not work at a handicap. For example, membership in a resident buying office will provide a great deal of information such as new resources, trends, hot items, economic forecasts, and promotional approaches for successful merchandising. Equally important as educational tools are regular reading of the appropriate trade papers, study of business periodicals, attendance at preseason fashion shows, working on the selling floor to listen to customers' requests, regular meetings with sales personnel to "pick their brains," "shopping " the major retailers to evaluate their merchandise offerings, and attendance at trade shows. Although this list is lengthy, it is by no means complete. Each buyer must become accustomed to exploring those informational resources that best serve his or her particular merchandise needs.

At a time when retailing is overcrowded with competition, the small store buyer must do a great deal of homework to meet and beat competitors.

## SUMMARY OF KEY POINTS

1. Buyers not only select merchandise, but are responsible for decisions in such areas as employee development, pricing, department management, and advertising.

2. The scope of the individual buyer's responsibility is based on such factors as the company's organizational structure, the department's volume, the merchandise, staff personnel, and the location and number of branches in the company.
3. Although many department stores have followed a plan in which the buyer has been responsible for sales personnel, many companies have changed to a system in which store managers and department managers now manage the sales force.
4. The merchandise manager is the buyer's superior. Buyers formulate pricing policies, discuss trends, plan promotions, plan research, and plan private brand utilization with the merchandise manager.
5. For the buyer to function effectively, he or she must have a meaningful and cooperative relationship with the store's other management personnel.
6. Successful careers as buyers require such qualifications as graduation from college, the ability to analyze, understanding of merchandise, leadership, and dedication.
7. Buying presents a great challenge to individuals. The field is open to men and women all over the country at salaries commensurate with and often superior to those in other careers demanding more formal preparation.

## REVIEW QUESTIONS

1. Is the buyer's responsibility limited to the selection of merchandise for the department?
2. Buyers in different organizations perform different activities. What factors determine the scope of their performance?
3. Do buyers purchasing for centrally managed chain organizations have as much instore involvement as buyers who work for department store organizations?
4. Describe the term *staff personnel.* What assistance do they provide for the merchandiser in a store?
5. What role does a buyer in a large department store play in the advertisement of a piece of merchandise?
6. Can the buyer function successfully as the manager of the department's sales staff? Defend your answer.
7. Describe the relationship between a buyer and a merchandise manager.
8. In what way does the knowledgeable department store buyer involve him- or herself with the store's personnel manager?
9. Is it at all necessary for a store buyer to work closely with the store's credit department?
10. Discuss the qualifications necessary for an individual to become a buyer.

11. If a salesperson has demonstrated expertise in the performance of his job, can he expect promotion to assistant buyer?
12. How important is product knowledge to the buyer? Do you believe buyers can make an easy transition from hard goods to soft goods?
13. Might a man be as successful as a junior sportswear buyer as a woman? Discuss.
14. Is it likely that a college graduate would enter retailing as a buyer? Why?
15. Describe the advantages and disadvantages of a buying career.

## CASE PROBLEM 1

About to graduate from college, Toby Rubin has been investigating the possibility of a buying career with several companies. During her last semester in school she participated in a number of recruitment sessions on campus. Personnel managers from the major retail organizations have interviewed her, and the time for a decision is drawing near. After considerable investigation and deliberation she has narrowed her choice to two companies, one a department store with 6 branches and the other a centrally managed women's specialty chain with 300 units. A summary of the two opportunities follows.

1. Roban's Department Store is located in Los Angeles. It has a main store downtown and six branches within a radius of 150 miles from the main store and expects to open five others within five years. It is a full-line department store featuring a full complement of hard and soft goods. Its prices are generally in the popular-to-better range. The store has an executive training program limited to 50 trainees each year. The trainees participate in a rotation system that brings them into many different retailing roles. At three-month intervals they are reviewed and evaluated. Successful trainees generally become executives within five years. The starting salary is $24,000. with increases to $31,000 after two years.
2. Centrally operated from Los Angeles, Gambit, Inc., operates 300 ladies' specialty stores located throughout the Far West and Midwest. It caters exclusively to those with family incomes of $35,000 to $50,000. Gambit has been in business for 58 years and expects to open stores every 6 months for the next 20 years. It does not have a regular executive training program, but provides on-the-job training in specific disciplines for new people. For example, a buyer trainee is hired to work exclusively in a particular type of merchandise and is assigned to work closely with the buyer and assistant buyers. The salary begins at $21,000 with periodic increases of $500 a month every 6 months for 5 years.

Ms. Rubin, who lives in Los Angeles, majored in retailing, has a B+ average, and is highly regarded by her professors and peers.

### Questions

1. Develop a list of criteria for Ms. Rubin to use in the evaluation of the two opportunities.
2. Which job would you recommend she choose? Why?

## CASE PROBLEM 2

Understanding the value of salespeople as excellent sources of buyer information, Carrie Blum has become dissatisfied with her company's attitude on the matter. During her five years as the children's wear buyer at Mangreen's Department Stores, Ms. Blum was responsible for the management of her department's sales staff. In addition, she was able to visit the company's eight branches regularly to get firsthand information from those salespeople as well.

Last year the company installed a computer system that provided periodic merchandise reports. With this assistance, Mangreen's felt that store visits would not be necessary and decided to increase the number of lines the buyer would be responsible for, since she would have additional time.

During the period under the new system, Ms. Blum has continually voiced her unhappiness. She believes direct input from branches is important in the proper merchandising of a department. Mangreen's maintains that the computer functions as well if not better.

### Questions

1. With whom do you agree?
2. Could Mangreen's institute a new system that might bring the information from the branches firsthand, while at the same time keeping Ms. Blum as the buyer of the additional lines?

# Chapter 2

# CENTRAL BUYING FOR CHAIN ORGANIZATIONS

## LEARNING OBJECTIVES

*Upon completion of this chapter, the student should be able to:*

1. List five characteristics of large retail chains.
2. Describe five qualifications necessary to success as a chain store buyer.
3. Explain centralization and the unique characteristics of centralized buying.
4. Discuss three centralized buying systems.
5. Write an essay on the shortcomings of centralization and the movement toward decentralization.

## *INTRODUCTION*

The chain organization is a retail operation that is experiencing greater growth than ever before in its history. Companies like The Limited, Inc., with divisions that include The Limited, shown in Figure 2–1, Limited Express, Victoria's Secret, Cacique, Lerner New York, and Abercrombie & Fitch, and Merry-Go-Round that operates more than 700 stores bearing that name or Boogies Diner and Cignal are just two that have selling arenas in major and minor malls all across the country. Their very presence indicates that chain organizations are here to stay and that the proper merchandising of these companies is necessary to make them profitable.

The role of the buyer in these and all the other chains, from the smallest to the largest, is becoming increasingly more important. Without the proper mer-

**FIGURE 2–1.** The Limited stores are primarily located in malls throughout the United States. *Courtesy:* Space Design International.

chandise assortments, acquired in a timely manner and for the best possible prices, profits could not be maximized.

As do all buyers, those who work for the chains have duties and responsibilities that are unique to these operations. The characteristics of the chain, and the qualifications needed by their buyers to function properly are offered in this chapter.

## *CHARACTERISTICS OF CHAIN STORES*

The American Marketing Association defines a chain store system as "a group of retail stores of essentially the same type, centrally owned, and with some degree of centralized control of operation." This broad definition covers everything from a two-store "mom and pop" operation to the enormous retailers whose units may be found throughout the country. In this chapter, discussion will focus on the large chains.

The great retailing chains usually have the following characteristics in common, which will be the basis for discussing chains and differentiating them from department and large speciality stores. Their methods of operation will be discussed in the next chapter.

1. There is a headquarters in which most of the operating functions are centralized. In the case of the very large chains, this home office may be augmented by regional offices, each of which is responsible for a cluster of stores in its vicinity.
2. The operation of a chain store is generally more complicated than that of a single unit. In chain organizations such functions as real estate, warehousing, and transportation are of great importance and require the efforts of specialized departments and an increased number of executives.
3. Because so much of the responsibility for the operation of the organization must be delegated to people far from the immediate supervision of the home office, the personnel department must use extraordinary care in the selection and promotion of employees. In recognition of this fact, most chains elevate the role of the personnel director to that of a major executive.
4. Chain operations are controlled at the home office. The effectiveness of this control depends in large part on the speed and accuracy of the information passed between the individual units and the decision-making centers.
5. The selling function is completely separate from the buying function. Buyers have very little responsibility and practically no contact with sales personnel.
6. Many chains make no attempt at fashion leadership. Instead, they seek a reputation for quality at moderate prices. However, chains such as J.C. Penney have attempted to become somewhat fashion oriented. Many

**TABLE 2–1** The Top 20 Chain Organizations, by Volume

| *RANK* | *COMPANY* | *TYPE* |
|---|---|---|
| 1 | Toys 'Я' Us | Toys |
| 2 | The Limited | Apparel |
| 3 | Kinney/Footlocker | Shoe/Sporting/Apparel |
| 4 | Radio Shack | Consumer Electronics |
| 5 | Circuit City | Consumer Electronics |
| 6 | Marshalls | Apparel |
| 7 | T. J. Maxx | Apparel |
| 8 | Gap, Inc. | Apparel |
| 9 | Zale | Jewelry |
| 10 | Volume Shoe | Shoes |
| 11 | U.S. Shoe | Shoes |
| 12 | Petrie Stores | Apparel |
| 13 | Waldenbooks | Books |
| 14 | Silo Electronics | Consumer Electronics |
| 15 | Kay-Bee | Toys |
| 16 | Levitz | Furniture |
| 17 | Charming Shoppes | Apparel |
| 18 | Woolworth Apparel | Apparel |
| 19 | Burlington Coat | Apparel |
| 20 | Highland Superstores | Consumer Electronics |

of these stores rely on self-service, with salepeople available if needed. Private labeling and goods manufactured to the chains' specifications eliminate comparison shopping and increase gross profits. This is another topic which will be given substantial coverage in a later chapter.

Table 2–1 features a list of the nation's largest speciality chains and the merchandise they sell.

## QUALIFICATIONS OF A CHAIN STORE BUYER

The chain store buyer is a specialist in a specific type of retail operation. He or she must therefore have special skills other kinds of buyers do not need.

### Thorough Knowledge of the Market

Because chain store buyers have no responsibilities on the selling floor, they are free to devote a major portion of their time to buying. This time must be used to develop an intensive knowledge of the market. Selection of vendors must be limited to those capable of handling enormous volume and complicated shipping requirements (often in small lots to several thousand stores). When in midseason a vendor is not able to meet the demands, the buyers' knowledge of the market must be such that they can find a substitute vendor immediately. Vendor selection is further complicated by the fact that many successful producers prefer not to deal with chains. Chains are fierce price negotiators, their packing and shipping requirements are expensive, and they take so much of the vendor's output that the vendor may not be able to satisfy other customers. This often results in overdependence on the chain, which may lead to dictatorial practices on the part of the buyer and, in the event of termination, a serious lack of customers. Unlike the case of the small store buyer, finding perfect goods is not nearly sufficient grounds for making a purchase.

## Thorough Knowledge of the Product

Like all other buyers, those who work for chain stores look for unique, noncompetitive styles at a price that is both attractive to customers and profitable to the store. Unlike other buyers, those for the large chains are able to do something about it. It is not unusual for a chain store buyer to become involved in the design of the merchandise and the selection of fabric or other raw materials. This may even be carried to the extent of buying fabrics and contracting out the manufacture of the finished product. The knowledge required for this is far beyond that necessary for other types of buying. In addition to an understanding of what customers want, the chain store buyer must know the value of fabrics and the details of manufacturing costs. The cost of adding a pleat to a skirt or a pocket to a pair of slacks may spell the difference between a successful item and an also-ran.

The removal of the selling responsibilities from the duties of these buyers enables them to devote their time to their product and their market. Theoretically at least, these "pure" buyers know more about their goods and resources than other buyers who are forced to devote time and energy to the selling floor.

## Writing Ability

It would seem that this lack of contact with the selling floor is an important advantage. While this is an undeniable fact, the inability of the buyer to speak to customers and salespeople is also a serious defect in the chain store operation. It is vital that selling personnel understand what merchandise was bought, why it was bought, what it should be coordinated with, and how it should be displayed and sold. Unlike a department store buyer, the chain store buyer cannot orally explain the goods to the sales personnel. The only contact is by bulletin. He or she must be able to communicate with, and even inspire enthusiasm in, salepeople by writing brief explanations and descriptions (anything over one page will probably not be read). Lack of contact is both a blessing and a curse to the chain store buyer. On the one hand, it gives the purchaser more buying time; on the other, it removes vital personal discussions. However, the buyer is still responsible for goods being sold properly. Because this can be done only in writing, the buyer must have considerable writing ability. The ability to communicate in this fashion is of great importance.

### Quick Decision Making

Another necessary qualification of a chain store buyer is the ability to make quick decisions. The buyer is responsible for keeping a large number of distant stores well stocked. This requires a constant flow of merchandise. Because of the distances involved and the relatively small orders going to each store, freight is an important part of the cost. It is impossible always to use the most expensive type of transportation if required profit margins are to be maintained. In addition, some goods must be warehoused before going to the stores. In some chains, managers are permitted to select the goods for individual stores from catalogs and other descriptive material prepared by the buyer. In short, there is a built-in time lag in chain store operations. This can be a very serious defect, particularly in the case of seasonal goods, and the chain store buyer who spends undue time in making buying decisions only adds to this problem.

### Accurate Forecasting

Because they are responsible for merchandising stores in a wide variety of locations catering to a wide variety of customer tastes, forecasting is a difficult problem for chain store buyers. Lack of direct contact with customers and sales personnel makes these predictions even more difficult. Forecasting for staple items is relatively simple. If the buyer knows the history of the store for past seasons, requirements for staple merchandise for the current period can be calculated with relative ease. Predicting the salability of high-fashion, seasonal goods is another matter. There is, however, one important aid that may be used by the large chains. Because of the wide-spread geographical distribution of the outlets, seasons arrive at different stores at different times; and the information gleaned from one store can be used to stock another. For example, bathing suits may be big sellers in New Orleans in March, but not in New York until June. By the time the orders for the northern areas must be placed, the buyer already knows the styles that have proved to be good sellers in the southern market. But this is not nearly as foolproof as it seems. A proved winner in Miami, Florida, may be a dog in Racine, Wisconsin. However, the seasonal lag is of considerable help. How much help depends on the buyer's experience and ability to use the information available.

Information about the success of the various stores in the chain organization with particular items of merchandise has other advantages. Chains that allow individual store managers to order goods for their own stores, as does J.C. Penney, send frequent bulletins to describe the success they have had to the other stores in the company. Figure 2-2 illustrates a typical J.C. Penney bulletin.

Western Region HOT LINE

Department: HARD LINES

AUTOMOTIVE: W. A. Ver Weire

A. *Checkouts*

| *Subdiv.* | *Lot #* | *Retail* | *M.U.* | |
|---|---|---|---|---|
| 960 | 8116 | 17.99 | JK% | Battery Charger |

Comments: • 1831, Anchorage, Ak., sold 14/24 in 2 weeks with 24 on hand and on order.

| | | | | |
|---|---|---|---|---|
| 960 | 8021 | 33.99 | GN% | Battery Charger |

Comments: • 29, Spokane, Wa., sold 3/12 in 4 days.
• 1831, Anchorage, Ak., sold 12 in 7 days. On hand and on order 48 units.

| | | | | |
|---|---|---|---|---|
| 981 | 0220 | 129.95 | GJ% | Quad 8 track Auto Stereo |

Comments: • 1069, Huntington Beach, Ca., sold 1 on second day of arrival of shipment.

| | | | | |
|---|---|---|---|---|
| 986 | 0967 | 15.99 | GC% | Auto/Home Perk Kit |

Comments: • 1614, Montclair, Ca., sold 13 in 3 weeks, reordered 36. Sales more than doubled when we mass displayed on end cap.

| | | | | |
|---|---|---|---|---|
| 986 | 4094 | 1.57 | JT% | Auxiliary Spot Mirror |

Comments: • 557, Whittier, Ca., sold 12 in 3 weeks, reordered 24.
• 1831, Anchorage, Ak., sold 48 in 30 days with 72 on hand and on order.

B. *Merchandising Comments*
Just a reminder to be sure you buy your December allocation of oil as per my letter.

**FIGURE 2–2.** Checkout bulletin—J.C. Penney. *Courtesy:* J.C. Penney Co.

## CENTRALIZATION

As noted earlier, the portion of the retail market that has been taken over by major chains in recent years is enormous and rapidly growing. They dominate such industries as groceries, and they are probably the largest single factor in such areas as low-fashion, moderate-priced clothing and appliances. The reason for their growth is that they are uniquely efficient. This is due to centralization. By this we mean that one group of centralized managers controls all the stores in the organization. In other words, instead of having buyers for each of the stores in the chain, one group of buyers has the responsibility for merchandising every outlet in the organization. This leads to greatly reduced buying costs, which, when added to the other efficiencies of centralization such as recordkeeping and advertising, give the chains a big edge over their competitors.

As the chains increase their sales volume and profitability, additional advantages of size and specialization become available to them. Size permits increased power over vendors and the opportunity for profitable self-manufacture. Specialization provides for a narrowing of the functions of personnel. In buying, specialization allows the buying function to be split up among a large number of people. Instead of one men's sportswear buyer, chains may have separate buyers for slacks, shirts, and so on. A person whose buying is restricted to one small area is certain to have more expertise in that market and product than one whose buying responsibilities include a host of varied products.

Standardization is another aspect of centralization that results in improved efficiency. It involves uniformity of procedures among all the operating units. Once a successful system has been agreed upon, it is used throughout the chain. This results in savings in the store layout, shipping methods, advertising, and other functions. It also permits a shopper to feel at home in any of the units of the organization and promotes confidence that the merchandise purchased is the same quality-for-price standard he or she has become accustomed to from experience with other units.

The responsibilities of the centralized buyer are considerably different from those of other buyers.

### *Separation of Buying and Selling*

Unlike small stores and many department stores, centralized buyers have neither responsibility for nor control over sales personnel. Except for a possible occasional visit to a nearby unit, the buyer has never even seen the vast number of outlets in the chain. This does not limit the buyer's involvement with selling. All buyers are judged by the amount of goods sold. The fact that salespeople do not know how to sell goods is not an excuse for chain store buyers. They are responsible for informing the stores of the manner in which the merchandise is to be sold. Since this cannot be done orally, it must be handled by a constant flow of written memos. If the sales pitch cannot be explained in writing, the buyer should not have purchased the goods. This places buyers in the unhappy position of explaining the way certain merchandise should be handled but having no control over the way it is actually sold. It is not unusual for a seasoned chain store buyer to pass up a salable item that requires a unique selling method.

### *Dependence on Reports*

Buyers for a large nationwide chain may be responsible for the merchandise on the shelves and a constant flow of goods to hundreds and even thousands of stores throughout the country. Some of these units are in warm climates, others in cold ones. They include suburban and rural stores. Their clienteles vary in ethnic, social, economic, and religious background. Despite these differences, each of the stores must be merchandised to fit the particular preferences of its customers. This includes promotion, display, advertising, and the whole gamut of a buyer's responsibilities. To compound the problem, the buyer has never seen the store and has no idea of the neighborhood or the competition.

If centralized buying is to be successful in these instances (and as we shall see, it doesn't always work), the buyer needs information. Since all the buyer's decisions must be based on reports on inventory position, sales, and so on, these must be prompt, accurate, and all-inclusive. The major chains are highly scientific in their methods of getting information from the stores, translating it into a format for use by the buyer, and getting it to the buyer promptly. Naturally, these sophisticated problems rely heavily on computers for solution.

**Computer-generated reports.** Obviously, in a large chain the amount of paperwork involved in reporting would be enormous. This has an adverse effect on both the accuracy and the timeliness of the output information. Because of this, the large-volume chains all use computers in their reporting systems.

Most chains use point-of-sales terminals, that is cash registers that are tied to the computer. When a sale is completed, the information such as price, size, style, classification, color, and anything else that is imperative to the store's merchandising system is fed into the computer. The majority of stores use one of two systems. One requires the cashier to enter each bit of information manually. While this feeds all the necessary data to the computer, a large sale that requires many key strokes may take a long time to record, thus slowing down the process and keeping customers waiting. The other system addresses this problem and eliminates the possibility of entry errors by employing a scanner. In this system, the cashier merely directs a "wand" or other device to the sales ticket and all the data is automatically recorded. When timeliness is important, the latter system is certainly preferable.

More and more chains are utilizing the Universal Product Code (UPC), a series of lines, a bar code, that is found on many products to record inventory information. Each line may be programmed or instructed to stand for a different bit of information such as price. Instead of using tags that indicate all the information in actual numbers and letters, the "bar of lines" holds the necessary numbers. High-volume chains such as supermarkets and home improvement centers use this system. Home Depot, the fastest-growing do-it-yourself home improvement center chain, uses the UPC system.

While these systems generate invaluable pieces of information that regularly inform the chain store buyers of inventory levels and merchandise statistics, it should be remembered that this is only one tool they must use to learn about sales. Such problems as customer complaints about proper fit of garments, requests for specific items, and others aren't made available through these point-of-sale systems. An open line of communication is necessary to solve some problems.

### *Long Lines of Supply*

The length of the supply lines between the vendor's shipping point and the far-flung units of the chain is a constant problem for chain stores. For one thing, small shipments for long distances are expensive; for another, the necessity for a constant flow of goods over long routes with varying shipping methods requires careful planning.

**Warehouses.** One method of improving the supply problem is the use of warehouses if there are sufficient stores in an area to justify a central warehouse. The use of these centralized merchandise depots provides two important advantages:

1. Expensive transportation costs for small lots to individual stores may be replaced by large shipments to central warehouses. Shipping from the warehouse to the individual store is limited to relatively short distances. Not only is large-lot shipping less expensive, but in the case of staple goods, where timing is unimportant, less expensive types of large-lot transportation may be used. For example, it would be cheaper for Safeway Stores, a large supermarket chain, to ship a freight car load to a central warehouse in the Los Angeles area than to ship by truck 10 cases each to all its stores in the area.
2. The use of central warehouses that are a short distance from the stores they service reduces the amount of inventory that must be carried by each unit. This reduces the total inventory carried and permits the stores to allot more of their expensive floor space to selling and less to stockroom facilities.

Naturally, the use of warehouses for long-term storage is less effective for fashion and short-season goods. Such merchandise has to be placed on the shelves in the shortest possible time, and warehousing delays can result in markdowns. Many fashion chains, however, do utilize regional receiving facilities to supply goods in specific areas.

### *Testing of Merchandise*

Making certain the customer will be attracted to the merchandise the buyer has purchased is certainly an enormous responsibility. When a buyer makes the commitment to buy, the order, especially in the giant chains, could be for several thousand units of one item. Not only must the item in question have the appeal to generate purchasing, but it must also have the quality to provide customer satisfaction. Merchandise that wears poorly will certainly bring returns and could, if it happens with great frequency, give the store a poor reputation.

The expansion of chain organizations, coupled with mass merchandising through catalogs, has led some of the larger companies to establish testing operations. Picture the problem associated with the inclusion of a product in a six-month catalog, only to discover it is faulty. The bad publicity generated could be disastrous. Complete installations that test for such specifics as color fading, permanancy of finishes, dishwasher proofing, and tensile strength of fabrics have become more and more evident in chain store retailing. The industry has found it need not rely on a producer's guarantee to safeguard its reputation.

The systems employed by retailers organized as centralized operations vary from company to company. That is, each company might need to employ a system that is somewhat different. Most retailers who engage in centralized purchasing make use of one of three systems. They are known as the central merchadising plan, the warehouse and requisition plan, and the price agreement plan.

### *The Central Merchandising Plan*

Under this system, the central office plays a most important part in the store's merchandising plans. It has complete responsibility for merchandise assortment, receipt, and management. Planning is done by a number of specialists, such as merchandise managers who plan budgets, buyers and assistants who purchase goods, and distributors who decide which units receive which goods in quantities determined by data previously collected from the stores.

Although under this system the store receives whatever the central office considers appropriate, there is some store input to central merchandisers and buyers to apprise them of particular needs.

While the system does offer advantages in the form of steady merchandise flow, control of styles, quality control, and so forth, it does not allow for individual store needs. Some managers become disillusioned under such a system, and this often results in less enthusiastic selling of merchandise. Chains like Lerner New York, Baker's Shoes, Hanna Barbera, and the new Bostonian shoe chain, pictured in Figure 2–3, use this plan.

### *The Warehouse and Requisition Plan*

Chains that specialize in staple goods often use this plan. The central buyer in this arrangement determines the merchandise assortment, but relies on the store manager to control inventory levels through the requisition of merchandise to replace what has been sold. Thus the store receives what the central office sends, but the assortment can be adjusted according to the quantities thought necessary by the store manager.

There is some flexibility in this plan in some companies. Although the central office initially sends the merchandise it wants the stores to carry, it sometimes permits managers to eliminate some items they consider unnecessary for

**FIGURE 2–3.** The new Bostonian shoe chain's flagship store in the historic Old South Building in downtown Boston. *Courtesy:* Space Design International.

their units. Managers are required to send their merchandise requisitions to the warehouse when merchandise is needed—hence the name warehouse and requisition plan.

### *The Price Agreement Plan*

The greatest amount of store merchandising independence is achieved with this system. The central buyer assumes the responsibility for selecting vendors and merchandise, while the store manager is left to choose from these selections the items the store will carry. The buyer is involved with all purchase negotiations, such as price and terms. After the buyer has made the decisions, he or she prepares a list for transmittal to the store manager, who in turn selects the merchandise he or she considers suitable for the particular unit's needs. This plan is being used successfully by many major chain organizations, such as J.C. Penney. Not only does it afford the company economy through centralized purchasing, but it allows each unit in the chain to offer the merchandise best suited to that particular location.

## *DECENTRALIZATION*

Thanks to the efficiencies inherent in centralization and standardization, the typical chain has undergone strong expansion. The process reached the point at which a buyer, expert in purchasing from New York vendors, had the full responsibility for the complete merchandising function for store 1897 in southeastern Texas. The buyer's duties, in addition to the selection of styles, colors, sizes, and quantities of merchandise, included advertising, display, and promotion. At this point, the system began to break down. The buyer was simply too far removed from the action to take over the total merchandising activity. His or her information was too scanty. It did not include such vital areas as customer habits and tastes and the activities of competing stores. Too often, a can of food was marked 49 cents while a competitor carried it at 35 cents. Obviously, part of the decision making had to be done closer to the scene. Some decentralization was necessary.

Most of the large chains began decentralizing by dividing the country into districts and delegating some of the central office's responsibilities to district managers who, being closer to the stores, had a better understanding of their problems. Most chains use a dual system of centralization-decentralization in all areas of operation. The degree of decentralization varies with the function and the type of goods involved. For example, the purchasing of merchandise that finds its way to the shelves of each individual store may be the responsibility of the regional supervisor or the manager of the store involved.

Another problem inherent in the centralized buying system is lack of selling enthusiasm in the stores. Store managers and salespeople who are not involved in the selection of goods may be uninterested and even critical of the selections of a buyer thousands of miles away. Written bulletins are a poor substitute for the enthusiasm built up by actual involvement in the selection of goods.

## *ORGANIZATION OF A NONFOOD CHAIN*

J.C. Penney operates a department store chain of over 1600 nongrocery outlets. Its principal source of volume is soft goods, but its stores carry appliances and other goods as well. The organization chart for Penney's merchandise function varies with the type of goods involved. For some fashion goods, the individual store manager is given a great deal of leeway. The buyers of these goods prepare catalogs of the merchandise available to the stores. From these pictures and descriptions, the individual manager determines a merchandise mix. This ensures that the goods will be hand-tailored to each store's customers. The stores retain their individuality and carry merchandise that conforms to customers' needs. Assortment plans and recommendations are sent along with the catalogs and price lists to help the manager with the choices. This may tend to blur the lines of authority, since store managers who do not use the "suggested" mix may be subject to criticism later.

This sort of decentralization keeps buying centralized but permits each manager some say in the merchandising of his or her own store. This leads to another problem. When the chain was fully centralized, the store manager's role was limited. The expansion of responsiblities to include merchandising resulted in higher-paid, harder-to-find managers. Their inefficiences are no longer covered up by skilled home office buyers. Finding 1600 talented store managers is a difficult task.

The catalogs from which the store buyers make their selections are prepared by the buyers as follows: staple items, once a year; seasonal lines, twice a year; fashion lines, four times a year. Very-high fashion goods such as dresses and other perishables are selected and distributed by Penney's centralized buyer, who must be sure that the selection fits the store's modest stock plan, in which the store manager plays an important role. Because of the short life span of these goods, there is simply no time for cataloging and manager selection.

Too much decentralization in the selection of merchandise by store managers is an error, because the store manager cannot be aware of the total fashion picture. For example, women's sweaters may be selling very well, and the manager may reorder them. He or she may not be aware, however, that the other stores in the group are doing spectacularly with a number the store has never carried. J.C. Penney gets around this problem by permitting the buyers to make substitutions where they feel it is necessary. Since the buyers have the overall picture, they can make sure that all the stores carry the "hot" items. Another way of ensuring the distribution of good sellers is through flyers such as the one illustrated in Figure 2–2.

Another example of buying decentralization at Penney's is the occasional visits of store managers to the vendor markets. These are limited to stores located near the markets and are done only with the knowledge of the buyer. The centralized feature of the buying is preserved by mandating that all orders be channeled through the buyer. On rare occasions, a store manager places an order directly with a vendor, but this can be done only with authorization from the buyer.

Warehouses are maintained in each distribution area. From these depots the goods are shipped to the stores or directly to customers, as is the case with major appliances. The procedure for this heavy, bulky merchandise is that each store carries samples, and customer deliveries are made from warehouses. Fashion goods are rarely warehoused. Because of the time savings involved, these are drop-shipped (sent directly to the various stores by the vendor).

While decentralization is necessary to the success of a retail chain, it has the disadvantage of overlapping lines of authority and responsibility. Who, for example, is responsible for poor sales figures if the buyer makes a substitution for the goods the store manager ordered? Would sales have been better if no substitution had been made? These are serious problems in an organization in which close supervision is not possible because of the distances involved. There are some who believe that the point-of-sale cash register will eventually provide such improved contact between the buyer and the stores that complete merchandising centralization may be possible.

## *ORGANIZATION OF A GROCERY CHAIN*

As is the case with nonfood chains, grocery chains operate under a system of centralized buying, warehousing, and regional decentralization. The organization chart of the merchandising and sales division of one of the leading chains in the field is illustrated in Figure 2–4. As shown in the illustration, the nation is divided into six semi-independent groups according to geographic location. Each group is supported by the number of warehouse units required for distribution within the area of its responsibilities. Each group is headed by a general

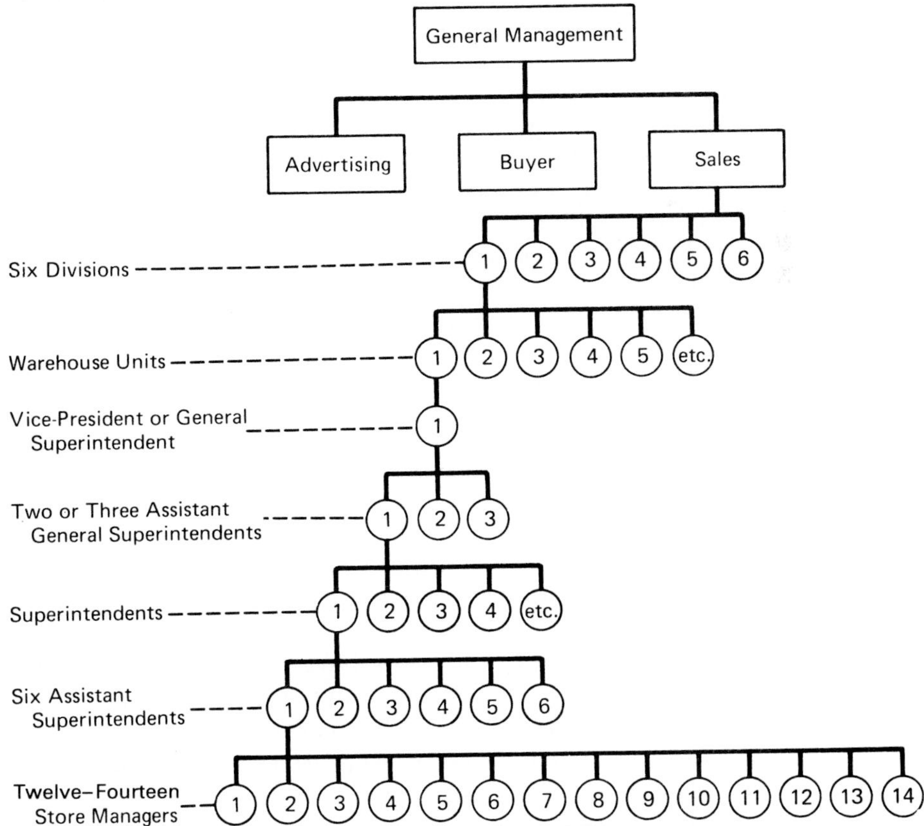


**FIGURE 2–4.** Organization chart of a giant chain operation.

superintendent, from whom authority flows through various subordinates to a number of assistant superintendents, each of whom is responsible for from 12 to 14 store managers.

Since there are considerable savings available to those who buy and ship in large quantities, all purchasing is done at central headquarters and shipped to the various warehouses. The merchandise is then trucked from the warehouses to the stores by requisition. The requisitions are in the form of inventory sheets. These are preprinted and distributed to the store managers, who periodically (usually weekly) fill in the number of units on hand in the space provided on the inventory sheet.

The sheets are forwarded to the home office, where the information is fed into the data-processing system. The computer compares the inventory on hand with the desired inventory and prepares a shipping order listing the goods that are in short supply on the store's shelves. If the computer indicates a lack of sales for a particular item, the merchandise may be dropped. The buyer may add new items to the shipment as he or she sees fit. Store managers are encouraged to be alert for customer requests for goods not in stock and to transmit this information to the buyer immediately. Warehouse inventories are constantly being compared to the warehouse's desired stock, and orders are sent to vendors for deficiencies.

Point-of-sale cash registers are now tied directly to these stores' computer. As each sale is made, the store inventory figures kept in the central office computer are immediately updated. The store manager is not required to take weekly inventories, and the shipment of goods from the warehouse to the stores need not be delayed. In addition, shortages in the warehouse inventory are determined much more quickly. As a result, out-of-stock situations, both in the warehouse and in the stores, are less likely to occur.

## A SUMMARY OF KEY POINTS

1. American retailing is dominated by large chain store operators. The characteristics of these organizations include central headquarters; highly complicated managerial functions; great emphasis on the personnel function; complete separation of buying and selling; and universal, high-quality, moderately priced merchandise.
2. The qualifications of a chain store buyer include intensive knowledge of the market, thorough knowledge of the product, writing ability, the knack of making quick decisions, and the ability to forecast accurately.
3. Central buying, having a small group of buyers responsible for the purchasing for all units, reduces buying costs considerably. As the number of buyers grows, each may be given a narrow range of goods to buy. This is called specialization. As the buyer's range of goods shrink, his or her expertise increases.

4. Separation of buying and selling is a problem for chain stores. The buyer is unable to instruct the sales force adequately in the selling procedures required by each type of goods.
5. Because of the geographic separation, there must be a constant two-way flow of information in the form of reports. All the information the buyer needs to merchandise the individual units depends on these reports. The use of computers has been a big help.
6. The long lines of supply between shipping points and the far-flung units of the chain is another problem. Transportation is expensive and time-consuming, and keeping the shelves stocked requires careful planning. Many chains use central warehouses in each area to cut down on time and transportation costs.
7. Because the central buyer in the home office simply cannot know enough about the customers of the individual units to merchandise properly, many chains allow the managers of the individual stores to become involved in decision making in such areas as merchandise selection, promotion, and markdowns. This is called decentralization.

## REVIEW QUESTIONS

1. Why do chain stores have more departments and executives than the single-unit operations? Give examples.
2. Explain the importance of the personnel function in chain stores.
3. Discuss chain stores as fashion leaders.
4. Does the chain store buyer need a better knowledge of the market than a single-unit buyer? Discuss.
5. Why do chain store buyers know the manufacturing process that goes into their product?
6. Explain the importance of written communication by a chain store buyer.
7. A chain buyer must be able to forecast accurately and make quick buying decisions. Why?
8. How do some stores in a chain generate information that helps the buyer forecast the needs of other units?
9. Define centralization. Explain the advantages available to centralized organizations.
10. Discuss the efficiencies of specialization in a large organization.
11. What is standardization? Why do chain stores standardize their operations?
12. Explain the advantages and disadvantages to a chain store buyer of the separation of buying and selling.

13. Why are speedy, accurate reports fundamental for a successful chain store buyer?
14. Discuss the importance of computers to a retail chain.
15. The chain store buyer must become a transportation expert. Why?
16. How do chains use warehouses? List several advantages of their use.
17. List and discuss the disadvantages of centralization.
18. Explain the store manager's role in a decentralized merchandising function such as that used by J.C. Penney.
19. What are the disadvantages of the kind of decentralization used by Penney's?
20. Discuss the effect of the use of point-of-sale cash registers on the operations of a food chain.

## CASE PROBLEM 1

The American Retailing Corporation is, by gross volume, the second largest retailer in the country. Its annual sales are counted in the billions. It has thousands of outlets of varying sizes spread throughout the country. Throughout the organization's 100-year history, the chain has undergone continuous growth and expansion. The stores operated by the corporation vary in their merchandise offerings. The largest units are operated as full-line department stores. The many small outlets are restricted to clothing sales. Women's clothes are the largest volume producers in the organization.

In addition to a central office where the major portion of the clothing purchases are made, the country is divided into ten regional groups, each responsible for the stores and warehouses in its area. Each regional group has one or more warehouses as required.

All the chain's clothing purchases are made in the central office and shipped to the various warehouses. From there the merchandise is sent to the stores by requisition. The organization uses the most up-to-date data-processing systems, including point-of-sale cash registers, which were recently installed in 800 of the largest units.

The store has a reputation for basic fashion, durable-quality ladies' clothes. Recently a proposal has been made to the merchandise management executive team to include high-fashion ladies' wear in the chain's offerings. It is argued that there is a market for these high-markup goods that the store is completely overlooking. Attracting a large bloc of shoppers who do not habitually use the store would improve all the store's selling departments. It is felt that since the store has been successful in every retailing area it has tried, it could do the job in high-fashion goods as well.

### Questions

1. Are you for or against this proposal? List your reasons.

2. If the plan is to be tried, how should the merchandising function be organized?

## CASE PROBLEM 2

The U.S. Sales Company, Inc., began business as a single-unit variety store in the Chicago area. From its inception, the store was very successful. Additional units were opened, first in the vicinity of Chicago, then gradually throughout the Mid-west, and finally nationwide.

In 1990, after 40 years of expansion, the central office, located in Chicago, supervised the operation of over 2000 stores throughout the country. The growth of sales volume and profitability and the building of new units remained steady until 1990, when the organization suffered its first setback in profits. A careful review of the operation revealed that the fully centralized merchandising procedures in use were at fault. Under these procedures, the various buyers had full responsibility for merchandising the outlets. A changeover to a decentralized system was indicated. Under the new system, each store manager was given complete authority over selection of the merchandise used in the stores. Selections were made through catalogs prepared by the central office buyers, who also placed the orders with vendors according to the instructions of the store managers.

By 1991 the new merchandising system was in operation throughout the chain. Although the slide in profits was arrested, the organization is still not living up to its full potential.

### Questions

1. Discuss the disadvantages of complete centralization of the merchandising function.
2. What are the disadvantages of complete control over the merchandising function by the store managers?
3. Suggest a merchandising plan that may be more effective.
4. Can you foresee any disadvantages with your plan?

# Chapter 3

# BUYING FOR FULL-LINE AND SPECIALIZED DEPARTMENT STORE OPERATIONS

## LEARNING OBJECTIVES

*Upon completion of this chapter, the student should be able to:*

1. Explain briefly the responsibilities of the following divisions and their component departments: (a) control, (b) advertising and publicity, (c) store management, and (d) personnel.
2. Discuss the role of the merchandise managers and list their duties.
3. Explain the authority of staff departments and describe the function of three staff departments reporting to the merchandise manager.
4. Describe the duties and responsibilities of the assistant buyer.
5. List and discuss four arguments for and four arguments against the separation of buying and selling.
6. Write an essay on the buyer's role in a branch operation.

## INTRODUCTION

Unquestionably, the success or failure of a retail operation depends principally on the buyers and other personnel involved in the merchandising function. A large retail operation, however, requires a host of other personnel if it is to function efficiently. Essentially, it is the function of these people to support and control the merchandising function. Simply put, the best merchandisers cannot operate effectively if someone doesn't turn on the lights or send out statements to charge customers.

To be fully effective, a buyer should know the relationship of the merchandising function to the other functions that make up the total operation, and the particular niche he or she occupies within the merchandise division. The buyer should have a working knowledge of the other divisions of the store and a specific knowledge of the duties of the people he or she is responsible to and of those he or she is responsible for.

The large retail stores are full-line or specialized department stores that operate from main or parent stores, or stores that are considered to be chains which function from central headquarters. While the concept might initially seem confusing, it is really quite simple.

One group operates so that there is a main or flagship store from which all merchandising is accomplished. The buyer is located in the main store and buys for that store as well as the surrounding units (branches). Examples of the former are Maison Blanche, a full-line traditional operation, and Saks Fifth Avenue, a specialized entry. The Maison Blanche flagship is featured in Figure 3–1. The buyer's responsibility, which often includes the selling floor, is for the main store and all the branches. The other type, as discussed in Chapter 2, operates from a central location (not a store) and requires the buyer to be responsible solely for purchasing. It should be understood, however, that it isn't always possible to categorize stores as either chains or department stores. J. C. Penney, for example, is a "department store chain" that crosses over into both types of organizational structures. Other functions, such as selling, are given over to each store manager. In this chapter discussion will be limited to large department and specialty stores. Table 3–1 is a list of the top 20 department stores in the United States. It should be noted that many are companies or divisions affiliated with major retail empires. In the ranking of the top 100 department stores, for example, The May Company owns 14 operations including Lord & Taylor and Foley's, both of which are in the nation's top 20 stores.

## FULL-LINE AND SPECIALIZED DEPARTMENT ORGANIZATIONS

To illustrate the buyer's role in the overall operation of the organization, it is necessary to study all the functions performed by a large retail organization and the duties of the various personnel responsible for those functions. The

**FIGURE 3–1.** Maison Blanche's anchor store, which occupies two floors in the Avenues Mall in Jacksonville, Florida. *Courtesy:* Space Design International.

organization charts of department and large specialty stores vary with each institution, but the differences are relatively minor. The chart illustrated in Figure 3–2 is typical of this type of organization. It is a five-function operation with responsibilities grouped under the controller, merchandise manager, advertising and publicity manager, store manager, and human resources manager.

Before going into the details of the merchandising function, of which the buyer is an integral part, a brief description of the other functions is in order.

## Control

The control function, which is supervised by the controller or treasurer, is responsible for safeguarding the company's assets. This part of the operation is usually divided into three separate departments: accounting, credit, and control.

### *Accounting Department*

This department is responsible for the recordkeeping involved with general accounting, accounts payable, insurance, taxes, payroll, inventory, and reporting. Buyers are very much involved with accounts payable, making certain that items were properly charged and that any questions concerning discounts, delivery charges, and so forth, were resolved.

**TABLE 3–1** The Top 20 Full-Line and Specialized Department Stores, by Volume

| *RANK* | *COMPANY* | *AFFILIATE* |
|---|---|---|
| 1 | J. C. Penney (Dallas) | Independent |
| 2 | Mervyn's (Hayward, Calif.) | Dayton Hudson |
| 3 | Dillard's (Little Rock, Ark.) | Independent |
| 4 | Macy's Northeast (New York) | R. H. Macy |
| 5 | Nordstrom (Seattle) | Independent |
| 6 | Dayton Hudson (Minneapolis) | Dayton Hudson |
| 7 | Macy's South/Bullock's (Atlanta) | R. H. Macy |
| 8 | Macy's California (San Francisco) | R. H. Macy |
| 9 | Saks Fifth Avenue (New York) | Independent |
| 10 | Neiman-Marcus (Dallas) | Neiman-Marcus Group |
| 11 | Bloomingdale's (New York) | Federated Department Stores |
| 12 | Foley's (Houston) | The May Department Stores |
| 13 | Lord & Taylor (New York) | The May Department Stores |
| 14 | The Broadway (Los Angeles) | Carter Hawley Hale |
| 15 | Marshall Field's (Chicago) | Dayton Hudson |
| 16 | The May Company California (Los Angeles) | The May Department Stores |
| 17 | Lazarus (Cincinnati) | Federated Department Stores |
| 18 | Hecht's (Washington, D.C.) | The May Department Stores |
| 19 | Woodward & Lothrop (Washington, D.C.) | Independent |
| 20 | Kohl's (Menomonee Falls, Wisc.) | Independent |

### *Credit Department*

With the large increase in charge customers in recent years, credit departments have grown considerably. This is a department with which buyers are rarely involved. Briefly, the responsibilities of this department include invoicing of customers, operation of credit offices, charge accounts, credit authorization, credit interviews, and deferred payments.

### *Control Department*

The organization's data-processing installation is operated by the control function. The system is used throughout the store. The part of the computer system that covers the buyer's operation is the responsibility of the control department. The personnel of this department are responsible for expense control,

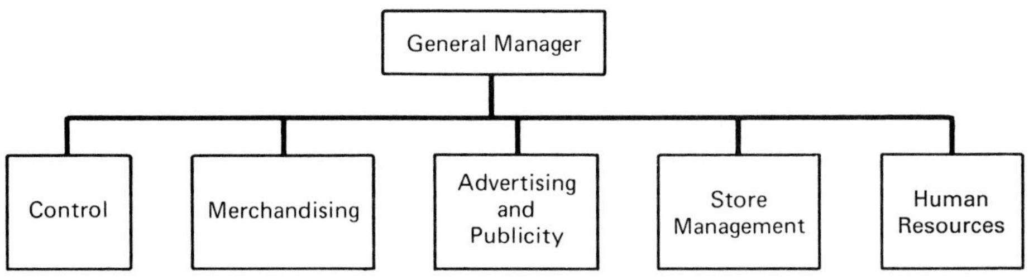


**FIGURE 3–2.** Five-function operation.

budget control, sales audit, and merchandise statistics and reports. Of the three departments under the control of the treasurer, this is the only one with which the buyer has direct contact.

The wise buyer would do well to have personal as well as professional contact with the people who make up the control department. It is from these people that the vitally important inventory and sales analysis reports come. As we will see in later chapters, these reports are used as a basis for many buyer decisions, and it is of great importance for buyers to meet with control personnel to have the reports set up in a way that can maximize their effectiveness. A buyer with close personal contacts among these people is in a position to communicate problems and needs to them.

Another responsibility of the control function is the preparation of reports to management. These will be used to evaluate the effectiveness of the merchandise function in general and the individual buyer in particular. Naturally, to be valuable these reports must be unbiased. We have already mentioned that various institutions have different organizational charts with various functions subordinate to one another. This should never be the case with the control department. To ensure fair, unbiased reporting, the control function must report directly to the general manager. Any other arrangement would be unworkable. That is, placing the control function under the merchandising manager would put the control people in the position of reporting on the effectiveness of their boss, to their boss. This would almost guarantee biased reporting.

## Advertising and Publicity

Although there is a degree of store-to-store variation, this function frequently consists of three departments: advertising, display, and public relations.

### *Advertising Department*

This department is responsible for media advertising. The personnel consist of artists, copywriters, layout experts, radio and TV programmers, and direct mail specialists.

### *Visual Merchandising Department*

The function of this group is the preparation and maintenance of interior, exterior, and window displays. They also maintain a sign room where price and other signs are made.

### *Public Relations Department*

These people are responsible for news releases about public fashion shows and other special events. It is the public relations people who work to get the store "free" publicity.

The place on the organization chart of the advertising and publicity division varies widely from store to store. On the organization chart illustrated in

Figure 3–2, this function is separated from the merchandising function and of equal strength. On other charts, this department is subordinate to and part of the responsibility of the merchandise function. Simply stated, it is a problem of who has the final say. Under all conditions the selection of the goods to be advertised is the responsibility of merchandising. In the organization indicated in Figure 3–2, the method, layout, and place in which the advertisement is to be shown are the responsibility not of the merchandising function, but of advertising specialists. Under these circumstances, conflicts must be resolved by the general manager. In situations in which the advertising function is placed under the merchandising manager, he or she makes the ultimate decisions.

Obviously, the advertising and publicity function is one with which the buyer is in constant touch. A close personal and working relationship is a necessity for effective cooperation. This is not always easy and requires effort if it is to be successful. Conflicts arise because it is impossible to judge objectively the reason for an unsuccessful advertisement. It is easy for the buyer to lay the blame on the advertisement, while the advertising department can as easily blame the buyer's merchandise. Because cooperation is so necessary between these two departments, each must treat the other with tact and understanding.

## Store Management

The store management function is responsible for projection, workrooms, service, maintenance, delivery, and receiving.

The housekeeping chores of the store management function are of relatively slight importance to the buyer, but some of the other responsibilities of this department are significant. These include receiving, delivery, workrooms, and service. Since these functions are vital to the buyer's effectiveness, he or she should know the personnel involved and be aware of their problems and weaknesses.

There is an ongoing question about whether or not the sales force should be placed under the buyer or the store manager. This will be discussed later in the chapter.

## Human Resources

The human resources function has the responsibility for interviewing, placing, and terminating employees. It also maintains personnel records, conducts training programs, and performs all the other chores involved with personnel.

The placement of the function varies from store to store. The organization chart illustrated in Figure 3–2 shows this function as an independent department. Other organizations include the function under the direction of store management or the merchandise manager. The reason for this is that the personnel department's involvement is principally in the area of merchandising personnel. This being the case, it is felt that the selection and training of these people can most effectively be supervised by the merchandise manager. In still other organizations, personnel is a staff function, with its role limited to advising rather than actual decision making.

Whatever the placement of the personnel function, buyers must be heavily involved in the hiring and training of the people they will be working with. Only by maintaining a close personal relationship with the personnel department can the buyer be certain of getting people who are properly trained for the job that will be required of them.

## Merchandising

Within the merchandising division the buyer's knowledge of the lines of authority and the duties and responsibilities of coworkers must be detailed. To show the buyer's place in this division, as well as that of superiors, those responsible to the buyer, and the staff information available, we present a diagram, Figure 3–3, which illustrates a typical organizational chart for the merchandise function.

The overall responsibility of the merchandising function is about the same as that of the buyers. It is to forecast the type of goods, quality, style, and price that will be wanted by the store's customers; to buy these goods as economically as possible; to encourage customers to buy the goods through effective sales promotion and salesmanship; and to create an atmosphere of goodwill that will build a permanent pool of customers.

### *General Merchandise Manager*

The head of the merchandising function is the general merchandise manager, who serves as both a policy maker and an operating officer. Since this job is of great importance, the general merchandise manager is a member of the policy-making unit, which sets the overall policy and objectives for the organization. As chief of the merchandising function, this manager is responsible for meeting the objectives by enforcing the policies.

In the large department store organization, the general merchandise manager delegates responsibility to a number of divisional merchandise managers, each of whom has, in turn, a number of buyers working under him or her. The divisions are generally set up according to merchandise categories and price lines. For example, a store might have a men's wear division, ready-to-wear (women's), children's, home furnishings, and so forth. Each of these has been designed with a particular type of merchandise in mind. There might also be a budget or basement division that does not restrict itself to merchandise classification but develops price lines which include many types of goods found in a budget or basement area.

In any event, it is the general merchandise manager who is the chief of the merchandising division. His or her duties and responsibilities might best be summarized as follows: to operate the merchandise division in accordance with the policies set. General store policy is defined by top-level management in

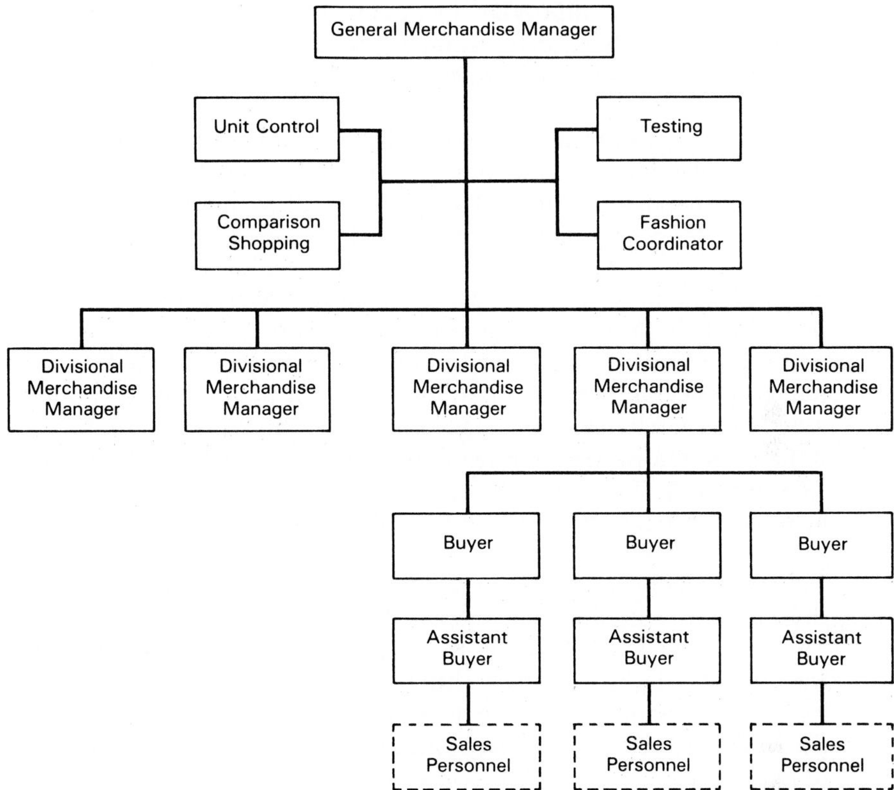


**FIGURE 3–3.** Organization chart of the merchandise function. *Note: Sales Personnel are indicated with a broken line to show that their placement is not always within the merchandising division.*

terms of price lines, quality, styling, and service. The merchandise manager is top management's representative to the division managers and buyers. He or she is responsible for carrying management's policy message to subordinates and seeing to it that they implement and adhere to those policies. The manager's role as representative to the merchandise division is reversible. Typically, the manager's is the only input the employees have to top-level management. The importance of the merchandise manager to the store's operation cannot be overemphasized.

### *Divisional Merchandise Managers*

Directly below the general merchandise manager are the divisional merchandise managers. Their numbers vary according to the size of the operation and the breadth of the offerings.

It is they who supervise the buyers in their divisions. They are responsible to the general merchandise manager and for the buyers. The following are some of their specific duties and responsibilities:

**Coordinate the efforts of buyers.** Every store has an image that must be uniformly presented to its customers. It is the responsibility of the divisional merchandise manager to unify the efforts of all their buyers with the purpose of achieving the image that has been decided on by top management.

**Keep buyers up-to-date on business trends.** Most buyers are completely familiar with their product. They know their market and are aware of price, style, and color trends within it. Frequently their deep involvement with their particular responsibility makes them less aware of the overall economic picture. The divisional merchandise manager must feed this information to them and see to it that their efforts are channeled in the direction of overall economic trends. For example, they must not be allowed to carry large inventories at a time when the economy seems to be heading for a recession.

**Advise individual buyers.** Probably the most important requisite for the job of divisional merchandise manager is that the individual have buying experience. This experience will provide the manager with a thorough knowledge of the many problems buyers face. Admittedly, in a large store with many departments, this manager's product knowledge will be limited. However, knowing the buying function will enable him or her to give effective advice in all but the narrowest of problems that concern specific product information. In areas in which product information is the basis of decision making, that advice must be carefully considered. Advice in this field, in which the buyer is much more knowledgeable than the merchandise manager, is often resented.

**Oversee the unit control system.** In retailing today, merchandising decisions are based on accurate, up-to-date information. As the buyer's representative to management, the divisional merchandise manager has the responsibility of providing them with the reports they need. He or she must be involved in determining the inventory and sales analysis reporting system needed to ensure the buyers of prompt receipt of reports, presented in a format that maximizes their usefulness. It is also the manager's duty to restrain the buying departments from requiring extra work of the computer system by the preparation of unnecessary reports. In short, when there is a conflict between the buyers and the computer personnel, the divisional manager must resolve it.

The divisional merchandise manager must pay close attention to the reports given to the buyers and must be as aware of the contents of each report as the buyers themselves. This will enable the manager to spot strengths, weaknesses, and future trends. Periodic scheduled meetings between the merchandise manager and each individual buyer are a must. The discussions at these meetings should be centered on—but not limited to—the reports. In addition, special meetings should take place as the need arises. Buyers who are not meeting budget figures or whose open-to-buy is being used up too quickly are typical of those who must be called in. Similarly, meetings must be held with buyers who are outstandingly successful. The reason for these meetings is twofold: to make the buyer aware that good work is recognized and to try to determine the reason for his or her success for possible use in other departments.

**Cooperate with buyers in planning.** Future planning, which involves sales forecasting and the budgeting of purchases, is of great importance. Too often this information is passed down from the divisional merchandise manager to the buyer with insufficient buyer input. This is a serious error. The buyer must play an important role in this task and be made to feel that it is his or her budget rather than one imposed from outside. Aside from the resentment an imposed budget may cause, leaving the buyer out of the planning decision results in a budget made without the participation of the one person who is expert in the field.

**Sales promotion.** In these times of fierce retail competition, advertising and sales promotion are crucial to success. The divisional merchandise manager must determine the effectiveness of the various promotion and advertising campaigns, coordinate campaigns that involve the activities of several departments, and make certain that all the departments involved conform their purchasing to the planned promotion schemes.

**Watch out for unusual talent.** Rapid expansion is the watchword for today's successful retailers. The success of any business depends on the talents of the people in positions of leadership. Expansion opens many new positions at all managerial levels. Providing people to fill these positions is the responsibility of all executives. They must be alert in their search for talent and make certain that the people who show the qualities for advancement receive the experience and training required for their new jobs. In-house promotions reward excellence and provide an incentive for all employees.

**Cooperate with other functions.** In stores in which such functions as personnel and sales promotion are organized as separate departments, the divisional merchandise manager has the responsibility of ensuring that his or her division gets the cooperation it requires. In the normal course of events, interdepartmental cooperation runs smoothly and can be handled by the buyers. In the case of conflict, however, the divisional merchandise manager must become involved.

### *Buyers*

The central theme of this text is the buyer. The duties and responsibilities of the position have been presented in the introductory chapter. Their applications will appear throughout the text.

### *Assistant Buyers*

As we saw in Chapter 1, the duties and responsibilities of a buyer are exhaustive. Obviously, in a large store a buyer requires the help of one or more assistants if all tasks are to be properly attended to. Many of the buyer's duties are clerical and time consuming. By delegating these to an assistant, the buyer may be free for his or her most important responsibilities, which are visiting the market and selecting the right goods. Among the duties usually assigned to assistants are merchandise control, supervision of sales personnel, customer relations, promotional assistance, and merchandise selection. It should be clearly understood that although the buyer may assign duties to assistants, the responsibility for the performance of those duties remains his or hers. Therefore the work of assistants must be constantly checked. Assistants are often responsible for the following:

1. *Merchandise control.* Sales analysis and inventory control are clerical in nature and may be easily delegated in stores in which such records are kept manually as well as those that are computerized. These chores include the following:

   a. Daily review of the stock for best sellers and other merchandise that requires reordering
   b. Daily updating of slow-mover lists for merchandise that requires marking down
   c. Recordkeeping on markdowns
   d. Daily reports on special and unusual merchandise
   e. In multiunit operations, balancing inventory between stores
   f. Responsibility for returns to vendors
   g. Follow-up of goods on order to ensure prompt delivery
   h. In stores that do not use computers, analysis of sales and daily posting to inventory control records
   i. Responsibility for proper price marking

2. *Supervision of sales personnel.* In companies where buying and selling are in the same division, assistants can free buyers from the responsibility of supervising the salespeople. To be effective in this task, the assistant must have complete knowledge of fashion, merchandise, selling, and promotion. The buyer must train the assistant in these categories so that questions and ideas of both salespeople and customers can be dealt with. The actual supervision of sales personnel includes the following:

   a. Training salespeople
   b. Scheduling personnel
   c. Assigning stock and housekeeping duties
   d. Observing sales personnel to prepare reports on outstanding or weak performance

3. *Promotional assistance.* The assistant buyer's responsibility in the area of advertising includes checking the on-order merchandise to ensure timely delivery and preparing salespeople and branches for the ad. When the department's goods are used for window displays, the assistant keeps track of the merchandise through loan slips. Other promotional assistance that can be delegated to the assistant buyer includes working with the sign shop and designing and maintaining counter and other interdepartmental displays.
4. *Customer relations.* Because the buyer spends so much time at the market, he or she must depend on the assistant to be a link with customers. As such, the assistant is charged with handling customer complaints, assisting in sales, and reporting customer wants and attitudes to the buyer.
5. *Merchandise selection.* The wise buyer thinks of the assistant as an executive in training. Since this is the case, the assistant must be trained in all aspects of the buyer's role. This includes merchandise selection. The assistant buyer should accompany the buyer on some buying trips. Not only will this give the buyer someone to confer with about decisions, but it will also promote a working relationship between the assistant buyer and the vendors. Too often buyers consider their assistants as competitors for their jobs. This attitude minimizes the amount of cooperation and help a capable assistant can offer.

### *Staff Functions*

As indicated in Figure 3–3, the merchandise manager has several staff departments available to himself or herself, which are also available to the division managers and the buyers. Typical of these departments are unit control, comparison shopping, testing merchandise, and fashion coordination. Since these are staff functions, they are outside the lines of authority; that is, they are neither responsible for nor responsible to the buyers. They are responsible only to the merchandise manager and, rather than supervising anyone, are available to all for advice.

**Unit control.** Prior to the widespread use of computers, this department was charged with the production of all sales analysis, forecasting, and inventory control. Today, with the help of the computer, unit control workers assist in budget preparation, supervise physical inventory taking, and check basic stock to see that the amount on hand is adequate. In some stores they independently analyze the computerized reports issued to buyers to ascertain whether or not the buyers are making prompt use of the information available to them.

**Comparison shopping.** The personnel in this department compare the assortment, service, and prices of competing stores with those offered by their own store. In addition, they check the effects of competitors' advertising.

Occasionally, when they find a competitor with a successful new item or an item that is lower priced but of equal quality to one their own store carries, they are authorized to purchase the merchandise and bring it back for study and appropriate action. For maximum effectiveness, they must take a shopper's point of view rather than that of a professional merchandiser.

Some stores consider comparison shopping to be a method of testing the effectiveness of the merchandising function. Under such situations, this department would make its reports to and be under the authority of some executive other than the merchandise manager.

Another function of the comparison shopping department is checking the merchandise displayed in the interior of the store and the store windows to make certain that such prominently displayed goods are of good value in comparison to competitors' offerings. For this reason, proposed advertisements are frequently checked by this department.

Comparison shoppers also check on the effectiveness of the services offered by the store. They investigate customer price and quality complaints and check on the store's salespeople by posing as customers while they note the appearance, attitude, and efficiency of the sales staff and compare the operation of their store's system with the methods employed by competitors. Although it is often resented by departmental personnel, a constant check on personnel seems to be a necessity.

**Testing.** Some stores maintain their own laboratories for testing the quality and other characteristics of in-stock goods or prospective purchases. This work may be done as standard procedure or at the request of a buyer. The maintenance of a testing laboratory is very expensive and is limited to such retailing giants as Macy's and J. C. Penney. Other stores use independent testing laboratories when the need arises. At present, the nation's attention is sharply focused on consumerism. As a result, the emphasis on this function has been expanding rapidly.

## A RETAIL BUYING FOCUS

### *J. C. Penney's Quality Control*

Recognizing the fact that customer satisfaction is of paramount importance in today's highly competitive retail environment, J. C. Penney has significantly expanded its product testing program. Its quality assurance program, as it is referred to by company executives, is a complete program designed to guarantee flawless merchandise.

Prior to 1991, the organization tested approximately 15,000 items, most of which fit into the apparel classifications. At the close of that year, their commitment was to test 40,000 individual items.

Motivation for the newly expanded practice was based upon the fact that the company sells approximately $3 billion through its catalog division, and anything less than perfection would result in a high rate of returns. Since catalogs are in print for long periods of time, unlike the ability to remove faulty goods from the selling floor, their inclusion in the catalog is for an extended period of time.

The Penney program is multifaceted. First, it has established a quality assurance factory evaluation system that rates each of the company's vendors. Those suppliers whose production falls below company standards are eliminated from future merchandise procurement unless changes are made. Second, the buyers are playing an important role in assuring that only quality merchandise will reach the consumer. Since the buyers are totally responsible for merchandise acquisition, they routinely interface with the manufacturers. They are required to impress upon them the need for quality items and that anything of a less desirable nature will not be tolerated by the company. To reinforce the buyer's responsibility for the purchase of quality merchandise, Penney's chief operating officer appeared on a videotape that was sent to each supplier and spelled out the goals of the program.

Buyers are motivated to exercise as much control as possible over the goods they receive. Those who demonstrate commitment to quality assurance in their buying activities are given an award as are the suppliers who provide the merchandise.

Through this stepped-up program, J. C. Penney expects to increase its share of the consumer market, improve its profit margin, and reward those responsible for the improvement. Buyers will receive recognition that will ultimately translate into monetary rewards, and vendors will become regular supply sources.

---

**Fashion coordination.** Fashion coordination is perhaps the most important of the staff functions available to the buyer. As the importance of fashion spreads from department to department, the efforts of a fashion coordinator increase in importance. Some of the major stores have more than one fashion coordinator in the main store, and one in each branch. The function of fashion coordination can be broken down into four areas: forecasting, purchasing and control, sales promotion, and training. Cutting across all these functions is the overall responsibility of seeing to it that the store is operated not as a series of independent, individually run specialty shops, but as an integrated unit with each department adding to the image that has been set for the store by top management. As a practical example, a customer who buys a coat in one department should be able to find such matching accessories as shoes, pocketbook, and gloves of the correct color, styling, and quality in other departments of the store.

All the fashion coordinator's efforts begin with a forecast of the coming season's fashions. Forecasting requires a complete understanding of the current market scene plus an educated estimate of next year's styling. This requires visits to all the important markets not only for made-up goods, but also for fabrics, fibers, and leathers. Requests to fashion magazines will produce information

**FIGURE 3–4.** A preseason runway show is used to introduce fashion coordinators to the new styles. *Courtesy:* Chicago Apparel Center.

about future issues that will be of value. Figure 3–4 features a fashion show attended by fashion coordinators to learn about the coming season's highlights.

Having gained the information required, the fashion coordinator's next step is to communicate that knowledge to the various buyers. Although the coordinator will be unable to suggest specific purchases, he or she can supply vital information as to colors, shapes, dress lengths, and the like. Another of the coordinator's responsibilities is to determine whether or not the suggestions are being carried out.

Once the fashion coordinator has made forecasts of the future season's styles, this information must be spread among the buyers that make up the coordinator's division. This should be done through both flyers and meetings with individual buyers. Group meetings with buyers should be held periodically to ensure interdepartmental cooperation—that is, to bring the accessory buyers up to date so that the store can offer a shopper a total ensemble.

When invited, the coordinator must find time to accompany buyers to the market to offer advice and opinions on purchasing decisions.

The coordinator must keep a careful check on the division's inventory position. Since he or she is the store's expert on style forecasting, this advice on which styles are apt to be "hot" and worthy of promotion should be carefully considered by buyers. For the same reason, the coordinator should comb the inventory for styles that are on the decline. These goods must be marked down at once.

Because the fashion coordinator occupies a staff position, he or she has no direct authority over the buyers. Success depends in part on personality characteristics. He or she must be convincing enough to prevail on the buyers of the various departments to buy matching, harmonious merchandise in the latest styles.

The fashion coordinator is involved in a variety of advertising and sales promotion areas. For one thing, he or she should suggest the styles to be featured. Although he or she is not responsible for writing copy, all fashion advertising and displays should be cleared through the coordinator for an opinion on the appropriateness of the message and the compatibility of the coordinated merchandise that is shown.

In sales promotion schemes such as fashion shows, which involve many departments, the fashion coordinator plays a major role. In this type of promotion responsibilities include selecting and coordinating the merchandise, writing the commentary, and staging the event.

Retailers that seek a high-fashion image find that a sales staff up to date in the area of fashion is a valuable asset. Within each department the buyer is the salesperson's source of information. However, a salesperson with knowledge of the total fashion picture is more effective than one with limited knowledge. Such a person can, for example, increase sales by suggesting accessories. The fashion coordinator, through flyers, group lectures, and informal discussions, is responsible for interdepartmental merchandising training. Some large retailers consider this type of training so important that they run periodic fashion shows for the sales personnel. Such events are the responsibility of the fashion coordinator.

## Separation of Buying and Selling

The salesperson is the link between the store and the customer. Consequently, salespeople are enormously important to a successful operation. The human resources department has the authority for hiring sales personnel, but in stores where the buyer is responsible for selling, the buyer has the final right of approval.

For many years the idea of separating the buying function from the selling function has been debated. In some department stores, the sales force is the direct responsibility of the buyer. This, however, is not always the case. Many stores are moving the selling function to the store's management division, as shown in Figure 3–5. The advocates of separation make the following case:

1. As style and fashion become more and more important, the buyer must devote an increasing amount of time to the market. This reduces the amount of time available for the selling floor. If the buyer is to be responsible for both buying and selling, both functions will suffer.

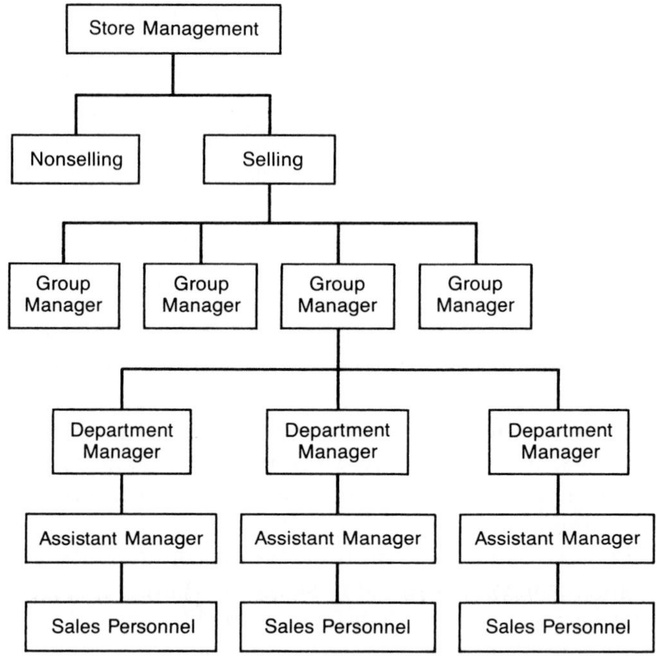


**FIGURE 3–5.** Organization structure where buying and selling are separated.

2. The characteristics required of a good buyer may be quite different from those found in a good sales supervisor. Rather than weakening one of these functions, wouldn't it be better to find the person who is best suited to each job?
3. The increasing ability of the computer to analyze consumer demand makes direct contact between the buyer and the public relatively unimportant.
4. With the growth of department and specialty store branches, it is virtually impossible for a buyer to manage sales personnel so far removed from the buyer's home working ground, the main store.

Arguments against the separation of the two functions include the following:

1. The use of assistant buyers as supervisors of sales personnel allows the buyer to be away from the sales floor as often as is necessary. Under such conditions, the assistant buyer can report customer attitudes.
2. The computer cannot analyze lost sales or customer attitudes. It is a historian of what has taken place rather than what might have taken place if the store had had the right goods.

3. The separation of the functions of buying and selling makes it difficult to fix responsibility on either group. Is a bad season the result of bad buying or ineffective selling?
4. Since the buyer's effectiveness is judged on the basis of sales volume, he or she is keenly interested in the operation of the sales function. Only the buyer can give the sales personnel the training and enthusiasm they need.

## Buying for Branches

Since the close of World War II, there has been a steady migration of middle-class families from urban centers to the suburbs. Faced with a drain of their more affluent customers, the downtown stores met the challenge by following their clientele to the rapidly growing suburban towns and villages. At present there are few, if any, large department and specialty stores that do not operate outlets at various distances from the home store. In recent years some of the branch stores have been running into difficulty because of increased competition and the general slowdown of the economy. On the other hand, many of the branch operations have proved more profitable than their urban parents.

Although there is sometimes unhappiness on the part of a branch manager with the merchandise assortment the buyer has selected, there is little, if any, movement toward having a separate buyer in department or specialty store branches. In some organizations, particularly the chains, as noted in the preceding chapter, store managers have some control over the merchandise they want for their units. But even in those cases, the store manager does not make any vendor contacts, except in rare circumstances.

### *Branch Variations*

When the downtown store buyer does the buying for the branch, the main problem is that the branch clientele may be different from the home office customers, particularly in the following ways:

1. *Different population.* Every classification of consumer characteristics must be studied separately for each branch to determine customer preferences. These include income level, family size, and age. On the basis of these population differences, the buyer must make decisions on price lines, styles, size mix, and type of merchandise that may be entirely different from the decisions for the downtown store.
2. *Different timing.* The flow of goods into the stores must meet certain branch buying habits that differ from the downtown store's experience. For example, Saturday is usually a bigger branch shopping day than the buyer is accustomed to. In addition, suburban customers seem to shop closer to their time of need. The buyer must learn and adjust to the timing differences as rapidly as possible.

### *Sales Analysis*

Because the buyer has relatively little contact with the branch selling floor, he or she depends on sales analysis and inventory control reports. The computer is a great help in this, and its reports must be quickly and carefully studied. Among the things to be watched are the following:

1. Branches are not usually stocked in depth. Fast sellers must be recognized immediately so that an adequate supply may be shipped to the store.
2. Because of the lack of selling space, slow goods must not be permitted to keep new goods off the shelves. Deadwood must be withdrawn, marked down, or transferred to another branch immediately.
3. Sales analysis provides the buyer with the best insight into the merchandise mix. Decisions on the most salable sizes, styles, colors, price lines, and so on, should be based on these reports.

### *Branch Visits*

Although this is demanding in terms of time, it is vital that the buyer be at the branch periodically. There he or she can personally review the stock and its display and presentation. In addition, the opportunity to talk to salespeople and managers about customer preferences and complaints, upcoming promotions, and future plans is certain to be fruitful. The best reporting system and use of want slips are no substitute for a person-to-person chat. A word of caution: Branch visits should never be unexpected. Much value may be lost if the branch people are not notified of the visit. To them, spot checks are indicative of a lack of buyer confidence.

Because the busy buyer can never spend sufficient time at the branch, written and telephone reporting in both directions must be encouraged. In addition, branch managers should be periodically invited to the home store. When possible, branch salespeople should be included in merchandise demonstrations, fashion shows, and sales meetings at the home office.

## SUMMARY OF KEY POINTS

1. This chapter focuses on giving students a general understanding of the various functions that make up department and specialty store organizations and a detailed understanding of the merchandising function.
2. The control function consists of three departments: the accounting department, which is concerned with bookkeeping; the credit department, which keeps track of charge customers; and the control department, which runs the data-processing system, including the reports used by buyers.
3. The advertising and publicity function is responsible for media advertising, window and interior display, and public relations.

4. The store management function includes responsibility for protection, workrooms, service, maintenance, delivery, and receiving.
5. The personnel function is responsible for interviewing, placing, training, terminating, and recordkeeping for all employees.
6. The general merchandise manager is the chief merchandising officer, and top management's link to the divisional merchandise managers and the buyers. This executive's overall responsibility is to put management's policies into effect. In large stores he or she is assisted by divisional managers, who are responsible for groups of similar departments headed by buyers.
7. There are several staff departments available for advice and assistance. These are unit control to report on sales analysis, inventories, and budgeting; comparison shopping to compare a store's merchandise, services, and prices with those of competitors; testing to determine the safety and quality of the merchandise; and fashion coordination to keep buyers informed of current fashions and coordinate their styling efforts.
8. Assistant buyers are executives in training. If used wisely, they can take over many of the buyer's tasks. This will enable the buyer to spend his or her time more effectively.
9. Many people feel that a department's operation will be improved if the selling function is removed from the buyer's control.

## REVIEW QUESTIONS

1. In what way is the buyer involved with the control function in a large department store?
2. Discuss the buyer's relationship to the advertising and publicity function.
3. What are the arguments against placing the advertising and publicity function under the merchandise manager?
4. Which of the responsibilities of the store management function have a direct bearing on the buyer?
5. Under what conditions does the buyer become involved with the personnel function?
6. Discuss the responsibilities of the merchandising function.
7. Explain this statement: The merchandise manager serves as both a policy maker and an operating officer.
8. In what ways can a divisional merchandise manager help buyers?
9. What is a divisional merchandise manager? What are his or her responsibilities?
10. Discuss the staff function of unit control.
11. List the activities of the comparison shopping department.

12. Give the arguments for removing the comparison shopping department from the authority of the merchandise manager.
13. What authority does the fashion coordinator have over buyers?
14. Discuss the most important function of the fashion coordinator.
15. Explain the training responsibilities of the fashion coordinator.
16. Review the duties that may be assigned to the assistant buyer in the area of unit control.
17. What is the importance of the assistant buyer's involvement with customers?
18. Why should the assistant buyer accompany the buyer on some market trips?
19. List some of the qualifications of an effective salesperson.
20. Why should the buyer visit the branch stores as frequently as possible?

## CASE PROBLEM 1

Wheatley's Department Store is one of the largest one-unit retailers in the country. Located in the downtown area of a large urban center, the store has been successful since its inception in 1910. Throughout this long history, management has been innovative and aggressive. This has resulted in steady growth in both sales volume and profitability. Wheatley's is, and has been for years, a model of how a large single-unit store should be operated.

As the store has grown in size, the responsibilities of the individual buyers have increased as well. As the load on these people increased, alert management was quick to supply assistant buyers to help ease the burden. By now, assistant buyers have taken over many of the nonmarket chores that had previously been done by the buyers. This has greatly eased the work load of the buyers, but since the ultimate responsibility for the assistant's work cannot be passed on, most buyers are rushed and perhaps do not work at maximum effectiveness.

To offset this problem, top-level management has before it a proposal that would remove the sales function from the buyer's supervision and place it under the authority of the store manager. It is argued that such a move will take a great deal of pressure off the buyer.

### Questions

1. Support the argument favoring the separation of the sales and purchasing functions.
2. What is the case against such a separation?

## CASE PROBLEM 2

Shortly after the close of World War II, Joseph and ELizabeth Betts opened a small women's clothing store in the suburb of a large city. The store began as a family operation, but thanks to capable management plus the stampede to the suburbs, the store became extremely successful. As the years passed and the store's profits grew, the Bettses added new departments to the store and greatly expanded the selling space. At present the operation is a medium-sized department store with emphasis on women's ready-to-wear. The operation caters to an affluent upper-middle-class clientele and has achieved status as a high-fashion retailer.

Mr. and Mrs. Betts divide the managerial operation of the store. They have reached the age at which they would like to limit their activities, take vacations, and otherwise enjoy their success. As a first step toward reduced involvement, they have hired a merchandise manager. The person selected has had great success in a similar job, and the Bettses have great confidence in him.

The new merchandise manager's first job is to prepare an organizational plan for the merchandising function. Included in the chart he has drawn up is the position of fashion coordinator. This is the first the Bettses have heard of such a job, and they have requested a complete explanation of the role of the fashion coordinator.

## Questions

1. Why is a fashion coordinator necessary?
2. Discuss the duties and responsibilities of a fashion coordinator.

# Chapter 4

# BUYING FOR CATALOGS AND HOME BUYING NETWORKS

## LEARNING OBJECTIVES

*Upon completion of this chapter, the student should be able to:*

1. Explain the types of catalogs for which the buyers purchase.
2. Discuss the difference between buying for stores and direct retailing catalogs.
3. Describe the use of cable television for direct retailing and some of its characteristics that make the purchasing task "unique" for buyers of this format.
4. Write an essay on how the buyer's role has been expanded when the individual is responsible for both in-store and catalog inventories.

## INTRODUCTION

As the 1980s drew to a close, there was considerable evidence that consumers had made significant changes in their purchasing habits. Until that time it was the department store that provided the assortments that captured the attention and dollars of the American citizen. But more recently, there have been serious indications that full-line and specialized department store organizations are failing to keep pace with other retailing forces. Names like Gimbel's, B. Altman & Company, Garfinkel's, and Bonwit Teller that once were legends in the industry have already hung up "going out of business" signs. What has prompted this turn of events? Quite simply, the American shopper no longer has the time necessary to spend making department store purchases. Specifically, the adult female member of the family is now employed.

At the same time the department store was experiencing difficulty in making profits, other methods to capture a share of the consumer's dollars were being expanded. Retailers who once used their catalogs sparingly, perhaps for the Christmas selling season or for some special sale, and new companies that operated totally in the catalog business were regularly blitzing the households with scores of catalogs. It became commonplace for families to receive as many as ten catalogs in one week, with some receiving even more.

At the same time another direct retailing method was heading for the shopper. Cable television featured shopping channels that would bring an enormous assortment of goods directly to the television viewer relaxing in front of the television set. Different types of merchandise shown could be ordered without the individual even having to leave his or her chair.

The catalog business began to grow by leaps and bounds, and the purchasing programs were being seen by tens of thousands of potential customers every hour of the day. Few stores, except for perhaps the national chains, could boast audiences of that size.

With trading areas fully extended beyond the reaches afforded the stores, more and more merchandise was now needed to satisfy the shopper's needs. Where buyers once were confined to purchase merchandise for a specific, narrow market, this new-found method of retailing demanded a greater assortment of merchandise and attention to its distribution that was quite different from what was practiced in the store.

In this chapter attention will focus on the different types of catalog operations and on cable television as a direct retail outlet and how the buyers' roles have been adjusted to make these methods of reaching the consumer market profitable for the companies they represent.

## CATALOG RETAILING

Before the buyer's role in purchasing for catalogs can be explored, it is necessary to study the types of companies that use catalogs to reach their markets. Some are department stores that have separate catalog divisions, others are chain operations that reach customers in this manner, and some are exclusively catalog operations that have no store outlets or other means of selling.

## Department Store Divisions

It would be difficult to find a major department store in the United States that relies solely on servicing the customer in the store. Recognizing the fact that there is a vast market to be served outside of the store, both full-line and specialized department stores have taken the route of catalog selling.

### *Full-line department stores*

On average such firms as R.H. Macy, Bloomingdale's, Dayton Hudson, Marshall Field's, Carson Pirie Scott, and Burdines mail catalogs to their customers at least two or three times a month. Regular customers whose names have been culled from the charge accounts and potential customers whose names and addresses have been supplied by market researchers receive merchandise offerings in the mail that include high-fashion women's apparel and accessories, men's haberdashery, bed linens, mattresses, furniture, dinnerware, video equipment, computers, and gourmet food items. Some of the merchandise is available for in-store shoppers; other items are distributed primarily through the catalog. Sears, for many years, has offered the in-home shopper items that weren't available on its stores' shelves. Using the catalog to merchandise low-demand goods, where stocking such items would be impractical given the space limitations imposed on retailers, the goods could be kept in centralized warehouses and delivered to the requesting customers.

### *Specialized department stores*

As previously discussed, some department stores specialize in one or more merchandise classifications. Typical of these are Saks, Neiman-Marcus, Bergdorf Goodman, Fortunoff, and Lord & Taylor. Their catalogs concentrate on one or a few merchandise classes. Fortunoff, for example, is an East Coast specialized department store that sells home furnishings; Neiman-Marcus predominantly features high-fashion apparel, accessories, and furnishings for the family, and Lord & Taylor offers clothing and some items for the home. As do its full-line store counterparts, Lord & Taylor is enthusiastically approaching its customers and potential purchasers via the catalog.

The following Focus examines the catalog operations of Neiman-Marcus.

**A RETAIL BUYING FOCUS**

*Neiman-Marcus Catalogs*

When Neiman-Marcus first invaded the retailing scene, its mission was to target the upper-income class in Dallas, Texas. With a host of expensive quality items, many of which were unique to Neiman-Marcus, the company quickly attracted a large number of followers. Throughout its history it regularly scouted the world for the unusual. In-store retailing was not its only vehicle for selling merchandise. For many years it has produced its now famous Christmas Book, a catalog that is legend among retailers and consumers. Not just another catalog to examine, this one featured, along with some traditional, up-scale fashions, a collection of "His and Her" items that was unlike anything else in the marketplace.

Buyers were called upon to sharpen their purchasing skills and come up with gift suggestions that were truly individual. In 1972, the buyers arranged for full-dimensional mummy cases that were facsimiles of the purchasers, his and her diamonds costing more than $1 million each were featured in the 1985 edition, and his and her LTV Hummers, motor vehicles used in Operation Desert Storm, at $50,000 each appeared in the 1991 Christmas Book.

Recognizing that the order of the day wasn't merely for exotic Christmas shopping, Neiman-Marcus expanded the Christmas Book to feature traditional wear alongside the exotic and also moved in the direction of expanding its catalog offerings in general. Buyers were now asked to tackle a broader-based market with purchases for other catalog offerings. In the "Neiman-Marcus by Mail" catalog, buyers are shown a host of items, some of which are available only through the mail. Some are designer-created goods, complete with recognizable labels, and others the creations of the company's own merchandisers and product developers.

With the direction toward catalog retailing moving quite rapidly, still another offering was developed by the company. Periodically, in "NM Edits," the buyers and merchandisers feature fashion forward items that are typical of the upcoming season. These books are regular presentations at the start of each fashion season.

Throughout the year, more than 50 catalogs are produced, each with a specific target in mind. There are special issues aimed at the men's wear customer, some exclusively for home furnishings, and others that concentrate on specific holidays. It should be understood that not every item is available in the stores; many are purchased only through mail and telephone orders. Bearing this in mind, it is easy to understand that the Neiman-Marcus buyers are called upon to select merchandise for two markets, those shoppers who come to the stores, and those who are satisfied through the mail. Figure 4-1 features the cover of the 1990 Christmas Book and some of the cover theme gift items.

## Specialty Chain Organizations

Although the chains have shown significant gains in in-store retail sales, they too have embraced catalog selling. One of the leaders in chain store organization is The Limited, with stores in many divisions all over the country; Ann Taylor, a fashion organization that features a wide assortment of private label merchandise; and Williams-Sonoma, a housewares specialty company with

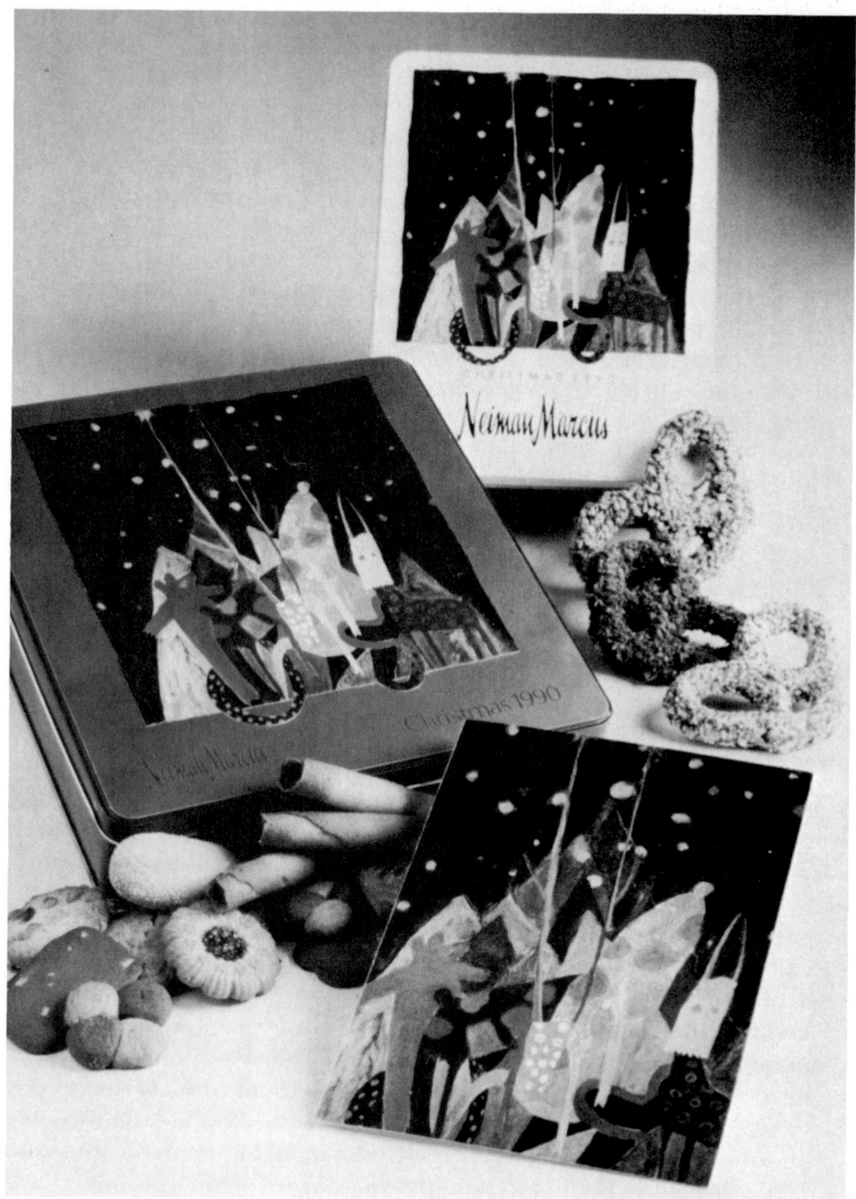


**FIGURE 4-1.** Christmas book from Neiman-Marcus. *Courtesy:* Neiman-Marcus.

stores all across the nation. These organizations offer merchandise in the catalog that may be found in their retail outlets or goods that are earmarked solely for catalog distribution. Victoria's Secret, the intimate apparel division of The Limited, distributes a catalog that also sells sportswear. None of the sportswear items is available in the stores.

While the catalogs of these operations are not as frequently utilized as are those of the department stores, they still bring in a significant amount of business.

## Catalog Operations

Retailing by mail is by no means limited to companies that retail outlets. There are more and more organizations being formed each day for the purpose of getting a share of the market that prefers to purchase at home or does so because of time limitations. Every conceivable product line and price point is available from catalog companies. Garnet Hill specializes in natural fiber merchandise, the Art of Food features unusual foods and cookware and offers ways in which they may be prepared, Back to Basics Toys offers toys and games that have been family favorites for many years, The Nature Company Catalog is full of nature-oriented products, and some like Spiegel feature a full line of hard goods and soft goods for the entire family. The buyers who buy for the aforementioned catalogs limit their selections in the same manner as the specialty or limited-line stores, while Spiegel employs a large merchandising team that is sent worldwide to find salable items. Order takers filling customer requests for Spiegel are shown in Figure 4-2.

**FIGURE 4-2.** Phone center for order taking at Spiegel. *Courtesy:* Spiegel Catalog.

The following Focus explores the Spiegel catalog and how its merchandise is acquired.

### A RETAIL BUYING FOCUS

#### *The Spiegel Catalog*

Spiegel, Inc., the nation's largest direct marketer and specialty retailer, was founded in 1865. It sells apparel, household furnishings, and other merchandise through semiannual catalogs and various specialty catalogs. Spiegel reaches 30 million households in the United States. While the business is primarily a catalog operation, it does have a few outlet shops that dispose of overstocked merchandise.

Buyers and merchandisers alike are provided substantial information about customer purchases from computer-generated reports. Such data includes customer demographics, behavioral information, merchandise preferences, and price points within the various markets. Through constant analysis, the buyers are better able to serve their customer's needs. In addition, primary research is a regular company undertaking. Studies are conducted which produce first-hand information about consumer preferences.

Typical of the consumer research taken was a questionnaire that was inserted in the company's spring/summer 1991 catalog. Many of the responses confirmed the organization's own merchandising thoughts, while some turned up requests that hadn't been considered before the survey. About 72 percent responded affirmatively to the store's customer advisory panel.

The success of the catalog is certainly due to the company's efforts to consider the consumer in the decision-making process; its mix of merchandise that includes both nationally advertised brands, many of whose items are specifically manufactured for Spiegel, and private label items; and buyer's careful attention to merchandise acquisition and development. Figure 4-3 shows size and measuring information provided by the buyers to facilitate purchasing. If problems arise, customer service representatives quickly address them as shown in Figure 4-4.

## *HOME BUYING NETWORKS*

During the early 1980s, television viewers were introduced to a new type of program. Rather than entertainment or a newscast, the audience was shown a variety of goods for their purchase. Initially, on some cable channels, displays of bargain merchandise was featured. For less than regular retail prices, viewers could order merchandise without leaving their homes. Towards the end of that decade, companies like K-mart and Dayton Hudson had entered the cable

## SIZE AND MEASURING INFORMATION

For a Perfect Fit:

**FASHIONS.** Order the size you usually wear. If you have any questions, our Ordertakers will be happy to assist you. You'll find Misses sizes for average figures, Petite sizes for women under 5'4" and Women's sizes 14 and up, as well as several styles in Tall Sizes (5'7½" to 6') and Women's Petite Sizes (under 5'4"). For men, we offer items in Big and Tall sizes.

Sizes 14W/14WP-26W/26WP. To assure the best fit, use the size chart below.

| Women's Sizes | 14W/14WP | 16W/16WP | 18W/18WP | 20W/20WP | 22W/22WP | 24W/24WP | 26W/26WP |
|---|---|---|---|---|---|---|---|
| | — | 1X | | 2X | | 3X | |
| Women's Tops* | — | 36 | 38 | 40 | 42 | 44 | 46 |
| Women's Bottoms* | 30 | 32 | 34 | 36 | 38 | 40 | — |
| Bust (inches) | 39-40½ | 41-42½ | 43-44½ | 45-46½ | 47-48½ | 49-50½ | 51-52½ |
| Waist (inches) | 30-31½ | 32-33½ | 34-35½ | 36-37½ | 38-40½ | 41-43½ | 44-46½ |
| Hips (inches) | 41-42½ | 43-44½ | 45-46½ | 47-48½ | 49-50½ | 51-52½ | 53-54½ |

*Women's top and bottom sizes (36-46 and 30-40) are simply identifying a size number and do not represent a specific garment or body measurement.

**SKIRT LENGTHS.** Skirt lengths are measured from **natural** waist to hem. The sketch below converts inches to real skirt lengths for a 5'6" woman.

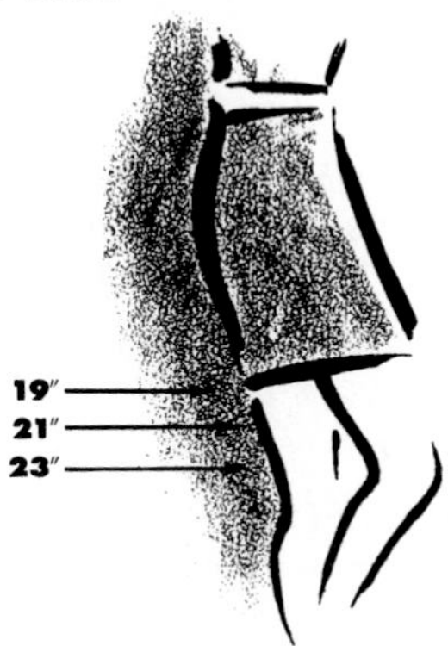


**Unisex sizes:** men's sportswear sizes with women's equivalents.

| Unisex sizes | XS | S | M | L | XL |
|---|---|---|---|---|---|
| Women's sizes | 4 | 6-8 | 10-12 | 14-16 | 18 |

**RINGS.** Order your normal size, or if you're not sure of your size, wrap a narrow piece of paper snugly over your knuckle and mark where it overlaps. Place the mark at "A" on the chart below. The left edge of the paper will fall at your proper size.

13 12 11 10 9 8 7 6 5 4 A

**SHEETS/BED RUFFLES.**
Most of our sheets are sized to fit standard mattresses.

| | | | |
|---|---|---|---|
| Twin | 39 x 76" | Full | 54 x 76" |
| Queen | 60 x 81" | King | 78 x 81" |

Some of our fitted sheets are available with corner pockets that will accommodate the new, deeper mattresses. These extra long pockets may also fit over feather beds or orthopedic cushions used on top of your mattress. To determine which sheets you need, measure the depth of your mattress at the corner.

Standard sheets fit mattress or topped depth of 7-9".
Deep Pocket sheets fit mattress or topped depth of 8-12".
Universal sheets fit mattress or topped depth of up to 14".

Bed ruffle lengths are measured from top of box spring to floor.

**RUGS.** To determine which size is right for your needs, use these guidelines:

- For dining areas, add 6 feet to the length and width of the table.
- Allow 3 feet on all open sides of a bed.
- Leave 8 inches of floor exposed around baseboards when covering an entire room.
- For entries and halls, consider the thickness of the rug and how the doors open.
- For added protection and cushioning, or to prevent rugs from slipping, we suggest using rug pads, grips or rug-to-rug pads.

**TABLECLOTH SIZES.**
To select the proper size tablecloth, determine the depth (in inches) of cloth overhang you'd prefer (usually 6-12 inches) and multiply it by 2. Add to the length of the table (in inches) as you intend to use it (with or without leaves). Repeat for width. Order the cloth size that corresponds to final dimensions.

**WALLCOVERINGS.** (a) Measure length of each wall to be covered (in feet). Do not subtract for door or windows. (b) Measure height from floor to ceiling. (c) Multiply height of each doorway and window by its width. (d) Multiply (a) x (b), then subtract half of (c) from this amount for the total square footage to be covered. (e) To determine the number of rolls you'll need, divide the total square footage by the applied coverage of each roll. (The applied coverage figure is found in the catalog description.) Add 10% for repeat patterns.

**FIGURE 4-3.** Size and measuring information help reduce merchandise returns and promote customer satisfaction. *Courtesy:* Spiegel Catalog.

**FIGURE 4-4.** The customer service department at Spiegel catalog. *Courtesy:* Spiegel Catalog.

home shopping arena only to leave the scene quickly. They were dissatisfied with the results and believed that the effort was unprofitable for them. By 1990, there were just a few home shopping channels on the air, and those that stayed found audiences that made their efforts worthwhile. Along with the Home Shopping Network, QVC dominates the field. In the accompanying Focus, the QVC approach is explored.

## A RETAIL BUYING FOCUS

### *QVC Network*

Throughout most of the United States, the QVC Network, which stands for Quality, Value, Convenience, may be seen by viewing audiences around the clock. Unlike the early cable shopping programs that featured closeouts and other bargain goods, this one offers a wide assortment of fashion apparel, accessories, precious jewelry, and home products. Careful programming helps to segment the merchandise into categories so that the audience need only to watch the featured merchandise they desire.

Periodically, the station presents a viewing schedule complete with times and merchandise classifications to be seen. "Ideas to Beautify the Home" might air at one o'clock, "Fashion Coordinates" at two, and so forth. In each spot, the items are carefully displayed. Models wear the item being offered for sale, which helps show the customer how it might look on him or her. Home furnishing products are often demonstrated, and every category is discussed by a commentator or program host. The prices are steadily shown on the screen listing the QVC price and the regular store price. The prices always promise savings to the purchaser.

As a means of providing some entertainment and motivation for viewers to tune in, QVC features a host of contests that award prizes to the winners. The network assures audiences they award 1500 prizes each week.

The success of their operation can be best stated in sales and numbers of orders. During a peak holiday shopping period at Thanksgiving, QVC boasted sales of well over $25 million on more than 300,000 orders.

With services such as speedy delivery and a liberal return policy, QVC has turned in-home shopping into a profitable venture.

## DIRECT RETAILING BUYER DUTIES AND RESPONSIBILITIES

The preceding chapters explored the duties and responsibilities of store buyers. Their roles included in-store management and involvement with other divisions in the store such as visual merchandising and human resources in addition to their buying chores. While the qualifications for buying for catalogs and cable television networks are much the same as those required of their store purchasing counterparts, the duties they perform are somewhat different.

Their major function is purchasing. They don't interface with a sales staff on the selling floor or select merchandise that will be promoted in advertising or display windows. They aren't concerned with the movement of merchandise or its visual presentation. They are concerned primarily with merchandise acquisition.

Traditional retailers draw their customer base from a well-defined trading area. That is, the customers they serve come from surrounding areas that are close to the store. Most trading areas are no more than 20 miles in any direction from the store and unless the company is a large chain or department store with branches, the audience they serve is quite limited. The buyers for these companies must only ascertain the needs of this narrow market and serve them well.

Catalogs and cable television shopping networks serve a much larger geographic market. Catalogs are readily distributed anywhere in the world and cable television reaches an enormous market. As a consequence, direct retailing buyers must purchase for a significantly larger geographic market than the store buyers. They also must concentrate on merchandise that has "universal" appeal so that the customer in Austin, Texas, will have the same interest as the one in Baltimore, Maryland. Store buyers can purchase items that might be appropriate only for a narrow audience.

Price is another important factor in purchasing for these outlets. Often, customers who use catalogs or cable television for their purchases want merchandise that is competitive with store offerings. Observation of numerous catalogs, for example, indicates many items that feature "special" prices. The buyer must be able to negotiate prices that enable their companies to sell at lower prices.

Some catalogs are published but twice a year as is the case with Spiegel. In such circumstances, the buyer must make certain the vendors will provide merchandise continuity for the life of the catalog. If this isn't carefully spelled out, and production isn't available for the entire period, the direct retailer will lose money and create ill will from customers who ordered but didn't receive the merchandise.

Since merchandise sold via catalogs doesn't have the benefit of a seller offering its advantages, it must be sufficiently attractive to catch the shopper's attention in print. Buyers must be able to assess how the item will look in print and whether or not, without the aid of a salesperson, it will motivate purchasing.

Without any of the advantages of store promotion, the buyer must make certain that every item will sell on its own merits.

## ACTION FOR THE SMALL STORE BUYER

The use of direct retailing methods is primarily concentrated in large store organizations or specialized companies. The enormous merchandise and capital requirements generally exclude the small store buyer from such activities. There are, however, opportunities for a smaller company to reach the consumer in the home or at the office.

Some small retailers belong to cooperative groups that share much of their buying responsibilities. By pooling orders, they often can negotiate better terms for their individual stores. Some even participate in catalog retailing as part of the team effort. In such cases, each small store promises to buy a minimum order of the same merchandise and have it featured in a catalog. Each store receives a number of the catalogs that bear the individual store's name, the only distinguishing feature of the catalog. The merchants then have their share of catalogs, with the store name imprinted, and send them to their customers. In this way the costs of the operation are shared, and each retailer retains his or her identity on the printed matter. Luggage and small leather goods merchants regularly cooperate in such joint ventures for the Christmas selling period.

Some small retailers are entering the direct retailing market by servicing the customer directly in the home or office. Customers are encouraged to call the store with apparel requests, for example, and have the store bring a selection to them. The acceptable merchandise is paid for and sometimes fitted for alterations and finally returned to the customer when finished.

With more and more people in the work force, and with less time to shop, even the smallest merchant must devise methods to capture the customer's dollars.

## SUMMARY OF KEY POINTS

1. With more and more women in the work force, the numbers who traditionally made their purchases in stores have been reduced in size.
2. Retailers who once sparingly used catalogs to bolster their total sales efforts are now using them on an increased basis, with some sending out as many as 50 per year.
3. Full-line department stores offer mixed merchandise catalogs to their customers as well as specialized ones that concentrate on a particular merchandise category.
4. Some retailers offer a different product mix in their catalogs than the assortments found in their stores.
5. More and more catalog operations, without retail outlets, are entering the field and reaching their target markets with a variety of merchandise.
6. Home shopping networks feature a variety of merchandise, around the clock, to most parts of the United States.
7. The individual responsible for catalog purchases has fewer responsibilities than his store-based counterpart.
8. Catalog and home shopping buyers must make certain that their offerings are more "universal" than those found in stores since their trading areas are significantly larger and more diverse.

## REVIEW QUESTIONS

1. For what primary reason does the consumer turn to alternate means of purchasing?
2. How has department store catalog utilization changed in recent years?
3. From which sources do major retailers choose names to whom catalogs should be delivered?
4. Which major retailer has been credited with a unique Christmas catalog? Describe its uniqueness.
5. In what way does Victoria's Secret in-store merchandise differ from its direct mail catalogs?
6. What merchandising approach do some major chains take in order to guarantee exclusivity in their catalogs?

7. Describe the manner in which the Spiegel buyers gather information for the purpose of merchandise acquisition planning.
8. How do you account for the success of the home shopping cable networks?
9. Explain how the QVC network alerts its customers to specific merchandise presentations.
10. In what ways do the direct retailing buyers' responsibilities differ from their store counterparts?
11. Why must the direct buyer make certain that his or her purchases are more "universally" acceptable than those made by store buyers?
12. Aside from universality, what other merchandise characteristic must be considered to make the catalog goods salable?

## CASE PROBLEM 1

Gallop & Litt have been successful specialty store merchants in Ohio, Missouri, and Kansas for more than 35 years. Today, they operate 48 stores in the three states. Their merchandise assortment focuses on understated sportswear and accessories for the middle-income female.

As is the case with other chain organizations, G & L, as the firm is usually referred to by its customers, operates a catalog division. The merchandise is acquired by the same buying staff for both in-store and catalog use and is basically the same for both divisions. That is, the most promising merchandise headed for the stores is earmarked for the catalog.

While the business has been generally profitable for all the company's years as a specialty retailer, management has decided it might be appropriate to expand the catalog division to make it even more profitable. After extensive brainstorming, the company's management team has narrowed the expansion ideas down to a few. They are as follows:

1. Instead of merely sending the store's catalogs to their regular customers in their trading area, as they have in the past, the operation should be expanded to serve markets from coast to coast.
2. The merchandise assortment should include other classifications than those featured in the stores and could include men's and children's clothing.
3. A separate buying team should be put in place for catalog purchases, with the present buying team relegated to in-store purchases.

At this point in time the company hasn't yet determined if they would utilize the three outlined changes.

### Questions

1. Could such changes prove to be a danger to the store's profit picture?

2. How should the team evaluate each of the suggested new approaches for catalog sales?
3. Which changes, if any, would you suggest be made?

## CASE PROBLEM 2

Anderson & Co., Inc., has been in the catalog business for 60 years. It features a host of gift items that are targeted for the upper-middle-class population. In addition to nationally advertised brands, about 25 percent of the assortment is private label. The catalogs are produced quarterly and reach upper-middle-class households throughout the United States.

For the past few years the company has considered an expansion of its business by opening stores in up-scale malls. After considerable discussion it has decided to test the waters and open three units. The locations are all within 60 miles of corporate headquarters where all decisions are made regarding policies, procedures, and merchandise acquisition.

Suzy Walker, general merchandise manager for the company, suggested that the buyers who are responsible for the catalog purchases be responsible for store merchandising. In addition to merchandise procurement, they should also be responsible for visual merchandising direction, advertising and promotion advisement, and direction of the sales staff. Gordon Parker, operations vice president, thinks the additional tasks would be impossible for the buyers to tackle. He suggests a separate team for in-store purchasing and management.

With the time to finalize its plans growing closer, the company still hasn't made a final decision as to what changes will be incorporated in the expansion program.

### Questions

1. With whom do you agree? Why?
2. What suggestions might you make that would improve upon those offered by Walker and Parker?

# Chapter 5

# RESIDENT BUYING OFFICES AND OTHER OUTSIDE INFORMATION SOURCES

## LEARNING OBJECTIVES

*Upon completion of this chapter, the student should be able to:*

1. Differentiate among five types of buying offices.
2. Discuss the independent office in detail, listing six advantages it offers a retail store.
3. Write a brief paragraph on eight of the services an independent office provides.
4. Describe five factors that should be taken into account in selecting an office.
5. Discuss the importance of reporting services to the retailer. Give five specific examples of such services.

## INTRODUCTION

The best informed store buyers are generally the ones who most successfully achieve their goals as the company's purchasing agents. In an era of competition for the customer's dollar, the retailer must provide merchandise that is palatable in terms of price, quality, function, and appropriateness. Buyers who operate in a vacuum without paying attention to internal and external indicators cannot possibly perform effectively. Without question, the resident buying office or market consulting organization, another name by which such companies are known, is one of the most valuable external sources of buying information. Small and large retail organizations make constant and meaningful use of resident offices.

Through the proper utilization of the services of a resident office, a buyer working on the selling floor in Spokane or Atlanta can feel the pulse of the market without being physically present. Since the buyer cannot possibly be in two places—the store and the wholesale market—at once, affiliation with a resident office provides the communication link between them.

In addition to the resident offices, buyers have available to them a number of other informative outside services. They include fashion and nonfashion reporting services, fashion forecasters, trade publications, and trade associations. The buyer who uses as many of these sources as possible makes the most intelligent purchases.

In this chapter, discussion will center on the various types of resident buying offices and other outside sources of buyer information, the services they afford buyers, and how, if efficiently used, they can increase purchasing effectiveness.

## CLASSIFICATION OF OFFICES

Unlike the retail stores to which it provides advisory services, the resident office is not located in an area that is important to the consuming public. Buying offices are located in wholesale markets, the largest of which is still New York City. Other important markets in which resident offices have set up shop are in such places as Los Angeles, Dallas, and the important foreign markets. The offices vary in size from a two- or three-person operation to the giant office that employs hundreds of specialized personnel. The merchandise runs the gamut from a single line such as women's dresses to the full complement of merchandise ranging from men's, women's, and children's wear to glassware, furniture, and dinnerware. The services offered by the offices may be restricted to the purchase of goods or run the spectrum from merchandise selection to the training of store sales personnel via audio and video tapes. Whatever the size and scope of activities provided, the resident buying office is primarily an advisory agency or market representative charged with the responsibility of transmitting vital market information.

**TABLE 5–1 The major resident buying offices**

| *BUYING OFFICE* | *TYPE* |
|---|---|
| Allied Stores | Corporate* |
| Associated Merchandising Corp. (AMC) | Cooperative |
| April-Marcus | Independent |
| Associated Dry Goods Corp. | Corporate* |
| Atlas Buying Corp. | Independent |
| Belk Stores Services, Inc. | Corporate* |
| Clothier's Corp. | Independent |
| Frederick Atkins | Independent |
| Henry Doneger Associates | Independent |
| Independent Associated Distributors | Independent |
| Macy's Corporate Buying | Corporate* |
| The May Merchandising Corp. | Corporate* |
| Men's Fashion Guild | Independent |
| Neiman-Marcus | Private |
| Promotional Buying Exchange, Ltd. | Independent |
| Retailers Representative, Inc. | Independent |
| Sears | Private |
| Specialty Stores Association | Cooperative |

*Division of a retail corporation

Although basically providing the same type of cooperation with the store buyer, there are different types of resident offices. They differ not in the services they provide but in their ownership. Table 5–1 lists a sampling of major resident offices.

## The Private Office

Retailers of enormous size with specific needs sometimes find it beneficial as well as economical to maintain a resident office specifically for their own needs. Although this type of operation is not commonplace in contemporary retailing (in fact they are few in number), some organizations deem the private office necessary to the success of their outlets. Neiman-Marcus, based in Dallas with units in other cities, maintains such an office.The nature of the Neiman-Marcus operation perhaps necessitates such an exclusive arrangement. The company caters to the affluent through a merchandising mix incorporating high price and unusual offerings, such as an offering in the 1990 Christmas Book of a one-of-a-kind Black Willow mink coat, carrying a $60,000 price tag. Where the specialization is so unique and the market so limited, affiliation with offices that represent several other retailers would be unsound. Figure 5–1 features an item so unique that it requires the personal attention of a private office to discover such an item.

This type of office is not restricted to the unique establishments such as Neiman-Marcus but is also available to those whose volume warrants exclusive attention. But without the necessary requisites such as uniqueness of product or vastness of size, the private office is not considered essential or economical.

**FIGURE 5–1.** "The Chairperson," a hand detailed, personalized, sculptured artwork by Philip Grace is a combination chair and portrait. *Courtesy:* Neiman-Marcus.

## Cooperative Ownership

Although such offices are few in number compared to independent offices, the cooperative office, sometimes called an associated office, accounts for an enormous amount of business. This type of buying office is owned, controlled, and operated by a group of stores. The retail operations involved have some common interest, such as merchandise assortment or price ranges. The stores are usually very large and demand attention that cannot be satisfied by membership in other types of resident buying offices.

Such policies as the scope of services to be offered are established by a board of directors, who are usually executives of the stores represented. The

Associated Merchandising Corporation, known in the industry as AMC, is an example of a cooperatively owned office that represents such department stores as Abraham and Straus, Rich's, and Bloomingdale's. In addition to the usual services offered by the independent office, AMC has sufficient coverage in foreign markets to enable member stores to avail themselves of merchandise from abroad. Another example of the cooperative office is Specialty Stores Association, whose affiliated stores are specialty women's stores rather than department stores.

While this type of resident office arrangement provides the member stores with more attention than membership in the less personal independent office, it might have a disadvantage. That is, retailers find invaluable the exchange of information available from their counterparts in other areas of the country. At periodic meetings at the independent office, retailers can achieve a great deal of insight into problems that confront others in the same situation. For example, a store in New York could learn of a noncompeting store's experience in Los Angeles with a certain line of merchandise. Although the cooperative resident office does have a number of different retail organizations in its group, the number of stores represented is certainly fewer than in the independent resident buying office, and the exchange of information is correspondingly limited. Private ownership provides no information exchange because representation is exclusive.

## Division of a Retail Corporation

In the United States there are corporations composed of chains of department stores structured in such a manner that a resident buying office is organized as a division of the company. An example of this type is Macy's Corporate Buying Division, a division of R. H. Macy. This buying office services the needs of such stores in the chain as Macy's Northeast; Macy's South/Bullock's, and Macy's California.

With this arrangement the office plays a significant role in the store's merchandising plans. Under corporate ownership, the resident office serves the member stores. With this structure, the buying office has the responsibility of formulating pricing policies and so forth, and seeing to it that stores adhere to these policies.

## The Independent Office

Most retailers in the United States are too small to satisfy their needs by maintaining private resident buying offices or the semiprivately owned cooperative ventures. The independent office (sometimes known as the salaried office), by far the largest type of resident buying office, offers operators of single stores and small chain organizations much needed market representation. Without the enormous investment of private or semiprivate office ownership, the smaller retailer can employ the services of a professional market representative at a cost commensurate with its needs.

For a fee, the retailer is entitled to all the services rendered by the resident office. The fees charged by the office are determined by the scope of activities offered and the particular requirements of the member retail stores. The actual charge is generally based on a predetermined rate for such items as postage, telephone calls, and desk space for visiting buyers. Purchases made by the office at the request of the individual retailer carry an additional expense in the form of a commission. At present the going rate is 0.5 percent to 1.0 percent of the store's net sales. Sometimes the commission applies only to the actual goods purchased. Figure 5–2 shows an example of a resident office contract.

The success of the independent office continues to increase. It is of primary importance to retailers who haven't the time to spend away from their stores to visit the wholesale markets frequently, or to those who are so far removed geographically that adequate market visits would be prohibitive in cost.

Gentlemen:

Confirming our understanding, we shall for the period beginning through place at your disposal the complete resident buying facilities of our organization, and shall, on your behalf, perform all services usually performed by resident buyers including the placing of your orders for merchandise and the furnishing of information regarding market conditions.

For our service, we shall receive from you the annual fee of $ payable in advance in equal monthly installments of $ each, plus postage.

Unless either you or we shall give the other written notice to the contrary at least 60 days before the annual expiration date, we shall continue our service on your behalf for the further annual periods.

Very truly yours,

Name of Company

BY________________________

AGREED TO:

BY________________________

**FIGURE 5–2.** Resident buying office contract

Member stores, by taking advantage of the multitude of services offered, can improve their retail positions.

The advantages of resident buying office affiliation include the following:

1. Merchandising effectiveness can be increased substantially so that small retailers can more knowledgeably compete with the large department stores and chain organizations. These large retail organizations, through their private or cooperative offices, have a constant insight into market conditions. Through membership in an independent office, the small retailer can gain the same timely market information. Without representation, the smaller store buyer, relegated to infrequent market visits, can easily miss market "happenings." Particularly in fashion merchandise, where a new fashion might be revolutionizing the current season, the buyer who is absent from the market might get the information too late to be meaningful. News of a new color or new silhouette could make the season a success.
2. The exchange of information by noncompeting stores provides the retailer with the point of view of a retailing counterpart. Under the resident office system, retailers from different parts of the country meet and can discuss their experiences. Thus a buyer from a northern region can meet with a southern retailer and "pick the latter's brains" about the current season's swimwear collection. Since the southern buyer merchandises swimwear all year long, the northerner can be led into the most appropriate merchandise before his or her season begins.
3. By belonging to a resident office, the smaller retailer immediately becomes more important to the vendors. Manufacturers and wholesalers recognize the important positions enjoyed by the offices merely because of their numbers of members. If a small store owner acts in unison with others in the group, the attention paid to him by the vendors increases significantly. Under similar conditions and circumstances, the retailer with representation in a resident buying office usually does better than a counterpart who "goes it alone." For example, if a retailer decides to return merchandise to a manufacturer because of poor fit or some other reason, the manufacturer must determine whether or not to accept the return. If the returner of the goods belongs to an office, the return is usually easier than for an unaffiliated retailer. The reason for this prejudice is simple: Unhappy members of resident buying offices may complain to their representatives, which could result in a boycott of the uncooperative vendor. (Unhappiness from the lone retailer might result in no future purchasing, but future business from other retailers is not likely to be affected.) By joining forces in the resident buying office, the individual business can bolster its position to compare with that enjoyed by the department stores or chain operations.
4. Careful utilization of the services rendered by the resident buying office can substantially reduce the risks faced by independent retailers. And these risks are many! Of primary concern to the store buyer is selection of

the appropriate merchandise. While individual stores must rely on the expertise of their buyers, the resident office, through experienced, skillful trading, can advise the buyers on purchasing and all its pitfalls. By narrowing down the available lines of merchandise and the available items to those that seem best suited to their members, the resident office helps the store buyer avoid purchasing errors.

In addition to merchandise selection, buyers are concerned with delivery deadlines. Because the resident offices provide vendors with most of their business, the stores they represent enjoy preferential delivery over unaffiliated independent retailers. Having the right merchandise at the right time can ultimately lead to fewer and lower markdowns and can substantially increase the efficiency of the retail operation.

5. One of the buying advantages enjoyed by the large department stores and chain organizations is the purchasing of merchandise made to specification and labeled exclusively under the store's name. Since private brand merchandising requires large purchases, small retailers are generally unable to participate in such endeavors. However, resident buying offices can and do provide their members with private brand merchandise that has been acquired for their exclusive distribution. Since the office represents hundreds of stores, its buying potential is commensurate with that of the large chains. The retailer enjoys this exclusive merchandise because it is available only at member stores and eliminates price cutting by competitors.
6. Initial orders need not be as large for resident office members as those placed by independent stores. Independent retailers, particularly those who are far removed from the wholesale markets, must place orders to cover their merchandise needs until the time of the next market visit or the road call from the vendor's salesperson. Stores with market representation are constantly being notified of new merchandise through brochures, telegrams, telephone calls, letters, and the like. These retailers enjoy the luxury of placing smaller orders, keeping their inventories "light," and being apprised of any hot items in the market. Authorization to their market representatives can bring the merchandise to the store as efficiently as if the store buyer purchased the merchandise directly.
7. The resident office, through its multitude of services, provides much more than the purchase and recommendation of merchandise available. These services, such as advertising and promotional suggestions, fashion show production, training of retail sales personnel through programmed presentations, and counseling on methods of inventory control, can contribute dramatically to the efficiency of the store's entire operation. Such services could cost the retailer considerable additional expense if purchased elsewhere. As part of the resident buying office's package to member stores, the costs involved are considerably reduced.
8. Recent years have seen an increase in the importance of merchandise produced abroad in the merchandising plans of American retailers. Few stores

in our country have the resources necessary for direct negotiation with foreign producers. The large resident buying offices have permanently based foreign branches or send representatives periodically to distant lands to survey the goods available for purchase. Through office association, small retailers can be alerted to foreign merchandise and can purchase goods without having to incur the expense of trips abroad. This enables the small retailer to compete on still another level with department store and chain organizations.

## ORGANIZATIONAL STRUCTURES

Resident buying offices may be as diversified in their offerings as department stores or may restrict their merchandise to that offered by the speciality store. The better known offices maintain departments in most of the lines found in the large department store, with emphasis on women's wear. The personnel organization of the larger offices generally follows the pattern of the stores they represent and acts in an assistance and advisory capacity. Figure 5–3 shows a five-function organization chart, with four divisions broken down and further subclassified according to major merchandise categories. The fifth division or function, operating vice president and assistant treasurer, deals with the operation of the resident office.

Figure 5–4 shows a more specialized type of resident buying office that caters exclusively to women's and children's wear. The structure shows three functions, with very little attention paid to operating services. Some resident buying offices restrict their merchandise lines even more than the one in Figure 5–4 and pay attention only to a single line, such as women's wear.

## SERVICES OF AN OFFICE

Services vary from office to office. The smallest office, with limited staff and facilities, may simply provide information concerning the purchase of merchandise. Larger, more diversified resident buying offices offer their members services ranging from the recommendation of specific merchandise to the preparation of promotional materials. The following services are among those available at the larger office.

### Buying Merchandise

In most cases, resident buyers provide assistance to the store buyers when the task of purchasing is at hand. Some buyers have the primary responsibility for purchasing and therefore come to the markets or see traveling salespeople at their own stores. Buyers seek the advice of resident representatives on buying matters but place their own orders. The buying actually performed by the resident buyers usually does not involve initial orders at the beginning of the sea-

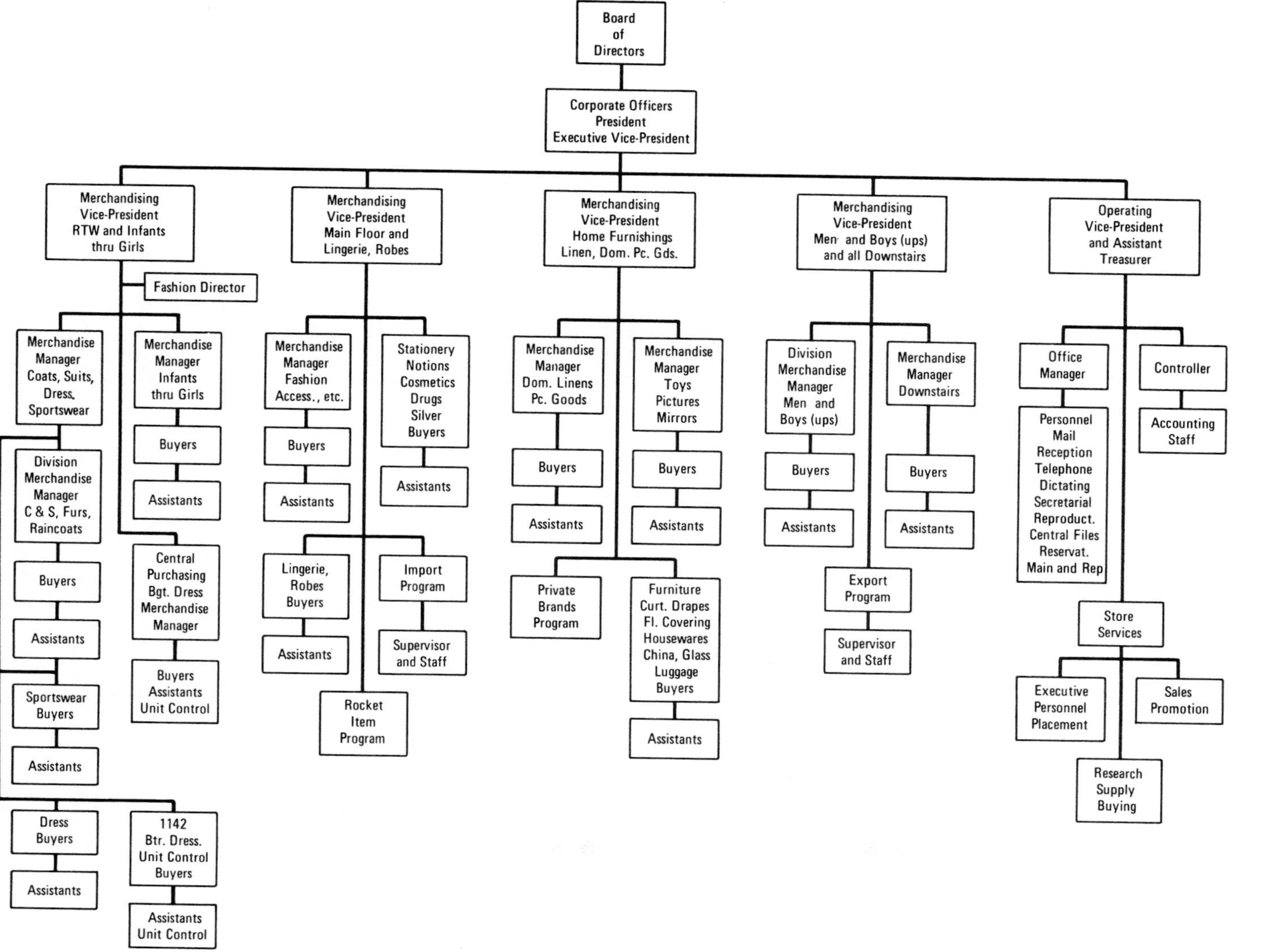


**FIGURE 5–3.** Organization chart—full-line resident buying office

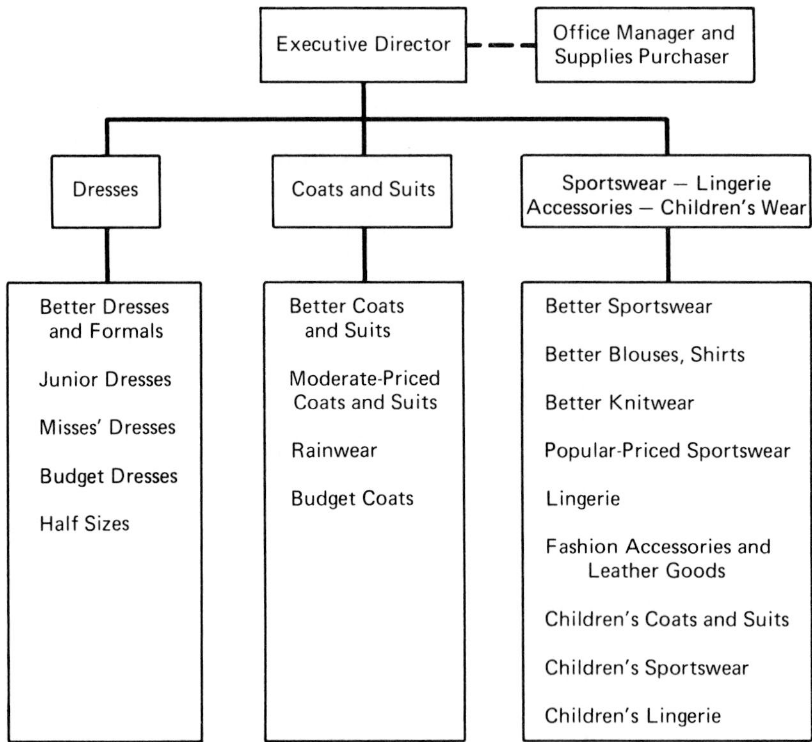


**FIGURE 5–4.** Organization chart—specialized resident buying office

son. Resident buyers, then, generally are directly responsible for purchasing of the following nature:

1. *Reorders.* A reorder is the replenishment of an item that has sold out. Buyers who can find enough salable merchandise that can be continually reordered can better guarantee a successful season. The timing of the reorder in terms of prompt delivery is essential to the store's business. Late arrival of reordered goods can seriously affect sales and lead to reduced profit. Stores often call on their resident offices to place the reorders. Since the office is located in the market and also enjoys the powerful position of representing many stores, it can more easily motivate the manufacturer to ship quickly. The manufacturer is certainly more likely to respond to the pressures applied by the resident buying office than to the independent retailer in Duluth, Minnesota. Figure 5–5 shows an example of a resident office reorder report.
2. *Special orders.* As the name implies, special orders are for merchandise not usually carried by the store. The "special" might consist of a size not usually stocked, a different color of an item in the store, or even an item unavailable at present. For example, a regular customer might want a dress

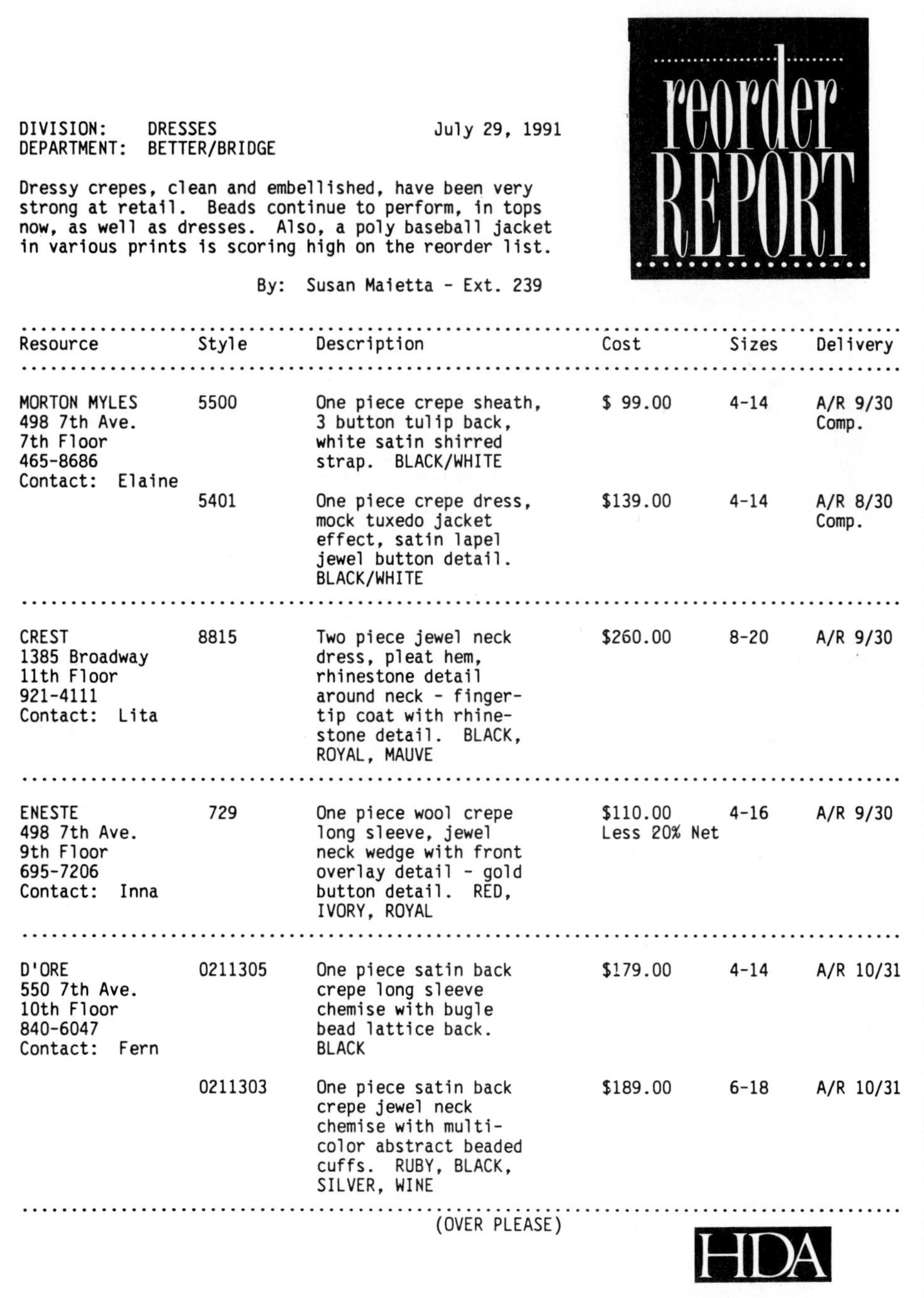



DIVISION: DRESSES July 29, 1991
DEPARTMENT: BETTER/BRIDGE

Dressy crepes, clean and embellished, have been very strong at retail. Beads continue to perform, in tops now, as well as dresses. Also, a poly baseball jacket in various prints is scoring high on the reorder list.

By: Susan Maietta - Ext. 239

| Resource | Style | Description | Cost | Sizes | Delivery |
|---|---|---|---|---|---|
| MORTON MYLES<br>498 7th Ave.<br>7th Floor<br>465-8686<br>Contact: Elaine | 5500 | One piece crepe sheath, 3 button tulip back, white satin shirred strap. BLACK/WHITE | $ 99.00 | 4-14 | A/R 9/30<br>Comp. |
| | 5401 | One piece crepe dress, mock tuxedo jacket effect, satin lapel jewel button detail. BLACK/WHITE | $139.00 | 4-14 | A/R 8/30<br>Comp. |
| CREST<br>1385 Broadway<br>11th Floor<br>921-4111<br>Contact: Lita | 8815 | Two piece jewel neck dress, pleat hem, rhinestone detail around neck - finger-tip coat with rhine-stone detail. BLACK, ROYAL, MAUVE | $260.00 | 8-20 | A/R 9/30 |
| ENESTE<br>498 7th Ave.<br>9th Floor<br>695-7206<br>Contact: Inna | 729 | One piece wool crepe long sleeve, jewel neck wedge with front overlay detail - gold button detail. RED, IVORY, ROYAL | $110.00<br>Less 20% Net | 4-16 | A/R 9/30 |
| D'ORE<br>550 7th Ave.<br>10th Floor<br>840-6047<br>Contact: Fern | 0211305 | One piece satin back crepe long sleeve chemise with bugle bead lattice back. BLACK | $179.00 | 4-14 | A/R 10/31 |
| | 0211303 | One piece satin back crepe jewel neck chemise with multi-color abstract beaded cuffs. RUBY, BLACK, SILVER, WINE | $189.00 | 6-18 | A/R 10/31 |

(OVER PLEASE)



**FIGURE 5–5.** This reorder report focuses on resources, styles, descriptions, costs, sizes, and delivery of better/bridge dresses. *Courtesy:* Henry Doneger Associates.

DEPARTMENT: BETTER/BRIDGE

| Resource | Style | Description | Cost | Sizes | Delivery |
|---|---|---|---|---|---|
| D'ORE<br>(CONT'D) | 0211021 | Three piece satin back crepe longer cardigan jacket with bead trim - beaded halter vest and slim skirt. SAPPHIRE, BLACK | $289.00 | 4-14 | A/R 10/31 |
| PARNES FEINSTEIN<br>530 7th Ave.<br>10th Floor<br>944-7788<br>Contact: Ron | 9213 | One piece acrylic blend long sleeve, jewel neck colorblock chemise with contrast trim.<br>ROYAL/BLACK/RED | $ 99.00 | 6-18 | A/R 9/30 |
| | 9210 | One piece acrylic blend chemise, red top jewel neck, long sleeve with stripe trim - solid black skirt, stripe scarf. RED/BLACK, CAMEL/BLACK | $105.00 | 6-18 | A/R 9/30 |
| CASTLEBERRY KNITS<br>530 7th Ave.<br>11th Floor<br>221-4333<br>Contact: Pat | 0917 | Two piece coin dot pleat skirt, double breasted shirt, knit trim.<br>SKIPPER/SILVER | $128.00 | 6-18 | A/R 9/30 |
| SCALA<br>498 7th Ave.<br>15th Floor<br>868-2244<br>Contact: Alby | 7257 | Sequin short sleeve top. FUCHSIA/BLACK, EMERALD/ BLACK, BLACK/BLACK, ROYAL/BLACK | $ 29.00 HDA<br>$ 39.00 Net | P-XL | A/R 10/15 |
| | 2703 | Sequin short sleeve top. RED/BLACK, ROYAL/BLACK, BLACK/GOLD, BLACK/SILVER | $ 29.00 HDA<br>$ 39.00 Net | P-XL | A/R 10/15 |
| GDT TOO<br>C/O JEN MAR<br>498 7th Ave.<br>2nd Floor<br>594-3118<br>Contact: Marty | 2984 | Poly zip front long sleeve baseball jacket.<br>PICASSO<br>BEIGE #3<br>FUCHSIA #4<br>BALLOON<br>BLACK #I | $ 66.00 Net | 1 Size | A/R 8/30 |

**FIGURE 5–5.** *(continued)*

for her daughter's wedding. The buyer might want to accommodate the request. Since a trip to the market might be impossible, an order bearing approximate specifications can be placed with the resident buying office. Since the office may have experience and expertise in merchandise the member store doesn't stock, the special order can more easily be accomplished by allowing the resident office to make the purchase.

3. *Initial orders.* Merchandise purchased for the first time is an initial order. Most stores place their own initial orders, but they sometimes call on their offices to perform this function. A store buyer might want to whet a customer's appetite with new merchandise but be unable to come to the market or have a salesperson make a store visit. Given an idea of price, style, color, and so forth, the resident buyer will purchase the goods for the retailer. In Figure 5–6 a photo of a recommended trend complete with pertinent information is sent to the store buyers for possible placement of an initial order. In instances in which the resident buyers have continuously purchased "the right numbers," stores come to rely on their judgment and increase the amounts of new purchases made by the offices. From their "spring 1992 trend overview" booklet, buyers are alerted to influences featured in Figure 5–7. Figure 5–8 shows an example of a form used by a resident office in the placement of an order for a member store, and a confirmation of placement of order is pictured in Figure 5–9.

Sometimes it becomes necessary for a store to cancel an order. Since manufacturers are more likely to accept the cancellation from the resident office, because of its important position, than from the individual store, the cancellation generally is initiated by the resident office. In cases where the store is a major department, chain, or specialty store, with purchases contributing to a major part of the manufacturer's production, cancellations are more readily tolerated. It is the small retailer, who doesn't have this clout, who finds that cancellations are often unacceptable to vendors. Figure 5–10 shows an example of the form used for the cancellation of an order.

## Finding New Resources

The key to successful merchandising is making desirable merchandise available to customers. The bringing together of vendors and retailers whose merchandise needs and offerings blend is a function of the resident buyer. Progressive retailers are constantly seeking fresh goods to satisfy the needs of their customers. It is true that retailers expend the bulk of their budgets on lines that are established and proved. To provide the excitement and versatility of creative merchandise, however, retailers need to purchase new lines. Although it is possible for individual buyers to scout the market to seek out new merchandise resources, none can do it as successfully and capably as the resident buying office.

Not only because of their close proximity to producers do resident buyers find new lines, but also vendors seek out the resident buyers. The manufacturer who can demonstrate to the resident office that it has innovative, timely, and desirable merchandise immediately has a whole world of prospective customers. If the manufacturers spent the time to locate new customers, the task would

**FIGURE 5–6.** The Euro-Folk fashion trend illustration alerts buyers to new merchandise. *Courtesy:* Henry Doneger Associates.

## EURO-FOLK

Fresh inspiration comes from continental Europe snow spots. Euro-Folk alpine patterns, folkalic prints and silhouettes glamorize winter dressing whether for Apres Ski, City Weekend dressing or soft dressing.

TARGET: All Markets

EMPHASIS/TIMING:
... Soft dressing - July - September
... Casual and activewear - September - November
... Strong sweater statement - 4th Quarter

FABRIC:
... Stretch
... Hi-tech textiles, ie, trilobal, matte and shine
... Corduroy
... Fleece
... Velour
... Mohair/hairy yarns
... Chunky knits - Ramie/cotton, wool or acrylic
... Rayon and silk for soft dressing
... Wools - flannel, boiled and plush
... Cashmere and cashmere blends
... Cotton knits for layering

COLORS: There are 3 color componixs to this trend -
... Impressionism brights
... Black - White combinations with color accent
... Winter White and fresco pales for 4th quarter

PATTERNS:
... Nordic designs
... New fairisles
... Tryolian and floral embroideries
... Peasant folkloric paisleys, florals and patchwork prints
... Colorblocking
... Border patterns

DESIGN:
... Wonderful hand knit pattern sweaters
... Christmas and animal motif sweaters and sweatshirts
... Cardigans - alternative to the blazer
... Oversize textured solid sweaters in great colors
... Cotton turtlenecks in solids, prints and borders for layering
... Novelty sweatshirts
... Stretch stirrups and leggings - wovens and knits
... Trilobal and fleece activewear sets
... Oversize blazers - plush and novelties
... Knit dressing
... Soft dressing - with pattern mixing, border patterns and/or texture

DETAILS:
... Fringes
... Quilting
... Zippers
... Embroidery

(OVER PLEASE)

**FIGURE 5–6** *(continued)*

CLASSIFICATIONS

**KNIT TOPS**

Layering pieces are the core of this classification. However, it will be the newness that will drive this business. Key retail for volume $9.99-$19.99.

Fabric:
... 100% cotton jersey, poly/cotton, and cotton/poly
... French terry
... Fleece
... Velour for 4th Quarter

Design Element:

The Core:

... Turtlenecks - definitely the backbone of a knit department. Target retail under $10.00. Color statement is key - along with White, Black, Red and Soft Pink, fashion colors from Titian, Minstrel, and Impressionism must be programmed. All over prints, dots and borders will be approximately 25% of the buy.

... Underwear Influences - the henley neckline is back in both solids and prints - with or without lace/picot edging. The henley is predicted to be the new fashion basic. Other underwear looks to be included for layering are the basic tee, pointelle tees, and ribbon or lace trims.
... Double collars with contrast trims will continue for budget.

The New:

... The Oversize 28"-30" Tee - is the silhouette to zero into. The cross-over item to feature with leggings and stirrups. Solids dominate with prints and stripes in the distance. Start to bring in for 5/30 delivery for wear now selling. Looks to include are:
... The deep V and double V's are a must-buy - A Predictable item!
... Trapeze and Swing Tops - have only scratched the surface. Look for this silhouette to make noise for Fall.
... Henleys are exaggerated with 8 to 15 buttons.
... Neck interest such as cowls, zipped funnels, drawstring cowls, turtlenecks and scarf necklines for early.
... Football Jerseys have a layered element.

... Cardigans have two directions:...trapeze shapes for Better, ... oversize and slouchy for Budget/Moderate.

**FIGURE 5–6** *(continued)*

be monumental and prohibitive in terms of cost. Thus the resident buying office provides the supplier with potential users and also gives the retailer new resources. The "marriage" of the two can make the retailer's business more successful. Figure 5–11 features the format used by a resident buying office to alert their customers to new resources.

## *Pop Present Tense* for Womenswear

A trend for the young or the trendy that is primarily item driven with broader influences in terms of color, fabric and styling details.

**1** *Funky color combos* for solids, prints, stripes. **2** *Bodywear, activewear and underwear.* **3** *Obvious synthetics* such as plastic, nylon, polyester. **4** *'70s Design details* including big collars, small shoulders, flare cuts. **5** *Pop prints* of motifs and personalities, past and present. **6** *'60s & '70s Accessories* such as platforms, long scarves, beads, sling-backs. **7** *Very soft fabrics* like jersey, chiffon, satin. **8** *Jeanswear* with '60s, '70s details in new colors, prints. **9** *Novelty handknits* with crochet effect. **10** *Knit dressing* in poor boys, bodywear, doubleknits. **11** *Extreme lengths* from hot pants to long flares.

## *Pop Present Tense* for Childrenswear becomes Pop-sicle

A trend for kids that concentrates on item business driven by personality licensing, young TV star role models and street style activewear.

**1** *Big baggy pants & tops* in lightweight prints. **2** *Oversize jeanswear* with '60s, '70s details, new colors, prints. **3** *Pop personalities* on t-shirts, usually oversized. **4** *Printed stretch bodywear* for both girls and boys. **5** *Active wear items* with sporting motifs. **6** *Bold graphics* as prints or yarn-dyes. **7** *Hot brights with dark* accents. **8** *State-of-the-art novelty fabrics* following hyper-color, holograms.

**FIGURE 5–7.** An excerpt from a spring 1992 forecast bulletin. *Courtesy:* Henry Doneger Associates.

BW
BURNSWINKLER
ASSOCIATES, LTD.
1372 Broadway, New York, NY 10018 (212) 764-0740

**SHIP TO:**
NAME
ADDRESS
CITY STATE ZIP

Purchase Order No.
11926

Dept. # ____________

ORDER DATE
VENDOR
COMPLETION DATE
TERMS
SHIPPING INST.

**BILL TO:**
NAME
ADDRESS
CITY STATE ZIP

**Send Duplicate Invoices To:**

**BURNS WINKLER ASSOCIATES, LTD.**

| STYLE | QUAN. | DESCRIPTION | COLOR | UNITS BY COLOR | | | | | | | | | | | WHOLESALE | NET COST | SUGG. RET. |
|---|---|---|---|---|---|---|---|---|---|---|---|---|---|---|---|---|---|

TOTAL COST

**ALL LABELS, HANDTAGS AND CARE INSTRUCTIONS MUST REMAIN IN GARMENT**
**NO SUBSTITUTIONS OR BACKORDERS, SHIP A STYLE COMPLETE**

11926

VENDOR

**See Notice On Reverse Side**

FIGURE 5–8. Resident buying office order form *Courtesy:* Burns Winkler Innovators.

**Certified Buying Service, Inc.**

CONFIRMATION OF ORDER NOTICE

YOUR ORIGINAL ORDER HAS BEEN PLACED FOR YOU AS FOLLOWS:

STORE .................................. CITY ...................................... DATE .................... 19 .......

ATT'N: ................................................................................ RE: ......................................

| MANUFACTURER | ORDER # OR DATE OF ORDER | DELIVERY DATE | REMARKS (CHANGES - IF ANY) |
|---|---|---|---|
| | | | |
| | | | |
| | | | |
| | | | |
| | | | |
| | | | |
| | | | |
| | | | |

BUYER: ..................................................

FIGURE 5–9. Confirmation form

**CANCELLATION NOTICE**

**Certified Buying Service, Inc.**

119 WEST 40th STREET
NEW YORK, N. Y. 10018

MFR.________________________ Date,________________19____

Address________________________

Please cancel the order for:

________________________

________________________

Order Date________________Order No.________Dept. No.____________

Style No:________________________

Acknowledged by:

MFR.________________________ CERTIFIED BUYING SERVICE, Inc.

Per________________________ Buyer________________________

FIGURE 5–10. A cancellation form

May 24, 1991

ATT: SPORTSWEAR DEPT.

Dear Client:

New resources and divisions are continuously opening in the market. The following is a listing and brief descripton of each.

Please add these to the current resource list.

ILENE COHEN
VP, Mdse. Mgr.

GAIL BARKEN - MODERATE/UPDATED MODERATE KNITWEAR

| | | | |
|---|---|---|---|
| Mfg.: | **NORTHEAST KNITTERS** | FOB: | RI |
| Address: | 202 West 40th St. 6th fl | Terms: | 8/10 |
| Contact: | Barbara | Sizes: | S-M-L |
| Phone #: | 704-0838 | | |

TARGET CUSTOMER: Updated Missy

BACKGROUND: A new company owned by Stanley Rutstein, formerly the president of Casual Corner and US Shoe Corp.

WHAT THEY ARE DOING: An item oriented novelty sweater line. An emphasis on bright colors in geometric intarsias and pattern interest makes this line perfect for weekend wear. Styles such as #1005, a ramie/cotton multi stripe jacquard with crochet edge at $42.25 and style #1011R, a ramie/cotton mock neck with large circle intarsia priced at $32.00. Prices range from $22.00 to $49.00.

| | | | |
|---|---|---|---|
| Mfg.: | **STATEMENTS BY PRONTO** | FOB: | NY |
| Address: | 1410 Broadway 8th fl. | Terms: | 8/10 |
| Contact: | Valerie | Sizes: | S-M-L |
| Phone #: | 921-5001 | | |

TARGET CUSTOMER: Updated Missy

BACKGROUND: New separate sweater division of Pronto, the well established knitwear company.

WHAT THEY ARE DOING: Whimsical, fun and sophisticated embellished ramie/cotton sweaters. Sequins, beading & embroidery look new & different when done on color block, with a novelty all over paillettes sweater style #3000 being a key item for Fall at $59.00. Prices range from $39.00 to $59.00.

(OVER PLEASE)

**FIGURE 5–11.** "Introducing Who's New," an announcement used for new resources. *Courtesy:* Henry Doneger Associates.

## Recommending Hot Items

A hot item may be described as one the buyer can't keep in stock because of great demand for it by customers. All buyers initially plan the purchase of merchandise with the hope that it will successfully sell and reorder. In reality,

GAIL BARKEN - MODERATE/UPDATED MODERATE KNITWEAR (Con't):

| | | | |
|---|---|---|---|
| Mfg.: | **STUDIO COLLECTION** | FOB: | Miss |
| Address: | 1411 Broadway 34th fl. | Terms: | 8/10 |
| Phone #: | 789-8900 | Sizes: | S-M-L |
| Contact: | Sandy Price | | |

TARGET CUSTOMER: Updated Missy

BACKGROUND: A new division of Oakhill Sportswear with Barbara Hodes designing the line, formerly a designer at Jennifer Reed. Gearing for upper moderate to opening price points in better.

WHAT THEY ARE DOING: Pretty, feminine, novelty handknit ramie/cotton sweaters in both pastels & bright colors. All patterns are original designs with lots of embroidery & surface interest. Incentively priced from $30.00 to $32.00 for Fall '91. Some key sweaters are style #7440 - Pastel "Patchwork" with blanket stitching at $30.00 & style #7445 - "Wedding Cake" with horizontal embroidered pattern & popcorn detail at $32.00. Holiday prices will range up to $42.00.

| | | | |
|---|---|---|---|
| Mfg.: | **KNITTING NEEDLES** | FOB: | NY |
| Address: | 1410 Broadway 9th fl. | Terms: | 8/10 |
| Phone #: | 921-1088 | Sizes: | S-M-L |
| Contact: | Susan | | |

TARGET CUSTOMER: Updated Missy

BACKGROUND: New division of I.K.L. International, a private label company making better sweaters for 10 years. The sales manager is formerly of Needleworks. Incorporating similar looks to Needleworks at less expensive price points.

WHAT THEY ARE DOING: Ramie/cotton and cotton beautiful handknit sweaters. Their strength is in intricate pattern intarsias and embroideries. Great novelty items perfect for the specialty store such as style #10022 - multi color raised embroidery rose & leaf pattern at $56.25 and style #10003 - embroidered scarf detail cardigan with fringe at $130.00. Sweaters priced at $45 - 67. Wool sweater coats priced at $95 - 130.

THERESA PARUOLO - UPDATED MISSY

| | | | |
|---|---|---|---|
| Mfg.: | **ANDRE SAUVAGE** | FOB: | NY |
| Address: | 525 7th Ave. 22nd fl. | Terms: | 8/10 |
| Phone #: | 840-7142 | Sizes: | 6-16 |
| Contact: | Pam, Les | | |

TARGET CUSTOMER: Updated Missy

BACKGROUND: New blouse division of Adamo, formerly a moderate missy blouse house.

WHAT THEY ARE DOING: Beautiful polyester print blouses in 3 bodies at incentive prices for HDA accounts. Choose from - The jewel neck at $19.00 ... the drape neck mock jabot at $25.00 ... and the 3 button crush also incentively priced at $25.00.

**FIGURE 5–11** *(continued)*

even the most seasoned buyers soon discover their share of less desirable items. They often must mark down some merchandise to dispose of it quickly. To ensure a successful season, the buyer actively searches for an item or items that will counterbalance the reduced profits from the slower-selling goods. A few hot items will do the trick! Resident buyers, through reports from member stores as well as from the manufacturers, are made aware of fast-selling numbers. This information is passed along to member stores in the form of newsletters, flyers, bulletins, and the like. Sometimes the resident office sends along order forms for quick delivery of merchandise. Figure 5–12 shows examples of the methods used to notify retailers of the hot items available and their success to date. One page features a drawing of the recommenced item; the other, the details of the recommendation.

## Following Up Orders

The placement of an order does not guarantee delivery of merchandise. Even the most careful and complete delivery instructions do not ensure that the buyer will receive goods on the prescribed delivery date. Receiving merchandise at the appropriate time is of paramount importance to the operation of the buyer's department. How vital timely delivery is may be best illustrated in a situation in which advertising is involved. A buyer might place an exceptionally large order for the express purpose of running an advertisement. Imagine how devastating it would be if the ad broke and the merchandise hadn't arrived on time. Sales could be lost and the store's reputation damaged. Customers might misunderstand the incident as being intentionally planned just to produce traffic.

Resident buyer assistants perform the task of following up orders to make certain that shipments will be forthcoming. The importance of the resident buying office to the manufacturer enables sufficient pressure to be applied to guarantee delivery. For an individual retailer to accomplish the same thing would be difficult. The distance between retailer and manufacturer, as well as the lesser importance of the individual store, makes it less likely that satisfaction can be attained as easily. Merchandise on order cuts into the efficiency of the store's operation, and the follow-up by the resident buying office helps get action. Figure 5–13 shows a form that is used to follow up orders for specific merchandise so that customers will be made aware of the status of the order.

## Group Buying

Occasionally resident buying offices can save the individual retailer money. By pooling orders, the office might be able to purchase a particular item at a lower price. Small retailers, because of their size, do not get the quantity discounts allowable on large purchases. Through the combining of orders, the resident buyer might enable the small retailer to qualify for a quantity discount. It should be understood that under the Robinson–Patman Act (to be discussed in Chapter 13), quantity discounts are allowable under certain circumstances.

## Handling Complaints and Adjustments

Buyers spend considerable time and effort in the merchandising of their stores. Diligent purchasers carefully scrutinize the merchandise offered and make their selections. Store buyers often find, however, that some manufacturers

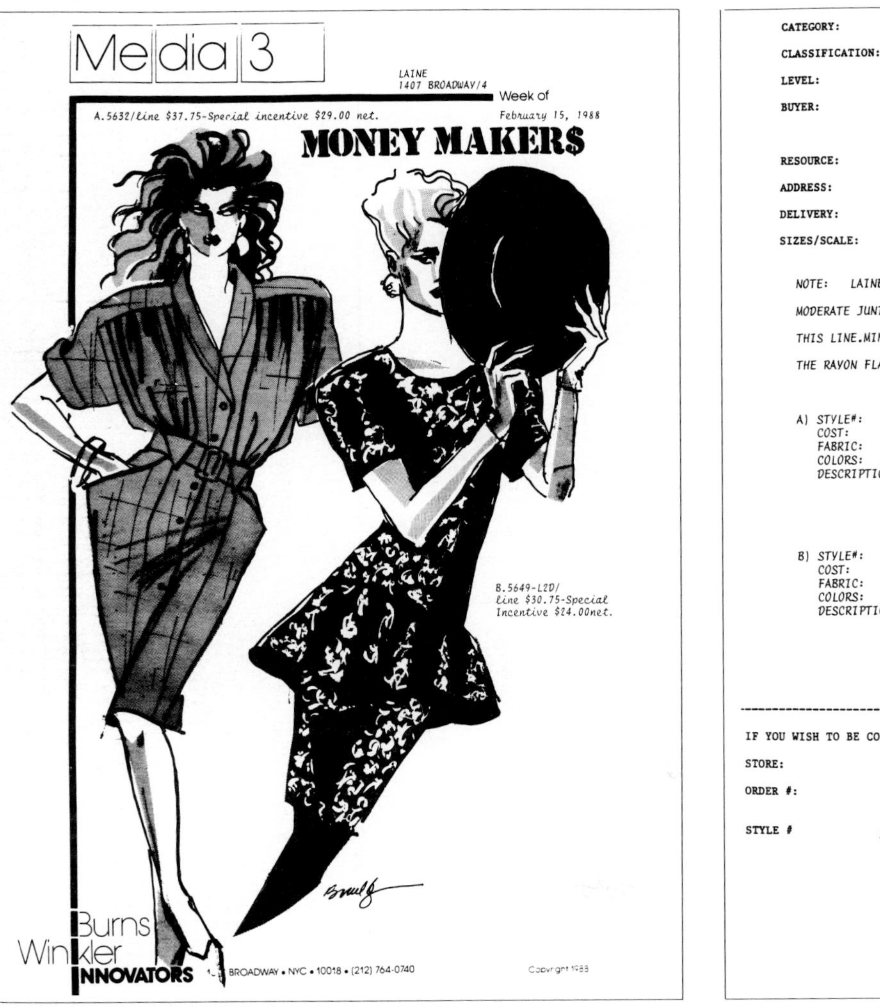


| | |
|---|---|
| **CATEGORY:** | JUNIOR DRESSES |
| **CLASSIFICATION:** | CAREER |
| **LEVEL:** | MODERATE |
| **BUYER:** | BARBARA HOCHSTEIN |

| | |
|---|---|
| **RESOURCE:** | LAINE |
| **ADDRESS:** | 1407 BROADWAY/4 |
| **DELIVERY:** | AR 3/30 |
| **SIZES/SCALE:** | 3-13 |

NOTE: LAINE OFFERS A STRONG COLLECTION OF CAREER 1 AND 2 PIECE DRESSES FOR THE MODERATE JUNIOR CUSTOMER. EASY PRINTS FEATURED IN POLY/RAYON ARE EMPHASISED IN THIS LINE.MINI FLORALS, ABSTRACT GEOMETRICS, MONOTONE CONTINUE TO BE BEST. ALSO THE RAYON FLAX GROUP LOOKS GREAT.

| | | |
|---|---|---|
| A) | STYLE#: | 5632 |
| | COST: | *Line price $37.75-Special incentive $29.00 net.* |
| | FABRIC: | *Poly/rayon/flax* |
| | COLORS: | *Cream, peach* |
| | DESCRIPTION: | *1 piece shirtdress button down front panel bodice, shawl collar, pull through belt slim skirt.* |

| | | |
|---|---|---|
| B) | STYLE#: | 5649-L2D |
| | COST: | *Line price $30.75-Special incentive $24.00 net.* |
| | FABRIC: | *Poly/rayon floral* |
| | COLORS: | *Red/white, navy/white* |
| | DESCRIPTION: | *1 piece drop torso, high low peplum, slim skirt.* |

---

**IF YOU WISH TO BE COVERED ON THIS MERCHANDISE, PLEASE INDICATE AS FOLLOWS:**

**STORE:** LAINE

**ORDER #:**

| STYLE # | COLORS | 3/4 | S 5/6 | 7/8 | M 9/10 | 11/12 | L 13/14 | 15/16 |
|---|---|---|---|---|---|---|---|---|

**FIGURE 5–12.** Money makers—a hot item notice. *Courtesy:* Burns Winkler Innovators.

Young Innovators

1372 Broadway
New York, New York 10018
(212) 221-7840

DATE: ______________________

TO: ______________________

☐ Young Innovators ☐ media 3

ATTENTION:

FROM:

REPLY REQUESTED: ☐ YES ☐ NO

MESSAGE:

FOLLOW UP INFORMATION:

RE: MANUFACTURER ______________ ORDER # ________ DATED ______________

☐ order placed
☐ order cancelled
☐ style(s) cancelled
☐ order extended
☐ return request

PLEASE SEE ABOVE FOR REMARKS

**FIGURE 5–13.** Follow-up order form. *Courtesy:* Burns Winkler Innovators.

are notorious for "substitution shipping." That is, different colors than originally ordered might be substituted, the wrong sizes might be sent, or materials that are inferior to the sample might replace the originals.

Knowledgeable buyers carefully examine shipments as they come into the store. Deliveries are scanned to determine quality, proper assortment, and so forth. In some cases, errors are found. Buyers who insist on "merchandise as ordered" usually return the unwanted goods. Although the manufacturer hasn't followed instructions, it is often remiss in handling the customer's complaint and refuses an adjustment. Once again the resident buyer can usually make the adjustment in accordance with the store buyer's wishes. Going it alone can result in frustration and dissatisfaction. Complaints can also include such problems as improper fit, late delivery, excessively high delivery costs, competitor price cutting, and poor merchandise wear.

### Assisting the Buyer During Market Week

The various types of new merchandise are made available to buyers periodically throughout the year. Typically, new women's wear lines are shown four or five times a year. These periods, called market weeks, are set aside for buyers to come to view the lines. They are hectic times for store buyers and thus for resident buying offices, which provide a great deal of assistance at that time. Store buyers may visit their markets more frequently than during market week, but it is during this period that all the buyers come to market. Since the trips are short, generally for one week, the resident buying office must plan carefully so that the visit can be a fruitful experience. The resident office plans for market week in many areas to make the buyer's trip more productive. In Chapter 10, these areas will be discussed in detail.

### Preparation of Promotional Activities

The small retailer often tries to emulate the large organizations through a variety of promotional activities. Unlike the giant retailer, the small business has neither the specialized talent necessary to handle promotional activities nor the capital needed for a great deal of outside assistance.

Large resident buying offices offer a number of promotional services that range from display suggestions to fashion show production. The office might supply its member stores with complete window display layouts or interior display hints. Very often newspaper advertising campaigns are recommended to help promote a particular line or open a new season. Even "canned" fashion show formats complete with commentary are made available to the stores.

### Foreign Market Information

With the enormous interest in foreign-made merchandise, a greater number of offices are offering information on those markets and goods to their members. The large offices provide continuous coverage of such areas as France,

Great Britain, Italy, and the Orient by maintaining branch offices in those countries. Smaller offices periodically send representatives to cover new openings such as the Paris haute couture collections, which feature high-fashion custom designs, *prêt-à-porter* or ready-to-wear merchandise, and lines that are demanding attention throughout the world. Small stores can thus avail themselves of the merchandise that was at one time available exclusively to the large companies. Figure 5–14 describes how one office assists its member stores with its import purchases. Since foreign markets have generated such excitement and play a significant merchandising role in contemporary retailing, more intensive coverage will be presented in Chapter 10.

## Private Label Development

To improve their average markups and profitability, most companies arrange to have merchandise produced for their exclusive use. By eliminating competition in this manner, they can charge prices without worrying about another company selling it for less. Since exclusive private label development requires enormous quantity commitments, this type of merchandising has been relegated primarily to the giants of the retail industry.

Resident buying offices have come to the rescue of the retailer who would like to be afforded private label goods, but individually, most have neither the resources nor the quantity potential necessary for their own programs. Most of the major offices are now involved in having goods produced, under their own label, and are making it available to their member stores. Since the stores involved are noncompeting (they are usually located far away from each other), the prices charged could be based upon a higher than normal markup. Major offices such as Henry Doneger Associates provide private label collections for their member stores.

## Training Sales Personnel

No one would argue that the training of salespeople remains the responsibility of the retail store. Nor is it suggested that resident buying offices are about to assume such responsibility. However, some offices do make available training material that can assist the retailer. Such devices as video tapes offer advice on how to sell a swimsuit have been made available. Likewise, booklets, pamphlets, brochures, newsletters, and so forth are prepared to be used as a starting point in sales training.

## Research

An area that is receiving more attention and generating more vital information for the retailer is research. Because of the similarity of their membership, resident buying offices are involved in research projects that can prove of value to all the stores they serve. The research ranges from informal studies,

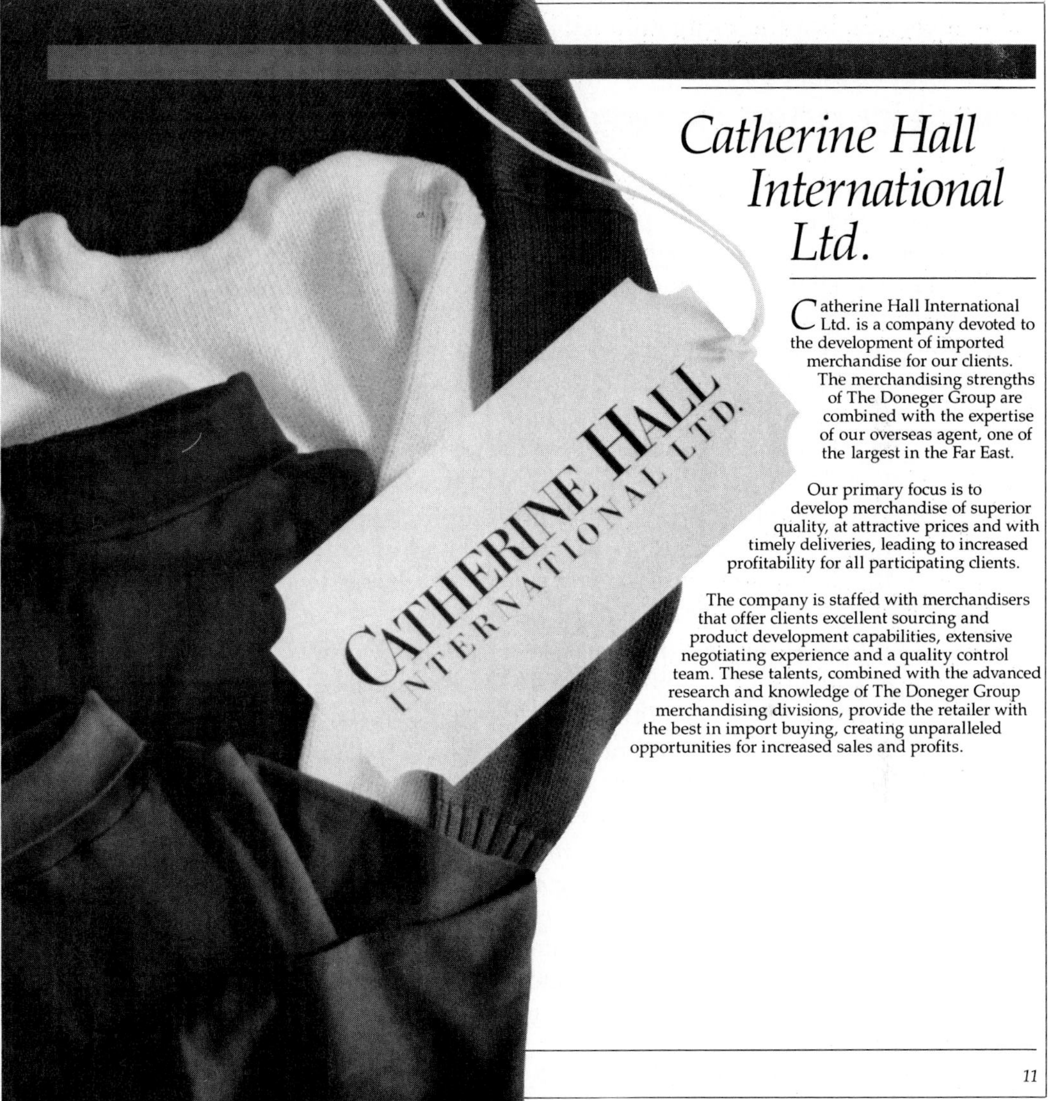

Catherine Hall International Ltd.
CATHERINE HALL INTERNATIONAL LTD.
Catherine Hall International Ltd. is a company devoted to the development of imported merchandise for our clients. The merchandising strengths of The Doneger Group are combined with the expertise of our overseas agent, one of the largest in the Far East.
Our primary focus is to develop merchandise of superior quality, at attractive prices and with timely deliveries, leading to increased profitability for all participating clients.
The company is staffed with merchandisers that offer clients excellent sourcing and product development capabilities, extensive negotiating experience and a quality control team. These talents, combined with the advanced research and knowledge of The Doneger Group merchandising divisions, provide the retailer with the best in import buying, creating unparalleled opportunities for increased sales and profits.
11


**FIGURE 5–14.** Import buying is made easy for stores when the resident office is involved. *Courtesy:* Henry Doneger Associates.

which might involve a telephone contact with key stores to find out what's selling, to the more formal approach, which involves observations, questionnaires, and personal interviews.

The research areas of interest to retailers include employee evaluation, price line dominance, methods used in the operation of a department store, return policies, promotional involvement, and cost analysis.

With resident offices providing such services, the retailer with neither the expertise nor the inclination for research can still benefit from it.

## *HOW TO CHOOSE AN OFFICE*

Large retailers are partners in cooperative ventures or maintain their own resident buying offices. It is the small retailer that must select from among the many independent resident buying offices the one that is best suited to its needs. It should be understood that the office's advice could contribute significantly to the store's success.

Before making the final decision, the retailer must measure a variety of factors. Among the questions to be considered are the following:

1. How large is the office? Are there a sufficient number of specialists to provide the information the store will need for its decision making?
2. Does the office provide the full complement of services the store needs to improve its operation? Some stores want only buying information and therefore might not have to incur the expense of belonging to a "full-service" resident office.
3. Which stores are members of the resident office? If competitive retailers already belong, joining would be inadvisable, since the customary exchange of information might divulge company secrets.
4. Are the stores represented by the office similar to the retailer's operation? This is important, since any information exchange in such areas as promotion, pricing policies, returns, and the like, can improve the company.
5. Does the office specialize in all the merchandise classifications the store carries? If you are operating a small department store, you should be able to get information in all the hard and soft goods lines. In such a situation, belonging to an office specializing exclusively in women's wear would necessitate belonging to still another office for other coverage.

## *OTHER OUTSIDE BUYING AIDS*

Although it is obvious from the discussion that resident offices assist the store buyer enormously, this is not the only outside source of information to which the buyer turns.

Capable buyers are aware of the great responsibility they have and always seek as much assistance in their planning as possible. Many different services are available to all buyers, whether their merchandise is hard goods, soft goods, or foods. Among the most important are the reporting services, magazines and trade publications, the many trade associations, nonprofit public relations organizations, and the latest innovation, video buying services.

## Fashion-Reporting Services

All buyers must be in constant touch with the trends that affect their products. Naturally, the more frequent and drastic the product change, the more important the information is to the buyer. In the field of fashion, the buyer must devote a considerable amount of effort on a daily basis to keep current. To satisfy this buyer in women's ready-to-wear, an information industry—fashion-reporting services—has been developed and is used by virtually all large fashion buyers.

### *Retail Reporting Bureau*

Typical of the fashion-reporting services is the Retail Reporting Bureau, an unbiased confidential reporting service. It normally makes monthly charges, depending on volume and the number of branches. In return for this fee, it provides its customers with 30 to 35 "merchandise news flashes" per month that contain information on the goods that are selling best and the places where these sales are being made. It does this by shopping daily a broad range of retail stores and regularly researching the wholesale market. It also studies the fashion advertisements on a daily basis and gets feedback from hundreds of buyers who cover the whole market. Figure 5–15 is a typical merchandise report from the Retail Reporting Bureau.

It should be pointed out that most of the fashion-reporting services concentrate heavily on the New York City retail market. This, however, does not limit the use of the service to retail buyers in that area. New York City is an important fashion center, and the city's major retailers are fashion leaders. Information concerning the important fashions being sold by the leaders is important to stores that are far removed from the metropolitan area. Even stores that are not interested in the specific goods shown will benefit from a knowledge of the "look," color, and tailoring of the strong-selling merchandise.

Other regular merchandise reports include those such as the ones featured in Figures 5–16 and 5–17.

### *Fashion Forecasters*

Companies such as Promostyl go one step farther than the typical resident buying offices and fashion-reporting services. They help buyers by predicting as much as 18 months in advance of the season what fashion trends could be expected. This helps the buyer with long-range planning.

## A RETAIL BUYING FOCUS

### *Promostyl*

Twelve years ago, a unique fashion forecasting service opened its first branch in the United States. Unlike the resident buying offices based in America that go

## REORDERS...BEST SELLERS

FASHION WATCH • AUGUST 19, 1991/VOL. 55/NO.24 • 800-251-4545

**DRESSES**

**S.G.GILBERT**
498 Seventh Avenue, NYC 10018
(212) 947-9150

**Style #6180**/sizes 4-14: Cotton double knit zipped front **TRAPEZE** in black with colorblock sleeves (yellow/orange/green). The zipper is yellow. (reo) Cost price: $69.00 Del: A/R 9-30

**SHOMAX**
498 Seventh Avenue, NYC 10018
(212) 760-9090

**Style #7012**/sizes S.M.L.: Long beaded constructed **GOWN** with all over multi color bead design. Short sleeved with hanging fringe beads, sweet-heart neckline and low open back, side slit are details. (reo) Cost price: $259.00 Del: A/R 10-30

**CARINE INTERNATIONAL**
(div. of Shomax)

**Style #1571**/sizes S.M.L.XL: Short **COCKTAIL** dress in black with multi color bead design at shoulders. 42" long, this dress has a jewelled neckline and a keyhole back opening. (reo) Cost price: $109.00 Del: A/R 10-30

**MICHAEL KATZ LTD.**
13 East 17th Street,NYC 10003
(212) 929-3976

**Style #292**/one size: **BLAZER** in silk crepe de chine with hand painted design (one-of-a-kind), notched collar with wide lapels, two welt pockets. (reo) Cost price: $750.00 Del: A/R September-November 30th
**Style #103**/sizes 2-14: **SHEATH** has deep scoop front (over the head entry) in solid colors (many varieties to match the jacket prints). The store can specify the length needed. (reo)
Cost price: $225.00 (sizes 16-20 slightly higher) Del: A/R 9-11/30

**RAINCOAT**

**GALLE RAINWEAR** at Tiezzi
498 Seventh Avenue, NYC 10018
(212) 947-5648

**Style #104**/sizes 4-14: Polyurethane zip front 33" **SWING** COAT. The red has pink turn back cuffs, stand up quilt collar.Also in silver. Cost price: $195.00 Del: A/R 10-1 (reo)

**SPORTSWEAR**

**SEGRETS**
1412 Broadway, NYC 10018
(212) 840-5050

**Style #P4890**/sizes XS-S-M-L: Long sleeved 100% cotton **TUNIC** designed with "Island Girl: illustration in front edged with navy/white border. **Style #P2804P**/sizes S.M.L.: Coordinating cotton/spandex stirrup **PANT** in 'Barkcloth' print - navy, white best colors. (best booking) Cost price: $24.50/$27.00 (from South Seas group) Del:A/R 11-30 cpt

**ALI & KRIS**
1407 Broadway, NYC 10018
(212) 819-1050

**Style #887**/sizes S.M.L.: Button front trapeze **BLOUSE** done in rayon acetate faille, detailed with shawl collar and sheer sleeves matching color of body. Black, white, orange, fucshia, chartreuse or royal. (reo) minimum quantity 3-6-3 of a style. Cost price: $15.00 Del: one week r/o

**MAGGIE MOODS** at Jatri
499 seventh avenue,NYC 10018
(212) 629-8410

**Style #13200**/sizes S.M.L.: All sequinned **TANK**. Sequins match the color of the silk chiffon body. Comes in matte or bright colors Cost price: $34.00 Del: A/R 10-15 (reo)

**AKA** at Jatri

**Style #7713**/sizes S.M.L.: Cuffed lurex **TUNIC**, slightly off the shoulder in silver, gold red,blue, or black. **Style #7721**/sizes s.m.l.: **LEGGINGS** in ribbed knit acetate lurex in silver to match. Cost price: $44.00 top; $24.00 silver leggings (colors $26.00) (reo)

**SPREE**
485 Seventh Avenue, NYC 10018
(212) 714-1666

**Style #5104**/sizes S.M.L.: Wool/acrylic blend **SWEATER** (on/off shoulder) in black, white or chartreuse has big cowl and all-over mirror paillettes detail. Long sleeves. (best booking) Cost price: $69.00 Del: 9-30/10-30

**FATIGATI & SMITH**
1450 Broadway, NYC 10018
(212) 575-1003

Note: New group called"Sparkle Farkle" heat transfer multi color paillette on interlock (wash & wear). (All are reo.numbers). **Style #2018**/sizes S.M.L.: Black interlock (multi paillettes silver/gold/red/prple/green/and blue)/ It's 3/4 sleeved **TUNIC** with crew neck, side slits. **Style #2017**/sizes S.M.L.: Black interlock **TOP** has 3/4 sleeves, rib knit cuff, banded bottom, Polo collar, (multi color paillettes). **Style #2016**/sizes S.M.L.: Black interlock **TOP** is crew necked, 3/4 sleeves, banded collar. rib cuff, (multi color paillettes). **Style #2019**/sizes S.M.L.: 24" walking **SHORT** also in black with 4" border that displays the multi color paillettes. Cost price: $49.00 on tops; $24.00 on shorts. Del: A/R 8-30/9-30 Also all styles will be done on black interlock with all-over silver paillettes for October delivery—for November the paillettes details will be red and green.

**FIGURE 5–15.** Reorders . . . Best Sellers merchandise report. *Courtesy:* Retail Reporting.

**RESOURCE REVIEW**

sportswear

**ADAM DOUGLAS**
498 7th AVe
NYC NY 10018
212-695-5244
PRICES $34-$149 SIZES PSML
DEL 9/30-10/30
MARKETS ALL MAJOR MARKETs

ADAM DOUGLAS is HOT! This year their sales have sky-rocketed..and after you shop this line you will see why. It is positively outstanding..offering casual to dressy "item" pieces that are well priced, feature plenty of detailing..are very special...and are sure to sell.

It's soft dressing all the way with CDC and sueded silks in two piece looks that are dyed to match... Brightly colored print or solid jacket/pant or tunic/pant sets are detailed with faux stones, sequins to gold embroidery

There is a sensational collection of item blazer jackets in wool crepes, silks, meltons, or flannels - each one spectacular.. "one-of-a-kind" looks.. detailed with emboidery, studs, pearls, stones, (some are a Criscione look at $79 & up)... They are 'must see' for Fall Holiday selling period.

More Great Holdiay Items include: a cotton interlock short sleeve T with all over paillettes in pastels, brights, silver, gold, black or white @ $69... A Tank dress @ $89 with all over paillettes..an item embroidered big shirt @ $49.....As well as a return of the infamous push up sleeve jacket in solid quilt ($89) or print ($110).

The retail business today is largely dependent on items. This resource offers you the opportunity to pick up a variety of the Hottest items in the market - all in one stop.

Adam Douglas
In Silk @ $79.00

**CHAVA**
at Project 2
209 West 38th
NYC NY 10018
212-575-2619
PRICES 18-42 SIZES SM-ML
DEL 9/15
MARKETS L.A. Dallas Atlanta

CHAVA has been in business for 17 years..but it has only been in the last three that this resource has really become recognized for its outstanding sweaters.

And this line is outstanding!... Chava sweaters are offered in 100% cotton and 100% cotton cashmere. Each silhouette comes in at least 15 color ways with some that come in as many as 40 color ways.

The silhouettes are predominantly long and sleek..tunic shapes that will merchandise perfectly with leggings to chiffon skirts - today's up-to-the-minute fashions.

Chava shapes include: long sleeve four-button oversize cardigans, generous long sleeve crew necks, roll necks, V necks, convertible double V-necks, cowl necks, off-shoulders, etc...all long and lean ..available in short or long sleeves.

This is a perfect collection for any store. the color palette is so vast, the sweaters can be used to accent just about any sportswear collection you buy. The quality is excellent.. and the styling perfect for today's fashion. Be sure and add this line to your shopping list, it's a 'must see'.

Chava
#18004 @ $28.00

AUGUST 19, 1991/FASHION WATCH **15**

**FIGURE 5–16.** A resource review for buyers. *Courtesy:* Retail Reporting.

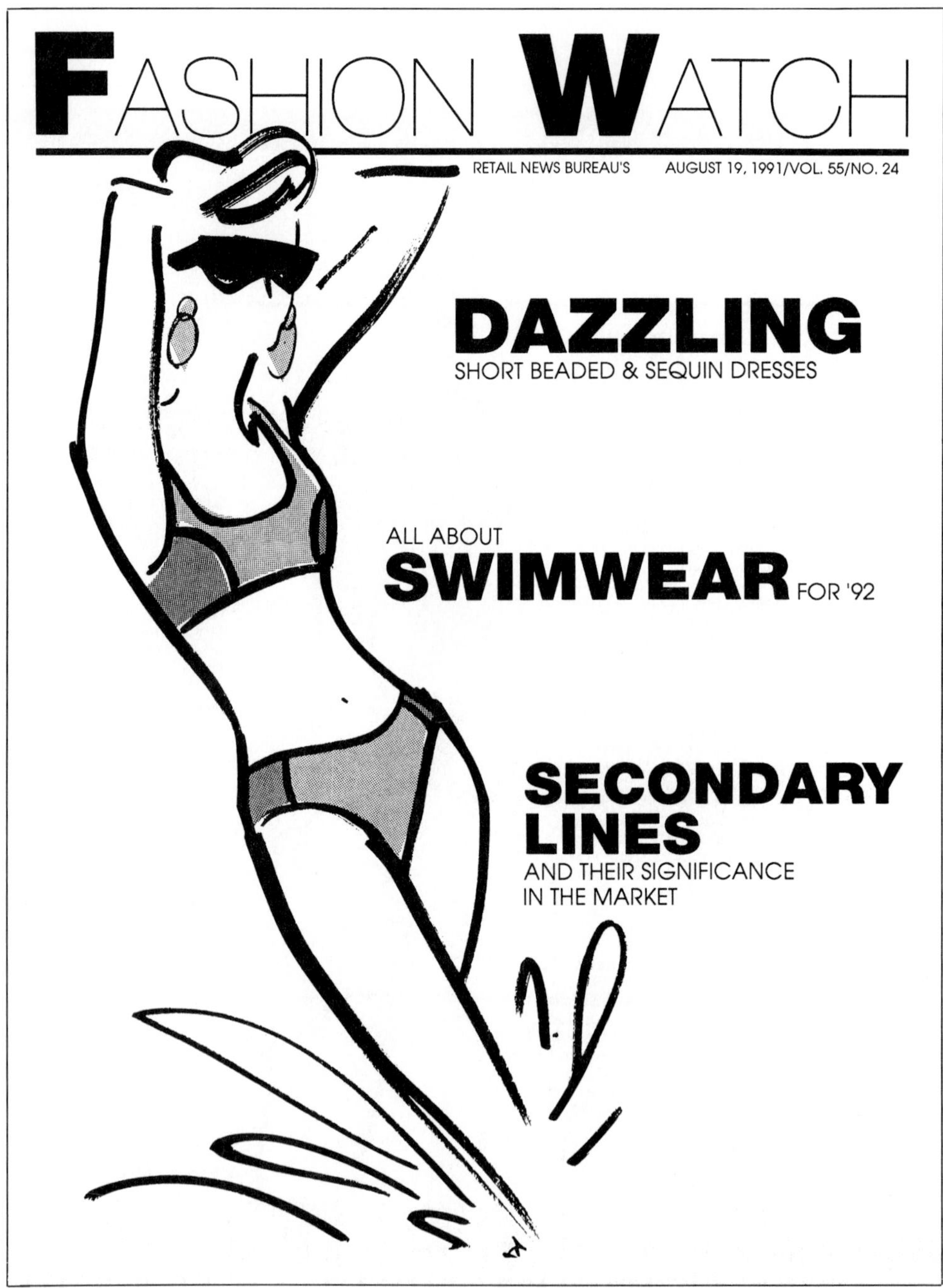


**FIGURE 5–17.** Fashion Watch, a weekly news reminder for buyers. *Courtesy:* Retail Reporting.

abroad to study the current offerings of foreign producers, or who have branch offices in these foreign countries, Promostyl has brought its fashion services to America.

Promostyl is a Paris-based company with branches in 21 countries throughout the world. Included among its staff is a creative and diversified team of designers, graphic artists, and marketing managers. Although fashion forecasting is the principal service they provide for stores and their buyers, they are involved in many other activities, such as designing complete lines. Promostyl designs, for private label use, men's wear, women's wear, and children's wear. Through this service, the buyer not only has merchandise for his or her store's exclusive use, but styles that are European-inspired and based on the forecasts of Promostyl's own diversified staff.

Trend books are the vehicles in which Promostyl publishes its predictions. Subscribers may select from books on ready-to-wear and knitwear, accessories and shoes, children's wear, and so forth. Each is produced twice a year and is received by the buyers 12 months in advance of the season. In this way a buyer can have a head start on making buying plans and an insight into what directions purchasing might take.

In addition, buyers receive fabric and silhouette updates twice a year, are mailed newsletters three times a year, have use of a New York–based fabric library in the wholesale market which features 4000 samples each season, and have access to audiovisual presentations and consultation privileges. Whereas the fashion-reporting services and resident buying offices provide current market information, Promostyl gives insights into the fashions of the future. Figure 5–18 features typical excerpts from Promostyl trend books; Figure 5–19, fabric and yarn samples for buyer examination; and Figure 5–20, the Promostyl newsletter.

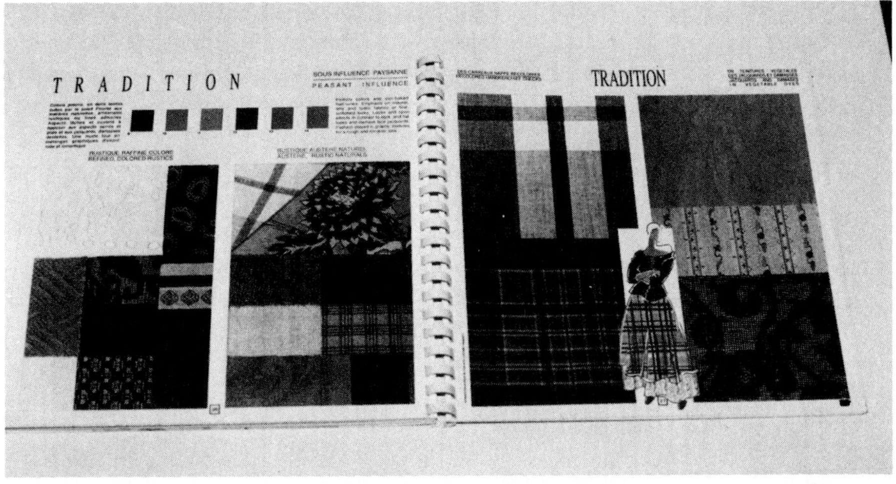


**FIGURE 5–18.** Promostyl trend books—fabrics, colors, and textures are featured. *Courtesy:* Promostyl.

**FIGURE 5–19.** Fabric and yarn library. *Courtesy:* Promostyl.

## Nonfashion Services

Among the services available to the buyer is a wide variety of generalized information not aimed at specific products. Typical of these services is one offered by Diversified Communications, Inc., which is currently being used by 150 major department and specialty chains and stores throughout the country. The program, called Help Your Sell-f, is a retail sales training program using standard audio cassettes. The service is organized to fit into a semi-monthly sales meeting. Each month the store receives one tape for store management and two tapes for sales personnel. The cassettes have been carefully prepared by an Emmy Award–winning TV and radio production firm, a group of retail training directors, and a consulting behavioral psychologist who checks the motivational and psychological material used.

Each sales training tape runs eight to ten minutes and serves as a core for the biweekly sales meeting. By inserting some humor, the producers have made the tapes enjoyable as well as instructive. The various departments take turns using the cassettes for their meetings.

All the tapes are retained by the store for selective replay for a specific salesperson when the department manager feels it is necessary. They are also used as the basis of the training program for newly hired personnel.

### *Magazines and Trade Publications*

The alert buyer must stay ahead of the selling floor in terms of new product trends. The fashion buyer should be aware of the latest couturier showings

PROMOSTYL NEWS * PROMOSTYL NEWS * PROMOSTYL NEWS

# PsN

FIRST AROUND THE WORLD

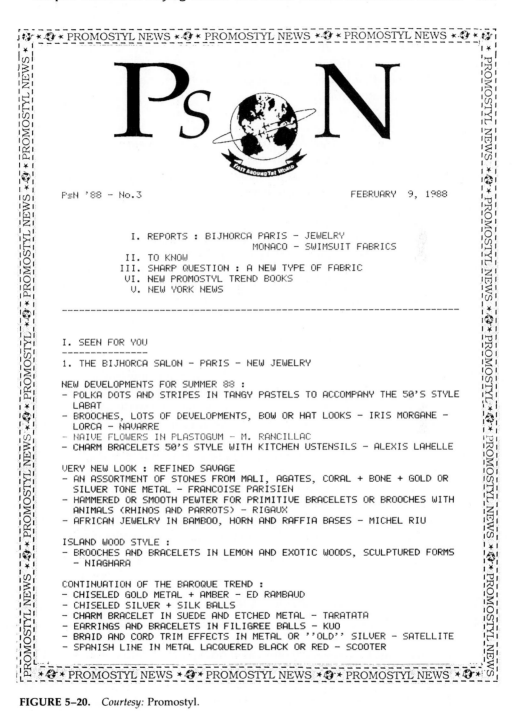

PsN '88 - No.3 FEBRUARY 9, 1988

I. REPORTS : BIJHORCA PARIS - JEWELRY
MONACO - SWIMSUIT FABRICS
II. TO KNOW
III. SHARP QUESTION : A NEW TYPE OF FABRIC
VI. NEW PROMOSTYL TREND BOOKS
V. NEW YORK NEWS

---

I. SEEN FOR YOU

1. THE BIJHORCA SALON - PARIS - NEW JEWELRY

NEW DEVELOPMENTS FOR SUMMER 88 :
- POLKA DOTS AND STRIPES IN TANGY PASTELS TO ACCOMPANY THE 50'S STYLE LABAT
- BROOCHES, LOTS OF DEVELOPMENTS, BOW OR HAT LOOKS - IRIS MORGANE - LORCA - NAVARRE
- NAIVE FLOWERS IN PLASTOGUM - M. RANCILLAC
- CHARM BRACELETS 50'S STYLE WITH KITCHEN USTENSILS - ALEXIS LAHELLE

VERY NEW LOOK : REFINED SAVAGE
- AN ASSORTMENT OF STONES FROM MALI, AGATES, CORAL + BONE + GOLD OR SILVER TONE METAL - FRANCOISE PARISIEN
- HAMMERED OR SMOOTH PEWTER FOR PRIMITIVE BRACELETS OR BROOCHES WITH ANIMALS (RHINOS AND PARROTS) - RIGAUX
- AFRICAN JEWELRY IN BAMBOO, HORN AND RAFFIA BASES - MICHEL RIU

ISLAND WOOD STYLE :
- BROOCHES AND BRACELETS IN LEMON AND EXOTIC WOODS, SCULPTURED FORMS - NIAGHARA

CONTINUATION OF THE BAROQUE TREND :
- CHISELED GOLD METAL + AMBER - ED RAMBAUD
- CHISELED SILVER + SILK BALLS
- CHARM BRACELET IN SUEDE AND ETCHED METAL - TARATATA
- EARRINGS AND BRACELETS IN FILIGREE BALLS - KUO
- BRAID AND CORD TRIM EFFECTS IN METAL OR ''OLD'' SILVER - SATELLITE
- SPANISH LINE IN METAL LACQUERED BLACK OR RED - SCOOTER

PROMOSTYL NEWS * PROMOSTYL NEWS * PROMOSTYL NEWS

**FIGURE 5–20.** *Courtesy:* Promostyl.

despite the fact that customers will not be aware of them for some time to come. Similarly, buyers in all product lines should be aware of changes in styling, new materials, and other innovations long before they are available to their clientele. To do otherwise would result in an obsolete inventory and a reputation for not having the latest products.

To keep up-to-date, buyers should subscribe to the major newspapers of the cities that are fashion centers. In addition, the fashion trends shown in such magazines as *Elle, Harper's Bazaar, Seventeen, Glamour,* and *Mademoiselle* are required reading for fashion buyers.

It would be difficult to find a retail activity that does not have a trade paper associated with it. These publications are carefully read by buyers for information on new styles, trends, technological developments, marketing schemes, trade shows, the effect of economic developments on the industry, and a wide variety of other important information. Among the more important publications are *Women's Wear Daily, California Apparel News, Daily News Record, Franchising Journal, Boot and Shoe Recorder, Stores, Chain Store, Body Fashions, Furniture Age, Jeweler's Circular-Keystone, Drug Topics,* and *Home Furnishings Daily.* Figure 5–21 shows a trade publication's regular feature.

### *National Retail Federation (NRF)*

Almost without exception, each retail activity has a trade association whose periodic meetings are widely attended to preview new lines, make personal contacts, and discuss matters relevant to the particular retailing area involved.

The NRF, an outgrowth of the National Retail Merchants Association (NRMA), is by far the largest and most important of the retailing trade associations. While not pointed at any specific retail product, this organization supplies information of interest to all retailers. Through lectures, panel discussions, publications, films, and periodicals of enormous depth and variety, it covers every area of retailing for both large and small stores. Its offerings are widely used by every retailing function, particularly merchandising, whose personnel require an intimate knowledge of the total operation. An indication of the importance of this organization is the wide attendance at its major meetings of retailers from all over the world.

## NONPROFIT PUBLIC RELATIONS ORGANIZATIONS

In their quest to keep current on merchandise trends and design directions, buyers often look to public relations organizations that represent particular industries. These groups, one of which is The Men's Fashion Association, play a twofold role for the industries they serve. First, they serve as a learning house for current data pertinent to the participants' own successes. Second, they act as liaisons between their members and the markets they serve. Specifically, the

**SCANNING THE MARKET**

# Fit for a princess

*Alexander Brown's dresses offer comfort and elegance.*

By DEIRDRE DUBE
*Features Editor*

**UPON HER RETURN FROM BUYING FABRICS,** Pamela Brown automatically flips her mass of dark, wavy hair to one side. This action, which she does several times an hour in hot weather, serves to reveal not only her olive-skinned shoulder, but also the gentle detailing of her long black dress. The dress hangs with plenty of breathing room on her trim little body. "You can kinda throw this dress on everyday," she says, smiling. "It's our signature dress—the Ruffle dress."

With Diane Alexander, Brown is co-owner of Alexander Brown, a company that manufactures elegant, carefree dresses that are blowing out of better stores nationwide. The two partners, age 26, never expected to have the immediate response their line has generated.

"It's really a dream come true," says Alexander, a Greek beauty who could pass for Brown's outdoorsy sister, adding, "we hope this is the beginning of a huge success."

Alexander, a former dancer, and Brown, who majored in business at UCLA, met in the summer of 1989 while both were employed at a Westside boutique. Each brought years of retail experience and a great sense of style to the partnership. Using tax return money as capital, they started work on a collection of samples from 50 yards of fabric in the summer of 1990.

Alexander Brown's lace princess dress.

PHOTOGRAPHY: RICK SWINGER

Alexander Brown's rayon crepe ruffle dress.

In the midst of small-scale production, Alexander was spotted wearing one of the Alexander Brown creations by a buyer at Fred Segal. He asked if she and Brown could design a few more. Using cutters and sample makers from the classified section of *California Apparel News*, they were able to fill the initial orders. It wasn't long before they hit Nordstrom with immediate goods.

Old-timers in the industry warned that it would take years to really get their business off the ground. A year later, as the partners prepare for their third season in their third downtown Los Angeles location, office manager Eden Small, one of the company's two employees, holds up a thick stack of accounts. Needless to say, sales representative Judy Kurgan is in seventh heaven.

"The dresses are magic. They practically sell themselves," says Kurgan from her eighth floor showroom in the CaliforniaMart. "Everyone is going crazy over them—especially me. You don't know me, but this is the style I wear all the time."

Alexander says she and Brown offer their own type of creativity and are able to "feed off each other" in terms of design. Brown derives inspiration from her own wardrobe, which she describes as "romantic, funky and mix and match." Alexander picks up ideas from a variety of sources, including travel to other countries. They both agree that what they initially thought were some of their bigger mistakes—weird hems, and strange cuts—have resulted in hot-selling items.

"We've been really lucky because people have helped us from the start and we've learned from our mistakes," say the dynamic duo. "But the thing is, your dream isn't going to come to you, you've just got to get out there and do it."

**FIGURE 5–21.** "Scanning the Market" is a typical of trade publication features. *Courtesy:* California Apparel News.

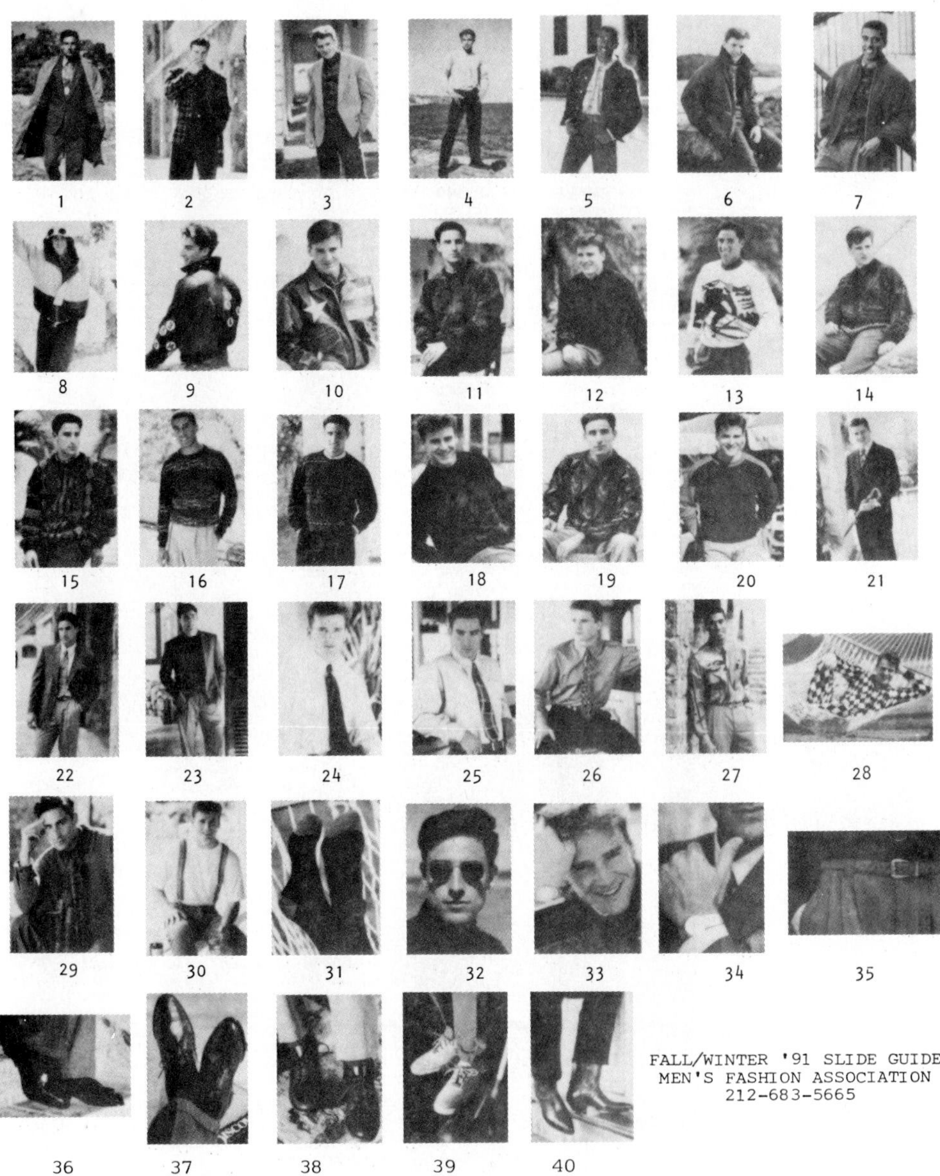


**FIGURE 5–22.** An overview of the season's trends. *Courtesy:* Men's Fashion Association.

markets are made up of the buyers and merchandisers who purchase for retail organizations. The organization presents an overview of the coming season's newest items in a typical release featured in Figure 5–22. The Men's Fashion Association, or MFA as it is referred to in the men's wear world, is examined in the following Focus.

### A RETAIL BUYING FOCUS

*The Men's Fashion Association*

Founded in 1956, the MFA is a nonprofit public relations organization that serves all levels of the men's wear industry, representing over 350 manufacturers, designers, and retailers. It provides a platform for all member companies to reach the print and electronic media with fashion and product stories.

Through a variety of means, the MFA is able to bring the men's wear designing and manufacturing industry closer to the retail outlets. Among the various promotional devices it employs to achieve its publicity goals are:

1. Semiannual seminars which feature an hour-long runway fashion show in which the press and retailers learn about the coming season's highlights. These shows give store buyers a glimpse of new product lines; trends in style, fabrication, and color; price changes; and information that will help them to plan for their purchasing needs.
2. Press kits which are provided and are used by the media to introduce their subscribers to the latest in the men's wear field. At the same time, the buyer learns what the consumer is being shown and can plan purchases to include those fashions in their merchandise assortments. When the public is made aware of "what is fashionably correct" by newspapers and magazines, the task of convincing the consumer of appropriate dress is simpler for the retailer.
3. Informational brochures which are periodically sent to retail organizations informing them of industry trends and areas of interest. For example, the MFA produces a quarterly newsletter, "Currents," which outlines recent news developments and story ideas about men's wear which keeps the buyer alerted to anything that might make his or her purchasing direction more meaningful. "Faxions" is a bimonthly news release breaking the latest in fashion tends.
4. Special programs including the American Image Awards honoring celebrated men of style and achievement, the Woolmark Fashion Awards saluting fashion creativity and leadership, and the Aldo Awards for outstanding fashion journalism. Each of these helps to make the men's wear industry more visible and provides the retailer with ideas on which to build store promotions.

## VIDEO BUYING SERVICES

The most recent innovation in bringing pertinent merchandise information to the buyer is the video buying service. While the same information provided by such a service comes to the buyer through other means such as resident buying office membership, the use of traditional reporting services, and fashion forecasters, this format is unique. It eliminates the costs of market visits, it features the season's highlights in full color and on models, and it enables the buyer to attend to more in-store duties and responsibilities. The Focus that follows describes The Merchandise Network, the first video buying service representing the New York market. The cover of its explanatory brochure is depicted in Figure 5–23.

## A RETAIL BUYING FOCUS

### *The Merchandise Network*

Promising savings in a number of areas such as travel, offering discounts on current lines of merchandise, and quickly relaying information on the season's hottest items, all with the use of videos, The Merchandise Network is a service that is attracting a great deal of attention in the fashion industry. By providing four videos a month that contain the highlights of numerous missy and junior sportswear, dresses, and accessories collections and by placing orders directly with the vendors for the merchandise selected by the store buyer, the retailer can feel the pulse of the market without ever leaving the store.

Specifically the service provides the user with the following:

1. Videos that include a minimum of five vendor's lines with the promise that each is the hottest in the market. In addition to showing the merchandise, the videos discuss up-to-the-minute styles and trends.
2. With their volume purchasing power, the company pledges to negotiate the most competitive prices possible.
3. The service doesn't select merchandise for you, as is the case when buying is left to the discretion of some buying services, but enables the store's own staff to make the buying decisions based upon the video presented information.

## ACTION FOR THE SMALL STORE BUYER

The major link to the wholesale market for the small store buyer is the resident buying office. No other institution so capably offers this buyer a significant, constant flow of information on which many purchasing decisions can be based.

For whatever reasons, small store buyers often operate without guidance or counsel from anyone in the store's organization. Membership in a resident buying office will provide information in almost every area necessary to purchase successfully. Such offices generate an overwhelming amount of materials that could improve the buyer's ability to make decisions, but examination and

**FIGURE 5–23.** Brochure cover of video buying service. *Courtesy:* Price Breakers.

evaluation of them all is a necessity. That is, allowing flyers, mailers, brochures, newsletters, and catalogs to lie unopened will not benefit the buyer. The interested small store purchaser must learn how the office to which his or her store belongs operates, what services it provides, how much individual assistance is offered, and how to derive the most benefits for the store. Too many small store buyers operate on whim and do not pay attention to the invaluable assistance provided by a resident buying office.

Most major offices, in some manner, describe how to get the most out of their services. Whether it is the regular brochures they use to communicate with their members or videotapes, they spell out the advantages of office affiliation. Just paying the fees to affiliate with an office will not give the buyer what it takes for effective purchasing.

## SUMMARY OF KEY POINTS

1. Of the various types of resident offices, the private office is least popular because of the cost involved in its operation.
2. Most resident buying offices are independently organized and represent smaller retailers.
3. Resident offices are structured in much the same way as stores. Some are full line and offer advice on hard and soft goods; some specialize exclusively in one particular line of merchandise.
4. In addition to the purchase of merchandise, the resident office assists the store buyer in making merchandise selection through the recommendation of new resources, information on hot items, handling of complaints, and assistance in the preparation of promotional activities.
5. One of the chief functions performed by the resident office is that of assisting the store buyer during market week.
6. Stores should choose office representation after considering such factors as the size of the office, the services offered, the member stores, the costs of joining, and merchandise specialization.
7. In addition to resident offices, there are a number of other informative services used by buyers. They include reporting services, trade publications, trade associations, public relations organizations, and video buying services.

## REVIEW QUESTIONS

1. Which type of office is most expensive? Why?
2. Why do some large retailers choose to participate in cooperative buying offices rather than establish a private office?

3. How are the independent resident offices paid?
4. What advantages are afforded small retailers through resident office affiliation?
5. Define the term *prêt-à-porter.*
6. Would it be more advantageous for a home furnishings store to join an office that specializes in that form of merchandise or one that offers a wide assortment of merchandise information?
7. For what reason might a buyer ask the resident buyer to place a reorder rather than placing his own?
8. Store buyers usually turn to the resident office to handle manufacturer complaints. Why?
9. The finding of new resources is usually accomplished better by resident buyers than store buyers. Why?
10. What methods do resident buyers use to notify member stores of hot items?
11. How can office membership result in lower merchandise costs for retailers?
12. Describe market week.
13. Are promotional activities the responsibility of the resident buying office? Discuss.
14. Can the store buyer get timely foreign market information from the resident office?
15. List three factors to consider in the selection of a resident buying office.
16. Discuss the use and importance of fashion-reporting services such as the Retail News Bureau.
17. Why should a buyer attend trade association shows?
18. What are the functions of the NRF?
19. How does a nonprofit public relations organization serve the retailer?
20. What are the advantages of membership in a video buying service?

## CASE PROBLEM 1

Spotlight Shops is a small speciality chain located in New England. The organization has five units and specializes in women's and children's wear. Since its inception 12 years ago, the company's sales have continued to increase. In fact, Spotlight has also continued to increase its merchandise assortments of women's and children's wear significantly. One factor that has enabled it to increase its volume is a recent addition to its merchandising philosophy. In addition to its regular offerings, Spotlight has successfully increased its sales picture through periodic promotional events. Every season the buyers prepare special promotion merchandise for disposal during three-day sales. The enormous success is becoming increasingly difficult to repeat because of the buyers' inability to obtain sufficient quantities of merchandise for these special events. It should be understood that merchandise is available, but their distance from the wholesale markets and their many chores at the store make it virtually impossible for the buyers to find time to seek out the necessary merchandise.

The company is currently deciding upon outside representation to help with the problem. Employing the services of a resident buying office is a consideration.

### Questions

1. What are the advantages of resident buying affiliation?
2. What kind of office should Spotlight join?

## CASE PROBLEM 2

For the past 45 years Caldwell's Department Store has successfully operated its main store and 18 branches in the Midwest. Its position as a Midwestern department store has improved steadily through the years. Competitors and noncompetitors alike consider the company to be one of the most progressive in retailing.

In the beginning, Caldwell's was a member of an independent resident buying office. With continued growth and expansion, the company decided that more personal attention was necessary for continued success. Ten years ago management moved in that direction by joining forces with 15 other noncompeting major department stores to organize a cooperative office. The arrangement proved to be successful; Caldwell's continued to grow.

At present the company is planning another expansion program. Management anticipates the opening of 12 high-fashion women's boutiques within the next ten years. Unlike the present organization, which features a full assortment of hard and soft goods at popular and moderate prices, the boutiques will feature high-fashion, expensive goods aimed at the affluent market.

Bearing in mind the expansion plan, some members of the top management team have suggested that the company organize its own private buying office. They believe the company's needs would be better served, particularly in light of the new expansion program. The remaining managers believe it would be wiser to remain with cooperative representation.

### Question

1. With whom do you agree? Defend your position.

# Section II

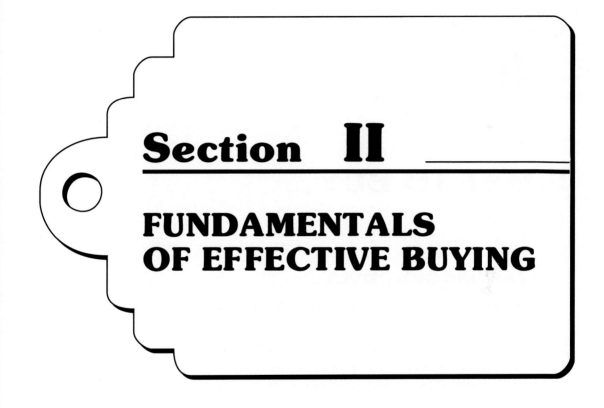

## FUNDAMENTALS OF EFFECTIVE BUYING

# Chapter 6

# WHAT TO BUY

## LEARNING OBJECTIVES

*Upon completion of this chapter, the student should be able to:*

1. Discuss the effect of the store's merchandising policies on the buyer's selection of goods. At least six factors should be included.
2. Explain the necessity of past sales information to the buyer. Include the importance of price, color, size, and style.
3. Discuss the importance of consumer research, citing four examples.
4. Speak about the role of sales personnel in the buyer's decision. Include want slip systems.

## INTRODUCTION

Today the merchandise assortment avaiable is greater than at any other time, and the number of retailers selling the merchandise has also increased significantly. Buyers, to attract customers and guarantee their return for subsequent purchases, must develop an image for their departments and stores. The establishment of this image and the development of a reputation depends on customer satisfaction. Knowing what the customer likes and at what price he or she is willing to purchase contributes enormously to the success of the store.

Although the computer provides the buyer with a greater variety of information than ever before, selection of merchandise is not a routine matter. How the buyer uses this pertinent information is of the utmost importance. Buyers, as well as all other retail executives, make a concerted effort to attract customers into their stores. What better appeal is there than the merchandise offered for sale?

Buyers have a great many sources available to them in their quest for information that will assist them in their merchandise selection. These sources may be divided into two categories. The external sources include resident buying offices, periodicals, trade associations, marketing research organizations, and reporting services, all of which were discussed in the preceding chapter. As important as these sources are, none can replace the information generated by the store's own efforts. In this chapter, discussion will focus on these internal sources of information, such as past sales records, customer surveys, sales personnel, want slip systems, and staff personnel. But before buyers can focus on what to buy, they must make certain they are completely sure of the store's merchandising policies.

## MERCHANDISING POLICIES

Whether the store is of the "mom and pop" variety or a nationally organized retail giant, its merchandising success depends on the buyer's understanding of the store's merchandising policies and the proper carrying out of those policies.

To cultivate a market of customers for the store, policies must be formulated and adhered to so that the prospective customer will know what to expect on entering the store. Smaller stores often tend to alter their policies and confuse their customers. For example, if the fall prices in an independent shoe store ranged from $40 to $55 and the spring prices rose significantly, not only could old customers be confused, but they could also be unable to afford the higher-priced goods. In large stores with merchandise managers to oversee the buyers, this is unlikely to happen.

Whatever the policy, the buyers must conform to it to make certain that the store's image, as perceived by the customer, is being preserved.

The merchandising policies of a store can include one or many points. Among them are the following:

1. Price lines to be offered
2. Quality of merchandise
3. Exclusiveness of goods
4. Variety
5. Timing of introduction of merchandise
6. Assortment
7. Price policy

### *Price Lines*

Rarely do stores offer merchandise at every price. They are limited by available space, customers in the trading area, and the need to merchandise differently priced merchandise in different ways. Retailers thus select the most appropriate price line(s) for their store to maximize profit.

### *Quality of Merchandise*

Goods in all classifications are generally available in many qualities. Two sofas, similiar in design, could be priced hundreds of dollars apart because they differ in such quality areas as materials, construction, and finishing. Stores must decide which route to take, then carry out a quality policy in actual purchases.

### *Exclusiveness of Goods*

Some of the more prestigious stores pride themselves on their exclusive offerings. Stores like Neiman-Marcus, Bergdorf Goodman, and Lord & Taylor appeal to their customers on the exclusiveness of some of their goods. Other stores feature the nationally advertised brands more commonly found in many stores. Still others take a completely opposite stance and carry only what is featured by most other stores so that they can easily appeal to the masses.

### *Variety*

Should a store feature contemporary furniture or all periods? The choice varies among retailers. The policy on variety must be adhered to so that customers will find what they expect.

### *Introduction of Merchandise*

The time when merchandise is offered for sale varies from store to store. Some are fashion leaders whose customers want new items "hot off the press." Others play it safe and introduce items only after they have been proved to be successful.

### *Assortment*

Should a wide assortment be available, or should the stock be limited? Should many colors be offered, or should the item be restricted to a few basics?

Should new fibers be introduced, or should the inventory reflect the regularly produced and accepted fibers? Whatever the policy, it should be adhered to for uniform store merchandising.

### *Price Policy*

To discount or not to discount? To compete with competitiors on price or disregard their prices and offer services to counteract price? This is an extremely important policy question. Some large retailers might actually offer both. They discount some hard goods but mark up their fashion items.

Whatever decisions they make, stores must carefully plan their merchandising policies and make certain they are carried out by the buyers. This will ensure that the right customers are attracted to the store.

## *INTERNAL SOURCES OF BUYER INFORMATION*

Although it is generally conceded that buyers consider past sales records their most vital source of buying information, it should be understood that different buyers place different emphases on the various sources available. The sources included in the following section are presented in no special order, but they include those generally examined by knowledgeable buyers.

### Past Sales

It's inconceivable that a buyer would plan purchases without careful scrutiny of past sales figures. Buyers for giant companies and small stores alike pay close attention to these records. In fact, many do not come to market without their inventory records, which indicate sales figures. It is common in wholesale markets to see buyers travel from vendor to vendor with these records tucked under their arms. They are generally organized into loose-leaf binders, affectionately called buyer's bibles.

Now, one might ask, how valuable are past sales if buyers must purchase items that haven't been available before? For example, if the new season introduces a fashion color not previously available, how in the world will previous sales of other colors be helpful? Analysis will not show a customer's specific like for the new color, but among other things, it will relate to the buyer the customer's reaction to last season's "new color." Certainly such information is not foolproof, but it provides some information about the customer's acceptance or rejection of something new.

Through the examination of past sales, buyers are able to make more intelligent predictions regarding new-merchandise acceptance. Naturally, the farther back into sales records the buyer can go, the better customer likes and dislikes can be anticipated. It should be borne in mind, however, that neither past sales records, as important as they are, nor any other source of information can by itself provide all the data on which buyers can plan their merchandise selections. Only through investigation of a host of information sources can a buyer clearly evaluate and formulate plans.

### *Recording Systems*

The past sales information that is generated for buyer use varies according to the needs of the buyer. Similarly, the systems employed in the collection of sales data are of a wide variety. Basically, the systems may be classified as hand recorded, as is still the case in many small retail outlets even though computers are now available for their use and computerized, as in the larger organizations.

**Hand recording.** Although we are in the age of computerizaton, the method most widely used by small retailers involves the ticketing of each individual piece of merchandise. The ticket includes such pertinent information as style number, size, price, and color. Each item is recorded in an inventory book. As merchandise is sold it is deleted from the inventory book, and as new merchandise comes into stock it is added. The following steps are typical of those involved in this type of recording, which is commonly known as a unit control system:

1. Vendors are listed in a contents at the beginning of the inventory book and are each assigned a code number. Table 6–1 shows an example of such a listing.
2. Continuing with the illustration, let's suppose the store receives a shipment of merchandise from Sheri Associates. On the page (or pages) assigned to Sheri Associates, the merchandise received is recorded. Included on the page would be any information the buyer deemed important for future purchasing. Such facts as style number, wholesale price, retail price, colors, sizes, and date of receipt of goods are recorded. This information will assist the buyer not only in merchandise selection but also in the determination of quantities and from whom future purchases will be made. Chapters 7 and 8 will deal with these matters in detail. Figure 6–1 is a

**TABLE 6–1** Table of contents—inventory book

| *CODE* | *VENDOR* |
|---|---|
| 1 | David Neil Sportswear |
| 2 | Style-Fit, Inc. |
| 3 | Caryn Joy Dresses |
| 4 | Sheri Associates |
| 5 | Craftstar Ltd. |
| 6 | Cameron Knitwear |
| 7 | Peterson Jeans, Inc. |
| 8 | The McCoy Company |
| 9 | Aristocratic Apparel |
| 10 | Loom and Sew Industries |

| SHERI ASSOCIATES<br>3780 Broadway<br>New York, New York<br>539-7420 | | | | | | | | | | | | |
|---|---|---|---|---|---|---|---|---|---|---|---|---|
| Style | Price | Colors | Sizes | | | | | | | | | |
| 7534 | $22.50 | Red | 8 | 10 | 12 | 14 | 16 | | | | | |
| Cotton | $45.00 | White | ~~8~~ | 10 | 10 | 12 | 12 | 14 | 14 | 16 | | |
| | Received April 20 | Yellow | 8 | 10 | (~~12~~) | 14 | 16 | | | | | |
| 6423 | $24.75 | Black | 10 | 12 | 12 | 14 | 14 | 16 | (~~18~~) | | | |
| Linen | $50.00 | Green | 8 | 10 | 12 | ~~14~~ | 16 | | | | | |
| | Received May 10 | | | | | | | | | | | |
| 1239 | $24.75 | White | 8 | 10 | ~~12~~ | 12 | 12 | ~~14~~ | 14 | 16 | 16 | 18 |
| Cotton | $50.00 | | | | | | | | | | | |
| | Received May 15 | | | | | | | | | | | |

Key: 4 – vendor code number
X – merchandise sold
ⓧ – sold but returned

**FIGURE 6–1.** Inventory page

sample page of the inventory book used to record merchandise purchased from Sheri Associates.

3. Before each piece of merchandise is placed on the selling floor, it is given a two-part tag that includes much of the information in the inventory page. In this way, as an article is sold the salesperson or cashier can separate the bottom part of the tag, store it until the end of the selling day, and use it to decrease the inventory by the merchandise sold. Figure 6–2 shows a merchadise tag used by many small retailers. The information indicated is keyed to an item of merchandise in Figure 6–1.

Using this system, the buyer in even the smallest boutique can quickly and positively refer to a complete inventory and sales history of the merchandise at any time. It is extremely important in reorder decisions, since inventory levels and salability can be clearly seen.

Some buyers even color key their entries to be able to determine how long it took for merchandise to sell: Instead of decreasing their inventories with black pencil or pen, they use a different colored pencil for each month. If a red marker was used for May and the item in Figure 6–2 was crossed off the inventory page in red, this would give the buyer an approximate idea of how long it took to sell the merchandise.

NO. 4
STYLE 7534
COLOR white
SIZE 8
PRICE $45
- - - - - - - - - - - - -
NO. 4
STYLE 7534
COLOR white
SIZE 8
PRICE $45

**FIGURE 6–2.** Merchandise tag

Different types of tags and information may be used in such a system. The buyer must determine which is most beneficial for the particular organization.

**Computerization.** Although the computer is being put to enormous use by the large retailers, the information recorded is no different from that which can be collected by hand. The computer, however, accomplishes the task more rapidly.

The systems employed vary considerably. The most frequently used system decreases the inventory immediately each time an item is purchased through a tie-in of the point-of-sale cash register to the computer. Information is fed into the computer by means of salesperson entries or with the use of scanners.

In determining merchandise selection, buyers rely considerably on the computerized reports. Fashion buyers in a large, well-known metropolitan department store gain much insight into color trends and customer acceptance of the colors in the weekly size and color sales report. Figure 6–3 shows an example of such a report. The report carefully breaks down the information offered.

### *Analysis of Information Given in Figure 6–3*

- *Class 18 pants:* This is the type of merchandise.
- *Vendor 103:* The particular pants are from Suzy's Pants.
- *Style 165:* The pants are pleated flannels.
- *Retail:* The pants sell for $35.
- *Store 5:* This report is prepared for store 5, Springfield.
- *Color 8:* The number 8 is the code for brown.
- *By size:* Each size featured in this style is coded: 1 is size 3, 2 is size 5, and so on.

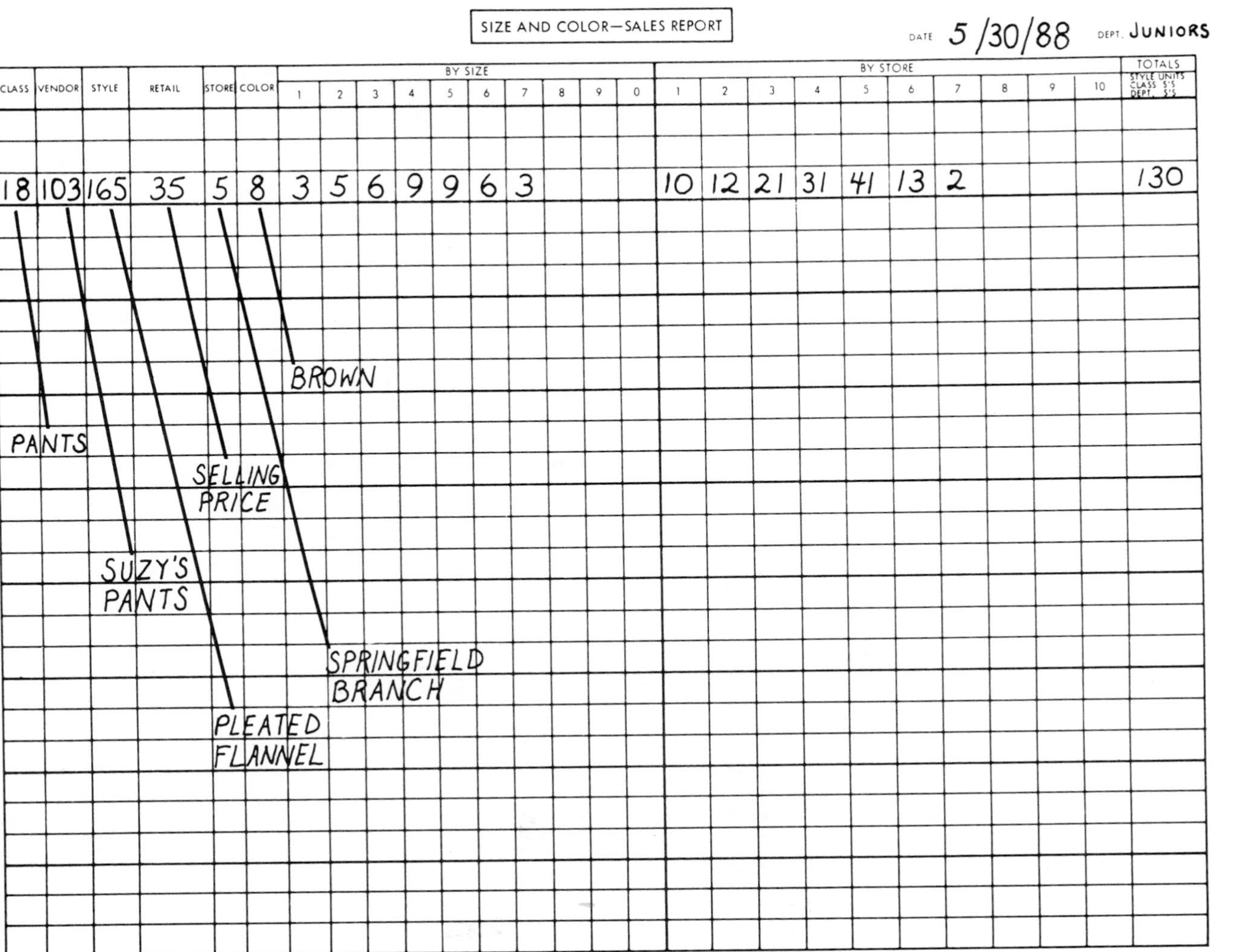

SIZE AND COLOR—SALES REPORT

DATE 5/30/88 DEPT. JUNIORS

| CLASS | VENDOR | STYLE | RETAIL | STORE | COLOR | BY SIZE 1 | 2 | 3 | 4 | 5 | 6 | 7 | 8 | 9 | 0 | BY STORE 1 | 2 | 3 | 4 | 5 | 6 | 7 | 8 | 9 | 10 | TOTALS STYLE UNITS CLASS $'S DEPT. $'S |
|---|---|---|---|---|---|---|---|---|---|---|---|---|---|---|---|---|---|---|---|---|---|---|---|---|---|---|
| 18 | 103 | 165 | 35 | 5 | 8 | 3 | 5 | 6 | 9 | 9 | 6 | 3 | | | | 10 | 12 | 21 | 31 | 41 | 13 | 2 | | | | 130 |



FIGURE 6–3. Size and color—sales report

- *By store:* Each store in the group is given a number; Springfield is store 5 and has sold 41 pieces.
- *Totals:* Total amount of style 165 sold in all stores. Springfield was the biggest user with 41 pieces for the time period.

This report shows that stores 3, 4, and 5 are successful with style 165, brown, with store 5 the leader. Store 1, 2, and 6 are doing less business; store 7 is showing no improvement at all. The buyer can quickly see a problem for store 7 with brown pants. Perhaps the merchandise should be moved to another unit, such as store 5.

### *Analysis of Information*

Buyers who receive the information from past sales records but do not carefully analyze the data are doing a disservice to themselves, their customers, and their companies. Not only does the information relate what has happened in terms of departmental merchandising, but it lays the groundwork for future merchandise selection.

Analysis should be in terms of the factors the buyer considers necessary in determining what should be purchased. These remain fairly constant among retailers and include classification, sizes, price, style, color, materials, frequency of purchase, and customer returns. Although the method of recordkeeping and analysis varies according to the individual company's preference, these factors are generally the basis of analysis.

**Classification.** Merchandise is grouped according to the classification in which it falls. Within each classification there may be many subclasses. (A full discussion of these will be found in the next chapter.) In staple goods the merchandise classifications change infrequently. For example, men's white handkerchiefs, children's tricycles, 60-watt bulbs, and snow tires have been in stock without change for many years. Staple merchandise is the "bread and butter" on which merchants count for reliable, continuous sales. Buyers are, however, aware generally of the sales levels for staples when it comes to the reordering of merchandise. In some cases, the computer may be programmed to reorder automatically a staple item if it falls below a predetermined inventory level.

It is in the merchandising of fashion merchandise that classification is continuously surveyed. Since fashions might be introduced and vanish because of customer nonacceptance, analysis is compulsory. In the 1970s men's fashion ready-to-wear buyers were on the brink of insanity because of their inability accurately to forecast the acceptance of the "leisure suit." Very close attention was paid to this classification because it was a new type of merchandise buyers had to evaluate. Since the overbuying of unsalable merchandise could seriously affect the buyer's season, he or she is particularly cautious in the approach of any new concept.

Buyers, in conjunction with their merchandise managers, keep watchful eyes on merchandise classifications and plan very carefully which to buy and which to eliminate. It should be borne in mind that stores do not usually make frequent classification changes even in fashion merchandise. A sign to the consumer that such a change is being made is visible in a store's policy in regard to the merchandise carried. Every so often a retailer will announce a discontinuation of a type of merchandise or a department and will sell out the remaining inventory at very low prices. The reverse is also possible. Stores sometimes expand their operations through the offering of "new" merchandise. One current trend is for prestigious men's shops to add women's departments.

**Price.** Buyers pay particularly strict attention to their past sales records, which include price information. Stores gain their reputations and images on many factors, price being one of the most important. By analyzing past sales records a buyer can determine which price is selling best, which isn't selling, and so forth. By studying price activity in many consecutive periods, the buyer may be able to determine a trend. For example, the records might indicate that customers have purchased higher-priced merchandise in each of the five preceding seasons. This may be an indication to the buyer that "trading up" (the stocking of higher-priced merchandise) is in order. Offering and successfully selling more expensive merchandise will increase store volume in terms of dollars, which could lead to greater profits. On the other hand, past sales records might indicate the need to "trade down." Figure 6–4 shows a class-price report, which provides information to the buyer according to merchandise classification and sales within each price. The individual stores in the company are listed, and sales figures for each are provided. From this information the buyer may be able to determine not only overall price information, but the results of each store's experience with the merchandise. Periodic analysis might indicate to the buyer that higher-priced merchandise is best suited for one branch and lower-priced merchandise for another.

The understanding of the class-price report requires familiarity with its subheadings:

- *CL Price.* The classification (or type) and price of each item in the inventory. The classification for A1 refers to half aprons and bibs, A2 to cobblers, and so forth. The prices are broken down for each particular price offered in those classifications.
- *Total.* The sum of all the merchandise sold by the *entire* company for that week.
- TOT UN. The sum of all the units sold, per classification.

The remainder of the columns across the top of the page show sales per store, with each store assigned a different color code letter. The minus figures show that returns were greater than sales for that particular period.

**Style.** The term *style* should not be confused with the term *fashion. Style* denotes the silhouette or shape of something, whereas *fashion* is a word used to indicate the style that is currently being accepted by consumers. (*Fad,* another

H

13 DEPT 492 CLASS-PRICE REPORT WEEK ENDING 02-16 PG 1

| CL PRICE | TOTAL | -B- | -J- | -H- | -N- | -U- | -L- | -R- | -G- | -W- |
|---|---|---|---|---|---|---|---|---|---|---|
| A1 HALF APRONS&BIBS | | | | | | | | | | |
| 1.00 S | 32 | 12 | 6 | 4 | 1 | 2 | | 3 | | 4 |
| 1.79 S | 22 | 11 | | 3 | 1 | 4 | | 2 | | 1 |
| 2.25 S | 23 | 5 | 1 | 6 | 1 | | 2 | 6 | | 2 |
| 2.50 S | 23 | 6 | 4 | 6 | | 6 | 1 | | | |
| 2.75 S | 17 | 4 | 2 | 5 | | 2 | 1 | 1 | | 2 |
| 2.99 S | 1 | 1 | | | | | | | | |
| 5.50 S | 18 | 4 | | 4 | 2 | 7 | | 1 | | |
| TOT UN S | 136 | 43 | 13 | 28 | 5 | 21 | 4 | 13 | | 9 |
| TOT $ S | .3 | .1 | | .1 | | .1 | | | | |
| A2 COBBLERS | | | | | | | | | | |
| 2.50 S | 50 | 19 | 3 | 5 | | 4 | 6 | 8 | | 5 |
| 2.59 S | 107 | 28 | 11 | 23 | 2 | 18 | 9 | 9 | | 7 |
| 3.00 S | 9 | 1 | | 4 | | 2 | 2 | | | |
| 3.50 S | 10 | 1 | | 1 | 3 | 3 | 2 | | | |
| 4.25 S | 2 | 1 | | | | | | 1 | | |
| 7.00 S | 1 | 1 | | | | | | | | |
| TOT UN S | 179 | 51 | 14 | 33 | 5 | 27 | 19 | 18 | | 12 |
| TOT $ S | .5 | .1 | | .1 | | .1 | .1 | | | |
| A3 BIBS & COVERALLS | | | | | | | | | | |
| 12.99 S | -1 | | | | -1 | | | | | |
| TOT UN S | -1 | | | | -1 | | | | | |
| TOT $ S | | | | | . | | | | | |
| A0 ALL APRONS | | | | | | | | | | |
| 1.00 S | 32 | 12 | 6 | 4 | 1 | 2 | | 3 | | 4 |
| 1.79 S | 22 | 11 | | 3 | 1 | 4 | | 2 | | 1 |
| 2.25 S | 23 | 5 | 1 | 6 | 1 | | 2 | 6 | | 2 |
| 2.50 S | 73 | 25 | 7 | 11 | | 10 | 7 | 8 | | 5 |
| 2.59 S | 107 | 28 | 11 | 23 | 2 | 18 | 9 | 9 | | 7 |
| 2.75 S | 17 | 4 | 2 | 5 | | 2 | 1 | 1 | | 2 |
| 2.99 S | 1 | 1 | | | | | | | | |
| 3.00 S | 9 | 1 | | 4 | | 2 | 2 | | | |
| 3.50 S | 10 | 1 | | 1 | 3 | 3 | 2 | | | |
| 4.25 S | 2 | 1 | | | | | | 1 | | |
| 5.50 S | 18 | 4 | | 4 | 2 | 7 | | 1 | | |
| 7.00 S | 1 | 1 | | | | | | | | |
| 12.99 S | -1 | | | | -1 | | | | | |
| TOT UN S | 314 | 94 | 27 | 61 | 9 | 48 | 23 | 31 | | 21 |
| TOT $ S | .8 | .2 | .1 | .2 | | .1 | .1 | .1 | | |

F3700-R2 (6-73)

FIGURE 6–4. Class-price report

term, is used to describe short-lived fashions.) *Style* is used to describe not only clothing, but also furniture, appliances, luggage, and so forth. For example, a refrigerator might be a two-door style, a lounge chair could be of contemporary style, and a suitcase might be styled as a car pack. Not only soft goods buyers, but hard goods buyers as well, are concerned with style.

Buyers periodically scan their sales records to evaluate the "movement" of their offerings in terms of which styles are selling successfully, trends of particular styles, inactivity of some styles, and the like. Whether the buyer is merely deciding whether or not to reorder a particular number or is preparing purchases for a new season, style informtion is of paramount importance in the final decision. Careful attention to the records will not only tell the buyer which styles are "hot," but also provide long-range information about each style in stock. The active style report in Figure 6–5 provides the buyer with style information, according to individual stores, in terms of two-day sales, weekly sales, sales for the past week, sales for the past two weeks, four-week sales totals, and the life of each style since its purchase.

An explanation of the various headings and analysis of one style will enable the reader to better understand the information.

- *Two-day sales.* The figures, broken down according to the various units in the company (B, J, H, etc. each denote a particular store), are for two days ending 2/19 (date at bottom of page).
- *Price.* The various prices available in the particular merchandise classification.
- *CL. Classification*—in this case it is all for A1 or domestic leathers.
- *HSE.* The house or vendor number.
- *Style.* The number of each particular item.
- *Week-to-date sales.* Sales for the entire week according to individual stores.
- *TOT.* Totals of two-day sales period per price and house.
- *One week ago.* Sales for the week before this report.
- *Two weeks ago.* Sales for the two-week period before this report.
- *Four weeks ago.* The total monthly sales picture.
- *Life to date.* The number of units sold since the style was placed in inventory.

If we analyze the first style on the page, we see that it was a good seller, but sales have declined; while the four-week total was 32, the past week's sales dropped to only 2. This *might* indicate that the style is no longer popular, the stores might not have sufficient inventory, or the like. In any event, it indicates to the buyer that closer inspection is necessary.

**Color.** Today, with the wide range of colors available to consumers, buyers are more than ever faced with color decisions. No longer is the buyer of household

## ACTIVE STYLE REPORT

| TWO DAYS SALES B | J | H | N | U | L | R | G | W | P |  | TOT | PRICE | CL | HSE | STYLE |
|---|---|---|---|---|---|---|---|---|---|---|---|---|---|---|---|
|  |  |  |  |  | ---- DOM LEATHERS |  |  |  |  |  |  | ---- | A1 |  | ---- |
| 1 |  |  | 1 |  |  |  |  |  |  |  | 2 | 13.99 | A1 | 000 | 0000 |
|  |  |  |  | 3 |  |  |  |  |  |  | 3 | 13.99 | A1 | 000 | 1022 |
|  |  |  |  |  |  |  |  | 1 |  |  | 1 | 13.99 | A1 | 000 | 1399 |
|  |  |  |  |  |  |  |  | 1 |  |  | 1 | 29.00 | A1 | 000 | 2900 |
|  |  |  |  |  | 1 | 2 |  | 1 |  |  | 4 | 19.00 | A1 | 020 | 0153 |
|  |  |  |  | 1 |  |  |  | 1 |  |  | 2 | 18.00 | A1 | 020 | 0183 |
|  |  |  |  |  |  |  |  | 1 |  |  | 1 | 24.00 | A1 | 020 | 0220 |
|  |  |  |  |  | 5 |  |  |  |  |  | 5 | 12.99 | A1 | 020 | 1400 |
| 1 |  |  |  |  |  |  |  |  |  |  | 1 | 22.00 | A1 | 029 | 3268 |
| 2 |  |  |  |  |  |  |  |  |  |  | 2 | 24.00 | A1 | 029 | 4414 |
|  |  |  | 1 |  |  |  |  |  |  |  | 1 | 16.00 | A1 | 029 | 9662 |
|  |  | 1 |  |  |  |  |  |  |  |  | 1 | 19.00 | A1 | 033 | 0953 |
|  |  |  | 1 |  |  |  |  |  |  |  | 1 | 19.00 | A1 | 033 | 0954 |
|  |  | 1 |  |  | 1 |  |  |  |  |  | 2 | 13.99 | A1 | 033 | 1109 |
|  |  | 1 |  |  |  |  | 1 |  |  |  | 2 | 8.00 | A1 | 048 | 0400 |
|  |  |  |  |  |  |  |  | 1 |  |  | 1 | 18.00 | A1 | 171 | 4778 |
|  |  |  |  |  |  |  |  | 1 |  |  | 1 | 21.00 | A1 | 171 | 4814 |
|  |  |  |  |  |  |  |  | 1 |  |  | 1 | 31.00 | A1 | 171 | 4976 |
|  |  |  | 1 |  |  |  |  |  |  |  | 1 | 15.00 | A1 | 172 | 0750 |
|  |  |  |  |  | 3 |  |  |  |  |  | 3 | 11.00 | A1 | 173 | 0022 |
|  |  |  |  |  | 1 |  |  |  |  |  | 1 | 15.00 | A1 | 215 | 0612 |
|  |  |  |  |  |  |  |  | 1 |  |  | 1 | 8.99 | A1 | 215 | 1218 |
|  |  | 1 |  |  |  |  |  |  |  |  | 1 | 34.00 | A1 | 215 | 3003 |
|  |  |  |  |  |  | 1 |  |  |  |  | 1 | 15.99 | A1 | 218 | 3006 |
|  | 1 |  |  |  |  |  |  |  |  |  | 1 | 39.00 | A1 | 247 | 1938 |
|  |  |  |  |  | 1 |  |  |  |  |  | 1 | 25.00 | A1 | 349 | 0503 |
| 1 |  |  |  |  |  |  |  |  |  |  | 1 | 23.99 | A1 | 349 | 0515 |
|  |  |  |  |  | 1 |  |  |  |  |  | 1 | 9.00 | A1 | 377 | 9268 |
|  |  |  | 1 |  |  |  |  |  |  |  | 1 | 13.99 | A1 | 386 | 1201 |
|  |  |  | 1 |  |  |  |  |  |  |  | 1 | 8.00 | A1 | 400 | 0400 |
| 2 |  |  |  | 1 |  |  |  |  |  |  | 3 | 31.00 | A1 | 462 | 1568 |
| 2 |  |  |  |  |  |  |  |  |  |  | 2 | 34.00 | A1 | 462 | 1702 |
|  |  |  |  |  | 1 |  |  |  |  |  | 1 | 10.00 | A1 | 479 | 6069 |
|  |  |  |  |  |  | 1 |  |  |  |  | 1 | 16.00 | A1 | 504 | 1637 |
|  | 2 |  |  |  |  |  |  |  |  |  | 2 | 15.00 | A1 | 504 | 2920 |
| 1 |  |  |  |  |  | 1 |  |  |  |  | 2 | 15.00 | A1 | 504 | 3292 |
|  |  | 1 | 1 | 1 |  |  | 1 |  |  |  | 4 | 17.00 | A1 | 504 | 4224 |
| 1 |  |  | 3 |  |  |  |  |  |  |  | 4 | 17.00 | A1 | 504 | 4227 |
| 1 |  |  |  |  |  |  |  |  |  |  | 1 | 19.00 | A1 | 504 | 9112 |
| 1 |  |  |  |  |  |  |  |  |  |  | 1 | 34.00 | A1 | 576 | 1152 |
|  |  |  |  | 1 |  |  |  |  |  |  | 1 | 35.00 | A1 | 600 | 3251 |
|  |  | 1 |  |  |  |  |  |  |  |  | 1 | 65.00 | A1 | 600 | 4252 |

| STYLE | WEEK TO DATE SALES B | J | H | N | U | L | R | G | W | P |  | TOT | ONE WEEK AGO | 2 WEEKS AGO | 4 WEEKS TOTAL | LIFE TO DATE | LIFE CUST RET |
|---|---|---|---|---|---|---|---|---|---|---|---|---|---|---|---|---|---|
| ---- | DOM LEATHERS |  |  |  |  |  | ---- |  |  |  |  |  |  |  |  |  |  |
| 0000 | 1 |  |  | 1 |  |  |  |  |  |  |  | 2 | 9 | 5 | 32 | 119 |  |
| 1022 |  |  |  |  | 3 |  |  |  |  |  |  | 3 | 1 | 1 | 11 | 20 |  |
| 1399 |  |  |  |  |  |  |  |  | 1 |  |  | 1 | 4 |  | 6 | 11 |  |
| 2900 |  |  |  |  |  |  |  |  | 1 |  |  | 1 |  |  | 1 | 9 |  |
| 0153 |  |  |  |  |  | 1 | 2 |  | 1 |  |  | 4 | 17 | 21 | 53 | 53 |  |
| 0183 |  |  |  |  | 1 |  |  |  | 1 |  |  | 2 | 8 | 16 | 30 | 30 |  |
| 0220 |  |  |  |  |  |  |  |  | 1 |  |  | 1 | 6 | 9 | 20 | 20 |  |
| 1400 |  |  |  |  |  | 5 |  |  |  |  |  | 5 | 8 | 12 | 36 | 36 |  |
| 3268 | 1 |  |  |  |  |  |  |  |  |  |  | 1 | 1 | 1 | 4 | 436 |  |
| 4414 | 2 |  |  |  |  |  |  |  |  |  |  | 2 | 1 |  | 3 | 126 |  |
| 9662 |  |  |  | 1 |  |  |  |  |  |  |  | 1 |  |  | 1 | 394 |  |
| 0953 |  |  | 1 |  |  |  |  |  |  |  |  | 1 | 8 | 2 | 11 | 11 |  |
| 0954 |  |  |  | 1 |  |  |  |  |  |  |  | 1 | 2 |  | 3 | 3 |  |
| 1109 |  |  | 1 |  |  | 1 |  |  |  |  |  | 2 | 10 | 2 | 14 | 47 |  |
| 0400 |  |  | 1 |  |  |  |  | 1 |  |  |  | 2 | 3 | 1 | 6 | 6 |  |
| 4778 |  |  |  |  |  |  |  |  | 1 |  |  | 1 | 3 |  | 4 | 4 |  |
| 4814 |  |  |  |  |  |  |  |  | 1 |  |  | 1 | 3 |  | 4 | 4 |  |
| 4976 |  |  |  |  |  |  |  |  | 1 |  |  | 1 | 1 |  | 2 | 2 |  |
| 0750 |  |  |  | 1 |  |  |  |  |  |  |  | 1 | 1 | 1 | 6 | 207 |  |
| 0022 |  |  |  |  |  | 3 |  |  |  |  |  | 3 |  |  | 3 | 3 |  |
| 0612 |  |  |  |  |  | 1 |  |  |  |  |  | 1 | 5 |  | 9 | 115 |  |
| 1218 |  |  |  |  |  |  |  |  | 1 |  |  | 1 |  |  | 9 | 267 |  |
| 3003 |  |  | 1 |  |  |  |  |  |  |  |  | 1 | 1 |  | 2 | 17 |  |
| 3006 |  |  |  |  |  |  | 1 |  |  |  |  | 1 |  |  | 5 | 81 |  |
| 1938 |  | 1 |  |  |  |  |  |  |  |  |  | 1 | 1 |  | 2 | 26 |  |
| 0503 |  |  |  |  |  | 1 |  |  |  |  |  | 1 |  | 1 | 2 | 24 |  |
| 0515 | 1 |  |  |  |  |  |  |  |  |  |  | 1 | 2 |  | 3 | 27 |  |
| 9268 |  |  |  |  |  | 1 |  |  |  |  |  | 1 | 1 | 1 | 5 | 108 |  |
| 1201 |  |  |  | 1 |  |  |  |  |  |  |  | 1 |  | 1 | 8 | 1117 |  |
| 0400 |  |  |  | 1 |  |  |  |  |  |  |  | 1 | 2 |  | 3 | 3 |  |
| 1568 | 2 |  |  |  | 1 |  |  |  |  |  |  | 3 | 2 |  | 5 | 5 |  |
| 1702 | 2 |  |  |  |  |  |  |  |  |  |  | 2 | 1 |  | 3 | 3 |  |
| 6069 |  |  |  |  |  | 1 |  |  |  |  |  | 1 |  |  | 1 | 1 |  |
| 1637 |  |  |  |  |  |  | 1 |  |  |  |  | 1 | 2 | 2 | 6 | 362 |  |
| 2920 |  | 2 |  |  |  |  |  |  |  |  |  | 2 |  | 1 | 3 | 3 |  |
| 3292 | 1 |  |  |  |  |  | 1 |  |  |  |  | 2 | 15 | 11 | 49 | 49 |  |
| 4224 |  |  | 1 | 1 | 1 |  |  | 1 |  |  |  | 4 | 7 | 4 | 31 | 31 |  |
| 4227 | 1 |  |  | 3 |  |  |  |  |  |  |  | 4 |  |  | 4 | 4 |  |
| 9112 | 1 |  |  |  |  |  |  |  |  |  |  | 1 |  |  | 1 | 1 |  |
| 1152 | 1 |  |  |  |  |  |  |  |  |  |  | 1 |  |  | 1 | 21 |  |
| 3251 |  |  |  |  | 1 |  |  |  |  |  |  | 1 |  |  | 1 | 10 |  |
| 4252 |  |  | 1 |  |  |  |  |  |  |  |  | 1 |  |  | 3 | 15 |  |

FIGURE 6–5. Active style report

linens able to satisfy the needs of customers with white sheets and pillowcases. Not only is color assortment wider in soft goods, but so is the range of colors available in appliances. Should the major appliance buyer stock heavily in a new color? Will men want prints, stripes, or bold solid colors in their dress shirt wardrobes? Will the customer be pleased with white dinnerware, or will contemporary patterns be requested? The color explosion has given buyers still another area of concern with which to reckon.

As with the other factors, color records are meticulously kept and religiously studied by buyers. The decision to buy a particular style might prove disastrous if the color in which it is purchased does not have customer appeal. It is true that certain colors are considered "hot" for the season, but they might not be so with a particular store's customers. Within a company that has many branches, color acceptance might vary from location to location.

Study of past sales records will not only point up the colors that sold best but will also, if properly analyzed, indicate overall color information. For example, if during the past season customers bought the "latest" color, pink, better than any other color, and in the season before that they bought the "latest" color, yellow, and so forth, a buyer could assume that these customers generally accept "the latest" color. It would then be comparatively safe to purchase whatever color is being promoted as the "latest" in the future. If, however, surveying past records indicates steady acceptance of "basic colors" (navy and white for spring) and reluctance to purchase "new colors," adherence to basics seems to be in order. Figure 6–1 shows that white is definitely the favorite of that store's customers. Figure 6–3 shows the size and color sales report used by a large retailer, in which color information is separated according to individual locations. As mentioned earlier, this will show how each store fares with particular colors.

**Sizes.** About 35 years ago, when American consumers went to purchase clothing they found relatively few size ranges. They would purchase what they found appealing and alter the merchandise for proper fit. Buyers didn't worry as they do today to make decisions about the quantities of each size needed. Contemporary retailing affords the customer as much size differentiation as there are colors. Men's wear buyers are offered regulars, shorts, longs, portlies, cadets, extra sizes, and so forth. Nothing, however, compares to the size madness of the women's market. Such size classifications as misses, juniors, women's, half sizes, petite, diminutive, and tall are commonplace. The department store buyer doesn't have nearly the size problem the small store operators face, since most department stores separate their departments according to the size classifications and each buyer is responsible for the purchase of one or two. Buyers whose job entails the purchase of many size ranges must carefully study past sales to see which of the many available ranges have had satisfactory customer acceptance. Stores very often eliminate (as well as increase) particular size ranges because of past sales records.

It should be borne in mind that sizes must also be carefully scrutinized in terms of available styles. A buyer cannot possibly separate sizes and styles but must evaluate each in terms of the other; that is, the buyer must know which styles sell best in which sizes.

**Materials.** The late 1960s saw a revolutionary change in the materials being shown in men's wear. For the first time men were being offered a departure from the woven woolens, silks, and cottons used in suits. Knitted polyesters were revolutionizing the industry. Today the soft goods industry has available hundreds of different "miracle fibers" as well as the old standby natural fibers in a variety of constructions. Materials confusion is not restricted to wearing apparel. Buyers of upholstered furniture, luggage, draperies, table linens, and carpeting must proceed with equal caution in the selection of their merchandise.

The proper analysis of those past sales records that include materials descriptions (see Figure 6–1) gives the buyer information on customer acceptance. Materials, like styles, change in terms of customer demand. The records indicate which are in demand at a given time. Buyers must also be aware of the fact that the material has yet to be discovered that will be all things to all people. In 1965 Corfam was introduced as leather's replacement in the shoe industry. History has shown that although some customers accepted Corfam, most preferred leather. Likewise, the polyester knit of 1970 was supposed to make men forget about the woven woolen suit. But in 1973 buyers who failed to stock woven woolens were found to be guessing wrong. Although all the new materials make the buyer's job more difficult, they are nevertheless a fact of life. Buyers must make certain their customers' needs are being met. There is no better way than through examination of past sales records.

**Frequency of purchase.** Many of the records depicted in this chapter provide information concerning frequency of purchase. Buyers simply cannot justify stocking merchandise that sells infrequently. Faced with a turnover problem (to be discussed in the next chapter), buyers must eliminate the merchandise that sits in inventory and ties up shelf space as well as capital. Weeding out the slow movers is very difficult. There isn't a buyer in the world who can buy perfectly. There is, however, sufficient information in past sales records to indicate definite slow sellers. These items contribute to lower profits and must be eliminated.

**Customer returns.** Occasionally buyers are puzzled by the poor showing of merchandise that seems to have all the earmarks of a winner but is still in stock at inventory-taking time. The problem may be due to faults other than price, color, style, and the like. Examination of past sales records might indicate that customers liked the merchandise and purchased it, only to return it to the store. The fit might be improper or the material faulty. Some past sales records provide information concerning customer returns. Figures 6–1 and 6–5 show forms that provide return information. Consistently returned merchandise could serve as an indicator to the buyer that further investigation is needed; this could lead to a correction of whatever was wrong or discontinuation of the item or vendor in question.

The past sales records available to today's buyers are more complete than ever before. Computer utilization is certainly responsible. The problem is not so much the information that is available, but the ability of the buyer to understand its implications. Only through careful use and analysis of past sales records can a buyer satisfactorily embark upon a purchasing program.

## Consumer Research

To make certain that the needs of the consumer are being satisfied, a buyer cannot rely strictly on past sales records. It is the responsibility of each merchandiser to participate in research efforts in some way. Research is being performed by merchandise managers, buyers, assistant buyers, fashion coordinators, and others in the store's merchandising division to make certain that consumer demand is understood.

In the larger stores, research departments are maintained to perform these functions. Their job, in terms of merchandising, is to provide buyers and merchandisers with information important to the decision making necessary for efficient purchasing.

With regard to the actual selection of merchandise, buyers are interested in determining customer reaction to price, style, color, materials, and so forth. Through the proper use of such survey devices as interviews, questionnaires, observations, focus groups, and college boards, buyers have still other sources of purchasing information available to them.

### *Interviews*

One of the methods employed to gather information is the personnel interview. The interview can be conceived simply to collect one or two important insights into customer behavior, or it can be extensive. For the simple interview, the store might call on salespeople to act as interviewers. For example, a buyer might want to know the customer's reaction to a new style. This might only necessitate that the salesperson ask each customer's opinion and then record the information. More complicated interviews would require the services of trained interviewers. Research departments use their own people or employ the services of an outside research organization.

### *Questionnaires*

Most retailers today have available customer lists just waiting to be surveyed. One of the most convenient and inexpensive methods of conducting a survey is through the insertion of a questionnaire in the customer's monthly statement. With the growth in the number of charge customers, retailers can easily find out their needs through this system. An ever-increasing number of retailers will agree that typical customers charge their purchases. Thus this group can provide significant information. Figure 6–6 shows a questionnaire that could be used to elicit information from charge customers for the purpose of assisting the buyer with merchandise selection.

Dear Charge Customer:

In an effort to more fully satisfy your shopping needs in the ladies' sportswear department, we are asking you to complete this questionnaire. With your cooperation we will be able to determine more accurately the type of merchandise that we will carry.

As a token of our appreciation, we are offering a surprise gift for those responses received prior to ________.

1. Are the prices of our merchandise consistent with your expectations?
____Yes ____No (If no, please explain)
____________________
____________________

2. What other types of merchandise, presently unavailable at our store, would you like to have us carry?
____________________
____________________

3. Can you usually find a color assortment to suit your needs?
____Yes ____No (If no, please explain)
____________________
____________________

4. Is the size assortment that we stock suited to your needs?
____Yes ____No (If yes, please indicate)
____________________
____________________

5. What is the occupation of the head of the household?
____________________

6. In which age group do you belong?
____20's ____50's
____30's ____60's
____40's

**FIGURE 6–6.** Sample questionnaire

Retailers do not limit their surveys to charge customers; they also employ other questionnaire methods such as the telephone interview. Each store must determine the best method of obtaining information and the best group from which to obtain it.

### *Observations*

One of the simplest tools used by buyers to gather style information is an observation technique called the fashion count. In place of interviewing people to get their merchandise reactions, buyers make use of the fashion count system of research, which merely requires observing and recording what people are wearing. The theory behind this technique is that if people are wearing some-

**TABLE 6–2** Fashion count, men's suits*

| *JACKET STYLE* | *PANTS STYLE* | *LOG STYLE* | *PATTERN* | *PREDOMINANT COLOR* |
|---|---|---|---|---|
| Two button | Pleated | Straight, plain | Solid | Black |
| Three button | Fitted (no pleats) | Straight, cuff | Check | Navy |
| | | | | Charcoal |
| Double breasted | | | Stripe | Brown |
| | | | Plaid | Tan |
| | | | Tweed | White |
| | | | | Camel |
| | | | | Green |
| | | | | Burgundy |
| | | | | Light gray |
| | | | | Other |

*Place in X next to the appropriate item.

thing, they must have liked it enough to make the purchase. It is important to observe those poeple who would be considered typical of the store's clientele. It is therefore necessary to carefully select the time and place in which to conduct the "count." The fashion count is particularly beneficial to buyers when taken periodically to show trends. The counts can be reliable only if those involved in recording the information fully understand the styles to be counted. Table 6–2 is an illustration of a typical form used in recording men's suits. The count is accomplished by the strategic placement of recorders at locations where people typical of the store's customers congregate. If this count were to be repeated a few times, it might indicate to the buyer changes in men's acceptance of style, pattern, and color. The information from this guide must be placed in the proper context and should be used as only one factor in future decision making.

### Focus Groups

The "consumer is king" philosophy has been painstakingly accepted by most retailers. Even those who had been reluctant to admit that only the consumer decides what he or she will purchase have come to acknowledge the power of the consumer. To provide themselves with firsthand consumer reactions, more and more retailers have organized consumer panels or focus groups. The varieties of panels are many, and the rules in each vary considerably. Some retailers have permanent consumer groups that meet regularly to discuss such merchandising concerns as price lines, merchandise assortments, fashion direction of the store, size ranges offered for sale, possible additional departments, and image. Other stores simply organize panels whenever a particular problem arises.

One major store has had considerable success with a teen panel. Each Saturday morning selected students from nearby high schools have a "rap" session at the store and tell what they like and dislike about the merchandise, services, and the like.

Whatever system is employed, the most important factor to the retailer is the composition of the panel. Extreme caution must be exercised in the formulation of the group to guarantee that the opinions will be typical of the clientele served. If the panel is not truly representative, the information could be misleading and could prove to be harmful in future decision making.

To motivate the participants involved in the focus groups, many retailers offer such incentives as discount cards, special gifts, and sometimes regular cash payments.

### *College Boards*

Most fashion-oriented retaiers have organized "college boards" for their junior departments. A college board is a group of students composed of one representative from each of several colleges. The representatives selected come from colleges likely to be attended by the store's college-bound customers. The board's primary function is to assist students with the selection of merchandise appropriate for their needs at the particular colleges they expect to attend. The board also provides the buyer with such information as which merchandise will probably be best accepted (a great advantage for early reorders) and which colors college students will probably prefer.

Although some buyers might consider this to be late information, it nonetheless provides an excellent link between the store and prospective customers.

## Sales Personnel

No information system is complete unless the sales staff is utilized. Nobody has closer customer contact than the store's sales personnel. Under organizational structures in which buyers are responsible for the management of sales staff, they enjoy a distinct advantage.

Salespeople, by the nature of their job, hear things computers cannot possibly record. For example, there are the reasons why customers *didn't* purchase. Among them are the following:

1. The merchandise desired wasn't carried by the department.
2. The item in question wasn't in stock at the particular time.
3. The fit was poor. How often customers try on merchandise, only to find that the fit is improper!
4. The size needed was unavailable, and larger or smaller sizes were being requested.
5. The color assortment was incomplete.

The information can best be brought to the buyer's attention through regular meetings with the salespeople. Most buyers agree that the salesperson is invaluable as a source of information.

While the regular meeting between the buyer and the salespeople is probably the best method by which to collect information concerning lost sales, it is not always possible to organize such meetings. Buyers who are responsible for the purchase of merchandise earmarked for branch stores generally find it difficult to visit those outlets on a regular basis. It is also true, even in the case of the buyer who operates from the parent store, that the multitude of duties and responsibilities prohibit personal meetings.

In an effort to bring customer requests for particular merchandise to the attention of the buyer when circumstances prevent meetings, some retailers have instituted want slip systems. These slips or forms are used to record information concerning merchandise requested but unavailable at the time of the request. The form is filled out by the salesperson or the customer, depending on the store's policy.

While want slip information can indicate to the buyer that particular merchandise has been requested, extreme caution is necessary in its analysis. For example, positive action on each request can lead to such diversification that the inventory can be overstocked and the store's image affected. Filling each request could result in the purchase of too many items desired by too few customers.

A criticism of the want slip system is that the information provided comes a little too late for maximum effectiveness. Careful attention, however, can provide the buyer with additional merchandise information that could be a guide in future purchases. Figure 6–7 shows the want slip used at Abraham and Straus, a full-service Campeau Department Store, that the salesperson completes. Home Depot, a leader in merchandise for the home, uses a system that invites the customer to fill out merchandise request forms.

SALES CLERKS If you could not supply an item exactly as the Customer wanted it,—record the item the customer described immediately after the customer leaves—even though you sold a substitute.

| ITEM CUSTOMER DESCRIBED (Style—Fabric—Etc.) | Color | Size | Price | No. Calls | Buyer's Disposition |
|---|---|---|---|---|---|
| | | | | | |
| | | | | | |
| | | | | | |
| | | | | | |
| | | | | | |
| | | | | | |
| | | | | | |
| | | | | | |

ITEMS LOW IN STOCK

| | |
|---|---|
| | |
| | |

CUSTOMER WANT SLIP

Sales Clerk No.________ Date________

Name________

**FIGURE 6–7.** Want slip

## ACTION FOR THE SMALL STORE BUYER

Buying that brings positive results to a store necessitates a considerable amount of planning by the individual reponsibile for purchasing merchandise. Large retail organizations spend considerable time and effort in research before major purchases are made, but the small store buyer is often known to make buying decisions based on whim or spur-of-the-moment thinking, or to be influenced by a high-pressure sales representative.

In determining what to purchase for the store, the buyer for a small company must perhaps plan more carefully than the department store or chain store purchaser. Those companies, which enjoy enormous traffic in their outlets, can more easily dispose of a "bad" purchase than the small store. Small store buyers cannot make too many errors and still turn a profit.

The smallest retailer must keep past sales records to be used for, among other things, giving the buyer historical data on which future buying decisions can be made. With the enormous advances in computers, which can be programmed to record vital past sales information, the smallest store could easily develop a system to assist the buyer in merchandise decisions. The prices are so relatively modest that even the smallest company could purchase such a system. If cost is still a factor, the hand-recording inventory system could be employed, with minimal cost and effort, and could be an excellent tool to use in determining what to buy.

In addition to past sales, the small store should develop other techniques to help forecast merchandise needs accurately. Devices such as questionnaires, fashion counts, and consumer panels, if carefully arranged, could provide a low-cost insight into customer needs. These sources, coupled with the data generated by past sales records, could let the smallest store buyer, with a minimum of expense, enter the market with as much expertise as the buyer for large companies.

Merely selecting "pretty things" no longer works. No matter how small the operation, the bottom line is profit. Attention paid to the techniques mentioned above will set the small store buyer on the right track.

## SUMMARY OF KEY POINTS

1. No outside information could be quite as important to the buyer, in terms of merchandise selection, as the information generated by the store's own efforts.
2. The single most important source of information is the store's past sales.
3. Store records are kept in a number of ways. Hand recording is used predominantly by small retailers, with larger ones making use of the computer.

4. Through careful recording and analysis of information, buyers can examine such merchandise factors as classification, price, style, color, size, material, frequency of purchase, and customer returns.
5. While it is obvious that not every buyer requires all the information discussed in the chapter, a buyer can select from what is available that which is important to his or her particular merchandise.
6. A considerable amount of customer research is performed by retailers. The research can sometimes be accomplished simply with the cooperation of salespeople. More extensive research involves the use of research departments.
7. Retailers survey their customers' needs through interviews, questionnaires, focus groups, and college boards.
8. One of the most valuable in-store information sources is the sales personnel. Because they have direct customer contact, salespeople can provide information otherwise unavailable to buyers.
9. In the absence of direct meetings with the sales staff, the want slip system reports many of the customer requests the store was unable to satisfy.

## REVIEW QUESTIONS

1. Contast the value of the store's internal sources of buyer information with outside sources.
2. How valuable are past sales records to buyers if the next season requires the purchase of new merchandise?
3. In what manner can the small retailer collect pertinent past sales information?
4. What purpose does the two-part merchandise tag serve?
5. Does color keying provide the small retailer with any additional inventory information?
6. Can present fashion color information provide the buyer with any assistance in future color selection even if the colors change?
7. Define the term *merchandise classification.*
8. Define the term *trading up.*
9. Why do buyers find it necessary to collect price information for each branch separately, rather than an overall report?
10. Differentiate between *fashion* and *style.*
11. Why do buyers have more problems related to size ranges today than in the past?
12. Data on customer returns provide valuable information for the buyer. In what way?
13. Who performs the research function in retail stores?

14. Describe the observation technique of gathering information.
15. How can the fashion count be beneficial to the buyer if he or she has already purchased the season's needs?
16. Retailers motivate customers to answer questionnaires and return them quickly. How do they accomplish this?
17. Focus groups provide retailers with pertinent information. What point concerning these panels must retailers approach carefully?
18. Discuss the value of the college board.
19. If the computer provides the buyer with a lot of information, why do many buyers find it rewarding to meet regularly with sales personnel?
20. Are want slips important? Explain.

## CASE PROBLEM 1

Pot Pourri, Ltd., opened its doors as a women's speciality store ten years ago. Throughout its first eight years of operation, Pot Pourri catered to the more affluent female, each year beating the previous year's sales figures. Sales volume last year was $900,000.

Last year the company decided to expand its operation by acquiring additional space in an adjoining building and by adding two additional merchandise lines. The store developed a program to include full men's wear and children's wear departments. The rationale behind the move was the ever-growing demand for these two lines by the company's clientele. After considerable investigation, Pot Pourri went ahead with its plans and opened the expanded operation six months ago.

Merchandising of the new department was assigned to Karen McGuiness, former women's wear assistant with the company, and Marc Litt, formerly the buyer in a large men's wear department of a medium-priced department store.

At this point Pot Pourri is disappointed with the new departments' business. Sales have been well below what was anticipated. The problem seems to be one of improper merchandise selection rather than customer traffic, because the store traffic has been considerable.

In an effort to correct the situation, management is planning to organize a research study. It is hoped that the findings will alleviate the present situation. The only management concern at the moment is cost. Although their thinking is progressive, both the size of the company and budgetary restrictions limit the type of research they could undertake.

### Questions

1. Do you think management's move toward expansion was correct?
2. Discuss three types of research the store could conduct, bearing in mind its organizational and financial situation.

## CASE PROBLEM 2

Janet Eastland has been hired as the children's wear buyer at Crompton's Department Store. The company grossed $18 million last year, with the children's department's share amounting to $1,500,000. Crompton's is based in the Deep South and consists of a parent store and eight branches. The branch stores are all located within a 150-mile radius of the parent store, in which Ms. Eastland has her office.

Crompton's, a progressive department store, has all the latest information systems in operation at the main store. The buyers receive numerous periodic reports such as style and color analysis, price analysis, and size status.

Ms. Eastland, formerly a buyer with a smaller company, uses all the buyer information she receives. She is, however, disappointed that all the functions she performs, coupled with the distance to the branches, make it difficult for her to get branch sales personnel input for merchandise decision making. Being a firm believer in sales personnel as an important information source, she is concerned about the lack of it at Crompton's.

At present management is trying to develop a method that would satisfy Ms. Eastland's wishes.

### Question

1. Develop a system that would enable the company to accommodate the buyer.

# Chapter 7

# HOW MUCH TO BUY

## LEARNING OBJECTIVES

*Upon completion of this chapter, the student should be able to:*

1. Explain the importance of a dollar merchandise plan and discuss its construction in detail.
2. Define model stock and differentiate between the buying of staple and fashion merchandise.
3. Define and give examples of classification and subclassification. Explain the use of these terms in stock planning.
4. Describe the function and method of construction of a distribution summary.
5. Provide the formula for open-to-buy and solve complicated arithmetic problems in this area (75 percent accuracy).
6. Discuss the importance of automatic reordering for staple goods.

## INTRODUCTION

Once the buyer has investigated all the necessary sources of information and has formulated a "merchandise attitude," he or she is ready to translate needs into quantitative considerations. It doesn't take a great deal of expertise to understand the consequences of buying more than was needed (overbuying). The dangers inherent in buying too little are of equal consequence. Almost no situation is as aggravating to the buyer as being unable to satisfy a customer's needs because of an insufficient amount of a particular kind of merchandise.

While it isn't always possible to plan perfectly, nonetheless buyers, in conjunction with their merchandise managers, carefully develop inventory plans. These plans, it is hoped, will provide assortments at levels that offer variety as well as proper quantities to meet demand.

Determining the appropriate quantities is no simple task. The buyer relies on a wealth of information from past records, as discussed in the preceding chapter, to set goals. A wide variety of forms helps the buyer establish the proper merchandise quantities. In collecting and analyzing the information needed for quantity decision making, the contemporary large store buyer has an advantage over his or her predecessor. The computer periodically provides the buyer with a wealth of information to use for future planning. Not only are more detailed printouts available, but they are obtainable more rapidly.

Whether employed by a large company equipped with a computer center or by a small organization that doesn't offer such sophisticated recordkeeping, the buyer must carefully examine the available information and determine how much to buy.

In this chapter attention will be limited to quantitative considerations and will include the dollar merchandise plan, model stock development, replenishment considerations, and inventory fluctuation.

## THE SIX-MONTH MERCHANDISE PLAN

To bring a net profit to the department at the end of the year, the buyer carefully develops a dollar merchandise plan. The most commonly used system in retailing is the six-month plan. The final budgetary allotment is determined after considerable effort has been made by the buyer, the merchandise manager, and the controller. Generally the buyer initiates the planning through the completion of a form similar to the one illustrated in Table 7-1. The prediction of the needs for the coming six-month period is exactly that, a prediction. It is based primarily on the department's past experience. In formulating the six-month plan, many stores use the figures for the preceding three years. Of major importance are the sales figures, stock, dollar markdown, and markup percent. After the form is completed, the divisional merchandise manager meets with the buyer to examine every figure on the plan. Such careful examination is

**TABLE 7-1** Six-month merchandise plan (computer printout), junior sportswear department

| | | *MERCHANDISE PLAN—FALL 1992* | | | | | | | | |
|---|---|---|---|---|---|---|---|---|---|---|
| | | *—MAIL STORE—* | | | *—BRANCH A—* | | | *—BRANCH B—* | | |
| *MO* | *YR* | *SALES* | *BOP STK* | *$MKD* | *SALES* | *BOP STK* | *$ MKD* | *SALES* | *BOP STK* | *$ MKD* |
| Aug | PL | 32.0 | 132.0 | 1.0 | 2.0 | 4.0 | | 1.2 | 3.0 | |
| | 91 | 23.2 | 119.4 | | 1.2 | 3.2 | | .3 | 0.4 | |
| 07 | 90 | 22.0 | 148.4 | 1.6 | 1.3 | 3.3 | 0.1 | .1 | 0.6 | |
| | 89 | 29.8 | 111.8 | 0.4 | 1.2 | 18.4 | 0.2 | .7 | 8.1 | |
| Sep | | 90.0 | 200.0 | 2.0 | 6.5 | 8.0 | | 2.0 | 1.5 | |
| | 91 | 85.8 | 218.6 | 2.1 | 5.7 | 7.7 | | .8 | 1.4 | |
| 08 | 90 | 66.4 | 214.2 | 1.2 | 5.1 | 9.3 | 0.1 | .3 | 0.9 | |
| | 89 | 80.2 | 203.0 | 2.0 | 6.0 | 30.3 | | 1.7 | 11.2 | |
| Oct | | 110.0 | 240.0 | 2.5 | 9.5 | 15.0 | 0.2 | 1.4 | 3.0 | 0.1 |
| | 91 | 104.8 | 280.0 | 2.6 | 8.6 | 19.6 | 0.3 | .9 | 2.2 | |
| 09 | 90 | 78.4 | 234.0 | 2.0 | 5.1 | 15.1 | 0.3 | .9 | 3.3 | 0.1 |
| | 89 | 91.2 | 159.6 | 0.8 | 8.6 | 32.2 | 0.7 | 2.3 | 7.7 | 0.2 |
| Nov | | 144.0 | 260.0 | 2.0 | 18.2 | 25.0 | 0.3 | 4.0 | 5.0 | |
| | 91 | 141.0 | 324.4 | 0.8 | 17.2 | 27.1 | 0.4 | 3.2 | 3.3 | |
| 10 | 90 | 103.8 | 211.8 | 1.7 | 7.6 | 16.2 | 0.2 | 1.8 | 4.3 | |
| | 89 | 133.2 | 209.0 | 0.2 | 13.3 | 31.9 | 0.3 | 2.0 | 8.0 | |
| Dec | | 258.0 | 250.0 | 3.0 | 35.0 | 23.0 | 1.0 | 12.0 | 7.0 | 0.4 |
| | 91 | 251.4 | 251.8 | 1.6 | 31.6 | 23.7 | 1.0 | 10.4 | 5.3 | 1.3 |
| 11 | 90 | 170.6 | 233.0 | 3.1 | 17.1 | 17.8 | 1.2 | 4.7 | 5.5 | 0.3 |
| | 89 | 193.6 | 236.8 | 3.9 | 23.6 | 28.3 | 1.1 | 7.9 | 8.3 | |
| Jan | | 112.0 | 190.0 | 3.5 | 12.0 | 18.0 | 2.5 | 3.5 | 4.0 | 1.0 |
| | 91 | 100.8 | 230.8 | 7.3 | 10.1 | 21.1 | 2.9 | 1.7 | 4.6 | 0.7 |
| 12 | 90 | 94.8 | 165.2 | 1.0 | 5.5 | 8.9 | 1.3 | 1.4 | 4.4 | 0.2 |
| | 89 | 95.6 | 181.4 | 6.8 | 5.5 | 18.6 | 2.3 | 1.7 | 4.6 | 0.1 |

| *SIX MONTH* | *TOT* | *MKD %* | *$ MKD, TOT* | *TOT* | *MKD %* | *$ MKD, TOT* | *TOT* | *MKD %* | *$ MKD, TOT* |
|---|---|---|---|---|---|---|---|---|---|
| PL | 746.0 | 3.8 | 14.0 | 83.2 | 4.8 | 4.0 | 24.1 | 6.2 | 1.5 |
| 91 | 707.0 | 4.0 | 14.4 | 74.4 | 6.1 | 4.6 | 17.3 | 11.5 | 2.0 |
| 90 | 536.0 | 3.9 | 10.6 | 41.7 | 7.6 | 3.2 | 9.2 | 6.5 | .6 |
| 89 | 673.6 | 4.5 | 14.1 | 58.2 | 7.9 | 4.6 | 16.3 | 1.8 | .3 |

| *MARKUP* | | *AUG* | *SEP* | *OCT* | *NOV* | *DEC* | *JAN* | *TOTAL* | *Approved Buyer* |
|---|---|---|---|---|---|---|---|---|---|
| % | PL | 55.0 | 54.0 | 51.0 | 51.5 | 50.5 | 50.5 | 52.0 | |
| | 91 | 56.8 | 53.8 | 51.0 | 51.4 | 50.8 | 50.7 | 52.1 | DMM |
| | 90 | 52.9 | 52.8 | 49.0 | 50.0 | 48.8 | 50.8 | 50.8 | MPV |
| | 89 | 50.7 | 50.1 | 53.6 | 52.1 | 51.3 | 51.2 | 51.8 | |

necessary, since the next six months' business will be affected by the amount of merchandise that is made available for sale. If there are errors in the planning, there could be insufficient merchandise, which could result in lost sales, or too much merchandise, which could eventually cause markdowns and thus affect the department's overall markup.

It should be understood that the past sales and stock figures should serve only as a guide. Naturally, if the past three years indicate a sales increase of 8 percent for each year, it is quite likely that the sales for the coming period will reflect an 8 percent increase as well. There are, however, situations in which other factors must be considered. For example, the economy might be headed in a downward direction. Economic indicators, such as unemployment figures, Federal Reserve Bank information, and so forth, may reflect conditions likely to adversely affect purchasing. The buyer for precious jewelry, furs, or any other items considered to be luxuries must carefully evaluate these implications, despite the fact that past years have shown a steady increase in sales.

The point is that external indicators can provide the buyer with information necessary for merchandise planning. Such sources as trade associations (the National Retail Federation, for example), the media, government agencies, resident buying offices, trade periodicals, and reporting services could assist the buyer in making plans. It is the inexperienced buyer who relies exclusively on past figures.

Table 7-1 shows a merchandise plan for one department in a three-unit department store organization. Before an analysis of the example in the Table can be presented, an understanding of the following abbreviations and symbols is necessary:

- MO—month
- YR—year
- SALES—sales, at retail
- BOP STK—beginning-of-period stock
- $MKD—dollar markdown
- TOT—total
- MKD %—markdown percent
- MKD TOT—dollar markdown total
- DMM—divisional merchandise manager
- MVP—merchandise vice president
- PL—planned

The buyer in the illustration was supplied with a printout that contained all the actual sales, stock, and so forth for each department (there are sets of figures for each of the store's units) for each month for a three-year period. Thus if we look at the August figures for the main store, we see that sales have been planned at $32,000, stock at $132,000, and markdowns at $1000. The junior sportswear buyer, in examining the figures for the preceding three years, has seen a decrease from 1989 to 1990 and a slight increase from 1990 to 1991. The "PL" numbers are the buyers prediction or projection for the coming August period. The jump from sales of approximately $23,000 to $32,000 might seem a little optimistic. As indicated earlier, however, merchandise planning does not rely solely on arithmetic calculations. The buyer's expertise in evaluating other factors contributes to the planning. Such an ambitious projection might have come from market forecasts of an increase in sportswear merchandise. The buyer must prepare for this possibility. If the market barometers had indicated a swing to dresses for the junior, the buyer would probably have been more conservative in planning.

Further analysis shows that for the main store, the buyer had projected greater efficiency in merchandising in September. While planned sales have been forecast at $90,000 (up over $4000 from the figure for the previous September), inventory has been set at $200,000 (down over $18,000 from inventory for the corresponding month of the prior year). This can lead to a more efficient operation, but it might indicate a little too much optimism.

Toward the bottom of the form, a total of the six-month plan is developed. These figures are a summary of the actual business and projections or plans.

At the very bottom the buyer enters the planned markup percent for each month. The percent he or she strives for must consider past figures as well as the future expenses he or she expects the department to incur. This percent must be carefully planned to result in a profit for the department.

In this particular company, the six-month plan is determined by the buyer, overseen by the divisional merchandise manager, and approved by the merchandising vice president. When all the signatures are affixed to the form, it becomes the official six-month plan for the department.

Among the typical factors a buyer might consider in addition to those discussed in the example are expansion of the department, the promotional budget, and shifts in population.

This is merely a dollar plan and in no way indicates how much particular merchandise must be purchased. It does not make provision for assortment in any way. Once a buyer has determined the six-month plan, however, he or she is on the road to the next important stage, that of developing the department's model stock.

## MODEL STOCK DEVELOPMENT

If a department is to be successful in satisfying the customer's merchandise needs, the buyer must carefully plan the proper assortment. An inventory that contains a satisfactory assortment at the time when customers are ready to purchase is known as a model stock. The development of the model stock takes considerable effort on the part of the buyer. The effort varies from department to department. For example, it is quite obvious that where the assortment to be inventoried is restricted to staple goods such as men's handkerchiefs, the involvement is not nearly as keen as in the case of fashion merchandise, where yesterday's fashion is today's "lemon." Since the planning of model stock varies so significantly between staple and fashion merchandise, individual attention will be focused on the two categories in order to underscore the different techniques involved.

## Staple Merchandise

Although the glamorous aspect of purchasing is generally regarded by novices as well as many seasoned buyers to be fashion merchandise, the steady profit realized by many retail operations is due directly to the merchandising of staples. Staples, goods considered basic to inventories that possess long-range salability such as birthday greeting cards, men's black socks, boxer shorts, and most groceries, have a place in just about every retail operation; in some, they are the only merchandise carried. Since the life of the staple is extremely long by comparison with the fashion item, the merchandising involved is not usually risky or tedious.

As discussed previously, the buyer generally establishes a dollar projection known as a six-month merchandise plan. Sometimes small retailers limit their projections to a much shorter period. (It is not that long-range planning isn't necessary or beneficial; it's simply that the small independents aren't always schooled along proper merchandising lines.) In any case the dollar figure that has been established provides the buyer with the sales projection and dollar inventory figure needed to reach the planned sales. This stock or inventory dollar amount must then be translated into an assortment customers will find palatable. How simple it would be if the retailer was confronted with only one particular item at one price that sold in equal quantities all year long! Realistically, this is impossible. Even in the case of a store that limits itself to milk, planning, although comparatively simple, requires quantity decisions on container sizes, chocolate versus regular, plastic jugs versus cartons, and peak periods in the business week.

Buyers of staples must then determine how to divide their dollar budgets so that ideal coverage is considered for all items. In the case of the vast majority of retail departments, most buyers are responsible for a merchandise mix that includes staple, fashion, and seasonal goods. Thus a beginning point is to examine past records to determine what portion of the dollar allocation for the designated period will be needed to fulfill adequately staple requirements.

For the purpose of better comprehension, the rather simple example of a candy department in a store will be offered. The candy department in this example is part of a large department store that develops the typical six-month plan for all departments. During the coming period from January 1 through June 30, the department's plans call for the following projection:

| *MONTH* | *STOCK (1ST OF MONTH)* | *SALES* | *MARKDOWNS* |
|---|---|---|---|
| January | 12,000 | 4,000 | 100 |
| February | 50,000 | 30,000 | 300 |
| March | 26,000 | 12,000 | 500 |
| April | 27,000 | 13,000 | 500 |
| May | 26,000 | 12,000 | 400 |
| June | 23,000 | 11,000 | 300 |

The projection has been based on past records as well as current trends regarding consumer weight consciousness.

Analysis indicates that candy consumption increases in the months containing holidays that motivate the consumer to purchase candy. February, March, April, May, and June include such holidays as Valentine's Day, Easter, Mother's Day, and graduation. This doesn't, however, merely signify to the buyer that the doubling or tripling of staple candies will satisfy the customer's needs. Easter requires stocking jelly beans, chocolate bunnies, candy eggs, and so forth. Thus careful planning must be exercised. Since this section deals with staples, we focus not on what "speciality items" to purchase, but on how much we will need for staple candies. Considering the staples, the buyer, with little risk of error, can stock and replenish inventory rather simply.

In this situation the first-of-month inventory is only one of a number of factors with which the candy buyer must be involved. The other decisions must include how often to replenish inventories, whether reorders should be automatic at certain levels, and which items must be ordered in limited quantities at more frequent intervals to avoid perishability problems.

Once the buyer has managed the buying chore for a given period, the purchase of the staples becomes second nature.

Later in this chapter, after the discussion of model stock planning for fashion merchandise, open-to-buy (merchandise needed for a period less merchandise available) will be explored to show its implications for the buyer's purchasing during a period.

## Fashion Merchandise

Buyers of fashion merchandise have a monumental task each season in trying to evaluate various sources of information to determine what they should promote for the coming season as well as how "heavy" the quantities should be. Once a buyer has decided how to approach the season in terms of style selection, he or she must prepare quantitative plans for each item to be purchased. The buyer must work within the framework of a dollar merchandise plan; quantity decisions must total to the dollar allotment. At the same time, the buyer must make certain that sufficient amounts of merchandise will be available to start the season. And the start of the season is the important time. Generally, once the season is under way, the fashion "winners" come to the fore and are reordered while there is demand, and slow sellers are sold off (it is hoped), never to be purchased again.

It should be understood that not every fashion decision is correct. In trying to feature the predicted hot fashion of the times, buyers sometimes purchase in quantities that turn out to be excessive. Now, trying to bury the quantity mistakes of yesterday, the buyer must calculate how much to buy for next season. In planning model stock the buyer must pay attention to several factors. These include the number of classifications in the department, the styles (or subclassifications) in each classification, price lines, sizes, and colors.

For the purpose of explanation, the examples used here will be based on the figures for September in the six-month merchandise plan for the main store's junior department (Table 7-1). The plan set forth will be for the department's needs on September 1.

### *Classification*

The term *classification* refers to the particular kinds of goods in a department. For example, the furniture department would carry such goods as bedroom furniture, upholstered pieces, lamps, and tables. In our example, the junior sportswear buyer would list the department's classifications and the quantities and dollar amounts sold during the last year. (See Table 7-2.)

In the "planned" column are the various classifications that fall within the junior sportswear department. The buyer translates plans for the future into dollars and quantities. Examination of the figures shows that the buyer is increasing the goals in sweaters, shirts, pants, and skirts; decreasing purchases of outer jackets and coordinates; and remaining constant in blazers. The information regarding the planned figures comes from a variety of sources. Since the merchandise is fashion oriented, reliance on past records alone is impractical and unwise. More than likely, planning has been based on such barometers as the trade papers such as the California Apparel News; trade association information (such as the NRF); reporting services; and conferences

**TABLE 7-2** Junior sportswear department classification summary, September

| | *SALES* | | *STOCK (DOLLARS)* | | *STOCK (QUANTITIES)* | |
|---|---|---|---|---|---|---|
| *Classification* | *1991* | *Planned* | *1991* | *Planned* | *1991* | *Planned* |
| Sweaters | $17,000 | $21,200 | $42,800 | $44,000 | 1,512 | 1,540 |
| Shirts | 7,000 | 8,400 | 15,200 | 16,000 | 760 | 800 |
| Pants | 22,000 | 24,000 | 54,000 | 58,000 | 1,350 | 1,400 |
| Skirts | 7,800 | 9,000 | 20,600 | 22,000 | 502 | 525 |
| Outer Jackets | 15,600 | 14,600 | 34,000 | 30,000 | 156 | 140 |
| Two-piece coordinates | 12,800 | 9,200 | 40,000 | 18,000 | 128 | 90 |
| Blazers | 3,600 | 3,600 | 12,000 | 12,000 | 150 | 150 |
| Totals | $85,000 | $90,000 | $218,600 | $200,000 | | |

with merchandise managers, fashion coordinators, and manufacturers. The following Focus describes the *California Apparel News* and its features, which help buyers plan their purchases.

**A RETAIL BUYING FOCUS**

***CALIFORNIA APPAREL NEWS***

While Fairchild Publications' *Women's Wear Daily* is the leading trade paper in the fashion industry, there are others, although lesser known, that provide pertinent and timely fashion information for store buyers. One of those that helps the West Coast buyer with buying plans is the *California Apparel News*. Published by MnM Publishing Corp., it is a regional periodical that concentrates on newsworthy fashion information for retailers located in Los Angeles, San Francisco, and other California shopping areas.

The paper is published weekly in standard newsprint stock, and prior to market weeks, it is produced in magazine format in full color.

Inspection of any issue immediately underscores its importance to fashion apparel buyers. Buyers are alerted to the latest in trends, merchandise offerings, the latest fabrications in the market, "hot" items and how they are selling in major retail organizations, market week showings throughout the world, and anything else that would be helpful in merchandising plans.

It should be understood that all the wholesale markets are explored, not only those found on the West Coast, since buyers travel great distances for merchandise procurement. Stress, however, is concentrated on information that would help make the California retailer a better and more informed merchant.

Since climate, customer needs, life-styles, and other characteristics make specific geographic regions unique, regional papers such as the *California Apparel News*, which focus on the West Coast, are considered mandatory for merchants in that area.

### *Style*

Once the information has been completed as in Table 7-2, the buyer prepares a detailed breakdown according to style or subclassification (see Table 7-3). Since the buyer must plan the department's assortments in a manner that will offer variety in each classification, he or she cannot rely solely on the classification summary for purchasing. For example, if, as in Table 7-2, he or she proceeds to buy 1540 sweaters, the buyer must make certain that all types are included. Thus it is necessary to plan even further. In continuing our example, we will use the "skirts" figures from Table 7-2 to further develop the model stock.

Breaking down the figures according to style, the buyer has further developed the model stock plan. At this point, he or she is equipped to purchase skirts in the necessary quantities by subclassification. The buyer is no longer

**TABLE 7-3** Junior sportswear department, style (subclassification) summary of skirts

| | *SALES* | | *STOCK (DOLLARS)* | | *STOCK (QUANTITIES)* | |
|---|---|---|---|---|---|---|
| ***Style*** | ***1991*** | ***Planned*** | ***1991*** | ***Planned*** | ***1991*** | ***Planned*** |
| Mini's—textures | $1800 | $3000 | $4800 | $8000 | 147 | 230 |
| Mini's—flannels | 1800 | 2400 | 4800 | 5400 | 140 | 170 |
| At the knee—textures | 1200 | 1400 | 2800 | 3000 | 40 | 50 |
| At the knee—flannels | 1400 | 1400 | 3200 | 3200 | 42 | 50 |
| Below the knee—assorted | 1600 | 800 | 5000 | 2400 | 133 | 25 |
| | $7800 | $9000 | $20,600 | $22,000 | 502 | 525 |

operating in the dark with meaningless amounts. In this particular case, analysis shows confidence in the desirability of mini skirts. The fact that he or she has substantially increased planned purchases in that style shows that the buyer believes demand will be greater. Eliminating longer skirts could be disastrous in terms of sales, since some customers change their habits more slowly and might still want the longer model. It is quite obvious that the most significant increase is expected in the mini category, in which the buyer has significantly increased planned purchases.

## *Price Lines*

The next step in planning involves further segmentation according to price. How simple it would be if the department carried merchandise at only one price! We all know, however, that there are always several prices from which to choose.

The buyer, continuing to refine the plan, prepares a price breakdown (See Table 7-4). An inflationary economy and a rise in raw materials' prices have caused the buyer to add an additional price line to the department. Whereas the past plan featured only two prices, the new plan calls for three. It should be borne in mind that the totals in Table 7-4 must agree with the numbers represented across the board listed after "mini—textures."

**TABLE 7-4** Junior sportswear department, price breakdown—mini textured skirts

| | *SALES* | | *STOCK (DOLLARS)* | | *STOCK (QUANTITIES)* | |
|---|---|---|---|---|---|---|
| ***Price*** | ***1991*** | ***Planned*** | ***1991*** | ***Planned*** | ***1991*** | ***Planned*** |
| $50 | $600 | $780 | $1800 | $2150 | 36 | 43 |
| 60 | 1200 | 1800 | 3000 | 4800 | 50 | 80 |
| 70 | — | 420 | — | 1050 | — | 15 |
| | $1800 | $3000 | $4800 | $8000 | 86 | 138 |

TABLE 7-5 Junior sportswear department, size analysis—$60 mini textured skirts

| | *SALES* | | *STOCK (DOLLARS)* | | *STOCK (QUANTITIES)* | |
|---|---|---|---|---|---|---|
| *Sizes* | *1991* | *Planned* | *1991* | *Planned* | *1991* | *Planned* |
| 5 | | | $ 360 | $ 540 | 6 | 9 |
| 7 | | | 480 | 720 | 8 | 12 |
| 9 | | | 540 | 960 | 9 | 16 |
| 11 | | | 720 | 1200 | 12 | 20 |
| 13 | | | 540 | 840 | 9 | 14 |
| 15 | | | 360 | 540 | 6 | 9 |
| | $1200 | $1800 | $3000 | $4800 | 50 | 80 |

## Sizes

Having completed the price analysis, the buyer must tackle the problems of converting these numbers into specific sizes to be purchased. It is not only a matter of buying 80 pieces at $60, but a problem of which size the 80 pieces should be ordered in.

Size allocation is based almost consistently on past records. Since customers usually remain constant from one period to another, it is safe to assume that the sizes needed will generally be the same as in the past. A departure from the buyer's typical size breakdown is necessary when the particular style lends itself better to a particular size. For example, large sizes might be eliminated if the style is one that overly accentuates the individual's figure. In the example used in Table 7-5, the planned size breakdown is similar in proportion to that for the previous year, since the style was basically the same. Only the amounts were increased to conform to the planned quantity increase.

## Color

Finally, the buyer must translate all the figures into the colors that appear to be important for the coming season. Since fashion colors usually change from one year to the next, the buyer cannot simply buy the colors that have sold well in the past and eliminate the slow sellers. Instead, the buyer must make an overall decision based on customers' acceptance of fashion colors in general. For example, if past records indicate customers to be fashion oriented, the buyer will safely purchase the new fashion colors of the coming season. Color sense and final decision making come as a result of consultation with resident buyers, examination and study of fashion periodicals and reporting service materials, meetings with the store's merchandise manager and fashion coordinator, and the buyer's own knowledge. Color plays an important role not only in the department's merchandise, but also in the development of the entire store's color "look" for the season. If color is properly selected and is compatible in all fashion departments, the customer can properly accessorize clothing purchases. If attention is paid to proper color coordination, sales will certainly build in all the

**TABLE 7-6** Junior sportswear department, color breakdown—$60 mini textured skirts

| | SIZES | | | | | |
|---|---|---|---|---|---|---|
| *Colors* | *3* | *5* | *7* | *9* | *11* | *13* |
| Black | 3 | 4 | 5 | 6 | 4 | 3 |
| Brown | 3 | 4 | 5 | 6 | 4 | 3 |
| Cranberry | 2 | 3 | 4 | 6 | 4 | 2 |
| Green | 1 | 1 | 2 | 2 | 2 | 1 |
| | 9 | 12 | 16 | 20 | 14 | 9 |

fashion departments. Table 7-6 shows an example of how the buyer might plan colors for the junior sportswear department's $60 mini textured skirts. Remember, since last year's colors will probably be unavailable or inadvisable for this year, the illustration will not include the old colors.

Notice that the total adds to 80 pieces, as planned in Table 7-5. In this case the buyer's emphasis is on gray and brown. These colors are to be purchased in all sizes, with heavy concentration in the typically stronger-selling sizes. Since the limit is only nine pieces in size 3 and nine in size 13 the buyer emphasizes the gray and brown and deemphasizes the cranberry and green, colors that are not expected to perform as well. It should be borne in mind that this is only an educated guess. Since all this planning is only for the initial model stocks, adjustments can be made once the selling season opens and customers begin to purchase. At that point reorders will change the stock to that which the customer actually wants.

## *Distribution Summary*

To work more easily with the figures that have been developed in all the categories already discussed, they are summarized into a more compact presentation. Table 7-7 shows a portion of the distribution summary that incorporates the figures prepared for the use in the development of the model stock for the junior sportswear department.

**TABLE 7-7** Junior sportswear department, distribution summary, skirts (excerpted)

| | | | | SIZES | | | | | |
|---|---|---|---|---|---|---|---|---|---|
| *Style* | *Price* | *Quantity* | *Colors* | *3* | *5* | *7* | *9* | *11* | *13* |
| Mini—textured | $60 | 80 | Black | 3 | 4 | 5 | 6 | 4 | 3 |
| | | | Brown | 3 | 4 | 5 | 6 | 4 | 3 |
| | | | Cranberry | 2 | 3 | 4 | 6 | 4 | 2 |
| | | | Green | 1 | 1 | 2 | 2 | 2 | 1 |

At this point the buyer is equipped with quantitative information for the various items carefully selected through investigation of the many sources of information available.

The plan developed thus far by no means demands purchasing from a particular source. In fact, purchases in a very narrow category may come from several sources. Look back at Table 7-7. The buyer may choose to purchase $60 black mini textured skirts from two sources rather than one, although with such a limited quantity he or she is more likely to restrict purchase to the single best resource.

The decision in regard to the source from which the purchases should be made will be based on his or her own expertise and a host of factors that will be discussed in the next chapter. It is the buyer who skillfully dovetails the elements "what to buy," "how much to buy," and "from whom to buy" who does the best job.

It is important to note that all the information necessary for planning this quantitative information is made easier with the computer. It should, however, be borne in mind that even the small independent retail operations plan these projections. Although the computer makes life simpler for the large store buyer, the small store counterpart makes the same plans from information that has been hand gathered and analyzed.

## THE BUYING PLAN

Having developed the dollar merchandise plan, which includes planned sales for each month, and a model stock plan, which breaks down the department's needs according to such factors as classification, style, price line, size, and color, it is necessary for the buyer to formulate a buying plan, which involves adjusting purchases according to merchandise on hand and commitments made.

This plan is organized by many different methods. In any case it should be carefully charted, with provision for marking off purchases as they are made. By doing this the buyer can easily see what has been purchased and what merchandise must still be bought.

In carrying out purchasing it is important that the buyer stay reasonably within the limits of the buying plan. This does not mean, however, that he or she should be inflexible. If something new is available and hadn't been planned for the department, the buyer should adjust the plan and revise the model stock. But caution must be exercised when making changes. The buyer should not be easily pressured by vendors, but should consider the merits carefully. The buyer who has planned judiciously will not have to make considerable changes.

Experienced buyers recognize the need for early shopping of the market and early placement of orders to guarantee prompt arrival of merchandise.

In carrying our their plans, buyers must carefully consider the nature of their goods and the fluctuations of their own stock levels. Since budgets must be strictly adhered to, buyers must be fully aware of inventory fluctuation, which includes analysis of stock position and open-to-buy calculations.

## Inventory fluctuation

If we look back to Table 7-1, we see that a department does not have a constant stock level. The reason is simply that sales fluctuate according to customer demand. For example, toys realize their greatest volume around the Christmas period, greeting cards at holiday times, and candy on Valentine's Day. To provide for the greatest efficiency, buyers try to plan their inventories at levels that will be in accord with expected sales.

Another aspect of stock fluctuation takes place within each business month. Buyers have greater needs at particular times in the period and less need at other times. There is also the increasing of certain types of merchandise and the decreasing of others. Sleds, for example, will be found in greater quantities before Christmas than after December 26.

Buyers must, then, continually increase and decrease their inventories as needed. To make certain that their inventories are at levels in line with budgeted dollar allocations, buyers must at various times determine their "open-to-buy."

### *Open-to-Buy*

Knowing how much money the buyer has to spend at a given point in time is extremely important. If a buyer locates a new item and wishes to purchase it during a season, there must be money in the budget. Thus buyers with experience try never to reach the absolute top of their budget so that they may buy goods needed to "freshen" and "spark" the inventories.

Buyers are always concerned with the open-to-buy and figure it frequently. Some stores have the open-to-buy figured weekly by the computer. Others have forms available that buyers complete monthly, having been provided with the proper figures. A typical form is pictured in Figure 7-1.

Whether or not computer printouts and standardized forms are available, buyers can easily prepare the open-to-buy. The formula used is as follows:

Merchandise needed for period—merchandise available = OTB

ILLUSTRATION The inventory at retail for shoes budget in Roban's Department Store figured at $30,000 on August 1, with an inventory planned at $40,000 on August 31. Planned sales were $14,000, with markdowns of $1,000 for the month. The buyer had already made commitments for August of $12,000 at retail. What was the open-to-buy?

ANALYSIS OF STOCK POSITION AND OPEN TO BUY
from
SALES & STOCK REPORT
of

______________________________
(Month) (Date) (Year)

| BUYER ______________________ | DEPT.#____ | DEPT.#____ | DEPT.#____ |
|---|---|---|---|
| On Hand (Sales & Stock Report) | | | |
| On Order This Month (Sales & Stock Report) | | | |
| Add'l Purchases Since Cutoff | | | |
| Total Liability | | | |
| Less: | | | |
| Balance This Month Sales | | | |
| Balance This Month Markdowns | | | |
| D.M.'s Not Journalized | | | |
| Cancellations from File | | | |
| Mark-Up Cancellations | | | |
| Others: | | | |
| Total Stock Reductions | | | |
| Estimated O.H. 1st of Next Month (Total Liability minus Total Stock Reductions) | | | |
| Stock Plan 1st of Next Month | | | |
| Difference (Plus or Minus against Plan) | | | |
| Monies Needed for Major Promotions (Plus or Minus) | | | |

COMMENTS (ACTION):

(use other side, if necessary)

**Figure 7-1.** Analysis of stock position and open-to-buy form

**SOLUTION**

| | | |
|---|---|---|
| Merchandise needed (August 1–31) | $40,000 | |
| End-of-month planned inventory | 14,000 | |
| Planned sales | 1,000 | |
| Planned markdowns | | |
| Total merchandise needed | | $55,000 |
| Merchandise available (August 1) | | |
| Opening Inventory | $30,000 | |
| Commitments | 12,000 | |
| Total merchandise available | | 42,000 |
| Open-to-buy (August 1) | | $13,000 |

Through an adjustment in the procedure, a buyer can figure the open-to-buy for any day of the month. This might be needed to determine if there are sufficient funds available to add an item immediately.

**ILLUSTRATION** Toby Rubin, sweater buyer for Avidon's Specialty Shop, is contemplating a sizable purchase of off-price merchandise for immediate delivery to be used in a January sale. To make certain she has the available funds, she must determine her open-to-buy for this date, December 19. The following figures were made available to her:

| | |
|---|---|
| Present inventory at retail (December 19) | $ 8,000 |
| Inventory commitments (December 19) | 1,200 |
| Planned end-of-month inventory (December 31) | 18,000 |
| Planned sales | 6,500 |
| Actual sales | 5,200 |
| Planned markdown | 175 |
| Actual markdowns | 150 |

Using these figures, the buyer can determine the open-to-buy.

**SOLUTION**

| | | | |
|---|---|---|---|
| Merchandise needed (December 19-31) | | | |
| End-of-month inventory (planned) | | $18,000 | |
| Planned sales | $6500 | | |
| Less: actual sales | 5200 | | |
| Balance of planned sales | | 1,300 | |
| Planned markdowns | $175 | | |
| Less: actual markdowns | 150 | | |
| Balance of planned markdowns | | 25 | |
| Total merchandise needed | | | $19,325 |

| | | |
|---|---|---|
| Merchandise available (December 19) | | |
| Present Inventory | $8,000 | |
| Commitments | 1,200 | |
| Total merchandise available | | 9,200 |
| Open-to-buy (December 19) | | $10,125 |

If computer-generated information reports are available, buyers can expect a report such as the one indicated in Figure 7-2. Notice that both last year's sales and this year's budgeted (planned) sales are included.

## REPLENISHMENT CONSIDERATIONS

Much of the stock that is in a department's inventory may be found with considerable regularity. That is, toothpaste, birthday greeting cards, canned goods, and combination locks are always available, since the needs they satisfy are always in evidence.

One of the by-products of a computerized inventory system is the automatic reordering of these and other staple merchandise. The program works this way. First it analyzes the sales patterns of every item involved in the system and determines its ideal inventory level for the particular time of the year. The ideal inventory level is then compared with the actual inventory, which is kept up to date in the computer's memory. The amount of goods already on order is considered, and when the inventory level is below the ideal level, the computer generates a printed order that is ready to be checked by the buyer and mailed to the source. Vendor lead time is taken into account. In a chain store operation, the reorder is not produced until every store in the chain has been studied for an excess inventory position. When this occurs, a store-to-store transfer is printed instead of a reorder from the vendor.

Obviously, automatic reordering saves considerable buyer time by removing tedious clerical tasks from the daily workload. It does not, however, reduce the buyer's responsibilities. The computer is only a machine, and the buyer must study the automatic reorders before they are sent out. If a buyer feels changes should be made, he or she should have the authority to make them.

It must be understood that the automatic reordering capability of a computerized system is only one of the by-products of an inventory control system. Shillito's, a department store chain located in and around Cincinnati, uses automatic reordering for some 150,000 staple merchandise items. Bearing in mind that separate inventory records must be kept for style, size, color, and the like, this is by no means its total stock.

Hills supermarkets operates a large chain in the northeastern part of the country. It claims to have increased its sales of health and beauty aids by 30 per-

SYSTEMS FOR RETAILING

DOLLAR OPEN TO BUY REPORT

PROG NAME: D1038-03 PAGE 0005

AS OF: 6/30/82
STORE: 2 SOUTH

| | BOM | ----------SALES---------- | | | | ------MKDNS------ | | | ---EOM INV @ RTL--- | | ON | OPEN |
|---|---|---|---|---|---|---|---|---|---|---|---|---|
| | INV @ RTL | LYR ACT | PLANNED | ACTUAL | $VAR | PLANNED | ACTUAL | RECPTS | PLANNED | ACTUAL | ORDER | TO BUY |
| DEPT: 26 INFANTS & CHILDRENS | | | CLASS: 033 | | | | | | | | | |
| FEB 82 | 17,896 | 5,566 | 5,567 | 4,458 | 19.9- | 76 | 251 | 3,700 | 29,672 | 16,887 | | |
| MAR 82 | 16,887 | 7,939 | 7,951 | 4,877 | 38.7- | 83 | 348 | 10,022 | 26,475 | 21,684 | | |
| APR 82 | 21,684 | 8,978 | 7,726 | 8,426 | 9.1- | 143 | 1,557 | 11,800 | 27,626 | 23,501 | | |
| MAY 82 | 23,501 | 8,917 | 7,792 | 6,294 | 19.2- | 107 | 464 | 6,258 | 25,982 | 23,001 | | |
| JUN 82 | 23,001 | 7,225 | 6,199 | 5,701 | 8.0- | 97 | 829 | 2,315 | 26,505 | 18,786 | | |
| JUL 82 | 18,786 | 6,387 | 6,379 | | | 108 | | | 27,522 | | 2,349 | 12,874 |
| AUG 82 | | 7,693 | 6,650 | | | 113 | | | 30,040 | | 5,362 | 3,919 |
| SEP 82 | | 8,469 | 7,014 | | | 119 | | | 28,956 | | 1,188 | 4,861 |
| OCT 82 | | 8,050 | 6,791 | | | 115 | | | 28,436 | | 786 | 5,600 |
| NOV 82 | | 8,236 | 7,263 | | | 123 | | | 30,706 | | | 9,656 |
| DEC 82 | | 9,993 | 9,133 | | | 155 | | | 27,573 | | | 6,155 |
| JAN 83 | | 6,630 | 6,657 | | | 113 | | | 27,883 | | | 7,080 |
| * DEPT TOTAL | | | | | | | | | | | | |
| FEB 82 | 40,136 | 8,204 | 8,204 | 7,027 | 14.3- | 204 | 234 | 8,684 | 42,338 | 41,559 | | |
| MAR 82 | 41,559 | 10,299 | 11,397 | 10,474 | 8.1- | 303 | 158 | 19,062 | 46,368 | 49,989 | | |
| APR 82 | 49,989 | 15,626 | 14,448 | 11,897 | 17.7- | 345 | 451 | 21,706 | 45,972 | 59,347 | | |
| MAY 82 | 59,347 | 15,644 | 15,136 | 10,474 | 30.8- | 304 | | 7,002 | 44,187 | 55,875 | | |
| JUN 82 | 55,875 | 16,204 | 15,876 | 10,619 | 33.1- | 308 | 193 | 4,960 | 42,776 | 50,023 | | |
| JUL 82 | 50,023 | 14,633 | 16,648 | | | 416 | | | 39,828 | | 2,700 | 4,169 |
| AUG 82 | | 14,493 | 14,499 | | | 362 | | | 40,289 | | 5,695 | 9,627 |
| SEP 82 | | 14,844 | 14,306 | | | 358 | | | 39,770 | | 3,230 | 10,915 |
| OCT 82 | | 13,729 | 13,089 | | | 327 | | | 39,947 | | 1,010 | 12,583 |
| NOV 82 | | 14,309 | 13,642 | | | 341 | | | 37,349 | | | 11,385 |
| DEC 82 | | 13,220 | 13,082 | | | 327 | | | 35,888 | | | 11,948 |
| JAN 83 | | 9,720 | 10,705 | | | 268 | | | 36,622 | | | 11,707 |
| ** STORE TOTAL | | | | | | | | | | | | |
| FEB 82 | 273,197 | 112,308 | 112,307 | 110,778 | 1.4- | 2,807 | 3,481 | 78,684 | 377,798 | 337,802 | | |
| MAR 82 | 337,802 | 115,578 | 116,662 | 115,153 | 1.3- | 2,916 | 2,749 | 77,635 | 363,230 | 297,535 | | |
| APR 82 | 297,535 | 121,549 | 119,555 | 115,865 | 3.1- | 3,039 | 2,986 | 95,780 | 350,250 | 274,411 | | |
| MAY 82 | 274,411 | 122,969 | 121,547 | 114,684 | 5.6- | 3,788 | 3,389 | 114,183 | 315,687 | 270,521 | | |
| JUN 82 | 270,521 | 121,879 | 120,753 | 114,622 | 5.3- | 3,019 | 3,200 | 125,231 | 321,433 | 277,930 | | |
| JUL 82 | 277,930 | 119,852 | 121,875 | | | 3,047 | | | 347,068 | | 148,373 | 45,687 |
| AUG 82 | | 121,050 | 120,164 | | | 3,004 | | | 331,243 | | 93,298 | 14,045 |
| SEP 82 | | 122,085 | 120,307 | | | 3,007 | | | 325,021 | | 60,308 | 56,784 |
| OCT 82 | | 119,725 | 118,169 | | | 2,954 | | | 321,083 | | 43,231 | 73,954 |
| NOV 82 | | 160,338 | 168,237 | | | 4,205 | | | 368,734 | | 33,231 | 186,862 |
| DEC 82 | | 188,431 | 192,250 | | | 4,806 | | | 320,025 | | 10,031 | 138,296 |
| JAN 83 | | 119,413 | 119,808 | | | 2,995 | | | 310,087 | | | 112,865 |

FIGURE 7-2. Computer-generated open-to-buy

cent by using its computer to tailor the inventory to the needs of each individual store. Hills' system involves the filling out of a weekly questionnaire by an employee; this requires about 2½ hours per week. Not only does the program produce the necessary orders, but it mandates the number of items on display and their shelf placement as well.

When you compare this system to the one it replaced, it is easy to understand the increase in volume. Under the manual system, shelf placement was arbitrary and random. Reordering was done manually by a clerk who studied the 900 items involved and looked for the ones that were in short supply. It is this clerk, by the way, who is the weak link in the computer system as well. If the clerk is careless or rushed in filling out the questionnaire, the results will be less than adequate. Hills' managers are so pleased with the results of the program in the health and beauty aids department that they are extending it to other areas of the store. They feel there is no reason why it could not be used for groceries and perishables as well.

Figure 7-3 shows the sort of report a buyer can get indicating the necessity for reordering. In this case the computer does not print the actual order, but it compares the stock on hand with the desired quantity and suggests the number of units to be reordered. Additional valuable information is also shown—for example, the "MIST CURLING IRON—COMPACT" last line figures indicate that store #6 has two weeks' supply on hand and should order 18 more pieces.

Another system used is to check the inventory book, where minimum levels are often indicated, and to reorder when that low point has been achieved. Small retailers sometimes rely on frequent physical inventories to determine their reorders. Whatever the system, there is no real danger of too much merchandise because its sale is relatively guaranteed.

By contrast, fashion items require extreme caution when being reordered. The last reorder might not sell and could cause substantial markdowns and eventual loss to the department. On the other hand, early stoppage of the reorder of hot items could curtail profits, since more of the merchandise could have sold. Knowing when to stop requires very careful examination of daily or weekly sales to discover any downshifts in sales. If there is a slight but steady downturn, the buyer should curtail further purchase of the item in question. Figure 7-4 features a computerized report that is typically generated for fashion merchandise replenishment. Even with the greatest of caution, the best buyer is sometimes left with "yesterday's winners" that become "today's monsters." Some buyers try to set limits at which to reorder fashion items. Having reached that point, they "get out of the goods" and look for another hot number.

Some merchandise falls somewhere between staples and fashion items. They need attention to make certain that new orders are warranted. Figure 7-5 features a report used by buyers for reordering such items.

Finally, perishables require the most sensitive and careful planning. Milk, bread, and fresh-cut flowers are not very salable if they have "withered." In dealing with perishables, however, retailers have found that in due time they can predict the needed quantities. Buyers of perishables are usually delighted once the stock is depleted, even if requests continue.

SYSTEMS FOR RETAILING — PROG NAME: 201VR017 PAGE 0001

I N V E N T O R Y   B E L O W   M I N I M U M

DEPT: 033 APPLIANCES — VENDOR: 300000 GENERAL ELECTRIC CO ------X

SELECTION BY DEPT: 33 CLASS: 113 VENDOR: ALL

| CLASS | STYLE | DESCRIPTION | SKU# |
|---|---|---|---|
| 113 | CS-6 | MIST CURLING IRON - COMPACT | 0330012-6 |

| UNIT COST | UNIT RETAIL | LAST RECEIPT | LEAD TIME | MIN BUY | MIN STOCK | MAX STOCK | ON HAND | ON ORDER | DUE DATE | AVG WKY SALES | WEEKS SUPPLY | STORE NO. | SUGG REORDER | |
|---|---|---|---|---|---|---|---|---|---|---|---|---|---|---|
| 7.49 | 12.99 | 09/28 | 21 | 6 | 12 | 24 | 8 | 12 | 11/15 | 2.3 | 3 | 01 | 6 | ---- |
| 7.49 | 12.99 | 10/05 | 15 | 6 | 18 | 30 | 6 | 6 | 11/15 | 2.8 | 2 | 02 | 6 | ---- |
| 7.49 | 12.99 | 10/01 | 17 | 6 | 12 | 24 | 6 | | | 1.5 | 4 | 03 | 18 | ---- |
| 7.49 | 12.99 | 09/17 | 18 | 6 | 24 | 30 | 7 | 12 | 11/15 | 4.3 | 2 | 04 | 12 | ---- |
| 7.49 | 12.99 | 09/26 | 16 | 6 | 12 | 24 | 5 | 12 | 11/15 | 3.8 | 1 | 05 | 12 | ---- |
| 7.49 | 12.99 | 10/08 | 15 | 6 | 18 | 30 | 7 | 6 | 11/15 | 3.2 | 2 | 06 | 18 | ---- |

STYLE TOTAL..... COST: 494.34 66 *

| CLASS | STYLE | DESCRIPTION | SKU# |
|---|---|---|---|
| | PRO-12 | 1200 W. FOLD-A-WAY DRYER | 0330018-7 |

| UNIT COST | UNIT RETAIL | LAST RECEIPT | LEAD TIME | MIN BUY | MIN STOCK | MAX STOCK | ON HAND | ON ORDER | DUE DATE | AVG WKY SALES | WEEKS SUPPLY | STORE NO. | SUGG REORDER | |
|---|---|---|---|---|---|---|---|---|---|---|---|---|---|---|
| 13.99 | 21.99 | 10/05 | 15 | 3 | 21 | 30 | 6 | 6 | 11/05 | 3.4 | 2 | 01 | 18 | ---- |
| 13.99 | 21.99 | 10/06 | 18 | 3 | 18 | 30 | 5 | 6 | 11/05 | 4.5 | 1 | 02 | 6 | ---- |
| 13.99 | 21.99 | 10/05 | 21 | 3 | 15 | 24 | 6 | 9 | 11/06 | 5.0 | 1 | 03 | | ---- |
| 13.99 | 21.99 | 10/04 | 24 | 3 | 21 | 30 | 9 | 3 | 11/06 | 4.3 | 2 | 04 | 18 | ---- |
| 13.99 | 21.99 | 10/04 | 20 | 3 | 24 | 30 | 32 | | | 4.0 | 3 | 05 | 0 | ---- *** OVER MAX *** |
| 13.99 | 21.99 | 10/03 | 18 | 3 | 18 | 27 | 6 | 6 | 11/18 | 3.8 | 2 | 06 | 15 | ---- |

STYLE TOTAL..... COST: 797.43 57 *

DEPT TOTAL...... COST: 1,291.77 123 **

VENDOR TOTAL.... COST: 5,468.23 477 ***

FINAL TOTAL..... COST: 10,544.73 672 ****

**FIGURE 7-3.** Vendor replenishment report *Courtesy* of CREATIVE DATA SYSTEMS, INC.

SYSTEMS FOR RETAILING PROG NAME: US025-03 PAGE 0001

UNIT SALES CLASS SUMMARY

DEPT 20 LADIES SPORTSWEAR WEEK ENDING 2/20/83 03 3

SELECTIONS: SEASON ALL STORE ALL DEPTNO 20 CLASS ALL GRPS 1=ALL 2=ALL 3=ALL 4=ALL 5=ALL VENDOR ALL

CLASS: 130 JEANS - DENIM AVG RETAIL SALES: 12.83 ON HAND: 14.82 REC: 13.61 ON ORDER: 13.59 SE: SP SPRING

| | TOTAL | 01 | 02 | 03 | 04 | 05 | 06 | 07 | 09 | 10 |
|---|---|---|---|---|---|---|---|---|---|---|
| THIS WEEK | 13 | | 1 | 3 | 2 | 4 | 1 | 2 | | |
| LAST WEEK | 14 | | 2 | 4 | 3 | 1 | 3 | 1 | | |
| 2 WEEKS AGO | 24 | | 6 | 3 | 4 | 6 | 2 | 3 | | |
| 3 WEEKS AGO | 18 | | 2 | 4 | 4 | 1 | 4 | 3 | | |
| 4 WEEKS TOTAL | 11 | | 1 | 2 | 3 | 1 | 2 | 2 | | |
| SEASON TO DATE | 80 | | 12 | 16 | 16 | 13 | 12 | 11 | | |
| TOT RECEIPTS | 305 | 23 | 91 | 33 | 38 | 38 | 38 | 44 | | |
| ON HAND | 225 | 23 | 79 | 17 | 22 | 25 | 26 | 33 | | |
| ON ORDER | 1,075 | 159 | 2 | 152 | 153 | 153 | 303 | 153 | | |
| $ SALES | | | 15.00 | 20.00 | 20.00 | 16.25 | 15.00 | 13.75 | | |
| $ SALES | 1,026 | | 154 | 205 | 205 | 167 | 154 | 141 | | |
| $ INVENTORY | | 10.22 | 35.11 | 7.56 | 9.78 | 11.11 | 11.56 | 14.66 | | |
| $ INVENTORY | 3,334 | 341 | 1,171 | 252 | 326 | 370 | 385 | 489 | | |

CLASS: 131 ACTIVEWEAR AVG RETAIL SALES: 8.81 ON HAND: 6.72 REC: 6.73 SE: SP SPRING

| | | 01 | 02 | 03 | 04 | 05 | 06 | 07 | 08 | 09 | 10 |
|---|---|---|---|---|---|---|---|---|---|---|---|
| THIS WEEK | 31 | | 5 | 4 | 8 | 7 | 3 | 4 | | | |
| LAST WEEK | 9 | | 1 | 1 | 2 | 2 | 2 | 1 | | | |
| 2 WEEKS AGO | 13 | | 2 | 3 | 1 | 3 | 3 | 1 | | | |
| 3 WEEKS AGO | 11 | | 1 | 2 | 3 | 1 | 2 | 2 | | | |
| 4 WEEKS TOTAL | 8 | | 2 | 1 | 1 | 2 | 1 | 1 | | | |
| SEASON TO DATE | 72 | | 11 | 11 | 15 | 15 | 11 | 9 | | | |
| TOT RECEIPTS | 120 | 12 | 12 | 28 | 17 | 17 | 17 | 17 | | | |
| ON HAND | 48 | 12 | 1 | 17 | 2 | 2 | 6 | 8 | | | |
| ON ORDER | | | | | | | | | | | |
| $ SALES | | | 15.27 | 15.27 | 20.83 | 20.83 | 15.27 | 12.50 | | | |
| $ SALES | 634 | | 97 | 97 | 132 | 132 | 97 | 79 | | | |
| $ INVENTORY | | 25.00 | 2.08 | 35.42 | 4.16 | 4.16 | 12.50 | 16.66 | | | |
| $ INVENTORY | 323 | 80 | 7 | 114 | 13 | 13 | 41 | 55 | | | |

CLASS: 634 NOVELTY TOPS AVG RETAIL SALES: 9.29 ON HAND: 7.10 REC: 5.86 ON ORDER: 6.11 SE: SP SPRING

| | | 01 | 02 | 03 | 04 | 05 | 06 | 07 | 08 | 09 | 10 |
|---|---|---|---|---|---|---|---|---|---|---|---|
| THIS WEEK | | | 1 | 2 | 2 | 3 | 3 | 1 | | | |
| LAST WEEK | | | 1 | 1 | 2 | 1 | 2 | 3 | | | |
| 2 WEEKS AGO | | | 1 | 2 | 1 | 1 | 1 | 2 | | | |
| 3 WEEKS AGO | 12 | | 2 | 2 | 2 | 2 | 2 | 2 | | | |
| 4 WEEKS TOTAL | 12 | | 2 | 2 | 2 | 2 | 2 | 2 | | | |
| SEASON TO DATE | 54 | | 7 | 9 | 9 | 9 | 10 | 10 | | | |
| TOT RECEIPTS | 971 | 259 | 129 | 133 | 133 | 133 | 114 | 70 | | | |
| ON HAND | 917 | 259 | 122 | 124 | 124 | 124 | 104 | 60 | | | |
| ON ORDER | 19 | | | | | | 19 | | | | |
| $ SALES | | | 12.96 | 16.66 | 16.66 | 16.66 | 18.52 | 18.52 | | | |
| $ SALES | 503 | | 65 | 84 | 84 | 84 | 93 | 93 | | | |
| $ INVENTORY | | 28.24 | 13.30 | 13.52 | 13.52 | 13.52 | 11.34 | 6.54 | | | |
| $ INVENTORY | 6,510 | 1,840 | 866 | 880 | 880 | 880 | 738 | 426 | | | |

**FIGURE 7-4.** Unit sales class summary *Courtesy* of CREATIVE DATA SYSTEMS, INC.

SYSTEMS FOR RETAILING PROG NAME: 201DS037 PAGE 0002

SALES REPORT - BY MAJOR DEPT

SALES DATE: THURSDAY 10/07 COMPARISON DATE: 10/08

MDEPT 130 HOUSEWARES

| | CURRENT DATE | | VAR | WEEK TO DATE | | VAR | MONTH TO DATE | | VAR | YEAR TO DATE | | VAR |
|---|---|---|---|---|---|---|---|---|---|---|---|---|
| | THIS YEAR | LAST YEAR | % | THIS YEAR | LAST YEAR | % | THIS YEAR | LAST YEAR | % | THIS YEAR | LAST YEAR | % |
| DEPT: 11 CALCULATORS, WATCHES | | | | | | | | | | | | |
| STORE # 2 | 57.99 | 44.49 | 30.3 | 57.99 | 44.49 | 30.3 | 57.99 | 161.10 | 64.0- | 119,828.39 | 124,148.61 | 3.5- |
| 3 | 63.47 | 47.16 | 34.6 | 63.47 | 47.16 | 34.6 | 63.47 | 224.26 | 74.0- | 110,129.60 | 97,105.93 | 13.4 |
| 4 | 42.17 | 39.69 | 6.2 | 42.17 | 39.69 | 6.2 | 42.17 | 251.50 | 83.2- | 88,796.66 | 87,048.19 | 2.0 |
| 5 | 110.11 | 98.53 | 11.8 | 110.11 | 98.53 | 11.8 | 110.11 | 196.55 | 44.0- | 76,890.95 | 75,342.66 | 2.1 |
| 6 | 25.73 | 12.77 | 101.5 | 25.73 | 12.77 | 101.5 | 25.73 | 413.98 | 93.8- | 111,138.42 | 100,235.97 | 10.9 |
| 7 | 36.00 | 31.25 | 15.2 | 36.00 | 31.25 | 15.2 | 36.00 | 273.20 | 86.8- | 110,196.88 | 97,396.21 | 13.1 |
| *DEPT TOTAL | 335.47 | 274.39 | 22.2 | 335.47 | 274.39 | 22.2 | 335.47 | 1,540.59 | 78.2- | 616,980.90 | 581,127.57 | 6.2 |
| **MDEPT TOT | 335.47 | 274.39 | 22.2 | 335.47 | 274.39 | 22.2 | 335.47 | 1,540.59 | 78.2- | 616,980.90 | 581,127.57 | 6.2 |

**FIGURE 7-5.** Sales report by major department *Courtesy* of CREATIVE DATA SYSTEMS, INC.

In conclusion, it should be understood that without strict attention to quantities, retailers will not be able to turn profits even if the merchandise itself is fantastic.

## ACTION FOR THE SMALL STORE BUYER

As with determining what to buy, considerations about quantity are imperative for all buyers no matter what the size of the store. All too often, small store buyers find themselves either overbought in particular items or short of merchandise in other categories. Purchasing too little or too much can be devastating to the overall profit they bring to their stores. In short, the small store buyer must be extremely diligent in determining how much to buy.

Lacking the help of merchandise managers, as is the case in the large companies, the buyer must often decide, alone, the quantities of each item that should be purchased. As was the case with "what to buy," an examination of merchandise records of past seasons, along with information from outside forecasters such as the trade papers, will help even the buyer of minimum quantities to project the dollar and unit amounts needed for the new season. By plotting trends of seasons gone by, the small store buyer can make model stock adjustments that reflect the historical data. That is, if each of the three past seasons has shown a 2 percent increase in skirt sales, it might be appropriate to increase skirt quantities at that rate. Since small store buyers usually have space limitations, they must pay attention to buying the right merchandise assortment in terms of colors, sizes, and styles. If they overbuy in skirts, for example, they might not have sufficient space to carry a full line of sweaters and blouses to complement the skirts.

With the introduction of smaller-sized, relatively inexpensive computers, medium to small firms can now "get in on the action." Minicomputers adequate for the medium-sized retailer start at about $3000; microcomputers, at about $1500. These devices require very little user expertise. Software packages (programmed instructions to the computer) are available for a wide variety of computer applications. While the minicomputer and microcomputer are no match for their larger cousins, the tasks they must perform are correspondingly smaller. Unquestionably, the output of the smaller computers will fall short of the total requirements of the small store buyer, but large store buyers are never fully satisfied either. In any event, the use of these smaller devices will substantially lessen the information gap.

Small store buyers should also discuss quantitative decisions with their resident buying office representatives. In this way, they can get some outside expertise. The offices will not, of course, have the store's past sales figures but will judge the store buyer's projections in terms of what trends the market is experiencing. A small store buyer should also be aware of the calculations associated with open-to-buy. By paying close attention to this concept, there will be little chance of overbuying.

Too many small store buyers with discriminating taste miss the the opportunity to turn a profit because of deficiencies in quantitative decision making.

## SUMMARY OF KEY POINTS

1. Buyers prepare dollar merchandise plans, generally for six-month periods, to determine the size of their budgets, in conjunction with their merchandise managers and controllers.
2. The six-month plan is based on sales, stocks, and markdown figures for approximately three preceding years.
3. The model stock refers to the appropriate assortment the customer is ready to buy at a specific time.
4. Determination of a model stock is much more involved for fashion merchandise than for staple goods, since the former is subject to rapid changes in customer demand while the latter rarely involve change.
5. In planning a model stock for a fashion department, such factors as classification, style, price, sizes, and color must be carefully analyzed, evaluated, and projected into particular goods.
6. Once the buyer has spent considerable effort in the development of a model stock, he or she must carefully dovetail the findings with the merchandise available in the market.
7. Many times within a season or period, buyers must make certain they haven't exceeded their dollar budget so that they can purchase additional merchandise. They accomplish this by determining open-to-buy. The merchandise needed for a period less the merchandise available equals the open-to-buy.
8. Care must be exercised in the reordering of merchandise. This is particularly true of fashion merchandise; today's hot item could become tomorrow's loser.
9. The new generation of minicomputers has made electronic data processing available to small- and medium-sized retailers, improving their competitive position.

## REVIEW QUESTIONS

1. Is it possible for buyers to plan so perfectly that they will not have to mark down merchandise?
2. What is a dollar merchandise plan?
3. In the formulation of six-month merchandise plans, which information from past records is examined most carefully?

4. Should buyers examine outside indicators in projecting their dollar merchandise plans? Why?
5. Define the term *model stock*.
6. Differentiate between staple and fashion merchandise.
7. Which merchandise, staple or fashion, is more difficult to plan in terms of quantities?
8. Discuss the merchandise term *classification*.
9. Why is it necessary for buyers to break down their classifications into subcategories?
10. For what reason does a buyer purchase a price line rather than restricting the offerings to a single price?
11. On what basis does the buyer almost consistently base size allocation?
12. Describe a distribution summary.
13. Define open-to-buy.
14. At what point in the month does the buyer figure the open-to-buy?
15. The finding of a "winner" can make the buyer's season. How does the buyer know when to stop the reorder of hot fashion items?
16. For what purpose is automatic reordering used?

## CASE PROBLEM 1

Having been in business for 35 years, Helaine's, a department store with five branches, has come through some difficult periods in the American economy. Some of the leaner years have necessitated that the store's merchandisers pull in the reins, tighten their belts, and proceed cautiously with buying plans.

Historically, no period has been as dangerous as the one the store now faces. The economy has been lagging, and management is troubled by the fear that buyers are overly optimistic in planning their purchases. Of particular concern are the luxury departments that feature furs, precious jewelry, pianos, and other merchandise of considerable cost.

A meeting of all the store's buyers was called to project an atmosphere of caution. Since this is the period in which buyers must begin their purchasing estimates with six-month dollar merchandise plans, an understanding of the situation is vital. Special attention was focused on luxury merchandise. Although the preceding five-year period has shown approximate storewide sales increases of 5 percent in most departments, furs has exceeded all others with a growth rate of 10 percent for each of the five years. Management still has asked the fur buyer to proceed cautiously with the dollar plan.

### Questions

1. If you were the fur buyer, which in-store indicators would you investigate in the formulation of your buying plans?

2. Which external sources would you survey in the planning?

## CASE PROBLEM 2

Caryn's Boutique opened five years ago and has grown by leaps and bounds. The operation began as a "corner" of an established men's shop; it has mushroomed into a separate retail operation apart from the premises it originally shared. The first year of operation (as part of the men's shop) saw Caryn's Boutique gross $47,000. Today annual sales are in the vicinity of $475,000.

Much of the store's success was based on the ingenuity of its owner, Caryn. Merchandise purchased was not carefully planned quantitatively but was based on a general "feeling" for additional goods. With the opening of the present operation, all the operational expenses have grown significantly. Caryn has found sales increasing beautifully, but the unsold merchandise has mounted considerably. In her previous operation Caryn bought sparingly because of limited space. Now overbuying has become a serious problem. Not in the habit of carefully planning model stocks, Caryn has found her inventory to be short in some items and overstocked in others. Obviously, the key to success of the business is the development of a model stock prior to actual purchasing.

For the coming summer season Caryn has shopped the market and decided to restrict her purchases to swimsuits, beachcoats, dresses, pant suits, pullovers, shirts, skirts, shorts, pants, tennis apparel, accessories (scarves, belts, etc.), and novelty items of the season.

Let alone applying the actual dollars to the merchandise needed, Caryn is confronted with the problem of the development of a model stock for the coming season. Understanding that action based on whim is no longer practical and could be devastating, she is open to suggestion.

### Questions

1. Briefly describe the first consideration of Caryn's buying plan.
2. How could she determine, in order of importance, the need for each type of merchandise indicated in the case?
3. List the various steps Caryn should plan before finalizing her purchases.
4. Should she plan to spend every dollar allocated for her initial investment? Defend your answer.

## CASE PROBLEM 3

R & L Stores, one of the largest of the nation's supermarket chains, has been having difficulties in recent years. The chain, which has been a household word for 50 years, has been showing small but troublesome losses. Its traditional operation has simply been unable to meet the price competition of discount competitors. The problem seems to be that during many uninterrupted years of growth and success, the company has allowed its costs of operation to reach too high a level.

The board of directors of R & L has appointed a team whose responsibility it is to study every level of the company's operation in search of areas in which costs can be cut.

In the area of merchandising, the team has decided that many of the buying departments can be joined together under a single head buyer. This would permit considerable savings, since many buying jobs could be phased out. They suggest that through an expansion of the automatic reordering program, such departments as cookies, cake, bread, and cereals can be placed on completely automatic reordering under the control of one buyer. Naturally, this would permit considerable savings in buyers' salaries.

## Questions

1. Will automatic reordering work?
2. Explain the system and its application.

# Chapter 8

# FROM WHOM AND WHEN TO BUY

## LEARNING OBJECTIVES

*Upon completion of this chapter, the student should be able to:*

1. Discuss the importance of good vendor relationships to both a large and a small buyer.
2. Write a brief paragraph on six important vendor characteristics in selecting a source.
3. Speak on the importance of periodic vendor evaluation. Explain the role of recordkeeping in this operation.
4. List and define four classifications of resources.
5. Give the advantages and disadvantages of using the following resources: manufacturers, store-owned resources, service wholesalers, and rack jobbers.
6. Discuss the ethics involved in accepting gifts from resources, including free lunches.

## INTRODUCTION

Buyers are charged with the responsibility for purchasing from those vendors who provide the merchandise that most closely satisfies the needs of the store's customers and provides the retailer with the greatest profit.

The buyer must not only choose from among the practically limitless number of resources, but also decide whether to purchase directly from the producer or from some intermediary institution such as a wholesaler and when the purchases should be made. These choices are not always made at the buyer's discretion but are often dictated by a number of factors. For example, in some industries, such as light bulbs, purchase from the manufacturer isn't available even to the giant retailer. Everyone must go to a wholesaler. On the other hand, the very nature of fashion merchandise necessitates use of the direct method of purchase by even the smallest retailer.

In this chapter attention will center on the factors to consider in selecting resources, the classification of resources, the reasons for purchasing from them, and the timing of the purchase.

## FACTORS IN SELECTING A RESOURCE

A buyer's success depends in large part on choice of resources. The buyer must always be aware of the fact that success is based on the amount and profitability of the actual sales of the merchandise rather than on the attractiveness of the selections. In other words, there is no point in ordering the most beautiful junior dress on the market if the vendor does not meet delivery dates. Determining which vendors to be used requires careful weighing of many factors. Ideally, the major portion of the purchases should be limited to a few key resources, with some ordering reserved for trials with new resources. Naturally, the number of resources and amount of experimentation will vary widely with the size of the store and the type of merchandise.

### Vendor Relationships

Mutual respect and cooperation between buyer and seller are necessary to ensure long-term profitability for both parties. Regrettably, this does not always occur. When a vendor has a hot line, the demand for the goods is such that it is often unable to fill all the orders. The decision on which customers are to be disappointed is generally based on the relative importance of each customer in terms of profits. If someone is to be hurt by a vendor, it is more likely to be a small "mom and pop" store than Sears. The same holds true with returned merchandise. The better the customer, the more liberal the return policy. While small stores can't hope to overcome the edge massive purchasing power gives to the retail giants, they can, by limiting their resources to a few key vendors, improve their relative position. The same holds true of competing large retailers. When there are insufficient goods, the largest user will generally get preference.

Another way for a small retailer to ensure fair treatment is by building a good personal relationship with suppliers. It is not unusual for a vendor to steal a few pieces from the order of a giant customer to please a small retailer who he knows gives him a large portion of his business and with whom he has built a friendly relationship over a long period.

To a large extent a buyer's relationship to vendors is built on the dependability of the resources in such areas as similarity between the goods and the sample; no substitution of colors, sizes, or styles without permission; acceptance of legitimate returns; and similar evidences of good faith.

Both large and small retailers, by limiting the majority of their purchases to a few resources, can improve their relationship with their suppliers. However, this should not be overdone. Some purchasing power must be saved for new goods and new vendors.

## Vendor Characteristics

Many other factors must be considered in the selection of vendors. These include the merchandise offered, its exclusiveness, shipping and inventory maintenance, vendor cooperation, and profitability.

### *The Merchandise Offered*

Naturally, no supplier should be considered whose offerings are not appropriate for the store in terms of price range, style, and customer preference. However, there are degrees of suitability, and the first judgment in vendor selection must be whether or not the wares are salable. For most goods, buyers require more than suitability. Fashion goods, for example, require uniqueness and originality. This may be accomplished through styling, durability, or even packaging.

The availability of goods when needed is also crucial. The vendor's season does not coincide exactly with the retailer's. Some vendors, to reduce their markdowns, start curtailing production when customers are still selling well. This may result in empty retail shelves when the retail customers are still in a buying mood.

A good resource should be maneuverable. When the opening line lacks certain colors or styles that have proved to be hot, the vendor should be able to knock off (copy) these winners in midseason while the demand is still strong. When this is not possible, the buyer should seriously consider using one vendor at the beginning of the season and switching to a more maneuverable vendor for later purchases. The vendor who plays it too close to the vest and refuses to go into a new style until it is proved must expect to lose some mid- to late-season business.

When the merchandise to be used is branded (carries an important label or private brand), selection of vendors is automatic. Decisions for this sort of merchandise are rarely left to the buyer alone.

Goods that are to be manufactured to the specific requirements of the retailer must be ordered from a vendor who is capable of following the specifications. This type of buying, usually reserved to large stores, has the effect of improving products by protecting them from competition. It is not unusual for the retailer to provide the raw materials and even the equipment needed.

### *Distribution Policies*

With the exception of highly advertised, branded convenience goods, no buyer wants to carry the same goods as the competitor across the street. In selecting vendors, the purchaser should attempt to find a seller who agrees to limit sales of the particular styles purchased to a well-defined geographic area. Legislation, however, makes this a difficult task. Manufacturers are no longer able to use the exclusive distribution policy at their discretion. Stores with the proper credentials, such as a good credit rating, cannot be denied the right to purchase from a company.

Manufacturers approach the problem in any one of a number of ways. They might require a minimum purchase in order to be eligible for a delivery. This requirement immediately discourages the less important stores from purchasing the line. Another approach is to restrict production and ship only limited quantities on a preferential or seniority basis. In this way it is possible to discourage unwanted accounts by not being able to guarantee shipments. Finally, some vendors have expanded their lines and arranged for "special" numbers to be allocated in limited amounts to specific customers. This still enables the competition to buy the "name," but not the exact merchandise.

### *Promotional Merchandise Policies*

Except for a few high-prestige stores, retailers generally find it good policy to run an occasional special sale. To be successful, the sale must offer the shopper a legitimate bargain. While some slow-moving merchandise may be marked down by the store and included in the sale, other promotional goods are usually needed to round out the assortment. Manufacturers often have incomplete assortments of merchandise that they are willing to dispose of at a reduction. These are called job lots or closeouts. The merchandise includes broken sizes, slow-moving colors and styles, and sometimes even "seconds" with minor flaws. Such goods are in demand by certain retailers that specialize in this sort of merchandise. Their buyers must select resources that will give them a fair share of off-price merchandise.

The opposite attitude toward off-price merchandise is found among some high-prestige stores. They would never consider a vendor who would sell closeout goods in an area in which their customers might compare prices.

### *Shipping and Inventory Maintenance*

Like retailers, suppliers vary greatly in size. Some will ship only large-quantity orders. Others, with limited resources, are unable to handle large orders. It is important that the buyer select resources that are not only able but eager to handle the order.

The shipping practices of the vendor are important in many ways. Primarily, the buyer must be sure the goods will be at the store on the specified delivery date.

Speed of delivery for orders or reorders is another important factor for fashion merchandise and other products. Many retailers that lack the space or financing to carry large inventories need suppliers who are close at hand and offer spot deliveries. In many cases they are willing to pay a premium to a wholesaler for this service.

Some retailers require suppliers to drop ship merchandise directly to customers. Not many resources offer this service.

The use of vendors that offer a broad assortment of merchandise permits savings in delivery expense and paperwork.

### *Vendor Cooperation*

Other types of vendor cooperation cover a number of areas from information sources to actual cash contributions for advertising and promotion.

When a buyer studies the offerings of one of the resources, the choices depend in large part, but not exclusively, on personal taste. Another vital factor in the buying decision is knowledge of the items that have "checked out"—that is, the specific styles that have proved to be hot items or good sellers. The salesperson has this information. This places the salesperson in an interesting position. Some of the goods are in no trouble; they may even be oversold. Other items are weak and slow moving. If the salesperson doesn't sell them, the company may face eventual markdowns. In selecting resources, the buyer must take the reliability of the salesperson into account. In the long run, honesty is the only policy. There is no future in hurting buyers, and if the salesperson's clients are successful, they may help him or her move some slow goods as well. It should be mentioned, however, that complete reliance on salespeople could prove to be dangerous, since some are notorious for telling untruths.

In instances in which the salesperson must explain or demonstrate the use of the item to retail customers, as in the case with certain hardware and appliance items, the resource selected must be one that is willing to provide the necessary training. Resources often send their own trained employees to work as demonstrators. The ultimate success of the goods purchased depends on the ability of the salesperson to sell the consumer, and when specialized knowledge is required to make the sale, the producer is best qualified to provide it.

Manufacturers and designers of fashion merchandise understand that one of the ways in which to assist the retailer with the sale of their lines is through in-store fashion shows. Recognizing the enormous amount of competition from other lines and private label collections, more and more vendors are helping themselves and their retail customers by participating in these fashion presentations. One such company, Liz Claiborne, routinely plays the "fashion show circuit."

## A RETAIL BUYING FOCUS

### *Liz Claiborne*

The name Liz Claiborne is recognized by most fashion consumers throughout the United States. In the late 1970s, Liz and two partners began what has become one of the most successful operations ever to reach the fashion consumer market. At first there was only one collection, but with its unique success, the company expanded and began to produce variations on its initial collection. A line of separates, Lizwear, was added as was a line for petites, dresses, and shoes and one for men known simply as Claiborne.

Through its successful but brief history, Liz Claiborne immediately recognized that it would be beneficial to cooperate with the retailers by helping them sell the merchandise. It participated in cooperative advertising as most fashion companies did, but didn't stop there. Taking a cue from the higher-priced fashion houses, it began to participate in fashion show presentations in the stores. In the early days, Liz would make in-store appearances in conjunction with a fashion show production. The promotions were immediately successful. Shoppers would see the line presented in runway format and hear the company designer discuss the various styles.

Today, the company is totally involved in cooperating with its customers to keep its name in the forefront of fashion. Although Liz herself has retired from active involvement in the company, the fashion show approach she began is an important part of the company's public relations program. Professionally trained company representatives regularly participate in in-store fashion shows. They provide commentary and are available at the show's conclusion to meet and greet customers and answer questions about the Liz collections and fashions.

Most retailers believe that the show generates a lot of customer enthusiasm and increases sales.

---

The producers of cosmetics, liquor, and many supermarket items often provide point-of-purchase aids in the form of counter displays, signs, and other display units. Some go as far as inventory control and housekeeping. These services can be of considerable help to a buyer and must be taken into account in the selection of resources.

Many producers willingly share the advertising burden with the retailer. This can take the form of advertising mats (paper composition printing plates) and layouts, outright cash grants, or advertising allowances that are to be deducted from their invoices. This practice is so widespread that some large retailers probably make a profit by sending out seasonal catalogs. Because the amount of help varies from vendor to vendor, the advertising policy of the resource must be considered.

It is frequently desirable to deal with resources that are able to ticket goods in advance of shipment. This service is an important one in terms of time, space, and labor savings. Preticketed goods may be moved directly to the selling floor. Cutting down the space required for merchandise handling allows more space to be devoted to selling. This factor is of critical importance, since retail space is vastly more valuable than warehouse or workroom space.

### *Prices*

Naturally, the only resources to be considered are those whose prices fall within the price lines offered by the store. The problem is, how many suppliers are needed for each price line? In the category of $30 to $40 men's sweaters, for example, will the addition of a second resource really add breadth to the line? Or will it merely reduce the store's effectiveness with each supplier and add to inventory? How about a third resource?

### *Profitability*

In the final analysis, the essential feature of a key resource is profitability. However, this is not always easy to determine, since it depends on all the factors discussed previously. It is simple to determine the resource that provided the most sales of a particular line; but is the markup adequate? Does the firm preticket? How about markdowns? Returns? Customer dissatisfaction?

## *PERIODIC EVALUATION OF RESOURCES*

Periodically the buyer must weigh the contribution of each resource in every price line for which he or she is responsible. The buyer must weed out the resources that are mere duplications and develop those that are to be key suppliers. When the profitability developed by one supplier is reduced, a decision must be made as to the future use of the resource. The buyer's job and the success of the organization depend on it.

### **Evaluation Aids**

Obviously, with the number of factors involved, decisions on resources cannot be made on a hunch basis. Instead, where possible, hard data are essential. This requires a considerable amount of time and effort, and often the cooperation of various service departments.

Because the number of factors involved in resource selection is considerable, it is generally agreed among buyers that bookkeeping should be limited to certain key areas. In the following pages, examples of the types of records buyers use will be discussed.

The resource diary illustrated in Figure 8–1 is a page of a loose-leaf book carried by the buyer. It describes in considerable detail the important characteristics of each resource. The resource diary must be kept up to date, and a copy should be kept by the divisional manager of a large store. A third copy is usually sent to the accounts payable department, since the terms of payment are specified. Note that the form requires semi-annual review to ensure its being up to date. This is usually done by the merchandise manager as well as the buyer.

Since each line and certainly each department has unique requirements, the back of the page may be used for additional notes.

The resource diary is particularly important to a new buyer, who at a glance can be brought up to date on the past and present operation of the buying function. This book is also important in the periodic evaluation of resources. Along with other documents, it provides information about which suppliers should be built up, which should be eliminated, and which require investigation because of problems.

Figure 8–2 illustrates a listing of principal resources ranked by the total dollar purchasing done with each supplier. The amounts in the upper left-hand corner indicate the total purchases of the department for each of several years. The central listing by supplier indicates the amount of business done with that resource by season and for the year. The use of columns for each year provides comparatives; that is, it gives a trend of growth or shrinkage with each supplier on a seasonal and annual basis. Of further interest would be a comparison of the percent of growth of each supplier with that of the department as a whole. Any shrinkage in the relative growth of a supplier calls for further investigation to determine whether the problem can be straightened out or the resource replaced.

Figure 8–3 illustrates a form for calculating the gross margin from each style of each vendor. The numbered columns contain the following information:

1. Goods on hand at the beginning of the season—40 pieces
2. Retail price per unit—$10
3. Total retail value—$400 [(1) × (2)]
4. Total cost—$200 [(1) × (8)]
5. Pieces received—100 [(7) + (6) − (1)]
6. Pieces on hand at the end of the season—20
7. Pieces sold—120
8. Cost per unit—$5
9. Original retail—$10
10. Number sold at the original retail—120 pieces

11, 12. Markdown price and number sold at that price

13. Total sales—$1200 [(9) × (10)]

RESOURCE DIARY

Dept. No.

Date

Resource

Merchandise Top Grade____Medium____Low-end____

Activity (Mfr., Jobber, Importer, etc.)

Sales Office Address Telephone ________

Factory or Warehouse Address

Company Officers and Titles

Buyer Contacts-State peculiarities or special handling required by

a. Sales Office

b. Factory

Rating-Dun & Bradstreet

Ethics of Firm

Ranking in Industry

Vendor Importance to Store

Store Importance to Vendor

Record of All Arrangements (Terms, Trade Discounts, Cash Discounts, Cooperative Advertising, etc.)

Remarks (State clearly any additional information not covered above that will guide any member of our organization who may have to deal with this vendor.)

Semi-Annual

Date By Whom

**Note:** It is recommended that this Resource Diary be kept in loose-leaf form.

**FIGURE 8–1.** Resource diary *Note: It is recommended that this Resource Diary be kept in loose-leaf form.*

Dept. ____________

$ COST PURCHASES

| Year | Dept. | Approved | Date |
|---|---|---|---|
| 19– | 343, 017 | | 2/17/- |
| 19– | 604, 359 | | 2/24/- |
| 19– | | | |
| 19– | | | |

$ COST PURCHASES

| Year | Dept. | Approved | Date |
|---|---|---|---|
| 19– | | | |
| 19– | | | |
| 19– | | | |
| 19– | | | |

| Resource – Key Contact | General Comment | Season | 19– | 19– | 19– | 19– | 19– | 19– | 19– | 19– | |
|---|---|---|---|---|---|---|---|---|---|---|---|
| Design For Living<br>M. E. Andrews, Pres.<br><br>Hobbies – Antiques and Stamps | Top quality maker – exclusive with us – nationally adv. – most cooperative – better than average markup – low markdowns<br>Class A Terms 2/10/60X | Spring | 37, 007 | 81, 116 | | | | | | | |
| | | Fall | 24, 119 | 59, 412 | | | | | | | |
| | | Total | 61, 126 | 140, 528 | | | | | | | |
| Modern Age<br>John Jackson, Sales Mgr.<br><br>Hobby – Fishing | Excellent novelty house – alert to new ideas – also sells Store A – very reliable and profitable – repairs at minimum | Spring | 16, 981 | 44, 051 | | | | | | | |
| | | Fall | 19, 128 | 38, 946 | | | | | | | |
| | | Total | 36, 109 | 82, 997 | | | | | | | |
| | | | | | | | | | | | |
| | | | | | | | | | | | |
| | | | | | | | | | | | |
| | | | | | | | | | | | |
| | | | | | | | | | | | |
| | | | | | | | | | | | |
| | | | | | | | | | | | |
| | | | | | | | | | | | |
| | | | | | | | | | | | |

**FIGURE 8–2.** Principal resource list.

| MERCHANDISE | STYLE NO. | SEASON | BEGINNING OF SEASON | | | | NO. REC'D | O.H. END OF SEASON | NO. SOLD | COST PER UNIT | ORIGINAL MARKDOWN | | | | TOTAL SALES | TOTAL COST OF MDSE. HANDLED | UNIT RETAIL END OF SEASON | CLOSING INV. RETAIL | CLOSING INV. COST | COST OF MDSE. SOLD | G. M. | G. M. % |
|---|---|---|---|---|---|---|---|---|---|---|---|---|---|---|---|---|---|---|---|---|---|---|
| | | | O.H. | UNIT RETAIL | TOTAL RETAIL | TOTAL COST | | | | | UNIT RETAIL | NO. SALES | UNIT RETAIL | NO. SALES | | | | | | | | |
| | | | 1 | 2 | 3 | 4 | 5 | 6 | 7 | 8 | 9 | 10 | 11 | 12 | 13 | 14 | 15 | 16 | 17 | 18 | 19 | |
| | | | | | 1x2 | 3x8 | 7+6−1 | | | | | | | | 9x10+ 11x12 | 4+5x8 | | 6x15 | 6x8 | 14−17 | 13−18 | |
| SLACKS | 112 | 575 | 40 | 10 | 400 | 200 | 100 | 20 | 120 | 5 | 10 | 120 | — | — | 1200 | 700 | 10 | 200 | 100 | 600 | 600 | 50 |
| TOTAL | | | | | | | | | | | | | | | | | | | | | | |

| SEASON | FALL OR SPRING YR. | FROM<br>TO | DEPT. NAME<br>DEPT. NO. | | BEGIN | END | VENDOR'S NAME<br>VENDOR'S NO. | GROSS MARGIN PERCENT |
|---|---|---|---|---|---|---|---|---|
| | | | | CUM. M.U. % | | | | |
| | | | | COMPLEMENT | A | B | | |

FIGURE 8–3. Vendor analysis form.

14. Total cost of merchandise handled—$700 [(4) + [(5) × (8)]
15. Unit price retail at end of season—$10
16. Closing inventory at retail—$200 [(6) × (15)]
17. Closing inventory at cost—$100 [(6) × (8)]
18. Cost of merchandise sold—$600 [(14) − (17)]
19. Gross margin—$600 [(13) − (18)]
20. Gross margin or markup percent—50%

Figure 8–3 is essentially an income statement for each line of each vendor. The effort required to complete this form is considerable, and in the absence of data processing it is rarely used for other than principal lines.

The forms illustrated are by no means the only sources of information available to the buyer for vendor evaluation. For example, customer returns and complaints, to name only two, should be totaled by vendor and used to evaluate resources.

## The Computer and Resource Evaluation

Retailers, both large and small, have a great deal of resource evaluation data available from computer-generated reports. It should be emphasized that there is nothing provided by the retail application of the computer that cannot be done manually. It is only when the volume of data is so large that it becomes a necessity.

Typical of the use of data processing for vendor analysis is the MPS (merchandise processing system) offered by IBM. The output of this system includes a vendor performance report that indicates the following:

1. The accuracy of the quantities shipped and billed by each vendor
2. The ability of each vendor to meet the delivery date
3. Pricing accuracy
4. Unauthorized substitution of items by each vendor
5. All returns to the vendor and the reason for such returns
6. The terms and allowances provided by each vendor
7. The vendor's compliance with shipping instructions
8. The vendor's adherence to special instructions for the marking of merchandise and cartons

Although the information provided by this report is very important to the buyer, the same information can be determined manually by the small store operator with no great expenditure of time and effort. Perhaps the greatest advantage of data processing is that the report is actually made, rather than having the information trusted to memory.

```
VENDOR  INQUIRY                                                    PROGRAM-NAME: 201US031
                                                                   PFKEY  1 - RESTART
 DEPT     20      LADIES SPORTSWEAR                                PFKEY 16 - EXIT
VENDOR  437801   LONGSTREET INDUSTRIES, LTD.
  DATE  06/8-

RECEIPTS:                    MARKDOWNS:

  UNITS        420             UNITS        56         ADV CONTRIBUTIONS:          .00
  @ RTL       6715.80          @ RTL        280.23
  @ COST      3156.43                                    # P.O.'S PLACED:          6
                             PURCHASES:
SALES:                                                    # SHIPMENTS:             5
                               @ RTL       7438.20
  UNITS        324             @ COST      4462.92        OVER SHIPMENTS:          0
  @ RTL       5389.77
  @ COST      3108.45        INVOICED AMTS:              UNDER SHIPMENTS:          1

RETURNS:                       INVOICE    3782.40
                                  DISC     231.18
  UNITS         23             FREIGHT      45.20
  @ RTL        367.77           RETAIL    6715.80

                                                        Press "ENTER" to continue *
```

**FIGURE 8–4.** *Courtesy:* CREATIVE DATA SYSTEMS, INC.

CDS Systems for Retailing provides another system for evaluating vendors. Figure 8–4 shows an illustration of what could be called up on a display station at the buyer's option. Another major computer program used by retailers is ACI's Retail Express, which furnishes complete information on vendor analysis.

## GETTING ALONG WITH VENDORS

It is very much to the advantage of the buyer to develop key resources. Generally such producers are in demand and become key resources for other retailers as well. Just about every resource wants to do business with a large-volume buyer, but even a large-volume buyer will get better service if it is cooperative and helpful. The following are important in achieving this goal:

1. It is important to the vendor's operation that the buyer give a definite answer as soon as possible.
2. Buyers should not be involved in having one vendor copy the merchandise of another.
3. Orders, once given, should not be canceled before their delivery date.
4. Charges for cooperative advertising should not exceed the cost of such promotion.
5. Discounts and anticipation (extra discount for prompt payment) in excess of those agreed on should not be taken.
6. Purchase orders should be sent promptly. They should be specific and detailed.

7. Merchandise should be returned to the vendor only when a return is justified by prior understanding, damages, overshipping, and so forth.

## *CLASSIFICATION OF RESOURCES*

There are many types of resources available to buyers. Principal among these are the following:

1. Manufacturers
2. Manufacturer's representatives
3. Store-owned resources
4. Service wholesalers
5. Rack jobbers

### Manufacturers

Buying directly from the producer certainly affords the buyer a number of advantages, but the choice is not always left to the buyer. Many manufacturers decline to sell directly to retailers no matter how much they might purchase. They distribute their merchandise through wholesalers. This is generally characteristic of foods, some appliances, and convenience goods.

Buying from manufacturers, when permissible, is done under certain conditions and offers some advantages. Included among the reasons for direct purchase are the following:

1. Manufacturers' salespeople are generally more knowledgeable than those of wholesalers and can provide better advice on merchandise, advertising, point-of-purchase displays, and the like.
2. When speed of delivery is extremely important, as in such merchandise as fashion goods, the use of a middleman would slow the distribution process. By purchasing directly from the producer, the fashion buyer can get the goods on the selling floor very quickly.
3. The direct purchase permits the buyer (usually limited to the large store purchaser) to have goods made to the store's own specifications and requirements. Many large stores actually have manufacturers produce merchandise according to designs they supply.
4. Of course, price is an important factor. The direct purchase usually results in lower prices. By eliminating the wholesaler certain costs are reduced, which results in lower prices for the retailer.

Since many manufacturers do require minimum orders, the small retailer must resort exclusively to purchasing from wholesalers. Recent years have seen the formation of buying groups made up of small retailers who pool their orders so they can participate in direct purchasing. In that way, many manufacturers now sell to a growing number of small retailers. Not only have the manufacturers found new customers, but the small retailer has been successful in reducing the cost of goods purchased.

## Manufacturer's Representatives

In most soft goods classifications, with women's wear the most notable example, many manufacturers are using manufacturer's representatives to sell their lines. Instead of establishing their own sales outlets and training their own sales staffs, many manufacturers are going the route of using reps, as they are referred to in the trade, to represent their lines. In this way the manufacturer can put all the effort into production and leave the distribution of the line to professional sellers.

The advantages it affords buyers are several:

1. The reps often represent more than one manufacturer, sometimes as many as ten, under one roof. This permits the buyer to cover many manufacturer's lines without the need to move from showroom to showroom.
2. The lines are often compatible. That is, a jeans collection of one manufacturer could be represented alongside the sweater line of another, providing the buyer with tops and bottoms that work together and ultimately could result in an easy sale to the customer.
3. Where manufacturers who operate their own showrooms find it too expensive to have many sales branches throughout the country, using reps could place the goods in all parts of the country with little expense. With this method, the buyer could view lines from across the country without incurring the expense of travel to a manufacturer who is not within easy reach of the buyer.

## Store-Owned Resources

While the vast majority of merchandise found in stores has been purchased directly from manufacturers or wholesalers, more and more retailers are involved in their own merchandise production. Small retailers, because of their size and merchandise requirements, purchase their goods from outside sources. Most of the larger retail department and specialty stores feature an assortment that includes goods purchased from outside sources and their own items. Macy's, for example, stocks more than 20 private label lines alongside of its designer- and manufacturer-produced brands. In food stores, there is generally a mix of regular brands as well as store-owned items.

Some retailers enjoy success by offering only their own items produced in company-owned plants for their use. Names like Gap, The Limited, and Banana Republic deal almost exclusively with their own items. The benefits of such

**FIGURE 8-5.** Lerner New York features merchandise from company-owned resources. *Courtesy:* Space Design International.

operations include exclusivity of design, price maintenance, elimination of middlemen, and greater attention to their customer's needs.

The Limited, Inc., is one organization that uses company-owned resources for its merchandise assortment. Figure 8-5 features a Limited division, Lerner New York, that primarily sells merchandise that it produces in its own factories.

## A RETAIL BUYING FOCUS

### *The Limited*

Whenever industry professionals and analysts discuss the most innovative and successful store organizations in the United States, the discussion often centers on Leslie Wexner and The Limited. Although the tale is now legend in retailing circles, it is important to understand that one of the reasons for the unheralded success is due to the fact that the merchandise mix is almost exclusively company designed and produced.

A careful examination of the merchandise at The Limited, Limited Express, Cacique, Structure, Victoria's Secret, and Lerner New York, all divisions of the company, immediately reveals private labels. Sweaters, pants, coordinates, coats, blouses, skirts, dresses, and accessories carry a "brand" that is owned by the organization and is produced in its numerous factories all over the world.

While producing one's own merchandise can often be considered dangerous because of the enormous investments it takes to produce such lines, The Limited tends to guarantee some of its decisions with careful research and planning. One technique that it employs is the introduction of a limited number of external manufacturer–produced items in "test stores" to evaluate customer reaction. The winners are carefully copied or adapted and reproduced under the company's own label in their own factories. This eliminates a great deal of guess work associated with introduction of new styles.

With the more than 2000 units in the organization carrying, for the most part, products that have been produced in-house, The Limited exemplifies the potential for success with store-owned resources.

---

## Service Wholesalers

A simplified definition of a wholesaler is that it is a business unit that buys merchandise from a producer and sells it to a retailer. These organizations play an important role in the distribution of goods. They are widely used by both small and large retail organizations, and it is important that buyers develop good relationships with them. The extent, if any, to which a buyer of a particular line uses wholesalers depends mainly on the manufacturer's selling policies and the size of the retailer.

### *Advantages of Purchasing from Wholesalers*

Wholesalers offer many advantages to manufacturers. They provide a sales force, minimize packing and shipping, reduce inventory-carrying needs, provide market information, simplify bookkeeping, and reduce credit risks. For these and other reasons, many manufacturers prefer to deal with wholesalers. This is particularly true in convenience goods and food lines, for which buyers have no choice but to use wholesalers.

Wholesalers provide the following services for their retail customers:

1. They carry a large inventory, which reduces the amount of goods the retailer is required to maintain. This permits maximum use of space for selling by reducing the warehouse requirements of the retailer.
2. To be successful, the wholesaler must carry the right goods. This requires forecasting consumer demand. This burden, usually borne by the buyer, is partially shouldered by the wholesale resource.
3. The wholesaler's responsibility is service. This includes prompt delivery, which is rarely available from a manufacturer. A retailer whose advertising special does better than expected has a better chance of getting a reorder filled promptly by a wholesaler than by a producer.
4. The use of a wholesaler minimizes buying risks. Since the wholesaler maintains an "in stock" position in inventory and rarely insists on minimum ordering, buyers may try out new items without undue risk.

5. Buying time may be minimized because the wholesaler generally carries the lines of several producers, which can be seen at one time. This characteristic also reduces transportation costs and paperwork, including bookkeeping.
6. Small retailers are often forced to use wholesalers because they offer more liberal credit terms. By giving long-term credit, these middlemen frequently attract marginal retailers whose orders are refused my manufacturers for credit reasons.
7. Since inventory requirements are minimized by dealing through wholesalers, the result is often an improved stock turnover rate. This enables the retailer with limited working capital to have a continual flow of fresh merchandise.
8. Wholesalers are generally large-volume buyers whose relationships with their resources are excellent. With regard to repairs, allowances, and adjustments, small retailers have an advantage if they have a wholesaler to plead their case with the manufacturer.
9. Ultimately, the wholesaler's success depends on the retailer's operation. For this reason it is to the wholesaler's advantage to offer a complete line of services to customers. This includes information on new-product development, inventory checking, merchandise planning, store modernization, marking up, and the training of personnel.

### *Disadvantages of Purchasing from Wholesalers*

The previous discussion indicates the many significant advantages involved in buying from wholesale resources. The disadvantage of this practice is that the wholesaler must make a profit also. As a result, goods bought through a wholesaler generally cost more. This raises the retail price above competitive levels or reduces markup; consequently wholesalers are generally used by small retailers with limited working capital who require extended credit terms and the "in stock" inventory system offered by wholesalers, and by large retailers in industries in which direct purchase from manufacturers is not available.

This does not mean that large retailers never use wholesalers. They all do, but only for a very small percentage of their total purchases. The largest retailers handle certain types of low-volume merchandise best supplied by wholesalers. They also use them for such spot purchasing as fill-ins. For example, if sales of blue sweaters exceed anticipated demand, the largest store may take advantage of the quick delivery offered by a wholesaler rather than waiting for a time-consuming reorder from the manufacturer. It is very much to the advantage of any retail buyer to establish a working relationship with wholesale resources.

As supermarkets have expanded into such nonfood items as drugs, cosmetics, and housewares, a new type of wholesaler, called a rack jobber, has grown in importance.

The operation works this way. The store sets aside a certain area for a rack jobber. The jobber sets up displays and merchandise. The jobber makes frequent visits to the store, filling the shelves and doing general housekeeping. The inventory on the shelf belongs to the rack jobber, and the store is not billed until an article is sold.

The advantages of rack jobbing are these:

1. Serving many retail outlets, the rack jobber is a volume buyer who is entitled to quantity discounts as well as jobber discounts not available to the store. As a result, the cost of the goods sold to the store by the jobber is only slightly greater than if the store bought directly.
2. Store managers and food buyers are experts in their lines, as rack jobbers are in their area. A rack jobber knows how to anticipate customer demand, how to price goods, and how to best display merchandise. The use of rack jobbers frequently makes a profitable department out of what could otherwise be a stepchild.
3. Since the inventory belongs to the rack jobber, working capital requirements are minimized.

A disadvantage of rack jobbing is that the profit is reduced.

## TIMING THE PURCHASE

Now that the buying plan has been prepared, in qualitative and quantitative considerations, the buyer must carefully plan the timing of the purchase. Such factors as which classification the resource fits into, market conditions, seasonal openings of the lines, vendor popularity, and the store's own merchandising philosophy play important roles in deciding when the buy should be accomplished.

Retailers have images and reputations which might necessitate early purchasing. For example, stores such as Neiman-Marcus, I. Magnin, Bloomingdale's, and Saks all subscribe to the "fashion first" concept which implies that they must show the merchandise as early as it is available. Their fashion-conscious clientele, usually uncaring about price, purchases early in the season. Off-price merchants, on the other hand, cater to a consumer who first considers price, and then fashion. In this case, the off-price buyer must wait to buy merchandise that the resource is willing to dispose of at a greatly reduced cost.

Those buyers who purchase from well-known companies that are in great demand must purchase early enough to guarantee delivery. The likes of Liz Claiborne, Perry Ellis, Jones New York, Anne Klein, and Norma Kamali warrant early purchase to guarantee early receipt of the merchandise.

Merchandise from great distances, such as the Orient and Europe, require an early purchase decision. With the problems associated with dealing with foreign countries, such as size variation, shipping complications, quotas and tariffs, early order placement is a must.

In many industries, such as women's and men's clothing, where market weeks are commonplace (discussed fully in Chapter 10), the lines open and often are sold out in this short period of time. When buying in such an industry, time of purchase is usually of the essence to ensure prompt delivery.

Market conditions also dictate time of purchase. If denim is in great demand and supply of the textile is limited, the early order will secure the appropriate number of garments needed for the selling period.

Some purchasers have the luxury of buying their wares from wholesalers. Since the very nature of wholesaling requires warehousing of the goods until the retailer needs them, those who buy from wholesalers can buy on a "hand-to-mouth" basis since delivery is often overnight.

Experience teaches us when the time to buy is best for our company's needs. Attention to this aspect of purchasing will result in having the merchandise exactly when the customer is ready to purchase.

## GIFTS FROM RESOURCES

It is always difficult for people to agree on what constitutes a bribe: a free lunch? theater tickets? Recent years have seen an enormous growth in complaints about bribery of buyers. This is without question the most unethical and immoral act in which a buyer can be involved, and it hurts everyone concerned. By paying off the buyer, the vendor increases its expenses. The cost of the goods must be increased by the retail store, since the supplier must increase the selling price to cover this hidden cost. And because the retail store is forced to pay more for the merchandise, it must charge its customers more as well. Perhaps the most severely hurt is the buyer. If he or she pays more than is necessary for the goods, the budget will suffer. In addition, being involved in a criminal act may threaten the buyer's moral well-being as well as his or her physical freedom.

## ACTION FOR THE SMALL STORE BUYER

Very often, buyers for small stores operate under a handicap when determining the resources from which they should buy. It is not always possible to buy from particular vendors because there might be a minimum order requirement that exceeds the buyer's needs. Some small store purchasers, overzealous to buy from a particular resource, will purchase amounts that far surpass their needs and find themselves with significant end-of-season markdowns.

Small store buyers must do everything possible to make certain their orders will be filled with the same attention paid to the large store buyers. If a particular vendor places the smaller orders "at the end of the line," a decision must be made for future purchases. No buyer, no matter how small the store, should be treated as a second-class citizen. If poor treatment persists from any resource, the line should be dropped and replaced by another.

It is imperative that the small store buyer become important to every vendor from whom purchases are made. By limiting orders to a smaller number of manufacturers, wholesalers, or manufacturer's representatives, the small store buyer will be able to increase the size of each order. If the opposite approach is used, there probably will not be one resource at which the buyer will receive decent treatment.

If the small store buyer makes the effort to evaluate each resource in regard to the professional treatment the store receives, it will result in a more profitable situation. In any merchandise classification, the smallest user can be satisfied. Competition is at a point where there are a significant number of vendors eager to sell to and service the small accounts. Small store buyers must make every effort to buy from those who best satisfy their needs.

## SUMMARY OF KEY POINTS

1. In large part, a buyer's success depends on the choice of resources and the relationship established with them.
2. Generally the more volume a buyer can place with a resource, the better the relationship with that vendor. For this and other reasons, it is to the buyer's advantage to limit the number of resources as much as possible.
3. Some of the vendor characteristics that must be weighed in the selection of resources are type of merchandise, exclusiveness, shipping, inventory maintenance, cooperation, prices, and profitability.
4. Because of the importance of resources, the buyer must periodically evaluate their effectiveness. This requires considerable recordkeeping, for which data processing is a valuable aid.
5. Good vendor-resource relationships can be cemented by thoughtful as well as ethical treatment on the part of the buyer.
6. Stores that own their own manufacturing facilities pose problems for the buyer. The most significant of these is that the choices are limited.
7. Large and small retail buyers depend on wholesalers as resources. Small stores use them because of limited capital, large stores for small-volume merchandise and quick fill-ins. Wholesalers offer many advantages, but they generally charge more than manufacturers.
8. Rack jobbers own the inventory and have charge of the display racks of their customers.

## REVIEW QUESTIONS

1. Why is it important that a buyer limit resources to as few as possible?
2. Should a buyer place all purchases with key resources? Why?

3. Discuss the advantages a large-volume buyer has over a small-volume buyer.
4. How may a small-volume buyer improve the relationship with his or her resources?
5. Discuss the importance of the "maneuverability" of a resource.
6. Some retailers will use only a resource whose closeout policy will benefit the store. Discuss.
7. Discuss the importance to the store of the amount of inventory carried by the resource.
8. What information can a buyer expect from resources?
9. Explain the importance of the periodic evaluation of resources.
10. What factors should be considered in the periodic evaluation of resources?
11. Discuss the role of the computer in the evaluation of resources.
12. In what way can the buyer's ethical treatment of resources improve buyer-vendor relationships?
13. What is meant by store-owned resources? What sort of retailers use them?
14. Discuss the advantages of buying through wholesalers.
15. What are the disadvantages of buying through wholesalers?
16. What sorts of retailers are apt to use wholesalers? Why?
17. Define rack jobbing and discuss the advantages it offers.
18. Discuss the effects of the gifts some resources give to buyers.

## CASE PROBLEM 1

Brown's Department Store is a high-volume, single-unit organization that for years has been a leading retailer in a downtown urban area. Although the store's profits have held up well during the past five years, the earnings seem to be somewhat below those of a nearby competitor. Somewhat disturbed by this, the store's executive operating committee has hired a new merchandising manager and instructed him to make a department-by-department analysis to determine weak spots.

After studying the necessary reports, the new manager has pinpointed ladies' sportswear as the worst offender. These are his criticisms:

1. While the original markup is high, excessive markdowns have resulted in an overall low figure.
2. The department's gross sales have remained constant, while the total for the store has shown a steady increase.
3. The average inventory has been high in relation to sales. This has resulted in poor turnover rates.

When confronted with this information, the buyer resigned in anger. The store's policy has been to promote from within, and the assistant buyer has been promoted. It has been decided that her first chore will be an evaluation of resources.

### Questions

1. What resource characteristics should she evaluate?
2. What information will she need?
3. Where will she find these data?

## CASE PROBLEM 2

Quality Foods, Inc., operates a chain of eight large supermarkets in the suburbs of a large midwestern city. The owners are young, talented, and aggressive. Thanks to their operating ability, they have been very successful, and the rate of expansion has been phenomenal. If anything, they have grown too quickly. While more conservative management would have waited until enough profits had accumulated to finance expansion, Quality Foods has opened new units on the credit available through its success. The costs of building and stocking new units has led to a weak working capital position.

All the departments in the store are owner-operated. At a recent directors' meeting, two suggestions were made to ease the shortage of working capital. Both concern nonfood merchandise, a source of considerable profit to the firm.

The suggestions are as follows:

1. Use wholesalers for nonfood merchandise.
2. Use rack jobbers for nonfood merchandise.

### Questions

1. List the advantages and disadvantages to the firm of using wholesalers.
2. List the advantages and disadvantages to the firm of using rack jobbers.
3. What information do you need to make a decision?

# Chapter 9

# PURCHASING "OFF-PRICE"

## LEARNING OBJECTIVES

*Upon completion of this chapter, the student should be able to:*

1. Discuss the concept of off-price buying and where it had its roots.
2. Give research-supported evidence that off-pricers sell for considerably less than their department store counterparts.
3. Explain the various reasons why the off-price buyer is able to purchase at prices well below the original wholesale price.
4. Relate why manufacturers often remove their labels from the garments that are sold to the off-price buyer.
5. Describe the terms of payment that are often required in off-price purchasing.
6. List three concessions given to vendors by buyers who purchase off-price.
7. Compare the traditional store's use of off-price goods with that of the off-pricer.
8. Mention the names of famous designers and manufacturers whose merchandise is available off-price.

## *INTRODUCTION*

Most retailers who can look back to the early 1920s recall a small, pale-faced woman carrying a large tote bag who made the rounds of the Seventh Avenue manufacturers. The word quickly spread throughout the market that Frieda Loehmann was in town to purchase quality merchandise that, for one reason or another, the vendor was unable to sell. Perhaps there was a broken range of sizes left, or colors that didn't easily sell, or it was just getting too late in the season for the manufacturers and designers to wait for reorders from their regular retail customers. Whatever the reason, Mrs. Loehmann was ready to deal with cash (the reason for the tote), so that she could drive a better bargain. She was in town to purchase "off-price." Her needs began to increase as her sales began to soar at her small shop in Brooklyn. Eventually accompanied by a driver, who kept moving the van (now needed to transport the merchandise to her store) from building to building in the garment center, her presence spelled relief for vendors who couldn't easily dispose of their wares. The Loehmann's organization, now a major force in retailing that stretches across many states, still practices the same type of retailing as its founder, Frieda Loehmann. Many in the field give credit to this woman as the originator of "off-price" purchasing. Figure 9-1 features Loehmann's "Back Room." In all the stores, this is an area set aside for high-fashion, "off-price" merchandise.

**FIGURE 9-1.** Loehmann's, "The Back Room." *Courtesy:* Loehmann's.

Those who are less experienced confuse the term "off-price" retailing with discounting. There is a distinct difference. Although both offer the consumer bargain prices, the "off-price" merchant buys for less than the regular wholesale cost and passes his or her savings on to the shopper, while the discounter purchases at the regular wholesale price and sells to the consumer at a reduced price. The former's markup is generally equivalent to that of the traditional retailer, with the latter's a lower markup. It is the ability to negotiate that enables the "off-price" store buyer to bring desirable merchandise to the consuming public at prices that are lower than at other stores.

Today the number of "off-price" merchants continues to grow and poses a threat to many traditional retailers. No longer a distinct minority, they are found from coast to coast, featuring a wide variety of merchandise, in free-standing stores, in malls that are predominantly off-price, and in clusters that have become famous as "off-price" merchandising centers. The main attractions in towns such as Freeport, Maine, North Conway, New Hampshire, Reading, Pennsylvania, and Secaucus, New Jersey, are the "off-price" centers. Major retail empires have taken to the "off-price" route with the likes of Melville Corporation (parent of Marshall's) and Zayre Corporation (owner of both T. J. Maxx and Hit or Miss).

A recent study shows that what Frieda Loehmann started in the 1920s now accounts for approximately 10 percent of retail sales.

A mall, specializing in bargains for the shopper, Sawgrass Mills, is the epitome of off-price merchandise. The following Focus explores retailing's major entry into this aspect of the business.

## A RETAIL BUYING FOCUS

### *Sawgrass Mills*

With the success of two malls dedicated to "bargain" shopping, the developers of Potomac Mills in northern Virginia and Franklin Mills outside of Philadelphia went to the drawing board and created what was to become the largest of such retail environments in the United States. Occupying land in Fort Lauderdale, Florida, that was far away from the traditional shopping centers but conveniently located for consumers, Sawgrass Mills was born. Under one roof, scores of merchants offer vast assortments of goods at below traditional prices in more than 2 miles of store frontage. Opened just prior to the Christmas selling season in 1990, the throngs that attended the inauguration as well as those who returned time and time again to grab the bargains seem to indicate that the concept will be around for a long time.

Many of the outlets are retail divisions of manufacturers and designers. Shops bearing such names as Unisa, Dexter, Vanity Fair, and J. G. Hook feature goods from their own production companies. Retailers such as Ann Taylor, Lillie Rubin, Wacamaw, and others that run shops all across the country on a traditional markup basis utilize these outlets to dispose of merchandise they otherwise might have to sell at a loss. The remainder of the stores are typical "off-price" specialists who deliver consumer goods at prices far below the normal retail. In these environments names like Cole-Haan shoes, Reebok sneakers, Prince tennis rackets, Levi's jeans, and other nationally advertised brands are commonplace at reduced prices.

The Mill is not just a "plain pipe rack" operation; it provides comfortable rest areas, a food court, and visual presentations that make shopping a pleasure.

One need only to look at the vast parking fields filled with cars to know that the shoppers are willing and eager to take home the specially priced merchandise that the store buyers have made available.

---

In this chapter, discussion will focus upon the role of the "off-price" buyer, the scope of his or her activities, how the deals are negotiated, and the markets explored to make these "bargain" purchases.

## OFF-PRICE: MYTH OR REALITY

While the off-price phenomenon is gaining momentum, many traditional retailers try to dispel the price differential by stating that the items offered at these new retail outlets are "second quality, manufacturer rejects, end-of-season closeouts, copies of the originals, unwanted colors or ill fitting." Is the merchandise offered by the off-pricer the same as that found in the typical department store, or is it some bargain goods mixed together with a smattering of "the real thing"? Is off-price myth or reality?

The research of Kirby and Dardes, "A Pricing Study of Women's Apparel in Off-Price and Department Stores," in the *Journal of Retailing,* indicates that there were, in fact, major differences between the off-pricers and department stores. "Average prices for all 20 items during 13 weeks were 40 percent greater in department stores than in off-price stores." The 20 items in the study included shirts, blouses, vests, sweaters, jeans, slacks, skirts, dresses, suits and jackets. This research, as well as information compiled from a variety of knowledgeable shoppers, indicates that there are bargains aplenty in the off-price stores. It is certainly no myth when the identical designer label could be purchased "off-price" at 30 percent less than the department store ticket.

## MAKING THE PURCHASE

If the merchandise is the same except for the price, how then can off-pricers sell for less? Is it magic or is it a different approach to the acquisition of the goods? The latter suggestion is the answer!

We have carefully scrutinized the manner in which the typical merchant plans purchases. A great deal of attention has been paid to both quantitative and qualitative considerations and in the majority of cases, most conventional retailers want to be first to receive the goods. Being first or early is perhaps the reason why this retailer pays top dollar. When you want to be the first on your street to drive the latest car, you generally have to pay more than your next-door neighbor who is willing to wait until the excitement generated by the new model dies down. This concept, along with others, enables the off-pricer to sell for less.

## Timing

Being willing to wait a little longer gives an edge to the retailer who deals in bargain prices. The traditional store generally purchases early so that the customers will be able to shop prior to the season. While this approach to purchasing does give the consumer the privilege of early shopping, it results in merchandise at the highest price. Retailers who subscribe to this buying plan are the "fashion forward" merchants who base their reputations on being the first to introduce the new line.

The off-price retailer's philosophy is different. While it would please him or her to be able to purchase early, price is what they offer their clientele. To do so, they must be willing to play a wait-and-see game. They don't plan for "market week" (a time when the traditional buyers visit the wholesale markets to see the new lines). This category of purchasers waits until the new lines have been shipped to the regular stores before they set out to make their deals. By playing by this new set of rules, they can visit the same vendors as do the department store buyers, only it is to see what goods these vendors have on hand and must unload to make room for the next season's goods. In fashion merchandising, where seasons are short and manufacturers are often hungry for business, there is always the resource who is waiting to unload. The department store has had a chance to test the merchandise and might reorder the hot items. In today's fashion world, though, reorders are becoming less and less popular, with merchants looking for newer merchandise all the time. Except for the possible winners in the line (and they are sometimes available as part of a closeout deal), there is always an abundance of well-known, designer merchandise available at closeout prices. By waiting patiently, the off-price buyer is able to make a purchase that is well below the original wholesale price. It should be understood that the merchandise acquired at discount is still within the "season."

Table 9-1 presents the comparison timing of the purchases of an identical style by both the department store and off-price buyer.

Analysis of Table 9-1 shows that the only conditions of the purchases that were different were date of purchase, delivery and price. Why was the price different? The department store buyer, in a quest for early introduction of the item, had to make an earlier commitment to the manufacturer—and by doing so paid

**TABLE 9-1**

| Style | Date of Purchase | Delivery | Description | Wholesale Price |
|---|---|---|---|---|
| | | *DEPARTMENT STORE* | | |
| 842 | March 1 | April 15 | red dresses | $52 |
| | | *OFF-PRICE RETAILER* | | |
| 842 | June 1 | June 1 | red dresses | $36 |

the higher prices. This ensured receipt of goods on April 15 for selling through the summer season, which concludes around the end of June. The off-price buyer didn't plan to specifically purchase style 842 but found it available late in the season. Since the merchandise was in stock, it was available for immediate delivery (no waiting period as in the first case) and at a reduced price, since it was getting close to the end of the retail selling season. Using the same information, later in the chapter we will explore the price charged to customers by both stores for the identical dress. Placement at a later date doesn't always guarantee a price reduction, but the off-pricers are willing to take that risk if price is the main factor in the purchase.

## Assortment

In Chapter 8, we learned that traditional buyers generally prepare a buying plan that centers on a model stock. By looking at past sales and investigating the sources of buyer information (trade papers, resident buying offices, and the like), the buyer develops a merchandise assortment in both breadth and depth. This assortment or model stock assures a good cross section of merchandise styles (subclassification) to fit the customers' needs.

The off-price buyer doesn't plan as perfectly as the department store buyer. While this buyer will buy only for a particular classification (dresses, suits, sportswear, etc.), no particular attention will be paid to specific color, exact size allocation or styles. Since price is the major factor, the off-pricer will forgo those requirements and will seek to purchase merchandise that is appropriate for sale in his or her store. When visiting a resource and negotiating the off-price purchase, the buyer often buys "incomplete size ranges" or assorted colors. The department store buyer must fit the purchase to the developed model stock. Table 9-2 shows the purchase orders of both types of buyers for an identical item.

In the preceding figure it is obvious that the off-price retailer is willing to buy a large quantity, perhaps the remainder of the manufacturer's inventory for that style, in colors and sizes that are available. For this, the price is considerably less than the department store counterpart.

TABLE 9-2

| | | | | | | | | | | |
|---|---|---|---|---|---|---|---|---|---|---|
| | | | | | *DEPARTMENT STORE* | | | | | |
| | | | | | *SIZES* | | | | | |
| *Style* | *Color* | *3* | *5* | *7* | *9* | *11* | *13* | *15* | *Total Pieces* | *Price* |
| 615 | pink | 1 | 2 | 2 | 3 | 3 | 1 | 1 | 12 | $50 |
| | blue | 1 | 2 | 2 | 3 | 3 | 1 | 1 | 12 | $50 |
| | | | | | *OFF-PRICE RETAILER* | | | | | |
| 615 | assorted | | | assorted size range | | | | | 85 | $32 |

## "Special Handling"

Buyers who purchase for their stores at full price often make special demands on the vendors. Some major retailers require that their store labels are sewn into each garment and that merchandise should be shipped on special hangers or in individual plastic casings. The resource is generally amenable to such demands, since the merchandise is being purchased for the top price. Those who consider price first are willing to forgo these special handling accommodations. It is equivalent to the shopper who buys a gift at Bloomingdale's or Neiman-Marcus and expects expert gift wrapping at no extra cost versus the customer who buys off price and is willing to wrap the purchase at home. The off-price retailer buys on a "no-frills" basis.

## Label Removal

Often, manufacturers of nationally advertised brands and designer merchandise remove their labels from merchandise purchased below the original wholesale price as a condition of sale. In that way they can somewhat protect their department store customers who have paid the full price and resell at higher retail prices. While the off-pricer would prefer recognizable labels (which attract a large segment of the consumer market), the concession is reluctantly granted to gain the price advantage.

Removal of the label might eliminate the most prominent identifiable mark of a particular manufacturer, but off-price merchants point to the other features that allow for ease in identification. The lining of a garment often features a designer logo, and the buttons might reveal a recognizable design. The shopper at off price is often an expert in the art of discovering the name of the manufacturer. Syms, an off-price chain that specializes in men's and women's clothing with the labels removed, boasts "An Educated Consumer Is Our Best Customer." Syms is saying that, with or without the label, their customers can easily discern quality goods. Label removal is thus a small price to pay for top-fashion merchandise at considerably reduced prices.

### Transportation

In the negotiation process, traditional store buyers often demand that the seller pay for shipping the goods. With large retail organizations, F.O.B. destination (the seller pays for the transportation) is generally a forgone conclusion.

The situation is quite different in off-price purchasing. Since the seller has agreed to a reduction in the purchase price, he trims the extras as well. One of these extras, the cost of shipping, is absorbed by the purchaser. Many off-price merchants make their own arrangements, either by private transporter or their own trucks, to transport the goods at their own expense.

### Terms of Payment

One major problem endured by manufacturers concerns the payments for merchandise. In Chapter 13, Negotiating the Purchase and Writing the Order, attention will focus upon the time a retailer takes before he pays for the goods. Retailers today demand as much time as they possibly can before they pay their bills. In some merchandise classifications, swimsuits for example, the manufacturer permits as much as four months for the invoice to be settled. This demand by the typical conventional retailer often causes a cash flow problem for the seller. By giving in to the buyer's demands for extended time in which to pay for the goods, the manufacturer's ability to run a business might be hampered. To compound the problem, many retailers take longer to pay their bills than allowed by the terms of the purchase.

## *PRICING "OFF-PRICE"*

Many people are under the impression that off-price merchants pay the same price as department and traditional specialty stores but work on lower markups. While some do work on a lower markup because they "turn" the merchandise faster and generally restrict their customer services, the vast majority mark up their goods to levels that rival a department store. The bulk of the merchandise is bought at discount but is marked up more than off-pricers have you think.

With the following numbers as an example, it is easy to see how the off-pricers can take the usual markup and yet customers still get "bargains."

DEPARTMENT STORE
COST: $ 52
RETAIL: $110

MARKUP (ON RETAIL): $\frac{58}{110} = 53\%$

The department store typically works on "keystone" markup, or doubling the cost. Sometimes the actual selling price is "keystone plus," which amounts to double the cost plus a little extra. Using the latter concept, the following markups and consumer prices are realized:

OFF-PRICE RETAILER
COST: $36
RETAIL: $75

MARKUP (ON RETAIL): $\frac{39}{75} = 52\%$

Although the markups are almost identical, the off-price retailer makes an excellent profit (after all expenses are paid) while the off-price customer is saved a significant amount of money. It should be understood that the off-price customer might not be able to buy early in the season or in surroundings that offer a variety of services, but the bottom line is savings. The majority of off-price merchants do not discount their goods; they just pay less for them and pass the savings along to their customers.

## INDIRECT PURCHASING

Although off-price merchants employ their own buyers, they, like the traditional retailers, aren't always able to cover the market as carefully and as completely as they would like. To get a better handle on market conditions, the traditional retailer often employs the services of a resident buying office. Figure 9-2 is illustrative of an off-price buying service. In recent years, many resident offices have opened off-price divisions to accommodate that segment of the retail market, and some have opened offices that concentrate exclusively on off-price merchandise. Companies such as Competitive Purchasing Service, Inc. and Price Breakers, are located in New York City in the midst of the wholesale action. Their major task is not one of service, as it is for the regular buying office, but one of finding merchandise at the lowest possible prices for their off-price customers.

### A RETAIL BUYING FOCUS

#### *Price Breakers*

Based in New York City, in the heart of the famous Garment Center, a relative newcomer to the resident buying field is holding forth. Price Breakers, as the name implies, is not the run-of-the-mill resident office; rather, it specializes in procuring merchandise at prices below the usual wholesale selling price.

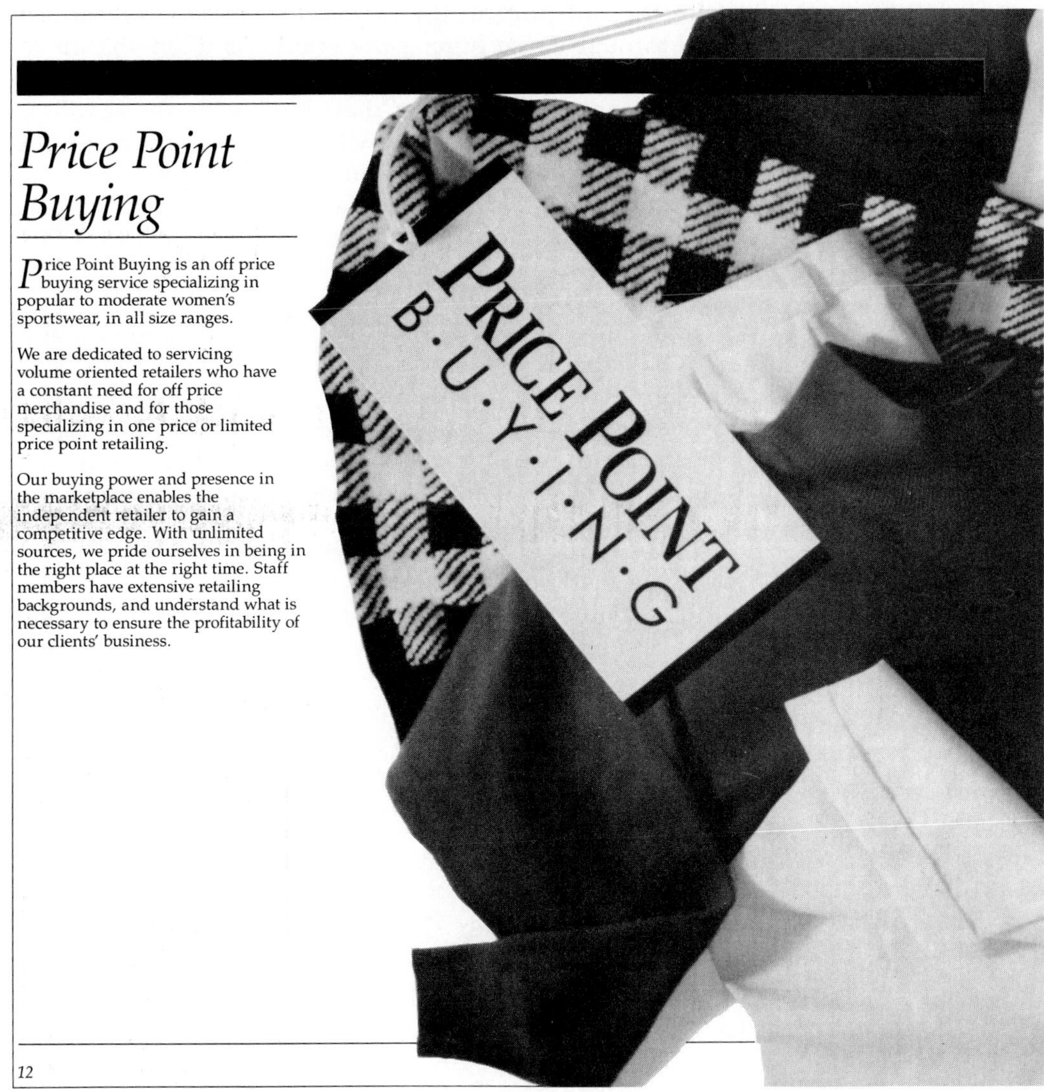

Price Point Buying
Price Point Buying is an off price buying service specializing in popular to moderate women's sportswear, in all size ranges.
We are dedicated to servicing volume oriented retailers who have a constant need for off price merchandise and for those specializing in one price or limited price point retailing.
Our buying power and presence in the marketplace enables the independent retailer to gain a competitive edge. With unlimited sources, we pride ourselves in being in the right place at the right time. Staff members have extensive retailing backgrounds, and understand what is necessary to ensure the profitability of our clients' business.
PRICE POINT
B·U·Y·I·N·G
12


**FIGURE 9-2.** Price Point buying service purchases off-price goods for member stores. *Courtesy:* Henry Doneger Associates.

With the emergence of off-price retailing, Price Breakers alerts retailers to merchandise at substantial savings. A staff of six people scour the market everyday to search for off-price goods that are still in season. Many merchants who operate off-price stores often find that goods at reduced prices are readily available at season's end. While many of their customer's are willing to wait for the lower-priced goods a little longer, many want the merchandise when it is still being featured for the full price at traditional department and specialty stores. Price Breakers, through mass purchasing efforts, is often able to convince manufacturers to break price at the season's peak. It consolidates the needs of its member stores, thereby making their buying power significant. Many manufacturers with cash flow problems willingly dispose of their offerings at lower prices when such quantity sales can be accomplished.

Unlike the conventional resident buying offices that require order placement as much as six months in advance of a season, Price Breakers works on a 45-day delivery period that falls within the specific season. In this way, merchants can avail themselves of goods later than they would traditionally have to buy and at prices that are lower. Rarely are minimum orders required that are different from the purchase made at full price. This enables even the smallest merchant to participate in the bargains.

The company specializes in moderate to better missy and junior sportswear, dresses, coats, accessories and lingerie. For those merchants without buying power on their own such as the giants like Marshall's and T. J. Maxx, Price Breakers is answering their call.

---

In times when manufacturers are overstocked and must make room for the next season's goods, they need a way to quickly dispose of the merchandise. While many of them deal directly with off-pricers, each negotiation takes time and effort. The off-price office which is right in the market is therefore easily accessible for discussions on the sale of goods at a reduced price. This setup is a perfect solution because the office has direct contact with many off-price merchants. Because of this, a producer might be able to sell his entire inventory to many outlets, with less complication.

## CONCESSIONS TO THE VENDORS

To gain access to the goods produced by the leading resources, off-price merchants must be willing to make certain concessions as a condition of the purchase.

### Store Location

One would hardly expect to find the same items, off price, in a mall that houses such prestigious retail names as Bloomingdale's, Neiman-Marcus and Lord & Taylor. The off-price merchants would never be able to convince a manufacturer to sell to them at lower prices, no matter how late it was in the season or even if the colors were not purchased by those stores. To gain the price advantage, off-price stores such as Syms, Marshall's, Loehmann's, and Hit or Miss locate themselves as freestanding stores or in neighborhood clusters that are far from the major shopping malls. In this way, the customer who frequents the major department and specialty stores will not be in the vicinity of off-price retailers. Some off-price companies have such clout that small shopping centers bearing their names (there is a Loehmann's Plaza in many parts of the country) are springing up, housing tenants with merchandise that is compatible but not competitive.

### Low-Key Promotion

The lifeblood of retailing is advertising and sales promotion. Without advertising of one sort or another, today's retailers will probably not attract shoppers to their stores. Much of the advertising is of a cooperative nature, with the producer gladly sharing in the cost with the retailer if the name of the label or manufacturer is prominently displayed. Buyers negotiate promotional dollars at the time of their purchases and quickly double the money earmarked by their stores for advertising.

In off-price negotiation, the manufacturers not only don't offer cooperative advertising money, but they generally insist upon anonymity for the merchandise they sell. In the print or broadcast media, it is rare for an off-price merchant to mention the brands of merchandise available at his or her store. The copy reads more like "20 percent to 50 percent Lower than Department Store Prices" or "Famous Designer Labels for Less." It is this condition that often enables the off-price buyer to purchase the same merchandise as the department store.

### The Final Sale

Although most suppliers do not take merchandise returns except in the case of damages, some will make exceptions for the major department store which wishes to return the goods. Some vendors will offer a discount to the purchaser so that a markdown could be taken and actually charged to the vendor.

The off-price buyer generally examines the merchandise before the purchase (it is usually in stock) and buys on an "as is" basis or under "job lot" terms. These conditions signify that the goods, once purchased, belong to the off-price retailer and cannot be returned even if there are damaged pieces. The off-price buyer's markups take the damages and ill-fitting possibilities into consideration. If a severe markdown must be taken, it is the off-pricer's problem and not that of the seller. In other words, the sale is final!

## *TRADITIONALISTS AS OFF-PRICE PURCHASERS*

Joining the bandwagon for off pricing, many retail organizations have started or acquired off-price stores. Dayton Hudson operates Pickwick, an off-price book retailer, as well as B. Dalton, the traditional bookseller. While these major companies and others practice off-price merchandising in separate divisions, some of the most highly regarded fashion forward retailers are involved in off-price acquisitions right in their regular flagships and branches.

If one carefully scans the advertising of department stores, the term "special purchase" will often be seen. Special purchasing is just another term used to describe purchases at off price.

To bolster their maintained or average markups, many traditional retail buyers will scout the market, well into the season, to obtain new salable items at reduced prices or additional inventory of merchandise that is already on the selling floor. By employing this approach, the buyer can "mix" the new inventory (purchased below the usual cost) with merchandise that was purchased at full price. A "special purchase" sale is then advertised in which the merchandise is offered at a discount. Since many of the new items were purchased "below cost," the total of the sum of the particular item brings the buyer an excellent "average" markup. Chapter 14 explores the concept of averaging.

Many manufacturers prefer to dispose of their extra inventory to the traditional store rather than to the off-pricer. This way they do not jeopardize their names, and they present a means of greater profitability to their regular price customers. The major stores often bring in these special purchases not only to improve overall markups but to keep the goods out of the off-price stores.

Of course, not everything that is earmarked for disposal by the manufacturer is wanted by the department stores, even if the price is exceptional. They might already be overstocked, or they might be close to the opening of a new season.

## *THE SUPPLIERS OF OFF-PRICE GOODS*

As much as they don't want to offend their traditional buyers, almost every manufacturer at every conceivable price point has something to dispose of. These are not the off-brands or the lesser known labels that don't ring a bell with the customer. Off-price buyers regularly make the rounds of fashion's elite suppliers and successfully purchase and sell below the regular price the products of Pierre Cardin, Liz Claiborne, Calvin Klein, Perry Ellis, John Henry, Albert Nipon, Adrienne Vittadini, and Anne Klein. No line is sacred if there is merchandise left over and a buyer is there to take it away.

### ACTION FOR THE SMALL STORE BUYER

While off-price purchasing is generally relegated to large purchases by stores who sell exclusively off price or department and specialty stores who make special purchases, the small store buyer can get in on the action. At promotional times, such as end-of-the-season clearances, many smaller retailers like to bring in merchandise, purchased below the original price, to mix in with reductions from their regular inventories. The routes that are least taken are to go to those suppliers from whom they regularly purchase, and to their resident buying offices. In the former situation, manufacturers always have something left over and are happy to dispose of it even in the smallest quantities, a perfect deal for the small store. For members of a resident buying office, the office often arranges for large off-price buys that are spread throughout their member stores. In this way, the smallest user can get a small amount of goods.

Many smaller merchants are finding that lighter purchasing early on, to be supplemented with below regular wholesale prices at the end of the season, offers a merchandise mix that is very profitable.

## SUMMARY OF KEY POINTS

1. The forerunner to today's off-price purchase policy has been attributed by many in retailing to Frieda Loehmann, the founder of Loehmann's.
2. Off-price retailing continues to grow and it is having a major impact on traditional retailing.
3. According to specific research, the average prices charged for identical merchandise at the off-price store sold for 40 percent more at the department store.
4. By purchasing later in the season than their traditional retail counterparts, off-price buyers are able to purchase goods at significantly lower prices.
5. In order to pay less for merchandise, the off-price purchasers pay less attention to assortment requirements, in terms of sizes and colors, than do department store buyers.
6. As a safeguard for their regular customers, producers who sell off price often remove their identifiable labels in the reduced price merchandise.
7. Instead of making demands to postpone payment of their invoices, off-pricers often buy for cash to receive price concessions.
8. It is common practice for both the off-price specialists and department stores to work on similar markups.
9. Concessions such as out-of-the-way locations, promises not to use manufacturer names in ads, and refraining from returning goods help off-price buyers to purchase at lower prices.
10. Every famous label is available in off-price centers since most producers, at one time or another, cannot dispose of their goods at the full price.

## REVIEW QUESTIONS

1. Who, in the early 1920s, was the first person to enter into what is now known as off-price retailing?

2. Differentiate between off-price retailing and discounting.
3. How much of today's retail sales are attributed to the off-price merchant?
4. What is the difference in the selling price, of the same merchandise, to the off-price customer buying at an off-price store instead of a department store, according to research published in the *Journal of Retailing*?
5. Discuss the "time" factor as it relates to the off-price merchant's ability to purchase for less.
6. How does "assortment" purchased by off-price buyers often differ from that of the department store buyer?
7. What type of special handling do department store buyers often require, which contributes to the cost of the goods?
8. In what way does the manufacturer, who discounts the merchandise for the off-price buyer, camouflage the goods so that comparison shopping could be undermined?
9. If labels are removed from garments, what other telltale signs are often left for ease in identification of a designer brand?
10. In negotiating the purchase, what transportation concession is generally made by the off-price buyer?
11. What terms of payment are generally found in purchases made by off-price buyers?
12. Is there a significant difference between the markups taken by traditional retailers and the off-price segment of the market?
13. If department stores and off-pricers generally price their goods on the same markup principle, how can off-pricers sell for less?
14. What is keystone markup?
15. Discuss three concessions made by buyers in the purchase of off-price goods that justify the lower price charged by manufacturers.
16. In what way are traditional retail organizations participating in off-price buying for their stores?
17. Are some traditional retailers joining the ranks of the off-pricers?
18. What fashion labels are regularly found in the offerings at the off-price outlets?

## CASE PROBLEM 1

Langtree's is a small department store located in Pennsylvania. In operation for 18 years, it has made its success on offering quality merchandise and service. Langtree's customers, who are upper middle class, purchase merchandise that sports labels such as Liz Claiborne, Perry Ellis, Calvin Klein, and a host of other reputable names.

About three years ago, Langtree's received its first taste of off-price competition. Clayton's, an off-price operation, opened a store 8 miles from Langtree's downtown location. The new venture, unlike Langtree's, was "off the beaten path" and freestanding. Although the two companies were not direct competitors, they both carried some of the identical lines. Since the new store was just a short car ride away, some of Langtree's customers visited Clayton's and purchased the same goods off-price for less. Some of the customers complained to Langtree's that although the service at Clayton's was poor, the price differential was significant.

Throughout the last few years, business slightly declined at Langtree's and management assessed the problem as price competition from the off-price retailer. Management held several meetings to determine a solution to combat shrinking sales. Three suggestions were made on coping with the off-price situation.

Mr. Birmingham, the general merchandise manager, suggested a plan to upgrade service to an even higher level and to ignore the price competition. He believed that the customer who shops at Clayton's is only a "fringe" shopper at Langtree's and that her business is not important. He felt that new, upgraded services such as personal shopping, VIP charge cards for preferred customers, and a new gourmet dining room would keep the better customers.

Mr. Austin, the store's fashion director, felt that a new promotional strategy to extoll the "fashion first" approach at Langtree's would help retain its share of the market. By promoting fashion clinics, special fashion storewide themes, and appearances by designers, Langtree's would separate its operation from Clayton's.

The third plan, the work of Mr. Laughton, was a radical approach to the problem. "If you can't fight them, join them." He was suggesting a total change in philosophy, one that would transform Langtree's into an off-price company. He suggested that their location would be perfect to attract scores of bargain hunting shoppers.

At the present time, the situation hasn't been resolved and pressure to make a change has mounted.

### Questions

1. Which, if any, of the three proposals seems to be the right solution? Defend your answer with knowledgeable reasoning.
2. Could you suggest another plan that might help Langtree's retain its profitable position?

## CASE PROBLEM 2

Patricia Reynolds recently fulfilled her dream of the past five years by opening a warehouse-type, off-price retail company. Fully aware that a mall or downtown location would make it difficult to purchase off-price (traditional stores wouldn't allow their manufacturers to sell to an off-pricer in the same location), Pat chose a warehouse that formerly housed a toy manufacturing company. The parking area was large and could accommodate more cars than she needed for a profitable business. She had no trouble buying since her location was far enough away from the traditional stores. She consented to buying later than the regular customers, having the labels removed and paying on a C.O.D. basis. Pat also promised not to take the traditional advertising route, which prohibited her from mentioning her resources in newspapers.

She opened her doors three months ago, and business was much below her expectations. Although she was surrounded by factories and other companies in the general vicinity, the customers didn't come in numbers necessary for success. She put up flags and banners around the building in the hope that they would attract attention, but still no luck. Her merchandise, the best that could be found and at low prices, sat on the shelves and racks. Her instinct told her to forget about her commitment barring "informative" advertising, but she knew such a breach would prevent her from getting more goods.

## Question

1. How could Pat promote her operation without violating her word to the manufacturers?

# Chapter 10

# A TRIP TO THE MARKET

## LEARNING OBJECTIVES

*Upon completion of this chapter, the student should be able to:*

1. Discuss the importance of the buyer's pretrip planning preparations.
2. List the reasons why the fashion buyer must make periodic trips to major markets.
3. Explain the role of the resident buying office in a buyer's market trip.

## *INTRODUCTION*

In an earlier chapter, there was a brief discussion of Market Week in terms of the resident buying office's relationship with the store buyer during this period. Typically, Market Week is a hectic period in the buyer's life, when all his or her preliminary research and planning for the next season must be reconciled with the merchandise actually available for purchase. In addition to the daily duties and responsibilities of involvement with top management, other divisions, vendors, outside agencies, and others, the store buyer must spend time in the market. For most buyers, the market is not convenient for weekly visits. It is usually located hundreds or sometimes thousands of miles from the store. The buyer whose merchandise is fashion must make several trips to these markets annually to assess and make selections for the coming season. Nonfashion buyers also find it necessary to make market visits, but it is the fashion buyer who has the additional strain of coping with the rapidly changing fashion scene.

The Los Angeles Women's Market, featured in the ad in Figure 10-1 is typical of the numerous market weeks that take place all over the world.

Attention in this chapter will focus on planning for the market visit, the specific activities involved in such a trip, and the work generated by such a trip once the buyer has returned to the store. Since the fashion buyer's market visit is generally more complicated and demanding than that of other buyers, the examples that follow will be fashion buyer oriented. It should be understood, however, that buyers of most types of merchandise have their work cut out for them during a market trip, and the information presented is generally pertinent to their buying requirements as well. Figures 10-2 and 10-3 depict the major fashion market in the United States and fashion merchandise headed for delivery to stores.

## *PLANNING FOR THE VISIT*

A trip to the market is undertaken at different times and at different intervals, depending on the nature of the goods, the store's proximity to the market, the season of the year, and business conditions. Some stores enjoy the good fortune of being located practically at the doorstep of the market and can use this to good advantage by making almost daily visits. The vast majority are too far away and can make visits only prior to the season's opening or in situations that demand inventory replenishment which cannot be satisfied from the store's headquarters. The latter two are major trips that require significant planning.

### Major Trip Involvement

Each industry has a specific number of major seasons for which the buyer must plan purchase requirements. For example, the men's wear industry has two major seasons, fall and spring; the women's wear market is more complicated, with four—fall, holiday/resort, spring, and summer. For these periods,

CaliforniaMart & Pacific Coast Travelers Present

# THE 1992 SPRING LOS ANGELES WOMEN'S MARKET

November 1–5, 1991

## RESOURCES

10,000 Lines. Womenswear & Accessories. Contemporary, Junior & Misses Ready-to-Wear. Designer Collections. Couture. Dresses. Sportswear. Swimwear. Bridal. Intimate Apparel. CaliforniaMart. Pacific Coast Travelers. New York Fashion Creators. Also Featuring 2,500 Menswear & Childrenswear Lines. All Under One Roof.

## EVENTS

Premiere Thursday & "A Day In L.A.," October 31. Buyer Orientation/Tours. Seminars. Fashion Show/Luncheon. Trend Reports. Networking Forums. Cocktail Receptions. Hospitality Rooms Daily. Call 1-800-CAL-MART For Information. 24 Hours A Day.

## VALUE

$35 Airfare Rebates For Buyers—Restrictions Apply. 3,500 On-Site Parking Spaces. $3.00 Parking With Validation On Weekdays. Buyers Park Free On Weekends. Shuttle Buses. Buyers Club. For Airline Reservations, Hotel & Car Rental Discounts, Call Executours At 1-800-323-7187 Or 213-622-0786.

The Los Angeles Women's Market. Open To Qualified Retailers And Press From 9 AM to 6 PM.

CM CALIFORNIAMART

**CaliforniaMart Is Open For Business 52 Weeks A Year.**
110 East Ninth Street, Suite A-727, Los Angeles, California 90079-2827.
For Buyer Information, Call 1-800-CAL-MART, ext. 231. For Exhibitor Information, Call ext. 316. For Leasing Information, Call ext. 260.

**Upcoming Women's Markets: January 17–21 Summer '92, April 10–14 Fall I '92, June 19–23 Fall/Holiday '92, August 28–September 1 Holiday/Resort '92, November 6–10 Spring '93.**

**FIGURE 10-1.** Trade paper advertisements for Los Angeles Market Week. *Courtesy:* California Apparel News.

**FIGURE 10-2.** Fashion Avenue—the major fashion market in the United States *Courtesy:* Ellen Diamond, Photographer.

**FIGURE 10-3.** Fashion merchandise headed for stores *Courtesy:* Ellen Diamond, Photographer.

the buyer must do a great deal of research to develop a buying plan that involves both qualitative and quantitative decision making. Such factors as price line adjustments, merchandise assortments, pricing policies, variety of offerings, vendor selection, model stock development, dollar allocations for merchandise, and so forth, as detailed in preceding chapters, must be carefully analyzed before a major market trip is made.

Once these factors have been addressed by the buyer, it is necessary to meet with management and any pertinent staff personnel before starting out on the market visit. In large stores, buyers are supervised by divisional merchandise managers whose responsibilities include making the final determination of the dollar allocations for purchases. The large store buyer would also have a fashion coordinator or director who has already scouted the market, to bring to the buyer's attention any trends in styling, color, silhouette, and so forth. Considerable time is spent with both these individuals to prepare the buyer for the market visit.

In smaller companies, the buyer is often the store owner and does not have much in the way of support personnel for advice. Some small store buyers are employees who work for the company owners; they rely on that individual for direction in terms of money to be spent for purchases, any changes in direction, and so forth.

Whether representing a small retailer, a large chain, or a department store, the buyer is the one who makes the decisions on merchandise selection. In cases where major changes will be made in merchandising, it is not uncommon for the buyer to be accompanied to market by a merchandise manager, a fashion coordinator or an owner. Otherwise it is the buyer who comes to the market, with an assistant buyer if there is one, to make the purchases.

Buyers also make interim trips to the markets as deemed necessary by themselves or their superiors. Often, inventory will need a shot in the arm to bolster sales, a new resource heralded by the trade papers will seem to have the right appeal for the store, and so forth. In these cases, if the buyer's schedule permits, a brief trip to the market will be made. For those conveniently located, it might be for a couple of hours; for others, perhaps an overnight visit. Whichever the case, these trips do not necessitate the planning involved in the major market visit.

## Resident Buying Office Assistance

The resident buying office, as we have already learned, is utilized by the buyer in many ways. A very important role it plays is the assistance it provides to the store buyer before his or her arrival at the market.

### *Personal Arrangements*

Whether it is New York, Dallas, Chicago, Los Angeles, Miami, or any other major market, the opening of an industry's lines often results in a shortage of hotel space. Market Week is a time when scores of buyers from all over the country converge on a city, so the accommodations they require must be planned in advance. The resident buying office makes hotel arrangements for the buyer and staff, if they wish. Reservations must be made at hotels that are close to the market and provide sufficient services to make the buyer's stay comfortable. Resident offices are service organizations, and this is just one that they offer.

### *Notification of Buyer's Arrival*

Whenever a buyer makes a trip to the market, the period of time allocated for the stay is usually insufficient to meet all the desired goals. That is, there never seems to be enough time to contact all the resources one would like to. The majority of the time is generally spent visiting those companies the buyer has had a positive experience with in seasons past, or resources that seem to hold excitement from publicity gained through the trade papers. These two types of destinations take preference in the buyer's work schedule and often leave little room for further market exploration.

One way to notify any interested resource of the buyer's coming to town is by publishing this information in the trade papers. *Women's Wear Daily* and *The Daily News Record,* the men's wear publication, offer features that indicate the buyer's name, the company represented, the length of the stay in the market, and the resident buying office affiliate if there is one. The resident office generally places the information with the trade paper as a service to the buyer. Through this announcement, any sales representative can contact the buyer's representative office, leave messages for the buyer, or even try to arrange for an appointment. As we will see later in the chapter, the buyer's first stop is at the resident buying office, a place where, in addition to other activities, the buyer can receive messages accumulated as a result of the announcement of his or her arrival in the trade papers.

### *Prescreening of Lines*

Time is of the essence when the buyer makes the trip to the wholesale market. To permit the store buyer to be more productive in accomplishing merchandise selection, prior to the market visit he or she often presents the resident buyer with a preliminary planning assignment. This can be accomplished on the telephone or in writing. In a visit during which the buyer might want to see an extensive number of lines, as is often the case at a season's opening, the resident buyers of the full service offices will screen the merchandise and/or lines that have been discussed earlier. This might require not only viewing these sources but locating particular types of merchandise from resources left to the resident buyer's discretion.

By previewing the merchandise, the resident buying office can offer the buyer the advantage of feeling the pulse of the market in such pertinent matters as style availability, color direction, price, delivery availability, and so forth, before the buyer sets foot in the market. Figure 10-4 shows an excerpted

## NEW AGE CLASSICS

*Traditional classic tailoring lightens-up with 90's modernism. Forget underlining, interfacing and rigid shoulder padding... Classic clothing is now looking very different. It is one of the most important changes happening in fashion, and the effects of this quiet, soft shouldered revolution will be felt throughout this decade. ✦Traditional tailoring gives clothing a semi-rigid shape of its own. Today's New Age Classics relate to the body as the basis for creating its simplified form and shape. ✦The fabric choices available to designers today are a triumph of new textile technology. The sophistication of touch and texture; their new suppleness and lightness provides the inspiration for the New Age Classics. ✦Garment design becomes more and more restrained. Simple, uncluttered shapes achieve a sense of perfection done in New Age fabrics whose touch and texture are a fashion statement unto themselves.*

6

**FIGURE 10-4.** Excerpt from fall 1991 "Fashion Elements"—guide to fashion purchasing. *Courtesy:* Henry Doneger Associates.

guideline from a brochure that leads buyers in the right direction during market week.

## THE MARKET VISIT

The length of the buyer's stay, for a buyer who is not located close to the market, is generally a week. The period, in the trade, is known as Market Week. During this time, the buyer will visit the buying office with which the store is affiliated, work with the office's buying and merchandise staff, make the rounds of the various manufacturers, visit the trade show if one is being held, plan preliminary merchandise acquisitions, "shop" the important stores in the market's city, and so forth.

### Calling on the Resident Office

The buyer generally arrives at the hotel the day before Market Week is to begin. This usually is a Sunday. The first call, on the morning of day 1, is made to the resident buying office. Although each office follows a plan specifically geared to the needs of its accounts, the approach is usually similar to the one about to be described.

Each buyer is given a schedule that indicates general meetings and events appropriate to all buyers, as well as appointment schedules that have been tailored to the buyer's specific needs.

Figure 10-5 is a sample schedule typical of those received by the store buyer. It specifies such agenda items as general merchandising meetings, specialized merchandise classification meetings, individualized conferences, fashion show presentations, market appointments, and so forth. The illustration is of an agenda for a men's wear fashion buyer. This buyer has a plan to follow that has been organized in a manner which permits maximum coverage of the market in the time allocated.

The entire first day, or at least a good part of it, is spent at the resident buying office for the purpose of familiarization. A general meeting is held for all the stores' merchandising teams to recognize what is in store for them during their time in the market as well as in the season before them. The agenda for such meetings is presented by the various merchandising vice-presidents or resident office merchandising managers, who discuss such topics as price changes; industry conditions; changes, if any, in import regulations; the status and general direction of private label merchandise offerings by the office; color, fabric, and texture directions; and so forth. Since this is a general meeting for all merchandise classifications, the presentations are general in nature and appropriate to all buyers and merchandisers.

At this point, the group disbands and reassembles into specific area groups according to merchandise classification. The major classifications, such

**STORE NAME** The Constable
**MERCHANDISE MANAGER** Philip Stern
**BUYER** John Richards
**ASSISTANT BUYER** Michael Fredrick
**MERCHANDISE CLASSIFICATION** Men's Clothing

*AGENDA*

*Monday (At Office)*

| | |
|---|---|
| 9:00–10:00 | General Meeting<br>Topic: Trends for the coming season<br>(All classifications) |
| 10:15–11:00 | Fashion Show<br>Topic: Men's wear, Fall and Winter |
| 11:15–Noon | Merchandise Presentation<br>Feature: Prices, fabrics, directions |
| Noon–1:30 | Lunch |
| 1:45–2:45 | Individual conference<br>Office representative: Carl Mann |
| 3:00–5:00 | Use of assigned workspace to review appointments, adjust plans, etc. |

*Tuesday/Wednesday*

| | |
|---|---|
| 9:00–5:00 | Attendance at NAMSB<br>Appointment schedule with specific companies will be distributed at individual conference. |

*Thursday*

| | |
|---|---|
| | Appointments at manufacturer's and designer's showrooms. |

Friday

| | |
|---|---|
| 9:00–Noon | Use of workspace to organize notes on possible merchandise acquisitions. |
| 1:00–2:00 | Meeting with office representative, Carl Mann |

**FIGURE 10-5.** Buyer's schedule—market week

as men's wear and women's wear, are usually presented in a fashion show. That is, men's wear buyers view a show of men's clothing and accessories, while the women's wear buyers are shown fashions appropriate to their departments.

In these shows, the merchandise that is featured represents the resident buying office samplings of what the market will be offering to the buyers. The resident office attempts to show a wide range of the styles offered in the "bread and butter" manufacturer's lines, numbers available from lesser known or new resources, merchandise available under the office's private label, or anything that is deemed appropriate for the coming season. Attention in these shows is paid to making certain the merchandise runs the gamut of all price lines and shows a cross section of the "fashion forward" and staple silhouettes, textures, colors, fabrics, and so forth.

This event enables the buyer to prepare for upcoming appointments in the market. He or she takes notes on the show that can be used when viewing the various lines. Table 10-1 shows a sample of a typical device many resident buying offices provide for member buyers to use in making selections from the

**TABLE 10-1** Note-taking form

| *OWENS AND LASHER, ASSOCIATES FASHION PRODUCTION: FALL AND WINTER* | | |
|---|---|---|
| ***Resource*** | ***Price*** | ***Description*** |
| Cambria Ltd. | $125.75 | D/B Glen Plaid Suit |
| O and L—Private Label | $ 92.50 | D/B Pinstripe |
| Pierre Cardin | $135.00 | 3 pc. Flannel (Wool/Poly) |
| Palm Beach | $ 89.50 | Sportcoat—Stripe |
| Jhane Barnes II | $110.00 | Blouson Jackets (Tweed) |
| Calvin Clothes | $115.00 | Tweed Blazer |
| O and L (P/L) | $ 69.50 | Sport Coat (Oatmeal Tweed) |
| O and L (P/L) | $ 95.00 | Leather Battle Jacket |
| | $ 95.00 | Leather Pants |
| Henry Grethel | $ 89.50 | Sportcoat (D/B) |

show. The selections made at this point are not necessarily for purchase; they merely serve as a reminder of items the buyers might seek out in the lines they will soon see. Figure 10-6 shows an item in the fashion show in which the buyer's notes in Table 10-1 indicate interest.

At the conclusion of the special fashion show, the buyers generally have some time to examine the garments that were shown. Frequently there are cuts of fabrics and other items available for closer inspection. This is a time in which buyers from all the member stores can exchange ideas and discuss anything of mutual interest. This exchange of ideas is done in an atmosphere free of worry in terms of competition. Since the resident buying office is a vehicle for non-competing merchants, the buyers are given the opportunity of talking with one another without the worry of giving away company secrets. Experienced buyers learn that this is a time when they can discover how other stores are dealing with similar problems.

Lunch is an extension of the preceding meeting period. It might involve speakers from the industry in formal or informal presentations, as well as time to recongregate with the other buyers in the company who have been involved in their own area fashion shows and meetings.

After lunch, it is appropriate for each store buyer to have a little private time, if needed, with a resident buying office representative. The time might be used to reexamine styles that proved interesting in the show, to discuss a new resource, to assess the office's feelings about private label or manufacturer's brand proportions in a model stock, and so forth. This is usually a hectic time for the resident buyer, since many store buyers want a piece of this time period. If necessary, the store buyer can arrange additional time with an office representative later in the week.

For the remainder of the first day of the buyer's visit to the market, time and space have been set aside at the resident buying office for use to review appointments, adjust plans according to what was seen or heard at the lectures, and so forth.

**FIGURE 10-6.** Selected item—men's wear fashion show Jhane Barnes II, Fall/Winter. By permission.

## Visiting the Resources

Following the schedule in Figure 10-5, the buyer spends Tuesday and Wednesday, days 2 and 3 of Market Week, in calling on specific companies represented at NAMSB. NAMSB, the National Association of Men's Sportswear Buyers, is the most important trade show in the men's wear industry. It presents under one roof (usually the New York Coliseum), approximately 1200 manufacturer's lines. About 25,000 retailers from all over the country converge on NAMSB to see the next season's lines. Other well-known trade shows are the Designer Collective, which features approximately the top 60 men's wear designers in the United States, and MAGIC, a Los Angeles–based men's wear trade show. (MAGIC stands for Men's Apparel Group in California.)

Figure 10-7 features a fashion presentation at the Midwest Men's Wear Collection in the Chicago Apparel Center.

At the trade show, the buyer calls on those resources with which appointments have been set. Each line requires a particular amount of time for viewing. The time varies, depending on how extensive each line is and whether the garments are featured on live models or on hangers.

**FIGURE 10-7.** Buyers view the fashions at a trade show. *Courtesy:* Chicago Apparel Center.

With each line, the buyer "takes numbers." This term is commonly used in the market and signifies a buyer's interest in particular styles or numbers. He or she records them for possible incorporation into the eventual purchase requisitions. Rarely do buyers "write" or authorize merchandise orders on first seeing a line, unless inventory replenishment is needed at once. This approach enables the buyer to compare all the merchandising offerings in the market in terms of prices, styles, colors, textures, and so forth. By digesting all the information and using the "numbers taken"as reminders, the buyer can more intelligently plan the merchandise assortment. Figure 10-8 shows buyers taking notes for future ordering.

When the time permits, most buyers will move from room to room at the trade shows to "discover" new lines that are suitable for their needs. It is when scores of resources are gathered into one centralized facility that the buyer can easily and quickly view lines he or she has never before purchased.

Thursday, or day 4, might be used to visit manufacturers not represented at the trade show. Some choose not to participate in a particular trade event. Their line may be at a higher or lower price point than that featured at the show. The collection might be designer oriented and better displayed in separate surroundings, or it might be decided that the trade show atmosphere is inappropriate to the merchandise. Figure 10-9 features a permanent manufacturer's showroom.

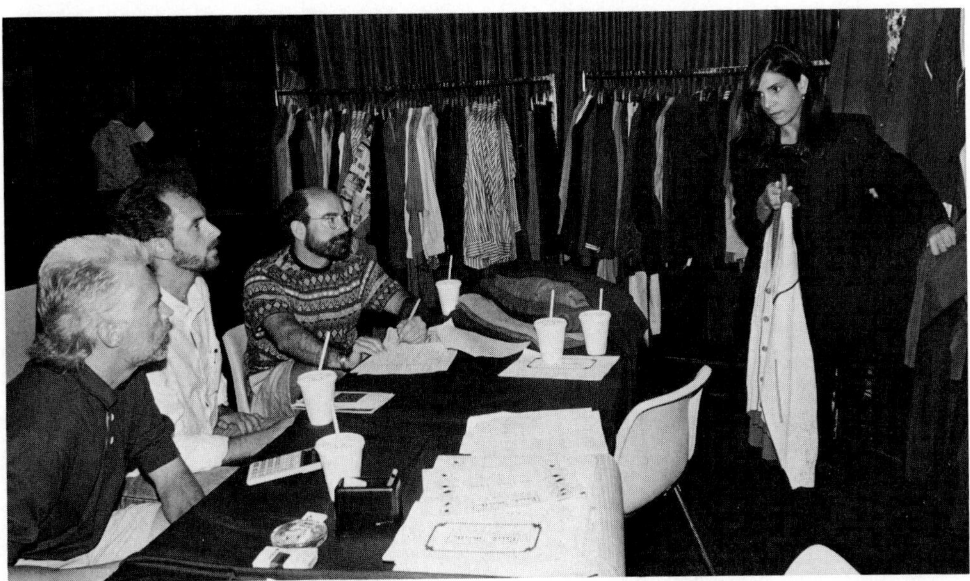

**FIGURE 10-8.** Buyers at Midwest Men's Wear Collective examine a line. *Courtesy:* Chicago Apparel Center.

Whether the sales team is located in the temporary quarters of a trade facility or in a permanent showroom, most manufacturers try to accommodate the buyers in every way to motivate them to buy. Some make available souvenirs with the company logo to serve as a reminder, others provide forms for "taking numbers" similar to the one shown in Table 10-1. The only difference is that the one provided by the manufacturer is assumed to be used for a particular line, while the other is used to recall interesting items featured by many producers in the resident buying office's fashion show. At Pierre Cardin, for example, each buyer receives a silhouette brochure to be used as a reminder of all the shapes available for the season, with pertinent buyer information for each design. The buyer might also use this brochure for "taking numbers" and jotting down notes.

On Friday, the final day of Market Week, the buyer generally returns to the resident buying office to organize the many notes taken on the offerings of the market. Not every item that proved initially interesting can be included in the final purchase requisitions. It is a time to reflect and plan. The office staff is available to answer questions and for further recommendations.

At this point, the buyer assembles all his or her notes and "numbers" and heads for home. It is back to the base of operations where further decision making concerning merchandise considerations must be made. The buyer, assistant buyer, merchandise buyer, and fashion coordinator will review every detail of each item to make sure it fits the store's plan.

It is at this time that the buyer must review all the fundamentals that went into the original plan for the market trip and come to a buying decision. The buyer, at this point, is ready to write the order.

The Tacchini Collection
Gene Graves
Ellen Becker
Robyn Simm
Lingerie by MAJ Enterprises
Mary Ann Cirullo


**FIGURE 10-9.** One of 650 permanent showrooms at the Chicago Apparel Center. *Courtesy:* Chicago apparel Center.

## ACTION FOR THE SMALL STORE BUYER

Too often, buyers for small stores depend on manufacturer's representatives who visit their stores for their merchandise needs. The reasons for resorting to this method of merchandise acquisition are many. Small store buyers are often also the store owners. They have other functions to perform, are fearful of the costs involved in making market trips, or sincerely believe satisfactory merchandise is always available from the vendors who call on them at their stores.

Knowledgeable buying is as important for the small purchaser as it is for the giant retailer. New resources, comparison of lines, and early viewing of merchandise are just some of the reasons for visits to the market. It is true that the small store buyer can feel the pulse of the market through a resident buying office, but first hand visits are necessary to evaluate market conditions.

The big store buyer is generally able to make frequent market visits. The small store counterpart must also make visits, even if they are fewer in number.

The proper timing of the visit is imperative when the number of visits is restricted. Small store buyers should, as a minimum, visit the market prior to each season for major purchases, and use in-store purchasing from visiting sales representatives to fill in the gaps.

It is the inexperienced or unknowing small store buyer who limits the time spent in the market. It is only through a trip to the market that good merchandising skills are honed to a level that is appropriate for competition with the giant retailer or other small retailers.

## SUMMARY OF KEY POINTS

1. A buyer's market is generally located far from the store and thus permits only infrequent visits.
2. Fashion buyers, more than any others, must make market visits because of the ever-changing nature of their merchandise.
3. Prior to the market trip, the buyer must plan in such areas as price line adjustments, assortments, vendor selection, model stock development, and dollar allocations for merchandise.
4. In addition to major market visits, buyers sometimes make interim trips for such purposes as checking out a new resource or selecting a new item to bolster sales.
5. The resident buying office provides services for the store buyer before he or she comes to the market in the form of making personal arrangements, notifying the press of the buyer's arrival, and prescreening lines.
6. Before visiting any resources, the buyer spends time at the resident office for the purpose of briefing, familiarization with current trends, and meetings with the office representatives.
7. The buyer makes the rounds of the market through visits to trade shows and specific manufacturer's showrooms.
8. Buyers generally do not place orders during a market trip, but only "take numbers" for future incorporation into orders.
9. When the buyer returns to the store, all the information gathered at the market is studied for the ultimate decision on purchasing.

## REVIEW QUESTIONS

1. Do most buyers make weekly trips to the market? Why?
2. For what two purposes are major trips generally made to the market?
3. What qualitative and quantitative factors must be analyzed prior to a major market trip?

4. With whom does the store buyer confer prior to the market trip?
5. In cases where major changes in merchandising policies are made, who would accompany the buyer on the market visit?
6. How does the resident buying office assist the buyer prior to his or her visits?
7. Why do resident buyers prescreen lines for the store buyers?
8. Define Market Week.
9. What purpose does the general meeting at the resident office serve for the buyer on the first day of visit?
10. If there are several meetings for the buyer on the first day of Market Week, why are individual conferences arranged?
11. Why do buyers from different stores feel comfortable in exchanging their ideas with other store buyers?
12. Name the two major men's wear trade shows.
13. Discuss "taking numbers."
14. For what reason do some manufacturers choose not to show their lines at the trade shows?
15. When do the buyers place their orders?

## CASE PROBLEM

Collins and Frost is a medium-sized department store located in northeastern Texas. It has a main or flagship store and three branches, all of which are within a radius of 70 miles of the main store. C and F, as it is known by the trade as well as its customers, is merchandised through its main store. At the head of the merchandising division is the general merchandise manager, Mary Cole, who supervises three divisional merchandise managers, one of whom is Jerry Williams, the DMM for all men's wear. As is the case with these organizations, each DMM is responsible for a number of buyers. At C and F there are 12 buyers, 3 of whom are men's wear division buyers.

For the past three years, Connie Rogers, the men's clothing buyer, has noticed a greater demand for men's designer suits and sportcoats. With each year's purchases, she has increased her initial orders for designer goods. At the last divisional meeting, Connie expressed her thoughts on the expansion of her department to feature a designer boutique. She feels that the steady increase in demand for such merchandise certainly warrants the new direction. Jerry Williams is in agreement and has taken the concept to Mary Cole, who has the ultimate responsibility for such decisions.

At this point, the merchandising division is in total agreement on the establishment of a men's boutique. The GMM and DMM want a little more input from other sources before making a final decision. They have directed the buyer,

Connie Rogers, to plan a trip to the market to gather more information pertinent to the department's new emphasis.

## Questions

1. Who should accompany Connie to the market?
2. With whom should they meet for general input? Why?
3. Should they visit their designer resources? Why?
4. Would you suggest they actually open the new boutique? Why?

# Chapter 11

# EVALUATING AND BUYING FROM FOREIGN MARKETS

## LEARNING OBJECTIVES

*Upon completion of this chapter, the student should be able to:*

1. List five reasons for purchasing foreign merchandise.
2. Explain the disadvantage related to the delivery of foreign goods.
3. Discuss seven other problems involved in purchasing from foreign sources.
4. Differentiate among four methods of purchasing from foreign vendors.
5. Explain the past growth and future trends of foreign purchasing.

## INTRODUCTION

Thirty-five years ago the purchase of foreign merchandise was generally restricted to particular types of goods as well as a limited number of retailers. Paris has consistently been a desirable market for the elite stores that purchase *haute couture* (high-fashion merchandise). This is by no means new. However, with the advent of the jet age, the various markets of the world have become more accessible. Goods from foreign lands have become common in the assortments offered for sale by stores not accustomed to carrying them. The merchandise currently being sold is no longer restricted to high-fashion goods, but includes the vast assortment of items, in every price range, that is found in the conventional department store.

The outlook for continued growth in the purchase of imported merchandise seems good. The implications of such merchandise are many for the retailer. What does the rest of the world offer to American buyers that they cannot find at home? In this chapter, attention will focus on the reasons for foreign purchasing, the arrangements available for purchase of such goods, the problems inherent in purchasing foreign-made merchandise, and the major foreign markets.

## REASONS FOR PURCHASING FOREIGN MERCHANDISE

American markets offer retailers an assortment of merchandise that cuts across almost every classification. From automobiles to fashion merchandise, and everything between the two, America has consistently provided limitless quantities of imaginative as well as functional items. Why, then, does the contemporary retailer continue to increase the amount of foreign made goods it offers in its inventory? Certainly it is easy to "cover" the domestic scene and convenient to buy goods produced at home. Foreign buying has increased for a number of reasons.

### Lower Cost

Merchandise found abroad that is comparable in quality, variety, and innovativeness to American-made goods often is less expensive. Contributing to the lower costs is the fact that usually the raw materials in the production of goods come from abroad and the factory workers are often paid far less than their American counterparts. For example, manufacturers produce their own brands "off shore" to compete with domestically produced men's clothing. By using materials produced there and paying wages much below our standards, they are able to offer American buyers merchandise comparable to American-made goods at significantly lower prices. In stores where fashion as well as lower price is of paramount importance to the consumer, carrying this imported merchandise could mean greater sales. Macy's, for example, produces its Alfani menswear in Korea. This reliance on foreign-made goods has enabled it to continue its fashion merchandising policy, while at the same time featuring prices somewhat below those of comparable domestic goods.

Lower price is by no means limited to imported men's wear. Merchandise of just about every variety, such as cameras, television receivers, women's wear, shoes, knitted goods, and home furnishings, is often available at prices somewhat lower than buyers could find at home.

## Quality

It should be understood that the United States can and does produce an abundance of quality merchandise. However, certain countries have consistently produced goods that are considered to be superior to ours. The reasons for the exceptional quality are many. First, the natural resources of a country might contribute to its quality. For example, Belgian linen is the finest in the world. The reason for this is that the pure water necessary for extremely fine linen is found only in the Coutral area of Belgium. Similarly, the quality of the mulberry leaves fed to silkworms for the production of silk is best in Japan.

Second, craftsmanship accounts for the quality of merchandise produced in some countries. Few can compete with the ability of the Irish in the creation of fine linen garments or the ability of Germany to produce lenses. The expertise involved in the production of the Rolls Royce automobile is found almost exclusively in Great Britain. Finally, the time necessary for the production of some goods is simply impossible in the United States at our hourly rate. A Persian rug, for example, might require a year of hand work.

## Greater Profit

The more efficient the organization, the greater the profit it will achieve. Efficiency can be increased in a number of ways. More efficient purchasing can contribute to greater profits. Goods produced in foreign countries often afford retailers higher markups (markup = retail − cost). This does not mean that the buyer can recklessly mark merchandise at whim; there is a great deal of competition in foreign merchandise. But there are occasions when buyers can purchase special goods that they intend to mark up more than usual. Retailers with the necessary financial resources can scout markets less frequented by most buyers. In fact, a large user such as a department store chain can bring an article to a foreign producer to have it produced for its exclusive use. Promising to buy all the manufacturer's production of the item guarantees the purchaser freedom from competition. This enables the buyer to work on a higher markup, and if the goods sell, a greater profit will be realized.

Many of the giant retailers are entering the foreign market to purchase the private label merchandise (goods sold only under the store's name) they used to buy domestically. The foreign-made product usually costs less than it would in the United States. "Bargain" television receivers are now purchased abroad by large stores and sold under private labels at lower prices; at the same time, they carry higher markups, which are attainable because of the exclusive arrangement that limits competition.

## Prestige

There is a segment of the consuming public that is enthralled with the notion of owning prestigious merchandise. This might be inconsistent with the advantage of a lower price. True, some goods from abroad are less expensive, but certain types of merchandise from foreign countries are available in extremely limited quantities, are expensive or are exquisitely designed and thus command an aura of prestige. For many years Paris has been known to fashion-conscious consumers as the fashion center of the world. Women discuss their Ungaros, La Croixs, Diors, and Chanels with the same excitement as football enthusiasts holding tickets to the Super Bowl. Women's wear bearing labels from Paris, bone china from Great Britain, and the man's suit made on Savile Row all provide interest to those so inclined. Figure 11-1 features a design that fits the prestigious haute couture category.

Wishing to satisfy customers who want prestigious merchandise, many retailers regularly feature such goods. To increase the air of excitement, some retailers produce periodic fashion shows to present their prestigious imported collections. These showings are often "by invitation only," which contributes significantly to the enjoyment of those interested in such goods. The

**FIGURE 11-1.** Ungaro Couture design *Courtesy:* Bloomingdale's.

merchandising of such goods is limited to a very few retailers, since the costs are high and the acquisition of such merchandise is costly and time consuming.

### Unavailability of Merchandise in the United States

Very often retailers find the need to round out their merchandise assortments with items that are unique to certain countries. For example, a growing number of specialty food stores feature foreign-made foods. Only these foods will satisfy the tastes and needs of some customers. While it is certainly recognized that domestic caviar will suffice for the typical American, the gourmet will not consider anything but Russian caviar. Likewise, hand-made jewelry from the Orient cannot be imitated in the United States without changing the methods of production and raising the cost. Hand-carved picture frames are extremely desirable and found in abundance in Mexico at extremely favorable prices. Duplication of such frames domestically would make their cost prohibitive.

Although copies of just about anything can be produced in the United States, the imitation usually comes off a poor substitute. Thus when merchandise at a desirable price and quality is unavailable in our own country, buyers very often scout distant markets in search of different wares.

### The Search for Fashion Trends

The highly sophisticated "jet setter" is often not satisfied with fashion that is accepted by the masses. Retailers such as Saks Fifth Avenue, Bloomingdale's, Neiman-Marcus, Gump's, and Bergdorf Goodman, which cater to the affluent, must constantly be "ahead" of fashion. To prepare themselves and their clientele with suitable merchandise, the buyers must formulate a fashion sense. This preparation often includes trips to the fashion markets of the world, such as Paris, where fashion has originated for decades. After making these visits, buyers are better able to accommodate the desires of their *haute couture* customers.

These trips abroad not only provide a buyer with the fashion direction for the upcoming season, but also enrich him or her with information that is relevant to the promotion of such merchandise. Since the sale of high-fashion, avant-garde merchandise often necessitates promotions that will tempt potential customers' appetites, the trips abroad can also serve the buyer in his or her capacity as a sales promoter.

## PROBLEMS RELATED TO FOREIGN PURCHASING

Although purchasing from foreign countries does afford the buyer the opportunity to significantly broaden both resources and the merchandise assortment, the problems inherent in imported merchandise are many. This does not mean that foreign goods are inappropriate, but it does underscore the fact that caution is necessary before a commitment is made. Buyers must weigh these disadvantages against the advantages and determine whether or not the purchase is worthwhile.

### Delivery

Buyers anticipate their needs and must make certain that attention is paid to their open-to-buy at all times. Since prompt delivery is extremely important to the buyer in preparing an open-to-buy and in satisfying merchandise needs, he or she must exercise extreme caution in placing orders. While it isn't always possible to guarantee delivery for domestic merchandise, the problem is compounded in the purchase of imported goods. This, as well as the inability satisfactorily to check on shipments, may contribute to delivery delays. It is not uncommon for a dock strike to tie up delivery for extensive periods.

Even the most careful planner cannot always foresee problems that might delay the delivery of goods. The buyer might have planned a promotion involving the imported goods, only to find that the promised delivery date could not be met. Buyers who make extensive use of merchandise from abroad must allow for all sorts of unforeseen problems so that they will not be caught with a delivery problem. How frightening it would be for the buyer who had planned an "import bazaar" promotional campaign to find that the merchandise will not arrive as scheduled!

### Quality Variations

The very nature of buying from foreign resources could prove to be troublesome in terms of the quality of the goods. Often the goods are ordered by a description, sample, or illustration, and when the delivery is made the merchandise is different than anticipated. The return of such merchandise might not only be difficult because of the time and the distance involved, but damage to the department can be realized in "short" inventories. Quality has been known to vary with each reorder even in American-made merchandise. However, experience shows that foreign merchandise presents the greater risk.

### Reorders

The key to the buyer's success usually lies in the ability to select merchandise that will be ordered again and again. It is this merchandise that helps the buyer maintain the markup necessary to show a profit. Lead time to guarantee delivery of reorders is virtually impossible. If the item is a staple such as a food product that is used all the time, the problem might be overcome through sizable reorders that allow for long delivery periods. This is fine as long as the item will continue to be in demand. In the case of seasonal goods, however, the reorder is virtually impossible. For example, the Italian-made bulky sweater might sell fantastically, but will require a delivery promise of three months for the reorder. In that case, the season could be over before the reorder arrives.

Buyers of such merchandise must fully comprehend the selling period for their merchandise and realize that promptly filled reorders are the exception rather than the rule.

## Early Selection of Colors

Fashion buyers are confronted with making color selections as part of their job. This is a necessary function. They can perform the job more efficiently by familiarizing themselves with color information. The information is available in both trade and consumer magazines, trade papers such as *Women's Wear Daily*, fashion-reporting services, and so forth. The only hitch is that this color news is not usually available at the time it is necessary to place orders for imported merchandise. Information is available for making judgments on domestic goods but not on foreign orders, because of the long lead time necessary to guarantee delivery of the imports.

## Size Discrepancy

Measurements vary from country to country. Those of Americans are the largest in the world. Thus shoes imported from France might not be salable to Americans, who require larger sizes. Goods purchased from the Orient might be in proportions not commensurate with the American figure. The actual sizes may also vary. A man wishing to buy a pair of shoes or a suit manufactured in Great Britain will find that they have no resemblance to our size structure.

In recent years, buyers have approached the size problem. Retailers who purchase in significant quantities can supply foreign producers with exact measurements or patterns. In this way they can capture the flavor of foreign design while making certain their American customers will be accommodated. When specification of size structure is impossible, buyers must exercise extreme care in their purchases. Failure to do so could result in an assortment of merchandise unsuitable for the American figure.

## Money Allocation

When buying from American manufacturers, retailers pay for goods in advance of shipment. Frequently manufacturers abroad insist on part payment for the goods at the time the order is placed. It should be clearly understood that this capital could be tied up for a long period. Retailers with limited capital might find such arrangements unprofitable. Even in situations in which money is required only at the time of delivery, there could be long delays. Thus capital might also be tied up for long periods.

## Time Involved

Visits abroad might require more time than it would take to cover the American markets. Aside from the distance, foreign markets are not as convenient geographically as American markets. Buyers on the American scene who might cover their resources in a matter of days might find equal coverage in foreign places taking twice the time. Even in the Paris fashion market, the couturiers are so spread out that it is difficult to move easily from one to the other. In other lines of goods, investigation of a few lines of merchandise might require movement through several different cities. Buyers with limited time to spend away from their duties and responsibilities could find coverage of the foreign market an impossible task.

## Capital Risk

Since the goods available for purchase from foreign countries are sold in currencies other than American dollars, a great deal of risk is involved in such purchases. The American dollar is worth different amounts at different times, with considerable fluctuation always a possibility. The American dollar fluctuates constantly in what it can purchase in foreign countries. Such changes could cause considerable problems for the buyer. For example, an item that could be considered a bargain at the time it is ordered could prove to be prohibitively expensive at the time when payment must be made because of money fluctuation. Extreme caution is the only approach for the buyer who must deal in foreign markets.

## Determining the Actual Cost

The price quoted for foreign merchandise generally reflects only the price that is charged by the producer. This is by no means the final cost of the goods. A number of factors must be considered to determine how much the buyer will actually pay for the purchase. One consideration is the delivery charge. Since the shipping distance might be considerable, transportation costs will undoubtedly be higher than for the domestic acquisition. Buyers in need of quick delivery must be fully aware of the expense of airfreight. Another consideration is the amount of duty that will be added to the actual purchase price. Complete understanding of customs duties is of paramount importance, since there is a great deal of variation according to the merchandise in question. A detailed discussion of import duties will take place in Chapter 12, Developing Import Programs. Items such as insurance for the goods, packing charges, and storage expense will also increase the actual price of merchandise.

Before the buyer finalizes a foreign purchase plan, a detailed computation to determine the *landed cost* should be undertaken. The landed cost is the actual cost of the goods to the retailer. Determination of landed cost is important so that the buyer can figure at what price he or she must finally retail the goods to realize a profit. Sometimes the buyer might decide in the final analysis that while the initial cost was appropriate for purchase, the landed cost was prohibitive in the ultimate cost of the merchandise to the consumer.

It might be assumed that seasoned buyers can automatically calculate the landed cost by adding a "typical percentage" to the initial cost. But what appears to be a simple expense for storage can turn out to be much greater because of an unexpected storage period.

The following is an example of the landed cost for the purchase of Italian men's accessories.

| | |
|---|---|
| Initial cost: 100 ties @ 8,000 lire each | 800,000 |
| 100 ties @ 10,000 lire each | 1,000,000 |
| Total initial cost | 1,800,000 |
| Less: 2 % discount | 36,000 |
| | 1,764,000 |
| Packing charge | 18,600 |
| 7 % commission (on initial cost) | 126,000 |
| Shipping charge | 90,400 |
| Storage | 16,800 |
| | 2,015,800 |
| Duty: 30 % (estimated) on initial cost | |
| Plus: packing charge | 558,600 |
| Total landed cost (lire) | 2,574,400 |

The buyer then must translate the Italian currency into American dollars at the current exchange rate. Since the exchange rates fluctuate on a daily basis, sometimes the costs might not be worth the effort of the purchase.

## Cost of Promotion

Nationally advertised goods are immediately known and accepted by a nucleus of the consuming public. The buyer's promotional budget (to be discussed in Chapter 16) is often enriched by cooperative advertising allowances. Even without the allowance, such goods generally require less promotion because of the consumer's awareness of the merchandise. Foreign merchandise, on the other hand, is often unfamiliar to the customer. To guarantee its acceptance, it is sometimes necessary to appropriate large amounts for promotional purposes, since foreign suppliers rarely give advertising allowances. Not only must larger than usual dollar amounts be expended, but the buyer must have specialists at home who can prepare a promotional campaign. It should be understood that not all imports require this careful attention. Every fashion-conscious customer immediately recognizes the Dior label, but an imported calculator might not be a household word and might require above-average promotional exposure.

The problems discussed thus far are by no means the only ones that could occur when foreign-made goods are purchased. Others, such as an additional expense attributed to larger than anticipated buying expenditures, damaged or soiled merchandise, or goods lost in shipping, are possibilities. Both apparent and unforeseen problems must be considered to ensure the success of the buyer's import purchases.

## METHODS USED IN THE PURCHASE OF FOREIGN GOODS

The purchasing in question may be achieved in any of a number of ways. The choice of methods is determined by such factors as the size of the company, the proportion of imported goods in relation to the store's total merchandise inventory, the time the buyer is allotted for the pursuit of merchandise, the size of the foreign markets, their distance from the United States, and the cost involved in the procurement of such goods.

Having examined these factors, buyers decide to accomplish their foreign purchasing in one of the following ways.

### Visits to the Foreign Market

This method of foreign merchandise procurement is restricted to the very large retail organizations. Buyers who represent department store and chain organizations in the United States frequent the foreign markets at regular intervals. It is not uncommon for large companies to send teams of key executives such as merchandise managers, buyers, and assistants on foreign buying expeditions. Very often the purchases involve significant expenditures as well as careful planning and necessitate a team effort.

Buyers can familiarize themselves with foreign markets through the U. S. Department of Commerce as well as by corresponding with the commerce departments of the countries in question. Many large retailers maintain relationships with foreign representatives, who plan for the American buyers' visits in much the same manner as resident buying offices in the United States. Figure 11-2 features a trade paper ad announcing numerous market exhibitions.

Although the availability of foreign merchandise cuts across just about every classification of goods, it is the fashion buyer who puts the most time and effort into visits to foreign markets. So demanding is the merchandising of fashion items that only through direct negotiation can the buyer execute a proper buying plan.

Buyers wishing to attend the "opening" of foreign lines must prepare well in advance of the trip. Plane reservations, hotel accommodations, and buying appointments must be attended to early. Some countries have organizations that regulate their industries, and are able to provide buyers with such pertinent information as vendors' locations, dates and times of merchandise presentation, and the like. No group in all the foreign markets plays as important a role in the regulation of an industry as the Chambre Syndicale de la Parisienne in its regulation of the fashion industry in Paris. Chambre Syndicale offers

*A selection of international fashion and textile trade events: For details, consult the local trade office at the Consulate of the host country.*

**BARCELONA:**
Oct. 16-19, 1992 Mostra de Tejidos (textiles)

**DUBAI (U.A.R.):**
Oct. 24-27, 1992 MOTEXA
(textiles & ready-to-wear)

**HONG KONG:**
Oct. 30-Nov. 2, 1992 Int'l Footwear, Handbags & Leather Goods Fair
Nov. 4-6, 1991 Interstoff Asia (textiles)
July 3-6, 1992 International Apparel Fair

**OSAKA:**
Nov. 4-6, 1991 TechTextil Asia (technology)

**HONG KONG:**
Jan. 13-16, 1992 Hong Kong Fashion Week

**TORONTO:**
Jan. 26-28, 1992 Mode Accessories International

**PARIS:**
Feb. 1-4, 1992 SISEL (sportswear)

**BARCELONA:**
Feb. T.B.A., 1992 Gaudí-Mujer

**DUSSELDORF:**
Feb. 2-4, 1992 Collections Premiers

**MILAN:**
Feb. 7-11, 1992 Modit (contemporary)

**TOKYO:**
Feb. 12-14, 1992
U.S. Ready-To-Wear Exhibition

**LONDON:**
Feb. 14-19, 1992 The London Show

**MONTREAL:**
Feb. 23-25, 1992 Quebec Market Week

**DUSSELDORF:**
March 8-11, 1992 IGEDO

**FRANKFURT:**
April 7-9, 1992 Interstoff (textiles)

**MOSCOW:**
June 6-9, 1992 Consumtech (all consumer goods) ■

**FIGURE 11-2.** A trade paper listing of international merchandise show. *Courtesy:* California Apparel News.

membership only to countries who meet certain specific requirements. Its jurisdiction includes rules concerning sale of merchandise, copying, and times that members can show their lines to prospective buyers. Such involvement helps protect the buyers in their purchasing endeavors and also enables them to attend all the important openings without having to choose between two lines being shown simultaneously. Many professional purchasers enjoy their buying experiences in Paris because the market is regulated by Chambre Syndicale.

It should be borne in mind that direct visits to other foreign countries also provide the buyer with advantages unavailable when buying at home through a middleman. Later in the chapter an overview of the principal foreign markets will be presented.

## Commissionaires—Foreign Resident Buyers

Unable to travel abroad to purchase merchandise, some buyers accomplish the task through specialists called *commissionaires.* These people also provide meaningful service for the American buyer who travels abroad. The counterpart of the American resident buyer, the commissionaire operates in foreign markets, scouting them for the best available merchandise. Being permanently located in these markets gives the commissionaire an edge. Whereas the American buyer might spend only a week abroad and is limited in both time and familiarity with the market, the foreign representative spends all his or her time in the market.

For a commission, generally 7 percent of total purchases, the commissionaire provides a variety of services such as purchase of new items, reordering of goods that have sold and are still available, arrangements for merchandise storage and transportation, and assistance to store buyers who visit foreign markets in their search for merchandise.

It should be mentioned that while the commissionaire provides valuable assistance in the procurement of imported merchandise, this method should be used with extreme caution. For example, permitting the commissionaire to purchase new merchandise might result in goods not really suitable for the American consumer. Whenever the commissionaire is used, the buyer must make certain that specific instructions are provided because any errors become the responsibility of the store buyer.

The very large domestic resident offices are represented in the major foreign markets throughout the world by exclusive commissionaires. Such American-operated offices are known as *foreign purchasing agents.* For example, Frederick Atkins, Inc., plays an important role in bringing import merchandise to its member stores, including such companies as The Broadway, Los Angeles; and R. H. Stearns, Boston.

Through its foreign division, Frederick Atkins International, the company offers commissionaire representation in such countries as Japan, England, Switzerland, Belgium, France, and Italy and anywhere the fashion market is "hot." These agents recommend items to the Frederick Wholesale Corporation for wholesale purchase programs. They also assist in the development of a particular item, arrange for negotiation of purchase contracts with foreign producers, and provide follow-up services on all orders.

While commissionaires usually work on a commission basis, some occasionally work for fixed fees when they perform exclusively for one organization.

## Importers

A study of the various methods by which foreign-made goods come into retail stores indicates that a significant number of wholesalers import merchandise specifically for this purpose. As the need for such goods has increased, the number of import wholesalers has also increased.

Merchandise available from the import wholesaler costs the retailer a little more than if the goods were acquired through a direct visit. It should be understood, however, the extra cost is certainly more appealing to the small retailer than the expense incurred by a trip abroad. When purchases are relatively small but the need still exists for foreign goods, the import wholesaler is the best solution for the buyer. Like traditional wholesalers of consumer goods, import wholesalers make available many lines of merchandise. This enables the retailer to compare foreign offerings without having to leave the wholesaler's warehouse.

Some buyers even argue that purchase through wholesalers does not involve higher cost. They believe the prices paid are not really higher because of the quantity discounts available to the wholesaler. Since the wholesaler pays a lower price than that usually paid by the retailer, the final price is not as high as it might appear to be.

Import wholesalers sometimes offer a wide variety of general merchandise, ranging from hard goods to soft goods and often including foodstuffs. Generally, however, these wholesalers restrict their offerings to specialties such as clothing, food, or appliances.

While the typical customer of the import wholesaler is the smaller retailer without access to the goods, the larger store in need of a particular item for immediate delivery sometimes uses this type of resource.

## Import Fairs

To service customers who cannot go abroad in search of merchandise, foreign producers have organized trade fairs at various locations in the United States to show their wares to retail store buyers. New York, for example, has been the scene of import fairs that offer a wide variety of photographic and recording equipment to retailers. The New York Prêt show staged semiannually in New York City features fashion merchandise. Figures 11-3 and 11-4 depict activity at the Prêt.

This type of selling is gaining in popularity and is being used throughout the country.

**FIGURE 11-3.** Buyers register for New York Prêt Fair. *Courtesy:* AETEC.

**FIGURE 11-4.** Buyers examine an import collection. *Courtesy:* AETEC.

### A RETAIL BUYING FOCUS

*New York Prêt*

Twice each year, the New York Prêt draws together leading designers and manufacturers from around the world for three days in New York City. More than 25,000 buyers and merchandisers attend these preview showings of apparel and accessories collections.

For two decades, the New York Prêt has helped launch the careers of new designers and made viewing simple for potential buyers of the lines. Under one roof, the retail buyer can examine each vendor's offerings individually in separate booths or get a taste of the flavor of the upcoming season by attending a variety of runway fashion shows.

In addition to making it simpler to see a host of American lines in one facility rather than having to go from showroom to showroom to preview merchandise, the New York Prêt features several hundred merchandise collections from all over the world. Lines such as Ansich Mode (Korea), Formosa Silk Development Co. Ltd. (Taipei), Friends Circle International Trading Corp. (Bangladesh), Kobo Ai (Japan), Krister Follin (Canada), Monos (Italy), and Vic Wood (Austria) are housed in a special international section that makes the purchase of imports easy to accomplish. While buyers for the major retail department stores and specialty chains often visit numerous offshore markets for merchandise acquisition, it is out of the question, because of costs and time limitations, for small merchants to go abroad. This show enables even the smallest boutique to avail itself of foreign designs.

Aside from offering a forum for American buyers to purchase goods from abroad, the New York Prêt also affords the foreign retail buyer an opportunity to purchase internationally designed collections. Examination of the 1991 roster of buyers from foreign countries indicates that the show is truly an international fair. About 20 percent of the total number of buyers represent retailers from such countries as Canada, Mexico, Great Britain, Japan, South Africa, Italy, France, Venezuela, and Australia.

AETEC, the sponsor of the New York Prêt, provides a great deal of services for the attending buyers in addition to the assembling of lines. It offers travel arrangements, hotel accommodations, and anything that would help the attendee to make the visit more profitable.

## Private Foreign Buying Offices

Some retail organizations have the capacity to deal in imported merchandise at such high levels that they find it beneficial to operate buying offices in foreign countries for their exclusive use. These offices are constantly searching for merchandise that will appeal to their home stores as well as seeking manufacturers to produce merchandise according to buyer specifications. Very often the American buyer finds an item that is available in the United States but that he or she would like to have produced abroad at a lower cost. The giant retailers, whose volumes permit such an arrangement, maintain foreign offices.

Unless a company is committed to substantial foreign merchandise purchases, the cost of operating a private office is prohibitive. Companies like the Associated Merchandising Corporation (AMC) have private representation because of their extensive interest in foreign goods.

The amount of foreign-made merchandise that comes into our country has been increasing each year. From all indications, the trend will continue, with buyers making even more use of the various techniques we have described.

## THE MAJOR FOREIGN MARKETS

Each year sees a tremendous increase not only in the amount of merchandise imported from abroad, but also in the number of foreign markets from which retailers are purchasing. For years, when retailers thought of foreign markets, Paris was the first city to come to mind. It is true that Paris is still considered by many to be the fashion center of the world, but it is by no means the only market abroad that offers fashion merchandise. Buyers travel far and wide to satisfy not only their fashion appetites but also their other merchandising needs, for such items as furniture, foods, cameras, television receivers, crystal, dinnerware, silverware, pottery, artificial flowers, and raffia baskets.

The following list includes the major foreign markets in which American buyers are currently satisfying their import needs.

| *EUROPE AND THE MIDDLE EAST* | | *CENTRAL AND SOUTH AMERICA* | *FAR EAST* |
|---|---|---|---|
| England | Italy | Colombia | Japan |
| Germany | Israel | Argentina | Hong Kong |
| Austria | Portugal | Mexico | Taiwan |
| Belgium | Spain | Brazil | Korea |
| Denmark | Switzerland | Venezuela | India |
| France | Sweden | | Philippines |
| Greece | Finland | | Thailand |

The importance of these markets may be seen from the fact that such resident organizations as Frederick Atkins, Inc., and AMC have representation in all of them.

## ACTION FOR THE SMALL STORE BUYER

Buying merchandise that has been produced by other countries, as we know, gives the buyer certain advantages. Not the least of these are better prices, quality, and prestige. While the major stores regularly have their buyers cover markets all over the world, the small store hasn't the time or dollar commitment for such trips.

Small store buyers in many merchandise classifications can avail themselves of such goods without ever leaving the country. Items of this nature can be purchased through wholesalers who specialize in foreign-produced goods. Many of these companies represent foreign producers in showrooms throughout the country. Another route to take in the purchase of imports is attendance at import fairs. Buyers can learn about the dates, times, and places by reading the appropriate trade papers. Resident buying offices, through permanent branch offices in foreign countries, or by commissionaire affiliation, often make imports available to their member stores.

By using any of these methods of acquisition, small store buyers can avail themselves of goods from international markets. They should, however, recognize such problems as possible variation in quality, slow delivery, difficulty with reorders, and price instability due to fluctuation of the dollar. Although the small store buyer might believe imports are a necessity, he or she must evaluate the real need for such goods. Very often, equally desirable goods are available from domestic resources. In such instances, the buyer should weigh and measure the benefits of imported goods and determine whether or not they are needed.

## SUMMARY OF KEY POINTS

1. Merchandise from abroad continues to grow in importance in contemporary American retailing.
2. Much merchandise is imported because of lower cost to the retailer.
3. For many years fashion-oriented retailers have purchased foreign-made merchandise strictly on the basis of prestige. Customers are often motivated by the prestigious labels rather than the particular goods.
4. There are many problems inherent in the purchase of goods from abroad, including delivery, reorders, quality control, and early outlay of capital.
5. The determination of the actual cost of imported merchandise is difficult owing to the fluctuation of the dollar.
6. Imported merchandise is subject to tariffs. The rates vary according to merchandise classification and the country from which goods have been purchased.
7. Large retailers generally visit foreign markets to purchase their import lines.
8. Small retailers may purchase foreign-made goods through commissionaires, wholesalers, and import fairs.

## REVIEW QUESTIONS

1. Discuss the outlook for American merchandising of foreign-made merchandise.
2. With all the production and expertise of American manufacturers, why do retailers purchase imports?
3. Cite specific products from abroad that are considered to be superior in quality to domestic goods.
4. In what way can the merchandising of foreign-made items increase the retailer's profit?
5. Is all foreign-made merchandise considered to have prestigious appeal? Discuss.
6. Why is it necessary for buyers to place foreign orders earlier than domestic orders?
7. How have the large retailers overcome the problem of size discrepancy in merchandise?
8. Define the term *landed costs.*
9. Since the tariff on foreign goods is not uniform, how can retailers predetermine the actual amounts?
10. Does it generally cost more or less to promote foreign merchandise than domestically produced goods?
11. Can the American buyer planning a foreign buying trip familiarize himself or herself with the various markets before making the trip?
12. What is the Chambre Syndicale?
13. Describe the role of the commissionaire.
14. Small retailers cannot afford the time and money involved in foreign buying trips. How, then, can they acquire import merchandise?
15. Import fairs are much in evidence in the United States. Discuss their importance to buyers.
16. Is it practical for companies to maintain private offices in foreign countries? Discuss.

## CASE PROBLEM 1

The Clothes Barn is a specialty retailer that operates three small units in Vermont. It has been in business for eight years and caters to an affluent market. Its merchandise offerings include dresses, coats, suits, sportswear, and accessories for the discriminating woman. Its reputation as a fashion leader has been established. Merchandise is purchased from prestigious manufacturers in the United States. In her continuous search for fashionable merchandise, Lisa Stone, the head buyer, has visited all the important markets in the United States. In the past few months exciting foreign goods have come to her attention through trade papers and customer requests. Much as she would like to satisfy her own curiosity and her customer's requests, there isn't sufficient money or time available for her to make trips abroad.

Management has suggested purchasing through importers. While this might be appropriate for some companies, Ms. Stone believes the store's reputation was achieved through careful merchandise selection and that such a plan would permit outsiders to make the merchandising decision. Now the need for imports has become keen, but the problem still needs a solution.

### Questions

1. Evaluate the possibility of the store's hiring a buyer solely for the purpose of foreign buying.
2. How could Ms. Stone remain at home yet still make her own purchases of foreign merchandise?

## CASE PROBLEM 2

First and Best, a supermarket chain, is located in the metropolitan New York City area. It has 12 units and is considered to be one of the finest supermarket chains in the area. Since it is small compared to its competitors, First and Best has been able to cater more carefully to the needs of customers. Its clientele, more affluent than typical supermarket customers, is offered such services as free delivery, telephone orders, and charge privileges.

In an effort to cater more fully to the needs of customers, the general merchandise manager has suggested that the company organize gourmet departments featuring foods of all nations. The company's owner is against the new program, protesting that purchasing foreign goods would present such problems as undependable delivery, large outlays of capital, enormous time spent purchasing the merchandise, and so forth. Further, he believes that America produces a sufficient variety of foods to satisfy even the most discriminating person's needs.

### Questions

1. What arguments could be used to support the merchandiser's position?
2. If the company agreed to the new plan, how would you suggest that it initially merchandise gourmet foods from all nations?

# Chapter 12

# DEVELOPING IMPORT PROGRAMS

## LEARNING OBJECTIVES

*Upon completion of the chapter, the student should be able to:*

1. Discuss the difference between purchasing ready-made merchandise abroad and the retailer's development of personal import programs.
2. Explain the government's role in the importing of merchandise by retail organizations.
3. Differentiate between dutiable merchandise and duty-free merchandise.
4. Describe the U.S. quota system for imports and why some goods are not bound by quotas.
5. List and describe the six qualifications that are considered to be beneficial to those who purchase abroad.
6. Plan and produce an itinerary for the buyer who is to purchase offshore.
7. Explain the various stages in the securing and use of letters of credit.
8. Define such terms as chief value, C.I.F., counter sample, tariff, exchange rate, and specification buying, all of which are commonly referred to in import buying.
9. Cite the import aspects addressed in the planning of a purchasing trip to a foreign country.
10. Discuss the importance of the "follow-up" in the purchasing of imports.

## INTRODUCTION

Careful examination of the merchandise at many of the retail giants indicates that the foreign label is more dominant than ever. The Burberry raincoat, a mainstay of the highly regarded British manufacturer, can be found in just about every fine shop in the United States that features top-of-the line rainwear. The line is by no means exclusive with any particular area merchant. Similarly, other well-known foreign labels and brands are integral parts of the model stocks of retailers.

As we have learned in the preceding chapter, prestige, quality, and price are some of the reasons cited for including this merchandise in American inventories. The lines which consumers know are stocked for these reasons. There is, however, a great deal of merchandise bearing the imported label that is generally unfamiliar to the consuming public. Labels that have a foreign ring fill the racks, but their names are not household words. In fact, unlike the famous foreign labels that abound in the American retail establishments, the newcomers may be found in only one company's offerings. Is it likely that the producer from abroad is relying on exclusive distribution in the United States, or is there some new approach to acquiring foreign produced goods? No, the manufacturer from abroad is not generally restricting a label to one company—the retailers are now in the game of developing their own lines of merchandise for import into the United States.

With the recent trend toward dominance by the giants of the retailing industry continuing, a widespread practice for these retailers is to become actively involved in producing merchandise for their exclusive use. Companies like The Limited, Inc., with divisions such as The Limited, Limited Express, Victoria's Secret, Lane Bryant, and Lerner Shops, and an overall total of approximately 2000 individual units, have entered the importing game on a grand scale. With outlets all across the United States, The Limited can easily dispose of more units of merchandise than most private manufacturers produce and sell to retailers. Through this practice, style as well as price can be controlled, and labels can be developed that are available only in their own stores. We have already learned about the importance of private label merchandise, of which this is a part, but there is a major difference being practiced by some such as The Limited. While most stores make arrangements to have outside manufacturers produce special items for their exclusive purchase, The Limited and others like them are involved in many aspects of the production of these goods. Unlike the typical store buyer who makes the trip abroad to purchase finished products, this new breed is involved in purchasing materials and trim as well as the ultimate styles that are manufactured.

In this chapter, attention will focus on retailers' development of their own import programs, the complications associated with the concept, the role of the buyer in the procedure, and the qualifications needed by these buyers to be able to participate in such a demanding undertaking.

## THE GOVERNMENT'S ROLE

While these importing programs offer significant benefits to those retailers who participate, they cannot operate as freely and as easily as they could if the production were done in the United States. First, it is important to understand why offshore production is undertaken. Some retailers say the lead time necessary to produce merchandise is less in some foreign countries, while others imply that the technology abroad is more sophisticated, and thus more creativity in manufacturing is attainable. Most will agree, however, that price is the dominant factor. In many of these markets, Hong Kong and Korea in particular, labor costs are significantly lower than ours. This enables the importing retailer to pay less for the merchandise and realize a greater profit. Figure 12-1 features the Hong Kong market, a major source for fashion merchandise.

Uncontrolled offshore production could easily destroy our domestic market and would lead to the eventual unemployment of our factory workers. Who would be able to compete with the price of merchandise manufactured by people who work at rates that are unheard of in the United States? In an attempt to avoid the disastrous results of such free trade, the U.S. government has imposed numerous restrictions on those who produce abroad and import their own goods. Through a variety of governmental measures, the unfair advantage of foreign competition has somewhat eased what could be the total downfall of American-made merchandise.

**FIGURE 12-1.** Hong Kong—a major offshore market for fashion merchandise *Courtesy:* Helaine Grossman.

## Duty Assessment

Most of the merchandise that is imported into the United States is subject to duty. Some, such as antiques, are duty-free; no tariff is charged for their entry into the country. The duty rate imposed on merchandise is a percentage of its appraised value. The rates of duty vary according to merchandise classification and the country of origin. Most goods are dutiable under the most favored nation (MFN) rates. Merchandise imported from countries which do not have this status is charged a significantly higher rate. There are rate concessions given to goods that come from least developed, developing countries (LDDC). Duty-free status is also available for specific items from developing countries.

Table 12-1 features an excerpted portion of the tariff schedules of the United States. In reading the chart it should be noted that column 1 lists the rates for the most favored nations and column 2 for those who do not enjoy that status. Comparing the identical items in each column, it is obvious that importing from the most favored nations affords the importer greatly reduced duty assessments. The term "free" in the columns indicates that no tariff is levied, no matter what the country of origin.

The rates charged are determined by the U.S. Customs Service. The stated rates change from time to time and should always be checked prior to importing merchandise. The Tariff and Trade Act of 1984 introduced significant changes in

**TABLE 12-1** Sample tariff schedules of the United States

| | | *RATES OF DUTY* | |
|---|---|---|---|
| *Article 3* | *Units of Quantity* | *Preferential Countries* | *Nonpreferential Countries* |
| Bamboo sticks for umbrellas | — | free | free |
| Rattan baskets | — | 25% ad. val.* | 50% ad. val.* |
| Bamboo curtains | — | 25 | 50 |
| Floor coverings (wool) | sq. ft. | 7.5 | 30 |
| Men's shirts | — | 21 | 45 |
| Leather footwear | pr. | 2.5 | 10 |
| Luggage and handbags | — | 8 | 35 |
| Jewelry (not over $18 per dozen) | doz. | 27.5 | 110 |
| Paintings, sculpture | — | free | free |
| Furs (mink, lamb, etc.) | — | 10 | 50 |
| Furniture (wood) | — | 8.5 | 40 |
| Rainwear (cotton) | doz. | 12.5 | 37.5 |
| Rainwear (other materials) | doz. | 16.5 | 65 |
| Dresses, sportswear | | | |
| Laces | | 40 | 90 |
| Cotton knit | | 17.5 | 45 |

*Ad valorem.

Source: U.S. Government Printing Office, Washington, D.C.

the Customs rules, regulations, and procedures, which thus have had great impact on the importing field. At the present time there is evidence that the United States may adopt a new customs tariff based upon the Harmonized Commodity Description and Coding System, which will replace the present system.

Since the assessed duty can contribute considerably to the cost of merchandise, it is vital that the buyer responsible for such purchases have a clear understanding as to what tariffs will apply to the goods to be imported.

## Duty-Free Status

Under certain conditions, the government authorizes importing merchandise that is not subject to duty. The major program allowing duty-free merchandise to enter the United States is entitled the General System of Preferences. Under this program, which became effective on January 1, 1976 and has been extended through July 4, 1993, a wider range of products (approximately 3000) comes ashore free of any tariff.

The terms of this agreement require that

a. The merchandise must be destined for the United States from one of the beneficiary developing countries (as listed by the Customs Service).
b. The Merchandise must be produced in a beneficiary developing country and not merely imported by that country and shipped to the United States.

The Caribbean Basin Initiative (CBI), is a program that also provides for duty-free entry of goods. Enacted into law on January 1984 and due to expire on September 30, 1995, the United States can import, duty free, from the following countries:

Antigua and Barbuda
Aruba
Bahamas
Barbados
Belize
Costa Rica
Dominica
Dominican Republic
El Salvador
Grenada
Guatemala
Haiti
Honduras
Jamaica
Montserrat
Netherlands Antilles
Panama
Saint Christopher-Nevis
Saint Lucia
Saint Vincent and the Grenadines
Trinidad and Tobago
Virgin Islands, British

## Quotas

A quota is the set amount of merchandise that a country's government allows to be imported in a specific category. Quotas are generally established for numbers of units rather than for dollar amounts.

To protect producers in the United States from unfair competition from certain countries, the federal government has established very specific quotas. At the present time the quota system applies to Far Eastern countries. Since their wage scales are so low, they can produce goods that would cost far less than their U.S. equivalents and could cripple industry in our country. European imports are not bound by quotas since their costs are comparable to ours.

There are two categories of quotas, absolute and tariff rate. In the case of absolute quotas, any merchandise that exceeds the established limit must be disposed of through a variety of means established by the U.S. Customs Service. Merchandise that is subject to tariff-rate quotas and is above the established limits may enter at a higher rate of duty or remain in a bonded warehouse awaiting the opening of a new quota. Strict adherence to these quotas is important because exceeding them could result in significant losses to the importer.

It should be understood that not all merchandise that is imported from Far Eastern countries, such as Hong Kong, Korea, China, Japan, Taiwan, and Singapore, comes under quota restrictions. Silk and silk products, for example, do not have quotas since most silk comes from these countries and the United States is not a silk-producing country. However, anything that we do regard as competitive, such as cotton, does come under the quota system. Table 12-2 shows the commodities that are subject to quotas administered by the Customs Service. Special attention should be paid to the different cotton types, according to staple length, and that each requires a different quota.

Note should be made that although certain cotton, wool, and manmade fiber articles that are produced in designated countries are not in the listing, there are certain controls that are administered by the U.S. Customs Service. These controls are imposed on the basis of directives issued by the chairman of the Committee for the Implementation of Textile Agreements to the Commissioner of Customs.

Often an importer uses up the assigned quota and still wants to import additional merchandise. Quotas may be purchased from holders of quotas who do not expect to use the entire quota allocated for a period. Thus, a major retail importer may avail himself of additional goods via this route. Sometimes additional quota isn't available by purchase, and importing must be suspended for the period. A well-known merchant recently made the transition from cotton sweaters to acrylics because no additional cotton quota was available.

Unlike the domestic purchaser who can order without restriction, those retailers who participate in importing their own goods must be fully aware of quota restrictions and changes so that their merchandise needs can be filled.

Import purchasers should carefully consider the exceptions to the general rules of duty and quotas. Sometimes by entering into relationships with countries that enjoy duty-free status or are not part of the established quota system, American retailers can produce and/or purchase goods that cost less than those imported from other countries.

So complicated are the rules and regulations which govern the tariff and quotas that it is good business practice to utilize experts who are more familiar

**TABLE 12-2**

*TARIFF-RATE QUOTAS*

Whole milk, fluid, fresh or sour
Fish, fresh, chilled, or frozen, filleted, etc., cod, haddock, hake, pollock, cusk, and rosefish
Tuna fish, described in item 112.30, Tariff Schedules
Potatoes, white or Irish; certified seed and other than certified seed
Whiskbrooms wholly or in part of broom corn
Other brooms wholly or in part of broom corn
Motorcycles, over 700 cc engine displacement

*ABSOLUTE QUOTAS*

Animal feeds containing milk or milk derivatives
Butter substitutes, containing over 45 percent of butterfat, provided for in item 116.30, Tariff Schedules, and butter oil
Buttermix containing over 5.5 percent but not over 45 percent by weight of butterfat
Cheese, natural Cheddar made from unpasteurized mild and aged not less than 9 months
Chocolate, containing 5.5 percent or less by weight or butterfat
Chocolate crumb and other related articles containing over 5.5 percent by weight of butterfat
Cream, fluid or frozen, fresh or sour
Milk and cream, condensed or evaporated
Ice cream
Cotton having a staple length under 1⅛" (except harsh or rough cotton having a staple length of under ¾", and other than linters)
Cotton (other than linters) having a staple length of 1⅛" or more
Cotton card strips made from cotton having a staple length under 1 3/15" and comber waste, lap waste, sliver waste, and roving waste, whether or not advanced
Fibers of cotton processed but not spun
Peanuts, shelled or not shelled, blanched, or otherwise prepared or preserved (except peanut butter)
Sugar, syrups, and molasses described in items 115.20, 115.30, 156.45, 183.01, and 183.05 Tariff Schedules
Steel, bars, rods, stainless, alloy tool steel
Coffee

with the situation. Misjudgment of Customs Service requirements could make an otherwise good deal into one that is riddled with problems. The end result could be a loss rather than a profit.

## IMPORT BUYER QUALIFICATIONS

Once the decision has been made that the source of merchandise should be foreign rather than domestic, the company must assign the purchasing to an individual or team with specific qualifications. While buyers of "on-shore" merchandise must have credentials that qualify them as professional purchasers, the "offshore" team must be even better prepared. Chapter 1 explored a buyer's general qualifications, such as educational requirements, enthusiasm, analytical excellence, ability to articulate, product knowledge, objective reasoning, dedication, leadership, appearance, and flexibility, as being essential. In addition to these, the buyer who travels all over the world should have even more.

## Language

With today's global market so important, the buyer who has a knowledge of languages other than English has a distinct advantage. Being able to directly communicate, without dependence on an interpreter, has tremendous value. Although interpreters play important roles in the consummation of a deal, something can be lost in the translation of one's concerns to another. Those with considerable import buying experience will generally agree that being able to directly communicate could make dealing easier and free from problems that result from misunderstanding. While markets like Hong Kong have large businesses with English-speaking representatives to deal with directly, some of the smaller companies don't enjoy this luxury. Although it might not be feasible to engage buyers who are fluent in many languages, it is important that those who purchase abroad have a basic ability to greet the seller and communicate key points of the purchase. Of course, those strong in language might not have the other essentials necessary for excellence in negotiation. A blending of some language with the other qualifications certainly provides a plus.

## Social and Cultural Awareness

Anyone who travels abroad will generally return home with a host of stories that center upon the strangeness of the country just visited. Tourists need not be as educated in terms of cultural differences as the professional businessperson. While a tourist might only offend the host country, a business executive's offensive behavior could destroy a deal.

Recently, a buyer returned from an Arab nation where he related that the deal wasn't ever consummated because of two offensive acts. One involved sitting on the floor. The American pointed the soles of his shoes directly at the Arab seller which, he later found out, was rude and unacceptable. The other was the typical question often used in American purchases, "How's your wife?" This error was a spoken one. The deal was never made. When traveling to a foreign land, it is imperative that the customs of the culture are carefully learned. It might not be the terms of the deal that turns the venture sour, but the words and actions might be offensive. While the removal of one's shoes might sound strange to Americans visiting Japanese homes, it is a necessity for making a good impression.

Many books and films are available to buyers which will prepare them for proper behavior and courtesies when dealing in foreign countries.

## Political Neutrality

In America we are often thrown into battle when we enter into the world of politics. Most professional businesspeople are aware that political differences are taboo in most business discussions. Although a good session with friends could become heated, generally all parties kiss and make up and resume their friendships. Many an onshore deal has been damaged, however, when politics are explored.

The buyer who purchases abroad should never engage in a political discussion with the foreign seller. While it is prudent to understand the basic political philosophies of each country to which buying visits are made, it is important to play a neutral role. In the United States we openly and freely criticize our president and other leaders, but in some countries this is unacceptable. Citizens of Great Britain typically justify anything that the Royal Family does, no matter how distasteful it might appear. One might detest the concept of communism, but when dealing with China it is not a topic to be considered. Too often Americans, used to speaking their political minds, kill a deal by engaging in political conversation.

## Technical Product Knowledge

The typical buyer, as discussed in Chapter 1, should have sufficient product knowledge to make appropriate buying decisions. When dealing with domestic merchandise, however, products that don't live up to expectations can often be returned to the vendor. In the case of imports, we have seen that many retail buying teams actually decide upon style, select fabrics, coordinate trims, and involve themselves in the product from inception to completion. They must be aware of the technology that is employed in the design: turn around time for the product, fit, and so forth.

If the items do not live up to what was expected, it isn't a simple task to make adjustments. The distance from the production and the time and expense incurred in making returns could turn anticipated profits into losses. An import buyer should be able to determine if the patterns are appropriate for American consumption. It should be understood that in clothing fit, there is often a discrepancy in the sizing of the merchandise. Such details are not generally addressed in domestic sourcing. Care must be taken that prior to the buyer's departure on a buying trip, a complete knowledge of the product, in terms of technical factors, has been mastered.

## Computational Skills

In the United States, buyers should have a basic understanding of the arithmetical concepts that are pertinent to buying plans. Discount calculation, markup, and so forth certainly play a part in the purchaser's daily routine. The computational skills must be even sharper for those buyers who not only participate in the products designed in foreign lands but who also must consider the variable costs that eventually lead to the retail price. While it might require nothing more than application of the fundamentals of arithmetic, the skills must be sufficiently honed to make certain that a profit will be achieved. Any error could affect the retailer's profit.

In the example of an "importing flow chart," it is clear how extensively detailed the computational skills of the import buyer must be:

## Importing flow chart

### *Product*

Factory Price + Inland Freight + Export Packing = *F.O.B. Vessel* (port of exit)
400 + 20 + 20 + 60 = 500

*F.O.B. Vessel* + Ocean Freight + Marine Insurance = *C.I.F.** (port of exit)
500 + 0 + 100 = 600

*C.I.F.* + Customs Clearance + Customs Duty = *Landed Price*
600 + 20 + 50 = 670

*Landed Price* + Inland Transportation = *Importer's Buying Price*
670 + 20 = 690

*Importer's Buying Price* + Markup = *Importer's Selling Price*
690 + 5% (34.50) = 724.50

*Importer's Selling Price* + Inland Transportation = *Retailer's Buying Price*
$724.50 + 20 = 744.50

*Retailer's Buying Price* + Markup = *Retailer's Selling Price*
744.50 + 744.50 (50% on retail) = $1,489

*C.I.F. denotes cost of merchandise from factory, insurance, and freight.

## Comprehension of Trade Terms

In making the deals, import buyers must be able to speak the language of international trading. Technical terminology is part of the everyday dialogue between buyers and sellers. The following list features some of the trade terms that require comprehension before a trip abroad can be made:

1. *Bill of lading*. Carrier's receipt of the goods which represents title to the merchandise. It also indicates the specifics of the shipping terms.
2. *Bonded warehouse*. Government-approved storage facility in which merchandise may be held without payment of duty. Ultimate release of the goods requires duty payment or export.
3. *Chief value*. Determination of that part of the goods that is its greatest cost factor and on which applicable duty is based.
4. *C.I.F.* Regularly used term that stands for initial cost of the goods, shipping insurance, and freight costs.

5. *Commissionaire.* Foreign resident buyer or agent who charges importers a fee for services rendered in participation of the purchase.
6. *Counter sample.* Corrected sample that incorporates changes made by the import buyer.
7. *E.L.C.* Estimated landed cost of the merchandise.
8. *Exfactory.* A term used to quote prices at the factory.
9. *Exchange rate.* The value of one company's currency as compared to another. Since the rates fluctuate on a daily basis, it is imperative for buyers to regularly check to determine feasibility of the cost.
10. *Landed cost.* Importer's final cost, which includes such factors as merchandise, shipping, packing, insurance, commissions, and tariffs.
11. *Letter of credit.* Used in financing most import purchases, it is a promise from the purchaser's bank to the seller that goods will be paid for.
12. *P.O.E.* The port of entry through which goods pass into a country.
13. *Prêt-à-porter.* French ready-to-wear or mass-produced merchandise.
14. *Specification buying.* Purchases that are made with input from the buyers. Such details as sizing, fabric selection, trimmings are specified by the buyer.
15. *Tariff.* Synonymous for duty, it is an extra cost that is added onto certain imports to make them more price competitive with domestically priced goods.
16. *Visa.* Permission granted to individuals wishing to enter certain countries. It is used in addition to the passport.
17. *Way bill.* A carrier-produced document that contains the details of the shipment.

## PLANNING THE TRIP ABROAD

Since buying trips abroad generally require a great deal of effort packed into the briefest amount of time, it is imperative that details are carefully addressed before the buyer departs. Attention to particular specifics prior to departure will help to ensure a trip that is profitable as well as free from mishaps. Problems that arise on domestic buying ventures are more easily handled than those that may occur offshore. Such elements as letters of credit, itinerary planning, hotel arrangements, and foreign agent contracts must be carefully planned. Slipups on any one of these could easily complicate the buyer's ability to negotiate the best deal.

*Letters of credit.* Most import purchases are made on the basis of letters of credit which guarantee that the purchaser's bank will pay the seller or the seller's bank for the goods that have been bought. Prior to leaving for the foreign countries, the buyer's company arranges for the bank to supply the necessary letter of credit to be used for each importing transaction.

To understand the various stages in the use of letters of credit, the following is presented:

STAGE 1. The retailer completes the bank's letter of credit application and returns it to the bank.

STAGE 2. The retailer's bank then sends the letter of credit to the foreign seller's bank.

STAGE 3. The receving bank forwards the letter of credit to the seller.

STAGE 4. Once the deal has been completed, the seller makes the shipping arrangements.

STAGE 5. Documents are then prepared, as outlined in the letter of credit, and delivered to the seller's bank.

STAGE 6. When the documents are in order, they are sent to the buyer's bank who pays the seller's bank according to the terms of the letter of credit.

When all the stages are complete, the retail buyer makes arrangements to have the goods delivered to his premises. If the details are not carefully planned before the buyer's departure for the trip abroad, extra time could be required to consummate the deal. In such dealings, where time is of the essence, improper handling of such details could kill the transaction.

It should be noted that in the development of these import programs where the buyer is actually involved in the materials and trimmings used in the production, letters of credit must be initiated for use with many suppliers. It is not uncommon for the various components of the merchandise to be bought from many different sources in different countries.

**Itinerary planning.** Import buyers live on schedules that leave little time for anything but travel from destination to destination. Itineraries or schedules are arranged for them, detailing arrivals, departures, airlines, and so forth, so that they will fit everything into the allocated time.

Figure 12-2 features a sample itinerary that details departures and arrivals in the cities to be visited. Some itineraries spell out hotels, appointments, and other details as well.

**Hotel arrangements.** Prior to departure, hotel accommodations should be made so that the buyer can be reached by the home office as well as by those with whom appointments have been made in the foreign country. It is imperative that those who will be working with the buyer will be notified of the buyer's hotel. In selecting a hotel, attention should be paid to those conveniences that will make the stay more productive. For example, English-speaking personnel might be needed to relay messages from the buyer's home office as well as to

March 4. 1992

ITINERARY

| | | | | |
|---|---|---|---|---|
| Ms. Sheri Litt | | | | |
| Monday, March 9 | BWI | Piedmont Flight 7872 | Depart | 3:05 PM |
| | JFK | | Arrive | 4:10 PM |
| | JFK | TWA Flight 705 | Depart | 6:20 PM |
| Tuesday, March 10 | Heathrow | | Arrive | 5:55 AM |
| Wednesday, March 11–<br>Friday, March 13 ................ London | | | | |
| Saturday, March 14 | Heathrow | British Air Flight 304 | Depart | 8:30 AM |
| | Paris-Chas. DeGau. | | Arrive | 10:50 AM |
| | Paris | Air France Flight 840 | Depart | 6:00 PM |
| | Heathrow | | Arrive | 8:20 PM |
| Sunday, March 15 ............... London | | | | |
| Monday, March 16 | Heathrow | Italiana Flight 459 | Depart | 10:50 AM |
| | Milan-Linate | | Arrive | 1:45 PM |
| Tuesday, March 17–<br>Thursday, March 19 ................. Italy | | | | |
| Friday, March 20 | Milan | TWA Flight 843 | Depart | 12:30 PM |
| | JFK | | Arrive | 3:20 PM |
| | JFK | Piedmont Flight 7987 | Depart | 5:05 PM |
| | BWI | | Arrive | 6:00 PM |

**FIGURE 12-2.**

translate messages from foreign representatives. Teletype facilities are usually a must so that telexes can be sent and received by the buyer, to or from his or her headquarters. With the time difference, telexes are often more appropriate than phone calls. With design emphasis so important to many business transactions, a fax machine is an added plus. If the hotel offers the fax service, the buyer can "send design" to his or her company and receive changes in a short period of time. If some business is to be transacted at the hotel, it is necessary to make arrangements for suitable business space to be available in addition to the buyer's sleeping quarters. Hotels that are centrally located and convenient to market visits should also be considered. Advantageous locations are time savers.

The more preliminary details that are worked out in hotel planning, the easier it will be for the buyer to function.

**Agent contracts.** Most companies make use of foreign agents to assist them with their vendor dealings. Some of the larger retailers have agents who work exclusively for them, while others, whose requirements are less stringent, employ agents on a free-lance basis. These agents are generally involved in every aspect of the buying trip, from making specific appointments to helping consummate the deal. Since they are capable of speaking the language of the country in which the import purchase is accomplished, they can make communication between the buyer and seller simple.

On buying trips that take the buyers to several countries, oftentimes one agent accompanies them for the entire trip. For example, on a trip to the Orient, a major area for mass-produced fashion imports, buyers travel to places like Hong Kong, Korea, and Japan within a week. Using one agent who speaks all of the languages and is willing to travel with the buyer makes the trip easier to accomplish.

Agents must be contacted far in advance of the foreign travel to make certain that they will be available as needed, that they can confirm appointments for the buyer, and that they can do any preliminary investigating necessary to make the buyer's visit one that will be productive. With time such a vital factor in foreign purchasing, the experienced agent is a must.

## MAKING THE PURCHASE

The various elements of the import purchase are similar to those of domestic purchasing. In the preceding chapters that concentrated on what to buy, how much to buy, and from whom to buy, and in the next chapter, negotiating the Purchase and Writing the Order, the specifics that the buyer must address to guarantee a profitable buy are explored. All buyers practice these principles, but the import buyer's task is a little more complex due to the various charges incurred that are not part of the buying from onshore manufacturers.

Of paramount importance in this type of trading is the cost of the add-ons to the merchandise. It must be remembered that initial cost is just as it implies, the first cost. The extra charges must be carefully determined to make certain that the merchandise under consideration warrants importing. When purchases are made in the United States, there are rarely additional costs (except for possible shipping charges which are often included in the initial cost) which increase the price, and often numerous discounts which actually lower the initial cost.

In making the purchase, after it has been determined that quality, style, trimmings, fit, and the rest are exactly what the buyer wants, and the initial price has been agreed upon, the buyer should evaluate and/or calculate the following costs and conditions of delivery:

1. *Delivery.* Regardless of the point of origin of the merchandise, imports take longer to deliver than do domestic goods. Completion dates for delivery should be firmed, with penalties negotiated in case the merchandise comes ashore late. By negotiating a penalty clause at the time of purchase, the vendor will do anything to avoid delivery after the agreed-on completion date.
2. *Overseas shipping.* The costs of getting the goods can vary depending upon the method used to ship the goods. Delivery by ship is the least expensive, but slowest; regular air is faster but more expensive; and overnight air express the most costly. By early order placement, slower delivery would be acceptable in most situations, and costs will be reduced. Some purchasers build into the contract that merchandise should be shipped at the lowest cost, but if delay in production is the manufacturer's fault, he will bear the additional costs of air express.

3. *Inland freight.* Not only must the costs be considered from the port of export to the port of entry, but also the costs of bringing the goods to the port of export. Inexperienced buyers might assume there is only one charge for shipping. Sometimes vendors will waive this charge if the order is large and the purchaser is a regular customer.
4. *Duty.* Although this is not a negotiable item, at the time of purchase it is imperative to determine into which category the merchandise falls and what duty will be charged.
5. *Packing charges.* If special packing requirements are necessary, the purchaser most often is responsible for this cost. It should be decided at time of purchase specifically what these costs will be.
6. *Storage costs.* Sometimes the merchandise arrives at the shipping point before the ship comes to port. In this case temporary warehousing is a necessity. The fees should be checked so that they can be considered in determining the actual or landed cost of the goods.

Miscellaneous charges may include such items as brokerage charges at port of entry, port charges, banker's fees, and freight from the port of entry to the retailer's premises.

A reexamination of the landed cost calculation, in the preceding chapter, should serve as a review of the details that must be addressed when making the actual purchase.

## FOLLOWING UP THE ORDER

Upon return to the United States the import buyer must carefully check all of the aspects of the purchases and particularly the arithmetic calculations. It is not rare that inappropriate yardage was mistakingly ordered or that a computational error was introduced into the purchase order.

Correspondence should be undertaken periodically as the time approaches for the goods to be received. The purchaser should receive progress reports, counter samples which incorporate any changes from the original design as requested at time of the order, fax reproductions, and so forth, to make certain that all is going according to plan. It is this followup that avoids any surprises which could affect the end result of the purchase.

### ACTION FOR THE SMALL STORE BUYER

It should be understood that small store buyers cannot, by themselves, develop import programs that take them offshore. They do not purchase in quantities that would qualify them to participate in these import programs.

Smaller retailers who wish to avail themselves of imports should do so by the more appropriate routes of purchasing at home from wholesale importers or through resident buying offices with commissionaire affiliates. Through these means, they are not troubled by the quota systems that complicate the lives of the large retailers, who are producing and importing their own designs, and merely have to concentrate on style selection. The rigors of developing such programs as faced by large scale counterparts is not for them.

## SUMMARY OF KEY POINTS

1. Numerous giant retail organizations are participating in the direct importing of merchandise, which involves them in merchandise acquisition from the design's inception to its delivery.
2. The federal government makes imported merchandise more competitive with domestically produced goods through duty assessment and quota restrictions.
3. Duty and quota restrictions come under the jurisdiction of the U.S. Customs Service.
4. Although all buyers should possess the basic, technical qualifications that make them better negotiators, import buyers should possess additional qualifications such as the ability to speak a foreign language, comprehension of international trade terms, and awareness of the social and cultural customs of other countries.
5. In planning a trip abroad, buyers should make hotel arrangements at establishments that feature English-speaking personnel, telex machines, and central location by the wholesale markets.
6. Itineraries are important so that buyers can complete their assignments without loss of time.
7. When making the purchase, special attention should be paid to those costs that are over and above the initial quoted price and to the details of shipping and delivery terms.
8. The follow-up of foreign orders is a must to make certain that the goods will arrive as scheduled.

## REVIEW QUESTIONS

1. To what extent do the giants in the retail industry now participate in import programs?
2. Why does the federal government impose import restrictions on merchants who choose to have goods produced abroad?
3. For what reason is duty levied on some countries' offerings and not on others?

4. Distinguish between the Customs Service's use of the MFN status and that of LDDC status.
5. Some imported merchandise comes into the United States free of duty. Why does the government make these exceptions?
6. Differentiate between absolute quotas and tariff rate quotas.
7. How does the government justify the imposition of quotas on merchandise produced in the Far East and not on European nations?
8. Is it advantageous for the import buyer's qualifications to exceed those of the domestic counterpart?
9. What additional qualifications should the buyer acquire in preparation for a career that warrants offshore negotiation?
10. Define the terms counter sample, exchange rate, and bonded warehouse.
11. How important is the letter of credit in purchasing from a foreign resource?
12. Which parties play the dominant role in the establishment of a letter of credit?
13. What purpose does the itinerary serve in the buyer's trip abroad?
14. Are there any special considerations in choosing a hotel for the buyer's stay in a foreign country?
15. In what way does the foreign agent participate in the import buyer's purchasing plans?
16. In addition to checking duty and quota restrictions, what aspects of the purchase need special attention?
17. Is the follow-up of orders a necessity for import purchasing?
18. Discuss the feasibility of the small store buyer as a participant in direct importing.

## CASE PROBLEM 1

Ever since they decided to go heavily into imported merchandise, Lucky Lady, a chain organization of 350 units, has realized a steady increase in profits. Initially, purchases involved buying from import wholesalers so they could test the market without making a major investment. Five years ago Lucky Lady had the buyers regularly visit foreign markets to purchase directly from the manufacturers. By utilizing this channel of distribution, their profits continued to increase. With the success of the imports in their merchandise offerings, the management at Lucky Lady decided to take the plunge into developing an import program in which they would purchase the materials, design the styles, and contract with a foreign producer to manufacture the goods.

Mr. Wheatly, the company's general manager, investigated several countries in which the goods could be produced and decided that Hong Kong would afford the greatest opportunity. With quote applications to be filed, duty assessments to be checked, and significant planning to be undertaken for the new operation, it took approximately eight months to set up shop. At once, the new venture was a success. It was so successful, in fact, that the established quotas were quickly absorbed and some of the best-selling items were no longer available. To compound the problem, new duty assessments were necessitating an increase in the ultimate price charged the consumer. Although once in an enviable position, Lucky Lady has had to make some changes.

Maryann Clark, the general merchandise manager, believes that the possible switch to a "beneficiary" country such as Haiti, where they enjoy duty-free status, would be a plus for the company. The landed cost of the goods would be considerably less than that of Hong Kong's imports.

John Langhorn, one of the divisional merchandise managers, feels that the switch to a European producing country, where there are no quotas, would enable an unlimited supply of merchandise.

Lucy Smathers, another divisional manager, is of the opinion that perhaps a return to American production would be the best solution.

Although an immediate decision is not urgent, long-term planning is necessary to guarantee that the store will continue to receive its merchandise.

### Questions

1. Which recommendation, if any, makes the most sense for Lucky Lady? Why?
2. Should the company continue to produce in Hong Kong? If so, how could the quota problem be resolved?

## CASE PROBLEM 2

Investigation of each season's past records indicates that there is growing demand for imported merchandise. Famous labels from the far corners of the earth dominate the inventory of B. Jeffries and Company, a specialty chain that offers upscale men's, women's, and children's clothing at its 12 units. The imported label seems to be the one factor that motivates the Jeffries' clientele.

Although the profit picture remains favorable, the various store managers are complaining more frequently to central management of price cutting by competitors. While the merchandise is high priced and not within reach of the mass market, the customers are still price aware. No matter how affluent the customer, few really care to see the same items available for less, and since the labels bear household designer names, price comparison is simple.

A call to the vendors requesting maintenance for their merchandise has fallen on deaf ears. Since the law forbids uniform pricing or fair trading in the store's trading area and the manufacturers are not about to offer Jeffries "exclusivity," price cutting seems to be a problem that will probably continue to plague the company.

Kate Frank, one of the company's buyers, has recommended private label merchandise, produced offshore, as a solution to the problem. The labels would still bear the names of the prestigious producing countries, but the styles would belong to Jeffries. By visiting a foreign producer and supplying the styling for exclusive consumption, the problem could be resolved. Through the elimination of the well-known labels, price cutting would be a thing of the past.

## Questions

1. Do you agree with Kate Frank's solution to the problem? Defend your answer with sound reasoning.
2. Is there another solution to the problem?

# Chapter 13

# NEGOTIATING THE PURCHASE AND WRITING THE ORDER

## LEARNING OBJECTIVES

*Upon completion of this chapter, the student should be able to:*

1. Explain the Robinson–Patman Act and its effect on purchase negotiations.
2. Discuss the importance of market and product knowledge in price negotiation.
3. Define and understand the importance of cash discounts to top management.
4. Define the following: anticipation, trade discounts, quantity discounts, seasonal discounts, advertising discounts, and postdating.
5. List and describe six factors that should be taken into account to reduce transportation costs.
6. Explain cooperative and consignment buying.
7. Discuss the following terms in relation to negotiating: limits, justification, splitting the difference, and future relationships.
8. Define each of the shipping terms listed.
9. Fill out a blank order accurately and completely, given the required information.

## *NEGOTIATING THE PURCHASE*

Most Americans traveling abroad are amazed at the amount of bargaining that goes on at the retail level. They really shouldn't be surprised, because in certain areas in the United States, consumer-retailer bargaining is quite common for such products as new and used automobiles, appliances, and other goods.

At the wholesale level, where buyers for retail stores operate, negotiations are an important part of the buying function. This is particularly true with seasonal goods. Manufacturers and wholesalers are as unhappy as retailers over the prospect of remaining with inventory at the close of a season. Consequently, as the season progresses they are often willing to reduce their selling prices to get unwanted goods off their shelves. In essence they too run sales, although the price reduction may not be marked on a ticket but must be negotiated. The people who sell manufacturers their raw materials are in the same boat. A mill supplying fabric for the spring line of a dress manufacturer will reduce its price to clean out all its goods before the season ends. This provides the manufacturer with room to negotiate. The catch is that the manufacturer will not tell the retail buyer about this, and the only way the buyer will get a reduction is by negotiating.

In negotiating price, the buyer must distinguish between regular goods, which must be "right" in terms of style, quantity, and timeliness, and "off" goods, which will be used for promotions and extra markup. It is the latter type of special goods that requires extra bargaining. It should be pointed out that some stores do the bulk of their business in special goods. Buyers for these organizations negotiate the price of practically all their purchases.

Negotiations between buyer and resource can be divided into three broad areas:

1. The price of the goods
2. Discounts
3. Transportation

### The Robinson–Patman Act

Before going into a discussion of price negotiation between buyer and seller, it is important to turn to an important piece of legislation involved in this bargaining. The Robinson–Patman Act of 1936 was designed to limit price discrimination. It is an attempt to protect small businesses by forbidding their giant competitors from getting an edge by using their size to obtain lower prices. The law, however, permits price reductions in the following instances:

1. When the price reduction is made to meet the low price of a competitor
2. When the lower price is based on cost savings in selling to the favored customer

3. When the price is reduced on goods that were obsolete or on the verge of becoming obsolete, as is the case with "job lots"

A vendor that singles out one customer for a price reduction must base the action on the fact that competitors have done the same, that costs will be reduced by the sale, or that the goods are obsolete or about to become obsolete.

It is important that all buyers understand the Robinson–Patman Act—the large buyer to keep from becoming involved in illegal activity and the small buyer to protect its competitive rights.

## Negotiating the Price of Goods

The most important factor in negotiating for merchandise, and one that must constantly be kept in mind, is that the goods must be "right." In other words, it must be the merchandise customers want. It is better to overpay for the right goods than to underpay for the wrong merchandise. The buyer's success in negotiating price may be greatly improved by knowledge of the market in general and the individual resource in particular.

### *Knowing the Market*

By being fully involved in the market, the buyer can pick up a great deal of valuable information. This is accomplished through frequent visits to various types of resources, conversations with salespeople, reading newspapers and trade journals, watching competitors' advertising and offerings, and studying the catalogs and price lists of vendors. From this information the buyer will bring to a negotiating session a wide knowledge of the availability of the goods, the prices being offered by competitors of the vendor, and the probable salability of the merchandise.

### *Product Information*

Buyers who understand the vendor's costs have a negotiating edge, since they can estimate the floor to which the resource will be able to drop a price. Admittedly this is a difficult task, and it is rare to find a buyer with perfect knowledge in this area. However, the more a buyer knows, the better his or her estimate will be. Therefore the buyer should always be ready to learn more about a product line. This information cannot be determined during a negotiating session. It is a long-term learning process that can be taught only by the various sources. Rather than trying to impress resources with how much he or she knows, the buyer should be constantly questioning to round out his or her knowledge. An inexperienced buyer should not consider a trip to a vendor successful unless he or she has gathered at least a shred of previously unknown product information.

## Negotiating Discounts

A *discount* is a reduction in the quoted price of merchandise that a buyer is permitted to deduct. There are many types of discounts. They include cash discounts, anticipation, trade discounts, quantity discounts, seasonal discounts, advertising or promotional discounts, and postdating.

Buyers must determine the type or types of discounts that are available from a specific vendor and attempt, where possible, to qualify for them. It is also the buyer's responsibility to know the traditional discounts allowed in a specific market.

### *Cash Discounts*

Cash discounts (accountants refer to them as sales discounts) are a reward vendors give to customers for prompt payment. For example, a vendor anxious to receive the money may permit customers to deduct a stated percent from their payment if they will pay their bills in a specified number of days. An invoice for $100 might state that the buyer is permitted to deduct 2 percent if payment is made in 10 days. Thus a bill paid within 10 days can be settled for $98. These terms are 2/10 n/60. If not paid in 10 days, the 2 percent discount is lost.

**Importance of cash discounts.** Cash discounts play a unique role in the buying function, one that is not easily understood. Top management in large retail organizations consider cash discounts to belong to the store rather than to the individual buyer. The discount is available because of the availability of money, and this is not the buyer's concern. In practice this means that a buyer who purchases a $100 item that after cash discount costs only $98 must calculate the markup on a $100 cost. The discount is kept as a profit cushion. This becomes an advantage to stores, since an accumulation of discounts can convert a break-even season into a profitable one.

Management is so insistent on buyers' getting discount terms on all their purchases that it often knowingly allows buyers to permit their resources to "load" their prices to make room for a discount. Thus if the buyer and resource agree on a price of $98, it is commonplace for the price to be set at $100 with a discount of 2 percent.

In most industries cash discounts are standard and are offered to all wholesale customers. Knowing this, vendors calculate the cost of discounts into their selling price in the same fashion as they do the cost of labor and materials. Consequently, in negotiating a price, if a resource that usually allows a 2 percent cash discount offers a 10 percent reduction to be paid without discount, it is reducing the price by only 8 percent.

The importance of cash discounts can be emphasized by some simple arithmetic. Assume that a 2 percent discount is permitted on a $100 invoice paid in 10 days. This can be done 36 times a year (36 × 10 days = 360 days). In other words, 36 × \$2 = \$72 can be earned a year on an investment of \$98, for about a 73 percent annual return on investment.

### *Anticipation*

Although not nearly as important as regular cash discounts, anticipation offers another opportunity for savings as a special form of cash discount. This is an amount, usually 12 percent per annum, that may be deducted for payment before the end of the cash discount period. A bill on which a cash discount of 2 percent plus anticipation is allowed if paid in 30 days may be settled with a 3 percent discount if paid at once—2 percent for discount and 1 percent for anticipation (12 percent per year divided by 12 months equals 1 percent per month). Large, financially strong stores fight for anticipation, which is not permitted by all resources. Where anticipation is allowed, top-level management often insists that buyers fight for long-term credit, since the amount of anticipation increases as the number of days increases. A bill due in 60 days allows twice as much anticipation to be deducted if paid at once than a bill due in 30 days. With the average large retailer's net profit at ½ to 2½ percent, the anticipation figure can mean the difference between profit and loss. The formula for anticipation is as follows: amount of bill due × rate of anticipation × days prepaid.

**PROBLEM** A bill for \$100 subject to terms of 2/10 n/60 dated March 1 is to be paid on March 7. If anticipation is allowed at 12 percent, what is the amount of the check required to pay this invoice?

**SOLUTION**

$$\$100 \times 2\% = \$2$$

$$\$100 - \$2 = \$98 \text{ amount of bill due}$$

$$60 - 6 = 54 \text{ days}$$

$$98 \times 0.12 \times \frac{54}{360} = \$1.76$$

then

$$\begin{array}{l} \$98.00 \\ \underline{-\ 1.76} \\ \$96.24 \text{ amount due} \end{array}$$

### *Trade Discounts*

In some industries the approximate retail price of an article is set by the producer. A trade discount is a percent that may be deducted from the list price. The percentage varies according to the resource's customer. A wholesaler may buy at list less a trade discount of 50 percent, while a retailer may be charged list less a trade discount of 35 percent. This type of discount is widely used by people who sell through catalogs. In such cases price adjustments can be effected by a change in the discount rather than an expensive reprinting of the catalog.

Frequently trade discounts are listed as a chain or series. An invoice may be marked $100 less trade discounts of 40, 30, and 10 percent. In such cases, to find the net cost, each discount is calculated and deducted from the price and the next discount is calculated on the balance:

| | |
|---|---|
| | $100.00 |
| Less 40%: | 40.00 |
| | $ 60.00 |
| Less 30%: | 18.00 |
| | $ 42.00 |
| Less 10%: | 4.20 |
| Net cost | $ 37.80 |

As is the case with cash discounts and anticipation, a buyer must be familiar with the trade discount traditions of a market as well as the trade discount policies of each resource. Some large retailers have attempted to take advantage of the extra trade discount offered to wholesalers by setting up their own wholesale organizations, which buy from the producer and resell the goods to their retail outlets. When such actions have been brought to court as a trick to reduce prices under the Robinson–Patman Act, the courts have generally disallowed the wholesale discount. However, when independent retailers have banded together to set up wholesale organizations, the courts have generally gone along, provided that the wholesale operation offers its services to outsiders.

### *Quantity Discounts*

Quantity discounts are generally permitted under the Robinson–Patman Act, since they can be shown to result in cost savings in such areas as bookkeeping and transportation. A quantity discount is the one that is keyed to the number of unit orders. An example of a quantity discount is the following:

| *DOZENS ORDERED* | *PRICE PER DOZEN* |
|---|---|
| 1–10 | $20.00 |
| 11–30 | 19.50 |
| 31 and over | 19.00 |

Sellers offer quantity discounts because of the savings that result. For the buyer, these discounts permit a reduction in the cost of goods. Naturally, a buyer must be aware of the quantity discounts available. Whether or not he or she takes advantage of them is another matter. Taking a quantity discount may require the purchase of more goods than the buyer can sell. While the decision depends on the buyer's judgment and knowledge of customers, it is true that quantity discounts are more frequently taken among staple than fashion or seasonal goods. Cumulative discounts are a type of quantity discount based on volume over a certain period. Whereas regular quantity discounts are on a one-order basis, cumulative discounts are concerned with the total business done with a resource during a period. For example,

| *TOTAL SEASON PURCHASES* | *CUMULATIVE DISCOUNT* |
|---|---|
| \$0–10,000 | 2% |
| \$10,001–20,000 | 3 |
| \$20,001 and over | 4 |

Cumulative discounts encourage buyers to place the bulk of their orders with one resource. When offered a cumulative discount, the buyer must bear in mind the fact that a percentage point or two is perhaps the least important element in the buying decision. All other things being equal, as in the case of some staples, the buyer should concentrate purchases to take advantage of any available cumulative discounts.

### *Seasonal Discounts*

Certain seasonal businesses such as paints, toys, and jewelry are enormously busy during certain periods of the year and inactive during the remaining months. If they remain dormant during the slow months, their overhead and the salaries of key people result in losses. Continuing with limited production to build up inventory for the busy season requires cash for labor, materials, and carrying inventory. Such resources often offer discounts to buyers who are willing to accept delivery (or at least title) to goods during the slow period. Because of the overhead and storage savings involved, these discounts are permitted under the Robinson–Patman Act if they are offered to all comers. Under these conditions a toy manufacturer who rarely ships before August might give a seasonal discount to a buyer who is willing to accept the goods and pay the invoice in the spring.

Given the opportunity to take advantage of a seasonal discount, the buyer must consider his or her own storage problems, the effect on the open-to-buy, ability to predict the success of the goods in the coming season, and the probability of a price change between the time the order is placed and the time he would normally place it.

### *Advertising and Promotional Discounts*

Many resources feel it is to their advantage to have retailers promote their goods locally. They are therefore willing to share part of this burden with cooperating retailers by giving a special discount. The Robinson–Patman Act permits such discounts when they are offered to all the resource's customers in proportion to the amount they buy. Such discounts are not limited to advertising, but are often given in return for a choice window or interior display location.

### *Postdating*

Another area of negotiation is for an additional period of time before which the bill becomes due. (This is also known as "extra dating" in the market.) For example, a bill dated March 1 with terms of 8/10 EOM (end of month) as of June 1 will allow an extra three months for payment as follows:

- *Without dating*—the customer, to receive an 8 percent discount, must pay the bill by April 10.
- *With postdating*—the discount period is figured from June 1 and is payable July 10.

Buyers often receive this extra time as an inducement to purchase and receive goods earlier than is usual.

## Negotiating Transportation Costs

Knowledgeable buyers can frequently effect important savings in transportation costs. Most of a buyer's purchases are sold F.O.B. factory. Under these conditions, title (ownership) passes to the buyer as soon as the goods leave the factory. Since the retailer owns these goods, all transportation and insurance costs must be borne by the retailer. The Robinson–Patman Act prohibits any special shipping deals, since they are in effect price reductions. On the other hand, the law specifically permits price cuts to meet competition. If a Dallas buyer can purchase an item from Chicago for $10 including transportation, a Los Angeles vendor can equalize its price so that the total cost, including transportation, equals the same $10 the competitor is asking. This is an interesting negotiating point.

Generally the purchaser pays all the shipping costs. However, since much transportation involves considerable distances, shipping arrangements are usually left to the vendor. It would be difficult for a Philadelphia store buying from a San Francisco vendor to make shipping arrangements. When shipping decisions are left to the judgment of the seller, it is apt to select the shipper that is most convenient for itself rather than the method best suited to the buyer. Because large sums are involved, buyers should familiarize themselves with the various shipping alternatives so that they may select the best one. The following are several areas a buyer should consider to reduce transportation costs.

**Size.** It is cheaper to ship a full carload than a partial one. When transportation costs are high in relation to the total cost, the buyer should consider timing purchases to take advantages of the savings that can be effected by ordering larger quantities less frequently.

**Timing.** Typically, slower carriers (waterways) are less expensive than rapid ones (airways). Where possible, ordering should be done far enough in advance to take advantage of this.

**Selection of carriers.** The various carriers have different price structures. Depending on the specifics of the merchandise involved, it might be cheaper to ship parcel post than by truck. Only an informed buyer can take advantage of this.

**Selection of the type of insurance.** The buyer must decide if insurance is necessary. If it is, he or she must decide whether a blanket policy on all incoming goods is preferable to individual coverage on each incoming order.

**Detailed instructions.** Since shipping instructions can be complicated and unusual for the vendor, care must be taken to state them on the order clearly and fully. Upon receipt of the incoming invoice, the buyer must make certain that the goods were shipped in compliance with instructions.

**Merchandise classification.** The rate structures of shippers vary with the type of goods shipped. Savings may be obtained by carefully describing the goods so that they will not be placed in a higher classification than necessary.

**Packaging.** Retailers agree that good packaging sells merchandise, but packaging also increases freight costs. Packaging materials, styles, and even the place where the packaging is to take place must be weighed against the additional freight costs involved.

Large retailers have a decided advantage over small ones in saving transportations costs. In addition to their obvious maneuverability in size and timing of orders, they can often afford to employ traffic managers. These are specialists in the complicated area of transportation. Small store buyers should consider dealing with independent specialists who are available for periodic audits of their shipping problems.

## Other Negotiating Considerations

There are many other alternatives a buyer must consider in negotiating goods. Among these are cooperative buying and consignment buying.

### *Cooperative Buying*

Small retailers, particularly in the food and drug lines, whose individual orders are too small to be considered by manufacturers, are forced to pay a premium for their goods by buying through wholesalers. It is not unusual under such conditions for these independents to pool their orders. The arrangements for such buying groups vary from occasional one-shot deals, in which the stores involved will share the shipment, to retailer-owned warehouses and buying offices that operate for the benefit of their members.

### *Consignment Buying*

A consignment sale is one in which the vendor retains title (ownership) to the goods although physical possession has been transferred to the retailer. It is not until the retailer has sold the merchandise to the consumer that a sale from the producer to the retailer is consummated. Consignment or memorandum buying is widely practiced in the jewelry business. While consignment buying reduces the risks a retailer takes, it also reduces the markup. In return for bearing the risk, the producer charges a premium price. Although most buyers prefer to take the risks and maximize profits, they should consider buying on consignment in at least the following situations:

1. On new types of goods when consumer acceptance cannot be adequately estimated. New toys are frequently sold this way.
2. For low-volume items that are carried more for prestige than for salability.
3. In special situations to help an important resource clean out inventory at a reduced price.
4. For a new, inexperienced buyer, who should take advantage of the safety factor involved.
5. When quantities are uncertain and the demand is sharp and short lived. An example of this situation is textbooks in a college bookstore. All unsold books are returned to the publisher; the store pays only for those that are sold.

A danger in consignment buying is that a buyer might stock his or her shelves with what might be less desirable merchandise.

## How to Negotiate

Like retailers, vendors generally maintain a one-price policy. However, even those resources that are willing to bargain claim to be one-price houses. It is up to the buyer to determine whether or not negotiation is possible. In wholesaling, as in retailing, price reductions are widespread when the demand for goods falls below expectations. Under such conditions the retailer runs a sale, reducing the original price to a lower, fixed price. The resource does the same, but that new, lower price is likely to be subject to bargaining.

Bargaining is an intensely personal act that must be learned from experience rather than a textbook. However, certain factors are more or less constant.

### *Limits*

Both buyer and seller approach the bargaining session with "limits" in mind. The buyer knows the maximum he or she is willing to spend and the seller the minimum he or she will take. In bargaining each party tries to improve on his or her limit. Naturally, knowing the other person's limit is a tremendous advantage. The buyer should set an intelligent limit in advance, stick to it, keep it secret, and try to determine the seller's limit.

On rare occasions a buyer might do well by stating the limit in advance. For example, a buyer of hardware might tell a resource that he is planning an advertised sale of hand tools at $2.00 each, for which he can afford to spend $1.25 (assume that $1.25 is below the vendor's normal asking price). At this point the bargaining is pretty well over; the vendor either offers the goods or doesn't.

### *Justification*

It is helpful for the buyer to give reasons for his or her offer. The buyer may build a case by discussing the retail selling price, the risk of consumer demand, the lateness of the season, and so on. Included in the justification should be such advantages to the resource as cleaning out the goods and getting cash in.

### *Splitting the Difference*

Somewhere along the way, usually after the negotiating has been in progress awhile, one of the parties always seems to suggest splitting the difference. That is, if the offer is $2 and the asking price is $4, they should settle at $3. The buyer should keep this in mind at all times, since this unspoken price is closer to the final result than either the bid or the offer.

### *Future Relationship*

It is unquestionably to the buyer's advantage to maintain a friendly ongoing relationship with resources. If allowed to get out of hand, bargaining can get quite ugly and leave scars that will hurt future relationships. The buyer must bear this in mind and not be unduly oppressive with resources. He or she must not negotiate over every price or take excessive advantage of the vendor's position. Naturally, a buyer must do the best he can, but there are limits beyond which he or she should not push. Buyers who get reputations as "chiselers" often find that prices are raised to provide room for their negotiations.

## Glossary of Shipping Terms

The following is a list of shipping terms a buyer should be familiar with

1. *Air Express.* Express service on regularly operated lines. Very quick and very expensive.
2. *Airfreight.* By air freight planes. Quick and less expensive than air express.
3. *EOM* (end of month). "2/10/EOM" means 2 percent is allowed before the tenth day of the month after the date on the invoice. Thus an invoice dated January 15 is payable on February 10 to qualify for 2 percent.
4. *Fishy-back.* Same as piggy-back, but ships are used.

5. *F.O.B. Destination* (free on board). Title to goods passes when it arrives at its destination. Since the vendor owns the goods until then, the vendor pays the freight.
6. *F.O.B. Factory.* Title passes at the point of shipment. Buyer owns the goods in transit and pays the freight.
7. *L.C.L.* Less than a full freight car load.
8. *Parcel Post.* A federally operated system for shipping small parcels. No pickup service is provided.
9. *Piggy-back.* A transportation system in which a truck trailer is loaded directly onto a freight car without costly unloading and reloading.
10. *ROG* (receipt of goods). Dating does not begin until the goods are in the hands of the buyer.
11. *UPS.* United Parcel Service.

## WRITING THE ORDER

After the buyer has made selections and the price and terms have been negotiated, he or she must write the order. This is an anticlimatic event that is often tedious and time consuming. It is also of utmost importance; carelessness and undue haste can be very costly. Buyers for large stores print their own order forms. This offers several advantages:

1. All departments are similar forms. These become second nature for the clerical and receiving personnel involved.
2. The form can be made to the requirements of the organization, including the desired number of copies.
3. It sets forth the legal conditions necessary for the protection of the store.

Figure 13-1 is an example of a six-copy store order form used exclusively by Abraham & Straus. It has been designed to fit all the specific needs of the departments concerned with the ordering of merchandise, such as the computer center, receiving, and merchandising departments. Copies of A & S orders are kept by the receiving department, the merchandise manager, the vendor, the order checker, the buyer, and the department concerned.

Careful examination of this order form will point up the features with which A & S is concerned. Some of the key features are as follows:

1. *Mfr. No.* Each manufacturer is assigned a number by A & S for the purpose of accurate recordkeeping. The number is inserted by the buyer in this place and is used again later on merchandise tickets.
2. *Direct Invoice and Deliver Merchandise to Locations Indicated.* The buyer must indicate to which branches in the company the merchandise, as well as the

**ABRAHAM & STRAUS** DIVISION OF FEDERATED DEPARTMENT STORES

| STORE | DEPT | 2806694 | MFR NO | ORDER DATE / / |
|---|---|---|---|---|

DIRECT INVOICE AND DELIVER MERCHANDISE WITH INVOICE TO LOCATIONS INDICATED:

| BROOKLYN | | | | |
|---|---|---|---|---|
| ☐ 15 GALLATIN PL | ☐ SERV BLDG., 20 JAY | ☐ CARLE PLACE | ☐ HUNTINGTON | ☐ GARDEN CITY |
| ☐ 20 ELM PL | ☐ BUSH TERM. BLDG # 22 | ☐ QUEENS | ☐ BABYLON | ☐ WOODBRIDGE |
| ☐ 167 SCHERMERHORN | ☐ BUSH TERM. BLDG # 24 | ☐ HEMPSTEAD | ☐ SMITH HAVEN | ☐ PARAMUS |
| | | ☐ MANHASSET | | |

VENDOR DUNS NUMBER

☐ CONFIRMATION OF ORDER DO NOT DUPLICATE

NAME

ADDRESS

CITY STATE ZIP CODE

TRANSPORTATION IS TO BE
☐ PAID BY VENDOR ☐ PAID BY DEPARTMENT
☐ PREPAID BY VENDOR

DISCOUNT

FOB SHIP FROM

DELIVERY DATE A&S CAN CANCEL IF NOT RECD BY

☐ SHIP VIA SPEADMARK ☐ SHIP VIA STANDARD ROUTING LETTER

TICKETING INSTRUCTIONS

| ACCTS PAYABLE USE ONLY | TOTAL COST THIS SHIPMENT | TOTAL RETAIL THIS SHIPMENT |
|---|---|---|

STORE TOTAL COST

| DATE | COST AMOUNT |
|---|---|
| COST BALANCE | |
| DATE | COST AMOUNT |
| COST BALANCE | |
| DATE | COST AMOUNT |
| COST BALANCE | |
| DATE | COST AMOUNT |
| COST BALANCE | |
| DATE | COST AMOUNT |
| COST BALANCE | |
| DATE | COST AMOUNT |
| COST BALANCE | |

| RECV'G | CHECKED BY | DATE | MARKED BY | DATE |
|---|---|---|---|---|
| 1ST | | | | |
| 2ND | | | | |
| 3RD | | | | |
| 4TH | | | | |
| 5TH | | | | |
| 6TH | | | | |

| STYLE NUMBER MFR | STYLE NUMBER A&S | CLASS | DESCRIPTION | COLOR NAME | COLOR CODE | UNIT COST | UNIT RETAIL | ORDER QTY | UNIT DES | SIZES | TOTAL COST | 1 | 2 | 3 | 4 | 5 | 6 |
|---|---|---|---|---|---|---|---|---|---|---|---|---|---|---|---|---|---|

F609 R (6 11 73)

**RECEIVING COPY**

BUYER SIGNATURE

D M M SIGNATURE

| TOTAL PURCHASE ORDER | M U % | RETAIL | COST |
|---|---|---|---|

TOTAL

**FIGURE 13-1.** Store order form *Courtesy:* Abraham & Straus.

invoice, is to be shipped. Frequently merchandise is earmarked for only some branches; this must be indicated on the order form.

3. *Transportation Charge.* As part of their negotiations, buyers arrange for the payment of transportation charges. This area on the form indicates to the accounts payable department the party that has responsibility for transportation charges.
4. *Discount.* Listing of any negotiated discounts.
5. *Delivery Date.* When the merchandise will be expected by the store. Usually it is not one date, but a "period" in which merchandise will arrive.
6. *A & S Can Cancel If Not Received by.* This is an extremely important item. Buyers of merchandise must work within their buying plans and expect merchandise to be received on time for maximum salability. This date is a cancellation date that allows the buyer to refuse any shipments after the date indicated on the order. This is of particular significance to buyers of fashion and seasonal merchandise.
7. *Ticketing Instructions.* Any special instructions pertaining to the type of ticket to be used are indicated here.
8. *Vendor's Dun's Number.* Each vendor has a number assigned by the credit agency Dun & Bradstreet. This number differentiates one vendor from another and simplifies recordkeeping by the computer.
9. *Store Total Cost.* Entire cost of the order.
10. *Cost Balance.* Since orders are often "part shipped," there will still be merchandise due from the vendor. This column provides for each shipment to be subtracted from the total cost with remainders to show the amount still outstanding and expected from the vendor.
11. *Receiving, Checking, Marking.* The columns at the far right of the order form provide space for the receiving department to keep track of the merchandise that has been received, checked, and marked.
12. *Style Number.* You might note that there is space for both manufacturer and A & S style numbers. For its computer system A & S must use four-digit style numbers. When manufacturer numbers are not four-digit numbers, A & S must assign a new number. Also, some manufacturers use names for styles instead of numbers. A & S must translate these into numbers.
13. *Class.* Classification of merchandise.
14. *Description.* Merchandise description.
15. *Color.* Each color is assigned a code number for the computer.
16. *Unit.* This requires the cost and the retail price.
17. *Signatures.* So that the order can be officially placed, it must be signed by the buyer and the divisional merchandise manager (DMM). The divisional merchandise manager's signature is necessary as a check to make certain that the buyer has a sufficient budget for the new purchase, the need for

the goods, and so forth. But it is the buyer's signature that is most important. This signature represents the signing of a contract between the store and the vendor. The buyer must make certain that he or she understands everything that is indicated on the order, since he or she will be legally bound to it.

18. *Total Purchase Order.* This space requires the markup percent for the merchandise, the retail price, and the cost.

Smaller retailers rarely have their own order forms. They rely on the manufacturer's or wholesaler's forms when ordering merchandise for their stores. In those cases it is incumbent upon the small store buyer to carefully read all of the aspects of the form so that they do not agree to any terms with which they are not in agreement. If the preprinted vendor forms have any details or conditions with which there is disagreement, the order form should be amended in accordance with the buyer's requirements. Figure 13-2 features a manufacturer's order form that places few conditions on the purchase. It should be noted that items concerning shipping and discount terms are completed at the time of the purchase. The only items that are preprinted are found in the lower left corner and address the company's conditions regarding claims, returns, and shipping liability.

Buyers' orders are usually made in many copies. This varies with the size and procedure of the store. A small retailer who is the buyer, bookkeeper, and receiving clerk can make do with two copies, one for himself and one for the vendor. A large organization might require copies for the vendor, the buyer, the receiving department, the bookkeeping department, the inventory control section, and branch stores.

Figure 13-3 features buyers writing their orders. It is good policy for buyers to wait until they finish their survey of each category in the market before writing orders for that category. In order to plan purchases, they make careful notes of the lines they have seen. This gives them the opportunity to compare notes on the offerings of the various vendors and make selections away from the pressure of salespeople.

Some buyers allow salespeople or assistants to write the orders for them. Under these conditions, buyers must bear in mind that they alone are responsible for errors, and they should check the order carefully.

## Preretailing

Once the merchandise purchased reaches the receiving department, it is important that it be marked and moved to the selling floor as quickly as possible. This operation can be speeded if the marking department knows the retail price of each item before it receives the goods. Some stores require the buyer to put the retail price of the goods on the order before sending a copy to the receiving department. When this procedure is followed, the buyer should be required to recheck the retail price when the goods are received.

| | |
|---|---|
| 39045 | |
| CUSTOMER NUMBER | |
| LOG NUMBER | |
| | |
| SPECIAL INSTRUCTIONS | |

**BASCO ALL-AMERICAN SPORTSWEAR CORP.**

Showroom: 58 West 40th Street, 10th Floor, New York, NY 10018, (212) 764-1730
Accounting: 118 West 22nd Street, 7th Floor, New York, NY 10011, (212) 255-4595

**DATE:** ☐ **WOMEN'S** ☐ **MEN'S** ☐ **NEW ACCOUNT**

| BILL TO: | SHIP TO: | SALESPERSON: | BEGIN SHIPPING: |
|---|---|---|---|
| | | CUSTOMER'S P.O. NO.: | COMPLETION DATE F.O.B. NEW YORK |
| | | STORE NO.: | SHIP VIA: |
| ZIP | ZIP | DEPT. NO.: | TERMS: |
| TELEPHONE ( ) | BUYER'S NAME: | | INPUT: |

| STYLE | COLOR | | DESCRIPTION | 28 | 29 | 30 | 31 | 32 | 33 | 34 | 36 | | TOTAL UNITS | UNIT PRICE | EXTENSION |
|---|---|---|---|---|---|---|---|---|---|---|---|---|---|---|---|
| | | | | 4 | 6 | 8 | 10 | 12 | 14 | | | | | | |
| | | | | S | M | L | XL | | | | | | | | |
| | NO. | NAME | | 36 | 38 | 40 | 42 | 44 | | | | | | | |
| | | | | | | | | | | | | TOTAL | | | |

**Claims:** All claims must be made within ten days of receipt of goods.
**Returns:** No returns accepted without our return authorization label. Address all requests for return authorization to Showroom.
**Ship:** Goods delivered to common carrier or sent via parcel post are at the risk of the purchaser.

**BUYER'S SIGNATURE**

**BUYER S COPY**

**FIGURE 13-2.** Vendor Order Form. *Courtesy* of Basco.

**FIGURE 13-3.** Buyers discuss terms of the order with the sales representative. *Courtesy:* Tickle Me!

It is becoming common for retailers to arrange for their merchandise to be premailed or prepriced. This service is arranged through the trucking companies that deliver to the stores.

## ACTION FOR THE SMALL STORE BUYER

Buyers for the large retail organizations have a definite advantage when it comes to negotiating the terms of their purchase orders. The mere size of their potential purchases often gives them the clout to receive better terms than the small store buyer. There are a number of instances, however, in which even the smallest store purchaser can negotiate with beneficial results.

By taking merchandise into the store prior to the traditional time, the small store buyer can often get a seasonal discount or terms that permit an additional period of time in which to pay for the goods. These buyers can often have shipping costs waived if they are persistent in their negotiations. An area that is often negotiable to the small-quantity purchaser deals with advertising allowances. Most small store buyers are not sufficiently sophisticated in their understanding of the specific legislation when it comes to promotional allowances. The Robinson–Patman Act guarantees that *all* buyers must receive the same advertising allowances by a company offering them. While the sales rep usually offers advertising dollars to the major stores, he or she is remiss in not doing the same for the small store. The informed small store buyer could easily avail himself or herself of such funds. By so doing, an otherwise generally weak advertising budget could be improved. Another technique to use for improving the small store's negotiating power is through cooperative buying. By purchasing as part of a group, total quantities to the vendors increase and place the buyers in better negotiating positions.

A positive attitude, coupled with knowledge of the market, could place the small store buyer in a better position.

## SUMMARY OF KEY POINTS

1. Negotiations between buyer and vendor are common in the areas of price, discounts, and transportation. The opportunity for negotiation is particularly common with seasonal goods.
2. Buyers should be aware of the provisions of the Robinson–Patman Act that affect price negotiations.
3. Before entering into negotiations, the buyer must be certain that the goods are "right." This requires knowing the product, the customers, and the vendor market.
4. A discount is a reduction in the price of goods. Discounts include cash discounts, anticipation, trade discounts, quantity discounts, seasonal discounts, advertising and promotional discounts, and postdating.
5. Transportation savings may be effected by careful planning in the following areas: size of the order, timing, selection of carriers, type of insurance, care in giving instructions, packaging, and merchandise classification.
6. By pooling their orders, small retailers are able to achieve lower prices. This is called cooperative buying.
7. A consignment sale is one in which the vendor retains title to goods that are in the physical possession of the retailer. Upon making the sale to a consumer, the retailer must pay the vendor.
8. In negotiations, the buyer must be aware of the limit he or she is willing to spend. It is helpful to be able to justify any reduction requested. Buyers should always remember that negotiations should not be permitted to get heated to the point that future relationships might be impaired.
9. Carelessness in writing the order can result in serious losses. Order forms are full of vital information and must be written carefully.

## REVIEW QUESTIONS

1. Explain the basic purpose of the Robinson–Patman Act. Who is being protected? From whom? Why?

2. Discuss three areas of price cutting that the Robinson–Patman Act does not affect. Give examples of each.
3. Why is it important for the buyer to know the market before beginning price negotiations?
4. Is it important that the buyer understand the resource's production problems before negotiating? Why?
5. What are cash discounts? How are they considered by top management?
6. Differentiate between anticipation and cash discounts.
7. How much cash would be needed to settle a $200 invoice, terms 2/60 with anticipation at the rate of 6 percent per annum, if it is paid in 30 days?
8. How do trade discounts differ from quantity discounts? Be sure to define each.
9. An invoice for $100 less trade discounts of 30, 10, 10 can be paid with a check for $______ .
10. Define seasonal discounts. Explain their relationship to the Robinson–Patman Act.
11. Why do retailers use cooperative buying? How does it work?
12. Discuss and give an example of consignment buying. What are its advantages and disadvantages?
13. Discuss negotiating in terms of the "limits" of the buyer and seller.
14. What is meant by ROG? F.O.B.? EOM?
15. Why do large stores print their own order forms?
16. Discuss the use of vendor-printed order forms for a small retailer.
17. A large retail organization prints its order forms in five copies. By whom are they used?
18. Define and discuss preretailing.

## CASE PROBLEM 1

The Acme Store is a large, successful one-unit retail store in a downtown urban area in the Midwest. The store was founded in the mid-1930s, and it grew steadily from its inception through the mid-1980s. Since then, though still profitable, its growth has been shrinking. This is due in large part to the departure of many of its customers to the suburbs.

The store's merchandising division has been and continues to be excellent. Thanks to aggressive, tasteful buying, the organization attracts far more than its normal share of the market. Moreover, the goods are sold at a markup in excess of that achieved by its competitors. It has become apparent to top management that the store's operation is not likely to be improved. Under such conditions, the continued shrinkage of volume and profits will be offset only by seeking out nonselling weak spots and applying corrective measures.

One area that seems to offer possibilities for savings is the reduction of transportation costs. A preliminary spot check of completed orders has revealed that most buyers indicate shipping instructions to the vendor by noting "best way" or "cheapest way."

You have been hired by the store as an expert in transportation. All the store's records are available to you.

### Questions

1. What will you look for?
2. What suggestions will you make?

## CASE PROBLEM 2

The swimsuit buyer for a large department store has been placing the major portion of his orders with a large, nationally branded manufacturer throughout the season. He has been successful with the merchandise and maintains an excellent relationship with the resource.

He has been informed that on July 1 the vendor plans a drastic price reduction on goods that have proved salable. From his past experience, the buyer knows that many of his store's customers have put off buying their swimwear in anticipation of an annual July 20 sale.

The buyer has a list of 14 styles he is interested in. These originally sold at $40 each. They will be offered at $20 each during the sale. For the sale to be a success, at least a 40 percent markup is required.

### Questions

1. What is the highest price the buyer can afford to pay for each swimsuit?
2. What information does the buyer need to carry on the negotiation successfully?
3. What concessions can the buyer try for in addition to a price reduction?
4. What will be the effect of the Robinson–Patman Act on the negotiations?

# Section III

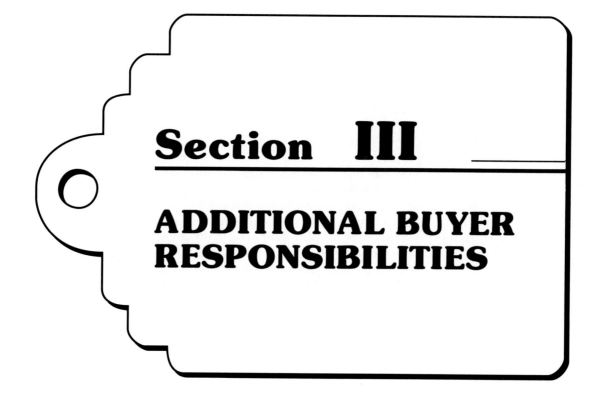

# ADDITIONAL BUYER RESPONSIBILITIES

# Chapter 14

# MERCHANDISE PRICING

## LEARNING OBJECTIVES

*Upon completion of this chapter, the student should be able to:*

1. Differentiate between the manner in which a large store buyer and a small retailer set prices.
2. Score 70 percent on a merchandising mathematics examination. The test should include problems on markup at retail, cost, related problems, cumulative markup, average markup, markdown percent, and turnover.
3. Write an essay on markdowns including timing, amount, and markdowns as a means of evaluating buyers.
4. Discuss the advantages and shortcomings of turnover information.
5. List and briefly discuss the factors that affect pricing policies.
6. Define price lines and discuss five advantages of their use.

## INTRODUCTION

Profits are the ultimate test of the effectiveness of the buying function. Profitability is measured by comparing the cost of an item with its selling price. The buyer therefore must be just as concerned with the selling price of goods as with their cost, since each of these functions affects profits equally.

## PRICING POLICIES

The success of a retail operation depends in large part on its pricing policies. Decisions on overall pricing are made on an executive level considerably higher than the buyer. In most instances, the buyer is given a target markup percent and volume for a particular period. This usually takes the form of a budgeted sales figure and a markup percentage (the difference between the cost and the selling price stated as a percentage). The success of a small retailer or of a buyer in a large store is measured by whether he or she falls short of, meets, or exceeds this budget.

Markup percents are never set uniformly throughout a store. Different departments, for a variety of reasons that will be discussed later in the chapter, are expected to yield varying profits. Although the markup percents are increased slightly year after year as operating costs increase, each department's increase generally remains in the same proportion to those for other departments in the store.

### Departmental Pricing

The buyer, then, is given a fairly rigid markup percentage to work with, and can expect to be called in to discuss any substantial variation from this amount. There is, however, considerable flexibility from there on. For example, a buyer who is told that the department is expected to produce a markup of 45 percent is not generally forced to fit every item into that slot. The 45 percent figure is an average markup, and she may, at her discretion, go above or below it on each item she buys. In other words, management is not concerned with the profitability of individual items. It expects a 45 percent average markup; how this is arrived at is the responsibility of the buyer. This allows for considerable skill and ingenuity. One mark of a good buyer is the way in which he or she handles this averaging.

### Pricing for the Small Retailer

The purpose of a pricing policy is to make certain that the excess of the selling price over the cost of the goods sold is sufficient to cover expenses and yield a reasonable profit. Naturally, this is as important to a small retailer as a large one. All retail stores, regardless of size, operate under a pricing policy set by top management. The difference is that the large store executive has to set up formal pricing guidelines to be carried out by subordinates, whereas the small operator need not be so formal, since he or she will do (or at least closely supervise) the buying. This lack of rigidity in following policy is one of the few advantages the small operator has over the giants.

## MERCHANDISING MATHEMATICS

Buyers are responsible for achieving a certain average markup. They arrive at this figure by averaging a variety of different markups on a wide assortment of merchandise. Obviously, they must become very proficient with the mathematics of markup calculation if they are to be successful at the job.

### Markup

Markup is the difference between the cost and the desired selling price of goods. As mentioned earlier, it must be sufficient to cover the expense of operating the business plus a desired profit. Thus if the cost of merchandise is $75,000, the operating expenses $15,000, and the desired profit $10,000, the goods must be sold for $100,000. Then,

| | |
|---|---|
| Sales | $100,000 |
| Cost of goods | 75,000 |
| Markup | $ 25,000 |
| Less: expenses | 15,000 |
| Profit | $ 10,000 |

The markup of $25,000 is the excess of sales over the cost of goods. It is sufficient to cover the expense and leave a profit of $10,000.

Retail (selling) price − cost = markup

#### *Individual Initial Markup*

Individual initial markup is the markup on an individual item that the buyer hopes to achieve.

PROBLEM A pair of slacks that cost $50 is offered for sale at $100. What is the markup?

SOLUTION Retail price ($100) − cost ($50) = markup ($50)

Markup, when referred to by buyers, is always calculated as a percentage. This is done by dividing the amount of markup by the cost or the retail price.

**Markup on retail.** In almost all instances markup is based on retail. Since sales figures are always available, the use of retail makes calculation much easier. For example, knowing a store grossed $2000 in weekly sales and that the average markup is 40 percent, it is easy to calculate the gross profit of $800 ($2000 × 40%). If the markup percentage were based on cost, it would be necessary to calculate the cost of the $2000 of sales before applying the markup percentage.

The formula for calculating the markup percentage on retail is as follows:

$$\frac{\text{Markup}}{\text{Retail}} = \text{markup percentage based on retail}$$

**PROBLEM** A scarf that cost $10 is priced to sell at $15. Determine the markup percentage based on retail.

**SOLUTION**

$$\text{Retail} - \text{cost} = \text{markup}$$
$$\$15 - \$10 = \$5$$
$$\frac{\text{Markup}}{\text{Retail}}\ \frac{\$5}{\$15} = 33\tfrac{1}{3}\%$$

**Markup on cost.** Though rare, some retailers use a markup percentage based on cost. A retail produce store whose selling prices vary greatly from day to day finds cost a more stable base for markup calculations.

The formula for calculating markup on cost is as follows:

$$\frac{\text{Markup}}{\text{Cost}} = \text{markup percentage based on cost}$$

The markup percentage based on cost in the preceding problem would be calculated in this manner:

$$\frac{\text{Markup } \$5}{\text{Cost } \$10} = 50\% \text{ markup based on cost}$$

## *Related Markup Problems*

There are related markup calculations with which merchandise buyers must be familiar. These require a slight rearrangement of the basic formula.

**Finding the retail when the cost and markup on retail are known.**

**PROBLEM** Find the retail price of a table that cost $84 and is to be marked up 60 percent on retail.

**SOLUTION**

$$\begin{aligned} \text{Retail} &= \text{cost} + \text{markup} \\ 100\% &= 40\% + 60\% \\ (\text{Cost})\ 40\% &= \$84 \\ 1\% &= \frac{84}{40} \\ 1\% &= \$2.10 \\ (\text{Retail})\ 100\% &= \$210.00 \end{aligned}$$

**Finding the cost when the retail price and markup on retail are known.**

**PROBLEM** Find the cost of a radio selling at $60 that is marked up 35 percent on retail.

**SOLUTION**

$$\begin{aligned} \text{Cost} &= \text{retail} - \text{markup} \\ \text{Cost} &= 100\% - 35\% \\ \text{Cost} &= 65\% \\ \text{Cost} &= 65\% \times \$60 \text{ (retail price)} \\ \text{Cost} &= \$39.00 \end{aligned}$$

### *Cumulative Markup*

As we will see later in the chapter, the buyer, although budgeted to a specific departmental markup, cannot achieve this desired profit on every item. Competition, for example, might force some of the goods to be marked up less than he or she would like. To offset this problem, the buyer can reach the goal only by marking up other items above the target figure. Under these conditions, the desired markup becomes an average of many varying individual markups.

Buying is an ongoing function. The buyer is constantly visiting manufacturers and wholesalers to purchase additional goods. Since it is necessary for the buyer to meet a targeted markup figure, he or she must know the markup percent on the goods handled to date. From this information, the buyer will know whether he or she needs high-markup, normal-markup, or low-markup goods. To determine the cumulative markup, the following formula is used:

$$\text{Retail price of all goods on hand} - \text{cost of all goods on hand} = \text{markup on all goods on hand}$$

then,

$$\frac{\text{Markup on all goods on hand}}{\text{Retail price of all goods on hand}} = \text{cumulative markup percentage}$$

**PROBLEM** At the beginning of the month, a clothing buyer had goods on hand that cost $10,000 and were marked up to sell for $15,000.

During the first two weeks she bought additional goods for $5000 that were to be sold for $10,000. What was the cumulative markup at that time?

SOLUTION

| | COST | RETAIL |
|---|---|---|
| Opening inventory | $10,000 | $15,000 |
| Purchases | 5,000 | 10,000 |
| Total goods on hand | $15,000 | $25,000 |

Retail − cost = markup
$25,000 − $15,000 = $10,000

then:

$$\frac{\$10{,}000}{\$25{,}000} = 40\% \text{ cumulative markup}$$

### *Average Markup*

Cumulative markup informs the buyer of the relationship between the markup on the goods already bought and the markup that has been budgeted in advance. From this information, the buyer is able to determine whether he or she is above or below goal and by what amount. The way in which the buyer uses the cumulative percentage in arriving at the target percent is a problem of averaging.

PROBLEM A retail dress shop plans to spend $12,000 during the month for merchandise. The purchases are to be marked up 40 percent on retail. During the first three weeks of the month, $6000 worth of goods are bought and offered for sale at $9000. At what price must the remaining budgeted purchases be marked to achieve an average 40 percent markup at retail?

SOLUTION 1. Find the total planned purchases at retail.

Retail = cost + markup
100% = 60% + 40%
60% = cost
60% = $12,000

$$1\% = \frac{\$12{,}000}{60}$$

1% = $200
100% = $20,000

2. From the total planned purchases at cost and retail, subtract the purchases already made.

| | *COST* | *RETAIL* | *MARKUP* |
|---|---|---|---|
| Total planned purchases | $12,000 | $20,000 | 40% |
| Purchases already made | 6,000 | 9,000 | |
| Balance needed | $ 6,000 | $11,000 | |

To average a markup of 40 percent, the remaining $6000 of purchases must be marked up to sell for $11,000. This yields a dollar markup of $5000 ($11,000 – $6000) and a markup percent of 45.45 percent:

$$\frac{\text{Markup ( \$5,000)}}{\text{Retail (\$11,000)}} = \$45.45\%$$

If there were goods on hand at the beginning of the month (opening inventory), they would be taken into account by being added to the total planned purchase. In the preceding problem, assume there were $1000 of goods on hand at the beginning of the month that carried a retail price of $2000.

| | | *COST* | | *RETAIL* | *MARKUP* |
|---|---|---|---|---|---|
| Total planned purchases | | $12,000 | | $20,000 | 40% |
| Less: opening inventory | $1000 | | $2000 | | |
| Less: purchases already made | 6000 | 7,000 | 9000 | 11,000 | |
| Balance needed | | $ 5,000 | | $ 9,000 | |

Under this condition the $5000 balance of purchases needed would have to be ticketed at $9000 to bring the average markup to 40 percent. The markup percentage on the goods to be bought would be determined as follows:

$$\frac{\text{Markup \$4000 (\$9000 − \$5000)}}{\text{Retail \$9000}} = 44.44\%$$

### *Maintained Markup*

If all merchandise was sold at the price it was initially marked, profits would soar dramatically. We all know, however, that for a variety of reasons this is not possible. Prices are reduced because the item didn't sell as well as anticipated, soilage, new merchandise is ready to be received and space is needed, the season is nearing an end, the item was a fad and therefore short lived, and similar reasons.

When these price reductions have been taken, the markup that is actually achieved is called the maintained markup.

**PROBLEM** A sweater buyer purchased 100 pieces at $30 and marked them to sell for $60. Toward the end of the season, he was left with 20 pieces which he reduced to $40 each. What was his maintained markup for the sweater purchase if he sold the balance for $40.

**SOLUTION** 1. Find the initial markup

$$\begin{aligned} \text{Initial markup} &= \text{original retail} - \text{cost} \\ &= \$6000 - \$3000 \\ &= \$3000 \end{aligned}$$

2. Find the initial markup percentage

$$\begin{aligned} \text{Initial markup \%} &= \frac{\text{initial markup}}{\text{original retail}} \\ &= \frac{\$3000}{\$6000} \\ &= 50\% \end{aligned}$$

3. Find the maintained markup %

$$\begin{aligned} \text{Maintained markup} &= \text{net sales} - \text{cost} \\ &= \$5600^{*} - \$3000 \\ &= \$2600 \end{aligned}$$

*80 sweaters sold @ $60 each = $4800

20 sweaters sold @ $40 each = 800

$5600

4. $$\begin{aligned} \text{Maintained markup \%} &= \frac{\text{maintained markup}}{\text{net sales}} \\ &= \frac{\$2600}{\$5600} \\ &= 0.464 \\ &= 46\% \end{aligned}$$

The buyer actually achieved 4 percent less than he originally hoped to obtain (50% − 46% = 4%).

## Markdowns

Markdowns are reductions in selling price. To understand fully the nature of markdowns, one must start with the concept that the original price is purely an estimate.

### *Reasons for Markdowns*

1. *Excessively high selling prices.* When selling prices are set at a level that discourages sales, markdowns become necessary. This may be a serious error, since the proper selling price may not be placed on the goods until too late in the season. This often results in lower selling prices than would have occurred had the merchandise been properly marked. This is not to be confused with intentionally high prices being set early in the season to attract customers who are willing to pay a premium to be fashion leaders. This practice frequently increases the cumulative markup.
2. *Errors in buying.* Buying errors are probably the most common reasons for markdowns. The most salable goods are valuable only if the quantities purchased are matched with an adequate estimate of consumer demand. When the amount of purchases exceeds the quantity sold, costly markdowns will result. Similarly, miscalculations in colors or sizes will force prices to be reduced. Markdowns of seasonal goods often occur when goods are ordered too close to the end of the season. Customers are simply not interested in buying winter coats in March at the regular price.
3. *Errors in selling.* Slow-moving stock must be marked down. Frequently sales are lost owing to poor display and weak sales personnel. It is often difficult to determine whether the loss of profits due to markdowns is a result of poor buying or of inefficient sales management. The best that can be done is constantly to evaluate the sales force and weed out the weak performers.
4. *Nonerror markdowns.* Not all markdowns result from buying or selling errors. Many seasonal goods depend on the weather. Snow tires are not sold in dry winters. A warm fall can be ruinous to outerwear. Occasionally new products appear on the market suddenly and make older goods obsolete. Stores that stocked expensive conventional tires had problems when steel-belted radials came out. Other goods may be marked down despite the best efforts of the most capable, hardworking people. There will always be shopworn merchandise and odd sizes that can be sold only at reduced prices.

Sometimes management encourages markdowns to earn the store a reputation for always having a full assortment of merchandise in stock. Management encourages late buying, which may result in markdowns. In other words, management is willing to pay the cost of markdowns for the image of carrying a full assortment.

### *Markdowns as a Means of Evaluating Buyers*

Markdowns are frequently a serious problem for buyers. Too often top management, in judging the efficiency of its buyers, gives too much weight to markdowns. A buyer should be judged by his or her overall record, of which markdowns are only a small part. Anyone can cut down on markdowns by playing safe and buying small quantities of relatively staple goods, a policy that will lose many, many sales. The best way to kill incentive, ingenuity, aggressiveness, and enthusiasm in buyers is to be overly critical of markdowns.

### *Timing Markdowns*

Markdowns are losses in selling price. The smaller the markdown, the less the loss. Timing is a crucial factor in determining the size of the markdown. The purpose of the markdown is to attract customer attention, but this can be done only when the shopper is in a buying mood. The less interested the buyer is in the goods, the more drastic the markdown needed to attract attention. Markdowns, then, can be minimized by being taken as early as possible in the season, when the maximum number of shoppers is interested. A small markdown taken *as soon as* demand for an item diminishes is more likely to move goods than a drastic slash late in the season. This will not only improve profitability, but also provide the buyer with the money to buy new styles in the middle of the season. Constantly bringing in new merchandise during the season is necessary to encourage shoppers to call again and again. Perhaps the most important factor in successfully marking down goods is the sales information available to the buyer. Sales reports must be accurate, prompt, and diligently studied to ensure proper timing.

Many stores, particularly exclusive specialty shops, postpone their markdowns to the end of the season and run a semiannual, storewide markdown event at that time. This practice, accompanied by heavy advertising, attracts many customers to the store and reduces the number of bargain hunters during the height of the selling season. Such sales are usually held in January and July. Most stores compromise their timing. Large stocks of slow-moving goods are marked down immediately. Semi-annual or monthly sales are used to move any goods left over plus odd sizes and shopworn stock.

Slow-moving merchandise of a staple nature is often warehoused and carried over to the following season rather than sold at a marked-down price. The advantages are obvious, since the goods can be sold at a higher price at the beginning of the next season. The disadvantages of this practice are the cost of storage, loss of freshness, possible damage, and tying up capital. Moreover, the most staple goods have a way of becoming obsolete owing to changes in style or the emergence of new fabrics or other materials.

Some stores mark down certain goods automatically. That is, after a specific period the goods may be marked down 25 percent. Several weeks later the prices are slashed again, and so forth. It is doubtful that such an inflexible policy can be widespread. It does not take into account such factors as a season that is delayed by unusual weather. The best known automatic markdown system is in Filene's Basement Store in Boston. Merchandise is marked down 25 percent after 14 days, 50 percent after 21 days, and 75 percent after 28 days and is given to charity if unsold after 35 days. Naturally, the system is unique. It is based on expert buying of closeout merchandise, coupled with rapid merchandise turnover, to bring the store a profit.

### *Amount of Markdown*

The purpose of a markdown is to attract customers to goods that have previously been ignored. Too large a markdown reduces profits unnecessarily. Too small a markdown will not produce the desired interest. The exact amount is a test of the buyer's ingenuity and must be based on the extent of customer uninterest, the amount of goods on hand, and the time left in the season. Often there is time for a second slash later in the season. Under such conditions, the initial markdown would be smaller than the later one.

### *Markdown Calculations*

Buyers are vitally interested in their overall markup percentage. Since this amount is affected by markdowns, the buyer must te able to calculate the markdown percentage on the sales of reduced merchandise.

PROBLEM A furniture buyer ran a sale on kitchen furniture. The goods had an original retail price of $10,000 and were reduced for the event by 15 percent. All the goods were sold. Calculate the markdown percent based on sales.

SOLUTION 1. Calculate the dollar markdown.

$$\text{Original retail} \times \text{reduction percent} = \text{dollar markdown}$$
$$\$10{,}000 \times 15\% = \$1500$$

2. Calculate the amount of the sales.

$$\text{Original retail} - \text{dollar markdown} = \text{sales (new retail)}$$
$$\$10{,}000 - \$1500 = \$8500$$

3. Calculate the markdown percent based on sales.

$$\begin{aligned}\text{Markdown \%} &= \frac{\text{dollar markdown}}{\text{amount sold}} \\ &= \frac{\$1500}{\$8500} \\ &= 17.6\%\end{aligned}$$

## Merchandise Inventory (Stock) Turnover

Merchandise inventory turnover is a ratio that indicates the number of times per period that the stock of goods has been sold and replaced by fresh merchandise. This information is widely used by management to check the efficiency of a department and by a buyer to find weak spots within a department. Good turnover generally indicates good management, since it measures the speed with which goods pass from the store to customers.

### *Calculating Turnover*

The formula for calculating turnover for a period is as follows:

$$\frac{\text{Sales}}{\text{Average inventory (at selling price)}} = \text{turnover}$$

Turnover can be calculated for a week, a month, a season, or a year. *Sales,* of course, means the sales for the period, and the inventory used is the average inventory at retail for the period. The average inventory for a month can be calculated by adding the beginning- and end-of-month inventories and dividing by two. If the turnover for longer periods is to be calculated, inventories at the end of each month are added, and the average is determined by dividing the total by the number of inventories totaled. When weekly inventory figures are available, weekly turnover may be computed.

**PROBLEM** From the following information, find the turnover for the six-month period.

| | | *SALES* | *INVENTORY AT RETAIL* |
|---|---|---|---|
| July | 1 | | $ 15,000 |
| July | 31 | $ 10,000 | 22,000 |
| August | 31 | 8,000 | 18,000 |
| September | 30 | 12,000 | 25,000 |
| October | 31 | 20,000 | 40,000 |
| November | 30 | 15,000 | 30,000 |
| December | 31 | 35,000 | 60,000 |
| | | $100,000 | $210,000 |

**SOLUTION** 1. Find the average inventory

$$\$210{,}000 \div 7 = \$30{,}000$$

2. Find the turnover.

$$\frac{\text{Sales}}{\text{Average inventory}} = \text{turnover}$$

$$\frac{\$100{,}000}{30{,}000} = 3.33 \text{ merchandise inventory turnover}$$

### *Advantages of Good Turnover*

Generally, the higher the turnover, the better and more quickly goods are sold. A good turnover ensures the constant arrival of new goods in the department. This improves traffic, store reputation, and the morale of the sales personnel. Goods that move quickly are rarely marked down. They remain fresh, and the amount of handling is reduced. Moreover, inventory that moves out quickly is easily financed. In short, all other things being equal, profits follow turnover.

Buyers should compare their turnover with both the published records of similar operations (see Table 14-1) and their own records from prior periods. In addition, by breaking down their operation by price line or groups of similar items, the weaknesses of certain areas can be identified and dealt with.

A major problem with the calculation of turnover is that the necessary inventory figures are not always available. The widening use of computers for inventory control has overcome this for the larger stores.

### *Shortcomings of Turnover Information*

While turnover offers an excellent yardstick for efficiency, it is of little use alone. One problem is that it does not indicate profits. A high turnover can be achieved by a poorly run operation. For example, by keeping the inventory low,

**TABLE 14-1** Turnover by merchandise classification

| *TYPE OF RETAIL FIRM* | *APPROXIMATE NUMBER OF STOCKTURNS YEARLY* |
|---|---|
| Gasoline service stations | 21 |
| Grocery and meat stores | 18 |
| Confectionary stores | 12 |
| Budget millinery | 11 |
| Liquor stores | 6 |
| Paint and wallpaper stores | 5 |
| Drugstores | 4 |
| Infants' and children's wear | 4 |
| Furniture stores | 3 |
| Family clothing stores | 2 |
| Retail shoe stores | 2 |

a high turnover can be achieved despite the fact that customers cannot find the goods they are after. Turnover can also be increased by insufficient markup. Bargain prices will increase sales, but only at the expense of profits.

## FACTORS THAT AFFECT PRICING POLICIES

Buyers for both large and small stores are forced to adhere to overall markup percentage policies. The buyer for a large store gets the information from management. The small store operator, though less rigid, needs a certain minimum markup percentage to survive. The exact percentage of markup is influenced by many factors.

### Store Image

Some high-prestige stores such as Bloomingdale's pictured in Figure 14-1 have been able to implant in their customers' minds an image that makes their clientele willing to pay a premium for goods bearing a highly prized label. Generally such an image carries with it a higher than ordinary cost of doing business.

**FIGURE 14-1.** Bloomingdale's, Chicago, a store with a high fashion image. *Courtesy:* Space Design International.

Such prestige is the result of expensive fixtures, highly paid personnel, and extensive service. Extra markup is necessary to cover the extra cost of the image.

### Services

Stores that offer such services as free garment alternations, individualized sales help, decorator advice, and the like must increase their markup to cover these additional costs. It is incorrect to regard price as the only factor influencing customers. Such stores as Saks Fifth Avenue, Neiman-Marcus, and Nordstrom run highly successful operations based on a clientele that knowingly pays a premium in return for additional services these stores offer.

### Convenience

Small local retailers are able to get higher prices than their giant competitors by cutting down on customer travel time or remaining open for longer hours.

### Competition

Perhaps the most important of the factors affecting price is the pressure of competition. There is a limit to the amount of premium customers are willing to pay for extra service, image, or convenience. Each retailer must find its own price niche, which carefully balances the operation against those of competitors by taking all influences on price into account.

### Private Labels

One way of getting around the problem of competitor pricing is by carrying merchandise that is unique and cannot be compared. Private labeling allows a store to stock goods that none of its competitors can carry. For example, the Charter Club label is carried exclusively by Macy's and cannot be comparison shopped. Private labels are available to smaller retailers though resident buying offices. Many small retail liquor stores carry goods bearing their own label. Since private brands require very little selling and no promotional expenses for the manufacturer, the retailer can often buy them cheaply and attach a higher than normal markup to them.

### Merchandise Characteristics

Certain goods have characteristics that dictate a markup policy. High-risk goods, for example, must be marked up sufficiently to cover markdowns and other losses. Fashion goods, perishables, and seasonal goods fall into this category.

Other goods have high overhead costs associated with them. Precious jewelry needs an expensive vault; bulky merchandise like furniture needs expensive floor space; expensive men's wear requires highly paid salespeople. Additional markup is necessary to cover the additional overhead required by such merchandise.

#### *Promotional Costs*

Advertising and sales promotion are extremely expensive, and the markup must be sufficient to cover such costs. This does not mean that heavily advertised merchandise is more expensive. Frequently big advertisers depend on quick turnover to keep prices low. However, in setting markups, promotional costs must be borne in mind.

#### *Leaders and Loss Leaders*

One way to entice traffic into a store is to offer a specific item of merchandise or a whole department at a selling price that is at, below, or near cost. Supermarkets regularly feature different items, each week, at cost or below.

#### *Discount Operations*

A discount operation is one that competes exclusively on a price basis. It offers minimal services, bare fixture, and no prestigious label. It seeks a rapid turnover at lower than usual markup. The buyer for such a store searches for quantity discounts on name brands as well as less known merchandise with which to sweeten the overall markup by getting normal or better than normal markups on these not easily compared items.

## *PRICE LINES*

No store can be large enough to carry an adequate stock of merchandise in every price range. To attempt such a "general store" approach would force so limited an assortment in each range that a customer would be offered very little to choose from. A woman shopping for a dress has a good idea of the amount she wishes to spend. Unquestionably, she will select a store with a wide assortment of dresses in that range. By definition, a price line is a situation in which a single price or range is used in place of a variety of prices.

### Selecting Price Lines

In general, the image of the store sets the overall tone of price lining. That is, a high-image, prestigious store will not carry low-priced apparel. Naturally, it will offer high-priced merchandise. However, within the term *high priced* there are many price lines available. For example, a "high-priced" man's suit can run anywhere from $600 to $1200. Establishing the proper price line for a particular store and the number of price lines to be carried requires particular care and constant control. These decisions depend on customer demand, and experience has shown that relatively few price lines are needed. Since customer demand varies, experimentation for price line changes must be continual.

An important consideration in the selection of price lines is that they should be far enough apart to make the difference in the quality of the goods easily apparent to the customer and the salesperson.

## Advantages of Price Lines

Price lines or price points, as they are often called, are widely used because of the advantages they provide.

**Increased sales.** Concentrating the merchandise at a price that has been determined as most appropriate to customer demand requires elimination of the slower-moving goods. This concentration provides the shopper with a wide variety of goods at prices he or she is willing to pay. The elimination of slow-moving goods increases sales and turnover while decreasing markdowns.

**Easier selection.** It is easier for a customer to choose between two items when their prices are similar. The shopper does not have to decide between a $50 pair of shoes and a $175 pair. If they are both marked in the range of $50–75, the decision may be based only on style and quality.

**Better control.** The effect of price lining is to decrease the number of items carried while increasing the depth of backup stock for each item. This results in fewer out-of-stock situations. In addition, fewer items require less salesperson time to find a particular piece and easier determination of the depth and condition of the stock. The decrease in assortment that results from price lining increases the salesperson's familiarity with the stock and reduces storage space.

**Reduced marking costs.** When there are a few prices that can be quickly learned by the personnel, savings may be effected in such overhead areas as marking, paperwork on returns, and remarking of returned goods.

**Better purchasing.** As the number of items becomes more concentrated, the number of possible resources supplying the store dwindles as well. The buyer, then, can be more specialized and become familiar with more vendors for the specific goods. Buying a wide assortment of goods limits buying visits to a relatively few vendors in each category. Price lining enables the buyer to concentrate on a few vendors. This increases the retailer's importance to them and enables the buyer to get preferential treatment in such areas as delivery date, price, and acceptance of merchandise returned to the vendor.

**Improved promotion.** Price liners are able to focus their advertising and display. Rather than being forced to spread out their promotional budget so that every area is touched, they concentrate on the merchandise their experience has shown to have the greatest demand. This leads to improved promotional efficiency.

## *UNIT PRICING*

During the present "age of the consumer," many agencies, both governmental and private, are offering suggestions to protect the buyer. Unit pricing is one such idea that has been adopted by many food retailers. Unit pricing requires that, in addition to the price of an article, the price per unit be marked as well. Typically, the supermarket shopper is faced with a buying decision that compares two items: The first offers 8½ ounces for $1.03, the second, 12¼ for $1.27. Which is cheaper? Many stores help the consumer by showing the cost per ounce of each package.

## ACTION FOR THE SMALL STORE BUYER

The bottom line for any retailer is profit. Selling a large amount of merchandise does not guarantee profits. Small store buyers are often more concerned with what and how much to buy than with spending the time properly pricing their purchases.

A thorough understanding of markup and the factors that affect pricing are a must. It is becoming more difficult each year for smaller merchants to compete with the chains and department stores. The giants in the industry have a definite advantage in terms of cost. The small store, however, does have one significant advantage over the big store: *service.* Customers who patronize the small store often do so for the individual attention afforded them. By offering a favorable shopping atmosphere, assisting each customer on a one-to-one basis, and providing services such as free alterations, the small store can often achieve a price that this particular customer is willing to spend. Most people are willing to spend a little more for the attention the big store is unable to offer.

Another area for consideration for the small store buyer is that of discounting, or working on a smaller markup. This seems to be a contradiction of the preceding discussion. Small stores sometimes have the advantage of being located in out-of-the-way places where rents are low. They can then, through lower operating costs, lower their prices. Many small retailers operate on such a basis and make their reputations by actually offering prices lower than those of the big stores.

Whichever approach is more appropriate, the small store buyer can successfully compete with the large companies and bring a profit to the store.

## SUMMARY OF KEY POINTS

1. Profitability depends on markup and pricing. Markup is budgeted in advance by the merchandising manager and serves as a means of judging a buyer's efforts.

2. The more important formulas involving markup are the following:

$$\text{Markup} = \text{retail} - \text{cost}$$

$$\text{Markup \%} = \frac{\text{markup}}{\text{retail price}}$$

$$\text{Markup on cost} = \frac{\text{markup}}{\text{cost}}$$

3. Cumulative markup is the markup on all the goods handled to date plus merchandise that is about to be purchased.
4. Average markup is the markup on all the goods handled during a period.
5. Markdowns are reductions in selling price. Markdowns may be due to excessively high selling price, errors in buying, errors in selling, weather, obsolescence, and the like.
6. Buyers are frequently judged by the size of the markdowns. This can be a serious error on the part of top management.
7. The timing of markdown is crucial. The earlier the markdown, the smaller the price cut.
8. The size of the markdown requires good judgment. It must be large enough to attract customers, but not so large that profits are reduced unnecessarily.
9. The formula for markdown percentage is as follows:

$$\frac{\text{Dollar markdown}}{\text{Amount sold}} = \text{markdown \%}$$

10. Stock turnover is a ratio that indicates the number of times per period that the stock of goods has been sold and replaced by fresh merchandise. It is a means of checking the efficiency of the buyer. The formula is as follows:

$$\frac{\text{Sales}}{\text{Average inventory (at retail)}} = \text{stock turnover}$$

11. A good turnover rate ensures the constant arrival of new goods and improves traffic, store reputation, and morale. However, there are shortcomings to turnover information. For example, it does not indicate profitability and can be achieved by carrying an inadequate inventory.
12. Some factors that affect pricing policies are store image, services, conveniences, competition, private labels, characteristics of the merchandise, promotional costs, leaders and loss leaders, and discount operations.
13. A price line is a situation in which a single price or range is used in place of a variety of prices. In general, the price line selected depends on the

image of the store. Price lining has the following advantages: increased sales by concentrating on the goods customers desire, easier selection by customers, better control, better buying, reduced marking costs, and improved promotion.

## REVIEW QUESTIONS

1. Why don't department stores allow each buyer to decide on the overall markup for a department?
2. A buyer is given an overall markup that he or she has to achieve. How does this affect the pricing of individual items?
3. Compare the pricing policy set by the owner of a small retail store with that set by executive management of a department store.
4. Calculate the markup on retail and the markup percentage on an item costing $7 and selling for $10.
5. Do any retailers base their markup calculations on cost? Why? Give examples.
6. Find the retail price of a sweater that cost $42 and is to be marked up 60 percent on retail.
7. Find the cost of a lamp selling at $120 that is marked up 35 percent on retail.
8. Define cumulative markup. Give the formula for its calculation.
9. Define average markup. How is it used?
10. Define markdowns. Give the formula for the calculation of the markdown percentage based on sales.
11. Discuss and give examples of markdowns that result from buying errors.
12. Give examples of markdowns that are caused by selling errors.
13. Do all markdowns result from errors? Discuss.
14. Discuss the importance of the proper timing of markdowns.
15. What factors must be taken into account in determining the amount of the markdown?
16. Goods with an original retail price of $5000 were marked down 30 percent; all the goods were sold. Calculate the markdown percentage based on sales.
17. Define turnover. Give the formula for its calculation.
18. What are the advantages of a good rate of turnover?
19. Can turnover alone be used to judge the efficiency of an operation? Discuss.
20. Discuss briefly six factors that affect pricing policies.
21. What are price lines? What advantages do they offer?

22. How should price lines be selected?
23. Define unit pricing. Give examples.

## CASE PROBLEM 1

John Douglas operates a small, moderately priced women's wear shop. The store has been open for two years and has barely managed to break even, after paying Mr. Douglas a small salary.

The proprietor has spent ten years as a salesman in a large, very successful store carrying the same type of merchandise he carries in his own business. From his experience he understands the store operation very well. In addition, he has excellent taste, which he is able to match to the requirements of his customers. As a result, he rarely buys the wrong goods. However, his experience is limited to selling and customer relations. He knows very little about buying procedures or proper planning.

His accountant has informed him that he needs a 40 percent markup on sales to cover his expenses and leave him a reasonable profit. For the season beginning September 25 and ending December 25, he planned to carry goods costing $60,000. On September 25 he had $10,000 worth of goods with a retail value of $15,000. By December 1 the goods he had purchased cost $45,000 to retail at $65,000.

### Questions

1. At what percentage must the balance of his purchases be marked up to achieve his desired markup?
2. Comment on Mr. Douglas's planning.

## CASE PROBLEM 2

You are the merchandising manager of the home furnishings division of a large urban department store. A year ago the floor coverings buyer resigned. After many interviews with applicants from both within and outside the store, you decided to hire Frank Thomas, one of the assistant buyers for the floor coverings department. Mr. Thomas is a young man who graduated from the store's executive training program five years ago. He has much less experience than some of the other applicants. However, you were impressed with his aggressiveness, intelligence, and regard in the eyes of his coworkers that you decided to go along with him. Naturally, since you are responsible for this choice, you are concerned about the results of his first full year's operation.

The year has just ended, and the only information available is the data necessary to compute the stock turnover.

| | | *SALES* | *INVENTORY AT RETAIL* |
|---|---|---|---|
| January | 1 | $ — | $100,000 |
| January | 31 | 35,000 | 100,000 |
| February | 28 | 45,000 | 220,000 |
| March | 31 | 55,000 | 200,000 |
| April | 30 | 60,000 | 180,000 |
| May | 31 | 50,000 | 140,000 |
| June | 30 | 45,000 | 130,000 |
| July | 31 | 40,000 | 100,000 |
| August | 31 | 40,000 | 100,000 |
| September | 30 | 45,000 | 200,000 |
| October | 31 | 60,000 | 230,000 |
| November | 30 | 85,000 | 150,000 |
| December | 31 | 40,000 | 100,000 |

During the last year the previous buyer was on the job, the stock turnover was 3.2 and annual sales were $510,000.

## Questions

1. Calculate the merchandise inventory (stock) turnover.
2. What conclusions can you draw from the turnover?
3. What other information will you need to make a definite decision on the new buyer's ability?

# Chapter 15

# THE DEVELOPMENT OF PRIVATE LABEL PROGRAMS

## LEARNING OBJECTIVES

*Upon completion of this chapter, the student should be able to:*

1. List five reasons for the widespread use of manufacturer's labels by retailers.
2. Explain the reasons behind the trend toward private labels.
3. Describe three methods of obtaining private label merchandise.

## *INTRODUCTION*

The development of the private label or brand is rapidly becoming the most significant method of coping with "off-price" retailers. At a time when manufacturers are selling their goods to retailers who function on less than the traditionally or conventionally accepted markups, buyers for every merchandise classification are using the private label as a competitive tool. It should be noted that off-price retailing is not limited solely to retail merchants; it has become a fast-growing method for manufacturers who operate their own outlets quickly to dispose of their merchandise at less than the "regular" selling price. Secaucus, New Jersey, and Reading, Pennsylvania, are two sites in which producer-owned outlets are achieving success to a point that is the envy of most conventional retailers.

Many manufacturers have gained their reputations by promoting labels and brands that have been recognized by consumers as quality products. As a result, most retailers have capitalized on the manufacturer's recognition and have stocked their own shelves with this merchandise. It has, in the past, resulted in maximum profits for the store. Today, however, with the competiveness of the off-pricers, retailers have started to evaluate the necessity of changing their merchandise mixes and are, in ever-increasing numbers, embarking on the development of private label programs.

While the majority of the major store buyers agree that some private labels are mandatory for the contemporary retailer, most must resolve such problems as these: What percentage of their offerings should be private label? Who should produce the goods? Should the merchandise bear a "recognizable signature" or the store's own name? How should it be promoted? This chapter will examine the rapid growth of the traditional retailers' private label development and its place in the merchandise mix, as well as the advantages the manufacturer's brand still affords most retailers.

## *MANUFACTURERS' BRANDS*

Until the present decade, most retailers would have agreed that a successful, recognizable manufacturer's brand meant a guarantee for repeat business and often a better than normal markup. Because of this, most retailers who operated in the traditional manner actively sought such merchandise for their inventories. Not only did the brand help presell the customer through the manufacturer's advertising campaigns, but it also brought customers to the store who might, while there, buy nonbranded or private label goods.

The advantages of the manufacturer's brands, to the retailer, can best be summarized as follows:

1. *Customer demand.* Successful producers' brands have an established following that will be attracted to the store that carries the brand. This will

increase the volume on the specific goods involved while at the same time increasing the store's traffic to the advantage of the other selling departments.

2. *Promotion costs.* The manufacturer bears the major part of the promotional costs of its branded items. This reduces the store's share of the advertising costs.
3. *Quick sales.* The characteristics of manufacturers' brands are usually well known to customers. This reduces selling expenses by saving the salesperson the time it takes to explain the benefits and uses of the product.
4. *Inventories.* Manufacturers of branded goods usually carry large inventories of their products, while they are willing to ship in small quantities. This has the effect of reducing the depth of inventory the store must carry.
5. *Quality control.* A successful manufacturer is usually a specialist in the manufacture of a branded item. Its equipment and control of costs and quality have the effect of reducing customer complaints and returns. In contrast, stores that involve themselves in private labeling are more diversified in their interests and often lack adequate controls.
6. *Prestige.* Being associated with a well-known, high-quality branded item tends to increase the store's prestige and attract additional customers besides those who come in for the branded goods.

Missing from the list of advantages is one that would have been there as recently as ten years ago—price maintenance. It was always expected that the manufacturer's brand would maintain price until the normal end of a selling season and, even at that time, that the price reduction would be small. The circumstance that alters this previously relied-upon advantage to retailers is the competition against the traditional department and specialty stores by the off-price merchants. Not only are manufacturers selling their goods "with the identifying labels affixed to the merchandise" to the off-price outlets, but many are successfully operating their own off-price units. This form of manufacturer-owned retailing affords the producer an outlet for "overcuts" (production greater than sales), slow-selling merchandise, store returns, and often current, up-to-date goods.

Given these conditions as the facts of life for today's retailer, there had to be an adjustment to the merchandising of the manufacturer's brand. Buyers cannot rely on the previous average markup of these goods, nor can they wait for the end of a season for their disposal. A visit to any major retailer will show the markdown of manufacturer's brands at any point in the season when sales begin to slip. It is not unusual for the heretofore "famous" brand to be marked down only a few weeks after introduction on the selling floor.

It should be understood that stores are not abandoning their manufacturer's brands and labels but are adjusting their merchandise mixes to maintain better markups. Thus, the boom in private labeling has made a strong appearance on the retail scene.

## *PRIVATE LABELS AND BRANDS*

Any discussion of a store's "own products" concept must begin with the examination of one of the retailing industry's giants. From the moment Sears opened its doors for business, it steadily built a reputation on merchandise that was its alone. Not that Sears manufactured its own lines: It developed private brands and labels that have become household names throughout the country. Sears has built a monumental reputation on names such as Coldspot, Kenmore, and Craftsman, all of which are exclusively Sears' but are produced by companies that also manufacture under nationally branded names. In the food industry, A & P has also capitalized on its own brands, especially Ann Page, and has continued to capture a significant part of the market by doing so.

It is ironic, however, that at a time when retailing is finally following the Sears and A & P lead, those two organizations are adjusting their offerings to incorporate a larger proportion of manufacturer brands into their merchandise mixes. Found alongside of their own brands, Sears now features merchandise bearing the Levi Strauss and Adidas labels.

Before a retailer can make the decision to alter its merchandising philosophy and embark on the private label concept, it is important to use the research tools necessary to evaluate customer reaction. Where retailers have, in years gone by, based their buying decisions on less sophisticated measures, today's merchandising team understands the value of in-depth research, especially in such an area as the introduction of the store's own-label merchandise.

### Determining Customer Attitudes

Many major retail organizations have taken surveys to assess consumers' attitudes toward manufacturers' brands and labels. The results of these surveys have shown, by and large, that customers are showing less reliance on the manufacturer's brand and relying more on the store's reputation for their merchandise selections.

In a telephone survey taken by the Newspaper Advertising Bureau (NAB), with 2705 men and women responding from an overall figure of 4000 calls, the findings were even more significant in favor of "store reliability" than most traditional retailers would have guessed. Table 15-1 clearly shows that 58 percent of the market makes purchasing decisions based on store reputation and reliability rather than a specific manufacturer's brand. This barometer gives buyers a positive signal to develop a private label or brand program or, if they are already

**TABLE 15-1** Customer's attitudes on brands and store image

| | *MEN* | *WOMEN* | *COMPOSITE* |
|---|---|---|---|
| Branded label merchandise gives me better quality and value | 45% | 35% | 39% |
| If the store is reliable, it makes no difference whose brand is on the merchandise | 53 | 62 | 58 |
| No answer | 2 | 3 | 3 |
| | 100% | 100% | 100% |

involved in one, to consider an adjustment in the merchandising mix to coincide with the figures revealed by the survey. Naturally, caution should be exercised to determine if the individual store's customers are those reflected in the NAB survey. Only a thoroughly researched investigation of its own customers would give the retailer the proper information.

## PROGRAM DEVELOPMENT

When a store decides to embark on the private label or brand concept, or makes a determination to expand its present program, it has three specific routes to take to achieve its goal. Retailers have the option of directly purchasing goods produced by manufacturers and affixing their own labels to the merchandise, buying goods with private label identification through resident buying offices, or establishing their own facilities in which to manufacture the goods.

Buyers do not make the ultimate decisions regarding the best road to private labeling, but they certainly have considerable input into this managerial decision because of their expertise with specific lines of merchandise.

### Direct Purchasing

#### *Purchasing from National Manufacturers*

To purchase directly from recognized manufacturers affords the buyer the opportunity to put private labels on goods that have already been proved. Since most of these manufacturers already produce merchandise under their own labels, the buyer can assess quality and standards. The most important part of any private label program is customer satisfaction with the product. The store must demonstrate that the product not only sells for less than the national brand, but is of comparable quality. The manufacturer's reputation is based on past performance, an advantage the buyer has in making an evaluation of the goods offered now under private label.

### *Purchasing from Private Label Manufacturers*

Some stores elect to purchase their "private label" needs not from the nationally recognized manufacturers but from producers whose manufacturing is exclusively limited to private label.

There are, in this country, manufacturing consultants who serve retailers with product development for private labeling. These are different from the national brand manufacturers who produce the highly recognized brands and variations under a store's private label. The consultant companies are dedicated to the development of merchandise with store buyers' and merchandisers' input. They offer retailers merchandise that will be theirs exclusively, designed and produced by experts who run no other type of manufacturing operation.

Mitchell Paige is one such manufacturing consultant. Working successfully for such nationally recognized major retailers as Marshall Field's, Saks, Sakowitz, Porteous-Mitchell-Braun, and Sanger's has made this company an important resource for private label goods. Mitchell Paige service begins with the design of the merchandise according to the buyers' specifications, coupled with its own expertise, and ends with delivery of the completed goods to the stores. In a very few years, the company has become a full-scale manufacturer with a network of 30 contractors in the East producing men's, women's, children's clothing, and fashion accessories. Given this enormous success, it is evident that the private label is the trend in retailing.

### *Labeling*

Once having made the decision to purchase "private label" from manufacturers, it is necessary to determine if it is best to develop a label that will be totally identifiable with the store, or one that bears a proven household name that will be sold exclusively to the store.

**Stores' own identifying label.** Predominant among retailers has been the route taken by Sears and other majors to develop their own identifying labels. Some have remained with the concept of a single label to identify the store's own brand; others have taken more aggressive approaches and have undertaken multiple programs.

Dayton's, a Minneapolis-based department store, began a private label project under the name Boundary Waters. The name was derived from a group of rivers, falls, and lakes forming the U.S.–Canadian border, which is 250 miles north of Minneapolis–St. Paul. Merchandise was limited to rugged men's and women's outerwear. The promotion set records for the company. After one year, the company made available better than 100 items using the Boundary Waters label throughout the store. The distribution included ready-to-wear, fashion accessories, housewares, gourmet food, and candy.

The Dayton's private label success was not based just on luck. It took an enormous promotional effort to help make customers aware. Some of the support given to ensure recognition and eventual purchase by the customer included

- Erection of a 400- to 600-square-foot shop in Dayton's main stores featuring summary displays that highlighted storewide items available as Boundary Waters
- Production of 200,000 color maps, suitable for framing by the customer, of the boundary waters region. The maps were made available with merchandise purchases
- Free color Boundary Waters shopping bags
- Institutional as well as promotional color advertisements in regional magazines
- Radio and television commercials from introduction day until Christmas

The results were outstanding. Fall 1982 showed private label penetration of 8 percent, with expected increases of double or triple.

Marshall Field's has an extensive private label program that goes one—or perhaps five—steps further than Dayton's. Field's promotes five labels in men's wear alone. Field's believes that separate and distinctive labels are the best approach to identify different categories of its men's wear offerings. It promotes private label merchandise in the men's classification, which makes up 25 percent of its men's wear offerings, as follows:

- Club Fellow for heavy-volume goods
- Field Standard for prestige and basic wear
- New Traditions for goods considered to be acceptable by trend-aware customers
- Field Sport for active and active-styled sportswear
- Field Gear for rugged wear

The merchandise marketed under the labels is both imported and domestic, with the imports making up the large proportion.

It would be hard to find a major retailer today who has not already incorporated a private label program using a well-known manufacturer for production, with the store's own label affixed to the garments.

An interesting concept of private labeling is one developed by Spiegel. Figure 15-1 spells out the details.

## Resident Buying Office Acquisitions

An alternative to direct dealing with the manufacturers and the origination of a store label for exclusive use is commitment to a resident buying office's brand. Although it doesn't afford the retailer total exclusivity, it does make

design
partnership™

You speak, we listen. And the result is Design Partnership—work clothes that reflect your point of view. Because they're shaped by your opinions, executed to your standards. How? Each garment comes with a response tag so you can tell us what you think. And you have. In fact, we've learned quite a bit over the past two seasons. Your preferences in styles and fabrics. Your insistence on quality. And as you'll see in our third collection, we hear you. Just who is the "we" you ask? Three working women bringing know-how in fashion design, retailing and real-life closets to the drawing board. Putting their experience—and your ideas—right on the hanger.

**FIGURE 15-1.** Design Partnership, a Spiegel private label. *Courtesy:* Spiegel Catalog.

possible the purchase of merchandise that will be distributed solely to non-competing member stores. This permits a relative amount of exclusive usage in a geographic area, as well as price protection.

The Frederick Atkins resident office has evolved a private label for its member stores. Committed to a two-year agreement, Atkins is merchandising men's and women's apparel under the Jonathan Stewart label. It is estimated that stores which agree to carry this private label will do so at the rate of 15 to 20 percent of their total merchandise offerings. To encourage member stores to sign on with the two-year commitment, Atkins has offered participants a national support system by way of advertising and promotional campaigns. Each store is to be provided a television commercial and statement enclosures, as well as 35mm slides, a videotape, and other materials for sales training on a cost-sharing basis. Other promotional materials made available by Atkins will include advertising preparation, in-store presentations, and research-oriented profiles of target customers. To round out the effort and make it appealing to the member stores, Frederick Atkins is demanding strict adherence to price stability. This will take away any fears of price tampering and will encourage the stores to promote the new private label with complete confidence.

Henry Doneger Associates, a resident buying office with more than 200 member stores, offers numerous brands under its own labels. Although it doesn't mandate usage by the stores of the private label merchandise, it reports that almost every store it represents carries some of the labels offered as shown in Figure 15-2.

By relying on private label programs initiated by resident buying offices, retailers can participate in programs that guarantee a degree of exclusivity without the problems associated with direct manufacturer contact and their own label development. Recent trends have continued to show an increase in

**FIGURE 15-2.** The private labels of Henry Doneger Associates.
*Courtesy:* Henry Doneger Associates.

the number of stores offering their own completely private labels as well as those offered on a "semiprivate" basis by the resident buying offices.

### Company-Owned Production

Many of the giants of the retail industry still produce their own merchandise, which is marketed under their store names. Marshall Field's was the chief practitioner of manufacturing goods with plants in seven states and in such foreign countries as China.

Although there are chains throughout the country that produce their own goods for exclusive sale in their own outlets, such as Edison Brothers, which manufactures the shoes for its own stores, such as Baker's, the majority of private brands look to others for their merchandise acquisitions.

## *INTRODUCTION OF A PRIVATE LABEL PROGRAM*

Once the store has made the decision for private label, it must initiate a plan to introduce it to the consuming public. Having planned the items to be incorporated in the program and developing the appropriate label hardly guarantees customer acceptance. Stores must be willing to make substantial dollar investments in these programs to motivate their customers to accept the new line.

Significant among the various approaches that have been taken by retailers to introduce their private labels are these:

- Creation of separate departments to feature the line
- In-store and window displays to dramatize the private label
- Extensive advertising campaigns in a multimedia approach
- Customer giveaways featuring the store's private label
- Sales training classes for employees to emphasize product knowledge of the merchandise
- Fashion shows and informal modeling of the items
- Promotions that feature, side by side, the private label item with a national brand item at a higher price
- Shopping bag giveaways displaying the new label

### A RETAIL BUYING FOCUS

#### *Macy's Private Labels*

One of the most successful department store organizations in the world is Macy's, with stores spread throughout the leading retail centers of the United States.

Macy's has kept pace, and often outdistanced its competitors, by paying attention to customer needs and providing them with what they have demanded. Its merchandise mix has long included the top names in fashion and hard goods lines. Clothing, accessories, home furnishings, furniture, and other merchandise classifications regularly feature the names of the industry leaders. In fashion, it offers the established designer lines such as Liz Claiborne, Ralph Lauren, Perry Ellis, and Calvin Klein as well as those who show promise in the field.

The store's product mix, however, is not limited to the lines that are available at other stores throughout the country. It has invested heavily in collections that are Macy's alone and market them under a variety of private labels. It is generally conceded that in the retail industry, Macy's is the leading retailer of private label goods. Names such as Jennifer Moore are featured extensively in the home furnishings department, Alfani and Christopher Hayes in men's wear, Aeropostale in the young men's department, Charter Club on the main floor, and Fantasies by Morgan Taylor in lingerie.

To the average customer, these, and other private labels, are goods that carry a well-known, branded label. This is certainly not the case since Macy's designs and produces the merchandise for exclusive use in their stores. What accounts for the success of these labels is the manner in which the company visually merchandises the lines and presents them along side of nationally branded labels. Charter Club, for example, is reminiscent of many Ralph Lauren items such as the famous polo shirt and is featured in close proximity to the prestigious designer's collection and in a similar manner. The major difference between the private label, Charter Club, and the Lauren line is the price. Through the exclusion of middlemen, prices for the former are in the customer's favor.

As do all merchants involved in private labels, Macy's makes its own lines appealing by carefully offering quality merchandise at popular price points. With careful presentation, all the lines are winners.

---

Retailers have hired outside consultants to work with their own staffs for ideas to incorporate in the introduction of their private labels. Only total involvement will ensure customer awareness of the private label lines of goods that buyers and merchandisers have provided for their stores.

## ADVANTAGES OF THE PRIVATE LABEL

Careful analysis of the information presented in this chapter indicates that the merchant who incorporates the private label into the store's offerings enjoys certain specific advantages. The list that follows is general in nature, but is appropriate to most large retailers. While small retailers cannot afford the luxury of large-scale private label programs, they can participate through resident buying office affiliation. The advantages of such programs are these:

1. Because the large retailers spend huge sums for advertising anyway, the high cost of promoting a brand does not require any additional outlay of funds. A change in the emphasis of the advertising copy at no additional cost may be all that is required to promote a private label.
2. The customer following that is built up by the brand belongs to the store rather than to the manufacturer. The price, styling, and quality of the goods are set by the store's merchandising team for the benefit of the store. In contrast, manufacturers' brand goods are merchandised for the benefit of the manufacturer.
3. Private branders do not have to deal with independent-minded manufacturers who may set strict policies on returns, tie-in sales, and the setting of retail prices. Private branders need not be concerned over the possibility that a brand that they have helped promote may be taken away at the whim of the manufacturer.
4. Because the brand is controlled by the retailer, price cutting, changes in style and quality, and, in fact, complete control of the merchandising of the goods are all in the hands of the buyer.
5. Merchandise that carries a manufacturer's brand can be found in other nearby stores. In a sense, a store that promotes such goods is doing it for competitors as well as for itself. This is not the case with private brands. They are exclusive to the store.
6. Goods carrying a private brand cannot easily be comparison shopped by customers. Although the goods may look exactly like competing goods, the brand name is different and the customer can never be sure. Retail stores with discount house competition frequently resort to private branding for this reason. The inability to comparison shop private brands keeps them from being price cut as frequently as unbranded merchandise.
7. Manufacturers' brands, particularly the national ones, are tailored to the tastes of a national audience. Frequently this does not correspond to the taste of the customers of a particular store. Private brands, on the other hand, may be designed to the specific tastes of a store's customers, which increases their salability.
8. A successful brand that has been able to build up a following of satisfied customers can usually support a better than average markup to the party that controls the brand. When the brand is a private one, the additional markup goes to the store rather than to the manufacturer.
9. The very large retailers, whose selling capacity is sufficient to require the total output of a large, efficient production facility, are able to increase their

profits by adding the manufacturing profits to their normal selling profits. A & P, for example, maintains canning plants to supply its stores.

10. In cases in which the merchandise that is to be privately labeled is bought from independent manufacturers, the cost of the merchandise may be reduced because the high volume involved reduces manufacturing costs and because the manufacturer is able to save promotion costs on the merchandise that is to be privately labeled.

## A RETAIL BUYING FOCUS

### *Will the Alligator Become Extinct?*

At a time when merchants are battling in their own minds the rationale concerning the expansion of private label programs and what percentage of these offerings will make up their merchandise mix, the question of the value of famous emblems poses a dilemma to many.

In the late 1970s, the rush for label recognition saw apparel of every type transfer the label and emblem from the inside of the garment to the outside. Izod, Ltd., with its nationally recognized alligator emblem, led the way for many years. Sales for the "Alligator" merchandise have increased ten times in the last decade and have continued to show enormous strength. Companies such as J. C. Penney climbed on the bandwagon with a Fox emblazoned on the Izod look-alike.

Has this type of merchandising peaked? Bloomingdale's has taken the direction of deemphasizing the label, believing that consumers want more individualism in their clothing choices.

While most retailers are staying with the emblem emphasis, many are beginning to pay close attention to the sales of these items. Izod had embarked on a program to feature more and more nonemblem goods in anticipation of the demise of the alligator.

Gant, a competitor of Izod in the knit shirt market, made the move for emblem removal five years ago. Its "Rugger" emblem was removed from the face of the garments.

Many reasons have been cited for this trend. Discounters have taken hold of the emblem products and have made them less appealing to traditional merchants and their customers; many promotional chains have gotten on the bandwagon and have marketed merchandise with an emblem such as "Hunter's Glen," an embroidered horse featured at K-mart; and flea markets have continued to feature everyone's emblem (most have been known to be counterfeits) at rock-bottom prices.

Given these conditions, it appears that more attention will be paid to private labels, affixed to the inside of the garment, and less to the emblem. The alligator might be laid to rest!

## ACTION FOR THE SMALL STORE BUYER

The movement to private label programs is quite evident among large retailers in this country. The use of such programs, however, need not be limited to the giants of the industry. Small store buyers can and should investigate the avenues available to them to avail themselves of such merchandise.

The easiest route to take is to meet with a resident buying office representative to discuss its private label merchandise. Most of the major offices have developed merchandise and labels for the exclusive use of their member stores. Since they have the potential for enormous purchases, which come as a result of being able to pool orders from member stores, the resident offices can negotiate with major resources to produce merchandise made to specifications. Of course, this route to private label merchandise necessitates joining an office that has such a program. In today's retailing picture, this is an important step, one necessary to compete with the department stores, chains, and off-price merchants.

Another approach is to organize a buying group made up of noncompeting small stores by pooling orders. The group will have enough clout to approach many manufacturers with specific merchandise needs. Although the organization of such a group might be difficult and time-consuming, it does afford the small store buyers an advantage that the resident buying office does not. In this situation, the buyers can "design" the merchandise they want. Through resident office affiliation, they can purchase only the private label merchandise available under the office's program.

In any event, it is imperative that small store buyers investigate the possibilities of private label merchandise in order to bring a higher average markup to their stores. With the growth of off-price retailing, the smallest merchant will be affected. If private label merchandise is used in the right proportion, it could increase the store's profits.

## SUMMARY OF KEY POINTS

1. The development of the private label or brand is rapidly becoming the most significant method of combatting off-price merchandise.
2. Stores still rely heavily on manufacturers' brands because of customer demand, quality, prestige, promotion of the goods by the producer, and the advantage of often being able to reorder quickly.
3. A disadvantage for today's retailer of manufacturers' brands and labels is price cutting of this merchandise by discounters and manufacturer-owned retail outlets.
4. Stores such as Sears, which have grown with the "private label only" concept, have started to adjust their merchandise mixes with the addition of manufacturer's brands.

5. Surveys indicate that a large percentage of customers are more concerned with a store's reliability and not the labels or brands it carries. This is a good reason to introduce private brands.
6. Much of the private label merchandise featured by stores is produced by manufacturers that also produce their own brands under different recognizable labels.
7. The giants of the retail industry also make private label acquisitions from manufacturers that do nothing but produce goods specifically for the store's private label needs and with input from the store's buyers and merchandisers.
8. Stores that do not have the buying capability often necessary for private label purchase use resident buying offices as sources of such merchandise.
9. In order to ensure success with their private label programs, stores spend enormous sums on promotions that include development of separate departments for the goods, extensive advertising campaigns, displays, and sales training classes.

## REVIEW QUESTIONS

1. What is today's major reason for growth in private label merchandise?
2. How are some manufacturers contributing to the problem created by retailers who sell off-price?
3. Are stores moving in the direction of eliminating the manufacturer's brand?
4. Does the manufacturer's brand offer the retailer the above-average markup it once did?
5. List three advantages of the manufacturer's brand.
6. Describe the "make up" of the goods generally featured in manufacturer-owned outlets.
7. How has Sears altered its merchandising concept?
8. Discuss the customer's attitude toward brand names and store image.
9. Why would a buyer purchase private label goods from the manufacturer of a famous brand?
10. What is a private label manufacturer?
11. How involved do buyers become with the private label manufacturers?
12. Compare Dayton's private label program with that of Marshall Field.
13. Can the small retailer offer private label merchandise to its customers?
14. Aside from purchasing private label from manufacturers and through resident buying offices, how can stores obtain this type of goods?
15. Describe how stores have highlighted their private label lines.

16. List five advantages of private label programs.
17. How has Izod approached the "no emblem" trend in merchandising?

## CASE PROBLEM 1

Peters-Blair is a retail organization consisting of three full-line department stores located in Dallas, Houston, and Los Angeles. Each of the stores is extremely successful in terms of both volume and profits. Although it operates only three stores, the combined sales of the organization rank it among the volume leaders of the country.

The stores are operated as high-priced, prestigious retailers. Their label is known and respected throughout the country.

Peters-Blair does no private branding. It carries all the high-priced quality brands in addition to a variety of unbranded merchandise. Its records disclose that the markup on unbranded merchandise is significantly higher than it is able to achieve on its branded goods.

The appliance buyer has made a proposal to the top merchandising team that the store establish a private brand for appliances. He reasons that the store's excellent reputation should make private branding relatively easy. His plan is to begin with refrigerators, and replace all the nationally branded merchandise with a line of privately branded products. If this is successful, he will go on to other items. You are the top merchandise manager.

### Questions

1. What other information do you want?
2. What do you think of the buyer's plan?

## CASE PROBLEM 2

Tailored Man operates a chain of 12 medium-priced men's wear shops in Chicago and its suburban areas. The stores carry a full line of medium-priced and promotional goods; each store is well established and operates at a profit. The chain has been expanding slowly, opening a new store every two years out of the profits accumulated by the other units in the organization. Accumulated profits are substantial, and the organization is in a strong financial position.

Several years ago the store began going into private branding. It accomplished this one department at a time by adding its own private brand to the established national brands. In addition, it has instructed its salespeople to push the private brands and emphasizes this by paying an extra commission on sales of store-branded goods.

You are one of the store's buyers. Your responsibilities are dress shirts, sport shirts, hosiery, underclothes, and handkerchiefs. The owners of the chain have informed you that they would like to begin private branding in your department next year. You have been asked to prepare a report indicating the goods you will brand and all the methods to be used to get into the private branding operation.

## Question

1. Prepare this report.

# Chapter 16

# THE BUYER'S ROLE IN PLANNING ADVERTISING, VISUAL MERCHANDISING, AND OTHER PROMOTIONAL ACTIVITIES

## LEARNING OBJECTIVES

*Upon completion of this chapter, the student should be able to:*

1. Discuss cooperative advertising, including the advantage and disadvantage of the operation.
2. Define and give examples of indirect advertising.
3. Write a brief essay on the effect of a store's merchandising policy on the selection of merchandise to be promoted.
4. Explain in detail the way in which the advertising request illustrated on page 340 of the text is filled out.
5. Differentiate among the following pricing terms: regularly, originally, comparable value, and value.

6. Discuss the buyer's role after the advertising request has been submitted. This should include layout approval, proof examination, use of tear sheets, notification of appropriate staff, and evaluation.
7. Define display, explain its importance, and give examples.
8. Explain the value of a special event to an individual buyer.
9. Define and give the advantage and disadvantages of a one-day sale, a three-day sale, and a warehouse sale.

## INTRODUCTION

At this point, having explored the many facets of retailing in which buyers are involved and for which they have responsibility, it can be appreciated that the buyer's job is not completely dependent on purchasing. Of enormous importance is the promotion of the merchandise once the buyer is committed to the purchase. Without exception, every experienced retailer spends considerable sums in an attempt to whet customer's appetites. Whether it's simply informing them of this week's supermarket bargain in the company shopping publication or presenting a department's special event centering on houseware imports, the buyer plays a central role in the promotion.

One might believe, then, that the buyer must be an expert in advertising, visual merchandising, and special event coordination. This is not true. Buyers initiate promotions, select merchandise that is to be advertised or featured in a store's window and interiors, arrange for cooperative advertising allowances and indirect advertisements, and provide the information that is finally utilized in an advertisement or promotion.

## THE PROMOTIONAL BUDGET

As in every business, top management decides the amount of money to be expended for promotion of the retail organization. Among the criteria considered in determining how much promotional money will be received by each department are its past sales volume and projected figures, its size, its relative importance to the store's overall merchandising, long-range experience that might indicate increases or declines, the percentage of sales as a result of past advertising and other promotions, and competition.

Having decided on the final budget allocation, some retailers further earmark specific amounts for advertising, visual merchandising, special events, and the like, while others give their buyers considerable responsibility by letting them decide how the money is to be used in their respective departments.

Whichever method is employed, few buyers ever concede that they have a sufficient promotional budget to satisfactorily expose their offerings to the consuming public. This being the case, management very often expects the buyers, through negotiation, to expand their promotional dollars with the assistance of the manufacturers and wholesalers from whom they purchase their merchandise. Knowedgeable buyers stretch their budgets through arrangements that include cooperative and indirect advertising.

## COOPERATIVE ADVERTISING

As a condition of a purchasing agreement, buyers who deal in significantly large quantities often insist that the manufacturer share the expense of advertising. The manufacturer agrees to such an arrangement for a number of reasons. First, it might be the only way the buyer will purchase the goods. Second, it provides the manufacturer with exposure to the consumer market. And, third, since the Robinson–Patman Act generally disallows quantity discounts, it permits the manufacturer to sweeten the deal for the buyer.

The allowance or the sum of money expended by the manufacturer is usually based on the amount of merchandise purchased by the store. The manufacturer might agree to pay for 50 percent of the advertisement for a sum that is equal to perhaps 5 percent of the buyer's purchase. For example, if a store purchases $50,000 worth of merchandise and is allowed 5 percent for an advertising allowance, which can be used to pay for 50 percent of the cost of the advertisement, then $50,000 × 0.05 = $2500 advertising allowance to be paid toward a $5000 advertisement. In this way the buyer can run a $5000 ad while incurring only half of the cost, thereby considerably stretching his or her promotional budget.

The money from cooperative advertising arrangements is used for newspaper, magazine, radio, television, and direct mail. Figure 16-1 shows an example of an advertisement that was cooperatively paid for by several manufacturers and the retailer.

While cooperative advertising has certain advantages for the store, buyers must be aware that this sharing of advertising expense might present some problems. The buyers' job is to purchase the most desirable merchandise available for their customers. This should be uppermost; they should not be motivated to purchase because of the advertising allowance. Over zealous buyers might seek out vendors who are prepared to offer huge promotional sums and thus allow the merchandise in question to take a back seat. Another pitfall of cooperative advertising is that it sometimes motivates buyers to order in excessively large quantities so that they can qualify for a bigger allowance. Buyers must not be guided by manufacturers' quantity demands for cooperative advertising, but must remain within the limits of their inventory plans. Seasoned buyers learn quickly that overpurchasing leads to markdowns, and these excessive price reductions can severely cut into the store's profit. Finally, the experts agree that advertising is not a miraculous catalyst in the movement of merchandise. Advertising will make salable items sell faster and in larger quantities, but

**NM opens today at 10 a.m., at Cherry Creek.**

**YOUR GUIDE TO NM CHERRY CREEK**

**Level One:** women's shoes and accessories, precious jewels, men's apparel and furnishings, hosiery, cosmetics, stationery, gifts, tabletop and decorative items, men's restroom.

**Level Two:** couture, furs, women's sportswear, intimate apparel, suits and dresses, gift wrap, executive offices, credit office, women's restroom.

**EVENTS IN-STORE THIS WEEK AT NM CHERRY CREEK**

**Monday, August 20**
**Mary Jane Marcasiano.** A fresh collection of creative and comfortable knitwear, with informal modeling from 11 to 3. Leisure Sportswear.

**Christian Dior Suits.** Classic career dressing for fall, with informal modeling from 11 to 3. Galleria Collections.

**Commemorative posters.** Don't forget your full-color "Denver 1990" poster, created especially by Neiman Marcus to celebrate our newest store! They're 10.00 each at special outposts on both levels, or free with a purchase of 50.00 or more in any department.

**Tuesday, August 21**
**Albert Nipon Suits.** The Fall '90 collection, with informal modeling from 11 to 3. Galleria Collections.

**Wednesday, August 22**
**David Navarro jewelry.** Exquisite materials and innovative design distinguish this collection. Accessories.

**Anne Klein II.** Timeless separates for mistake-proof career dressing, with informal modeling from 11 to 3. Sport Shop.

**Clearly superior.**
Our collection of fine crystal reflects a global perspective: American Steuben, Irish Waterford, French Baccarat, and the remarkable Japanese designs of Hoya, ours exclusively in Denver. Come in soon and see all the shining examples. The Galleries, on Level One.

**Thursday, August 23**
**Go Silk.** Luxurious yet casual separates that glide effortlessly into fall, with informal modeling from 11 to 3. Leisure Sportswear.

**Robert Comstock for men.** Inspired by his own adventurous lifestyle, this all-American designer creates ruggedly sophisticated separates. Men's Sportswear.

**Friday, August 24**
**Robert Comstock, in person.** Meet the designer as we present his dramatic new collection for women. Designer Sportswear.

**Saturday, August 25**
**Linda Allard for Ellen Tracy.** Looking good has never been simpler than with these updated classics. Informal modeling from 11 to 3. Sport Shop.

**On your feet.**
From classic styles by Ferragamo and Bruno Magli to the most current innovations from Manolo Blahnik and Robert Clergerie, the NM footwear collection has something for everyone. Shoe Salon on Level One.

**DKNY for fall.** Donna Karan's very modern approach to casual style. Informal modeling from 11 to 3. Leisure Sportswear.

**Commemorative posters.** Don't forget your full-color "Denver 1990" poster, created especially by Neiman Marcus to celebrate our newest store! They're 10.00 each at special outposts on both levels, or free with a purchase of 50.00 or more in any department.

Neiman Marcus

**Cherry Creek**
3030 East First Avenue, (303) 329-2600
**Store Hours:** Monday–Friday 10 to 9, Saturday 10 to 6, Sunday noon to 5.

In addition to the Neiman Marcus Charge Card, we welcome the American Express® Card.

**FIGURE 16-1.** A cooperative advertisement that features numerous designers. *Courtesy:* Neiman-Marcus.

it will not sell unwanted goods. Buyers who are preoccupied with advertising allowances may find themselves settling for second-rate merchandise. While the buyer's advertising budget might increase significantly through advertising allowances, he or she might also find the inventory stocked with items that customers won't buy.

## *INDIRECT ADVERTISING*

As an inducement for buyers to spend large amounts on their lines of merchandise, some manufacturers offer to mention the buyer's store in their own advertisements. Many manufacturers advertise heavily in magazines and on television to attract consumer attention. In an effort to make certain that the merchandise can be found easily by the consumer, the manufacturer mentions key stores where the goods are available. There are two major differences between indirect and cooperative advertising. In the case of indirect advertising, the ad is fully paid for by the manufacturer and the message concentrates on the product with only a mention of the store, which is considered an indirect advertiser.

## *SELECTION OF MERCHANDISE TO BE PROMOTED*

Whether the item to be promoted is earmarked for a window display, a direct mail piece, a newspaper advertisement, or any other kind of promotion, its selection must be carefully considered. Not every piece of merchandise is worthy of promotion. It is the general opinion of merchandisers that slow-moving items will not sell better if they are promoted. Advertising and other promotional techniques are reserved for goods that are proved sellers or those that deserve special attention. The person best qualified to select the most appropriate items is the buyer. Since the buyer pays close attention to the sales activity of the goods included in inventory and has a keen awareness of the hot items that the market has to offer, he or she is in the best evaluative position.

Each store determines its merchandising policy, and that usually dictates to the buyer the type of goods that are to be promoted to the consuming public. For example, stores like Saks Fifth Avenue and Neiman-Marcus, with powerful fashion images, will advertise the latest style without waiting to determine its salability. They run the risk of promoting something that might not sell. Another retailer, also fashion oriented but not necessarily determined to introduce new styles, will wait and use its promotional dollars for proved fashion items. Still other retailers will concentrate strictly on price and run advertising only when they can undersell their competitors. It should be understood that few retailers have so rigid a policy, and many run advertisements on unknown as well as proved sellers. Buyers, however, should not lose sight of the fact that advertising and other promotions cannot sell unwanted merchandise.

## THE BUYER'S ROLE IN PREPARING ADVERTISEMENTS

Most large retail operations (small stores generally operate in a haphazard manner) begin the preparation of an advertisement after it has been initiated by the buyer of the merchandise to be advertised. Similarly, displays are created after the request has been made by the buyer.

Figure 16-2 shows an advertising request form that is typical of large department stores throughout the United States. Careful examination of the form underscores the important role played by the buyer in the advertisement of his or her wares. The buyer must complete a great deal of preliminary planning before the advertisement is published to help guarantee that the results will produce increased sales.

The buyer's advertising involvement in most retail organizations is generally along the following lines.

### Completion of the Request Form

Occasionally the information in an advertisement is incorrect or incomplete. This makes it rather difficult for consumers to make a fair judgment of the merchandise. It might be that an air conditioner advertisement neglected to indicate the necessary power for proper utilization or an ad for luggage available through mail order omitted the choice of colors. Many ads have been completely unsuccessful in terms of sales because of these fundamental errors. To make certain that those responsible for the artistic creation of the ad have the information necessary, the buyer must complete the form carefully.

A detailed examination of an advertising request form will be made here to underscore its importance and the involvement of the buyer and others in its proper compilation.

Since newspaper advertising is used most extensively by retailers, its importance is indicated by the amount of space it is given on the form compared to other media. This does not mean, however, that the newspaper is best suited for every consumer product. For example, a stereo sale might be more appropriate on television, where both the visual and audio qualities can be appreciated.

In selecting the medium to be used for particular merchandise, the buyer must determine which would be most appropriate. This requires not only the selection of the newspaper, for example, but which of those available should be chosen. In addition, the size of the ad (or the time allocation in radio and television) is most important. To make the proper determination, experienced buyers call on other experts for advice. The advertising manager, the advertising agency, and the store's research department (if it has one) are all excellent sources of market information. Studies and research undertaken by these parties produce the information that is needed for the buyer to run the ad in the appropriate medium at the best time.

# ADVERTISING REQUEST

CIRCLE ONE | Z | DI | X

THIS FORM WILL NOT BE ACCEPTED UNLESS INFORMATION IS COMPLETE

**DEPT. NO.**

| | DATE | SIZE | | DATE | SIZE |
|---|---|---|---|---|---|
| ☐ TIMES | | | ☐ COLONIE | | |
| ☐ NEWS | | | ☐ AMSTERDAM NEWS | | |
| ☐ POST | | | ☐ SUFFOLK SUN | | |
| ☐ L.I.P. | | | ☐ OTHER (LIST) | | |
| ☐ NEWSDAY | | | ☐ | | |
| ☐ WEST. GRP. | | | ☐ | | |
| ☐ N. H. REG. | | | ☐ | | |

MERCHANDISE FOR NEW ART WORK IS DUE IN 15th FL. LOAN ROOM WHEN PINK SHEET IS DUE

EXCEPTION: Ready-to-wear merchandise is due directly after weekly Merchandise Review Meeting. Bulk merchandise should be available on the floor for movement to studio, or for sketching, when called for. Merchandise in LOAN ROOM? Yes | No

Do not request New Art Work BEFORE checking file FOR OLD ART.

| No. of Illus. | Illustrations to be featured. Points to be emphasized |
|---|---|
| No. of New | |
| No. of Old | Date and medium in which old art ran last (attach proof) |

OTHER MEDIA. ☐ MAGAZINE NAME ______ ISSUE ______ ☐ SALE BOOKLET ☐ OTHER DIRECT MAIL ☐ RADIO ☐ TV

MAIL ORDERS Yes ☐ ☐ No PHONE ORDERS Yes ☐ ☐ No COUPON Yes ☐ ☐ No

TOTAL AMT. OF MDSE. AT RETAIL $ ______ NO. OF UNITS ______ DAY SELLING IS TO BEGIN ______ NUMBER OF DAYS ON SALE ______

ON SALE AT: (CIRCLE) ALL STORES - H. S. - R. F. - HUNT. - B. S. - JAM. - W. P. - PARK. - FLAT. - NEW HAV. - QUEENS - COLONIE - NEW ROCHELLE - SM. HAV.

ABOUT THE MERCHANDISE: (NOTE: Please complete the following IN DETAIL.)

| ITEM | STYLE NO. | CURR. RETAIL | ADV. PRICE | QUOTE PHRASE & PRICE* | SIZES | COLORS |
|---|---|---|---|---|---|---|
| 1. | | | | | | |
| 2. | | | | | | |
| 3. | | | | | | |
| 4. | | | | | | |
| 5. | | | | | | |
| 6. | | | | | | |

MOST IMPORTANT SELLING POINTS (from customer's view) AND SUPERIORITY TO COMPETITIVE ITEMS. (Use other side if necessary.)

IMPORTANT: PINK SHEETS WILL NOT BE ACCEPTED UNLESS THE FOLLOWING INFORMATION IS PROVIDED.

| 1. TEXTILE FIBER PRODUCTS<br>List all information on the product label. If available, a fiber identification tag may be stapled in place. | 2. NON TEXTILE PRODUCTS<br>Copy from label or tag all information relative to composition of parts of product including finishes. | 3. ELECTRICAL ITEMS<br>Copy all name plate ratings including volts, amps, watts, horsepower, BTU, CFM, etc. Indicate if UL approved. |
|---|---|---|
| | | |

THIS IS A ☐ SALE LAST PREVIOUS DATE ______ LAST PREVIOUS PRICE ______

☐ CLEARANCE ☐ SPECIAL PURCHASE ☐ MFG'S CLOSE-OUT ☐ OTHER

INFORMATION ON COMPARATIVE PHRASES: (Note: Complete in detail as applicable.)

1. ☐ "REGULARLY" - means temporary reduction. Refers to price immediately before sale and price to which merchandise will return following sale.
   (a) period during which merchandise was selling on floor at regular price ______
   (b) approximate number of units ______ Is this the normal selling rate? ______
   (c) Is stock to be augmented with merchandise which is not identical? ______
2. ☐ "ORIGINALLY" - means first price during the recent course of business. (Recent course of business is current selling season for seasonal merchandise such as apparel and sporting goods, etc. and not more than 12 months for non-seasonal merchandise such as furniture, appliances, etc.).
   (a) period during which merchandise was selling on floor at original price ______
   (b) approximate number of units ______ Is this the normal selling rate? ______
   (c) Is stock to be augmented with merchandise which is not identical? ______
3. ☐ "COMPARABLE VALUE" - merchandise of equal grade and quality in all material respects,
   OR
   ☐ "VALUE" - identical merchandise selling in other stores.
   Indicate stores at which merchandise is likely to be found. ______
   ______ If in Macy's stock, indicate style # and price ______

BUYER OR ASST. BUYER | MDSE. ADM. OR V.P. | COMP. OFFICE REPRESENTATIVE

PART 1 ADVERTISING DEPT. COPY

FIGURE 16-2. Advertising request form

Many retailers find that a substantial amount of merchandise can be sold through telephone as well as mail order. Buyers wishing to sell via telephone and mail must indicate that the advertisement should include this information. To facilitate ordering by these means, the ad often will include an abbreviated order form that customers can use.

Sometimes, as an inducement to purchase at a lower price, advertisements will contain a coupon that customers must redeem in the store. Another reason for a coupon is to enable the buyer to determine the success of the ad. The number of coupons redeemed will tell the buyer exactly how much business the ad was responsible for in comparison with the product's total sales.

Many of us have experienced the unhappiness associated with being motivated by an advertisement, only to find that the store doesn't have sufficient quantities of the merchandise. For this reason, many stores require the buyer to indicate the dollar amount and number of units of the merchandise to be advertised. If the amount is low, the store might decide to warn its customers about the limited supply and save itself from harmful repercussions. Some advertising managers are directed by top management to return the request forms to the buyer if the merchandise supply is limited.

Merchandise information facts such as style number, current retail price, advertised price (if it differs from current retail), sizes, and colors are indicated in the appropriate spaces. In addition, the buyer must provide any important selling points that might motivate the consumer to purchase. Since the buyer is the most qualified person in terms of product knowledge, he or she can best indicate selling points. Advertisers merely follow the buyer's suggestions and incorporate them into the advertisement.

Such specific information as fiber content, nontextile information, and electrical terms should be indicated to guarantee appropriate use.

One of the most important portions of the request form is the information on "comparative phrases." Many consumer complaints are registered with better business bureaus and consumer affairs agencies because of misunderstanding on the customer's part, carelessness on the part of the buyer, or intentional misrepresentation. Many states have enacted legislation that clearly defines the often confusing price-related words such as *regularly, originally, comparable value,* and *value.* These terms are not interchangeable and should not be so used. Briefly defined, they indicate the following:

1. *Regularly.* The merchandise in question normally sells at a particular price and is reduced only for a specific time. At the end of the period, the goods will return to the regular or normal selling price.
2. *Originally.* An item that sold at the beginning of a selling season or period at a higher price but has been reduced to a new price. This is usually associated with fashion or seasonal goods or any merchandise the buyer is trying to dispose of.
3. *Comparable Value.* This term is the most confusing to the consumer and is sometimes abused by the buyer. Merchandise advertisements that include

the term *comparable value* or *value* do not indicate that the merchandise ever sold at a higher price, but that *in the buyer's opinion* it is equal in quality to merchandise currently available at other stores.

4. *Value.* A term used to indicate a lower price for identical merchandise at other outlets.

The misuse of these terms is not only illegal in some areas, but often detrimental to the store's reputation. Customers who feel they have been misled can cause considerable damage. Through curtailment of their own shopping at the delinquent store and through word of mouth, they can affect a store's sales. With the enormous amount of competition faced by retailers, it is a smart policy to make certain that customers are satisfied and not misled by shoddy advertising practices.

After the form has been completed, it is signed by the buyer (or appropriate assistant buyer), the merchandise administrator (commonly known as the merchandising manager), and the advertising department representative.

## Layout Approval

The request form, usually accompanied by the actual merchandise to be advertised, is sent to the individuals responsible for the artistic preparation of the advertisement. A loan tag or merchandise receipt is attached to each garment that leaves the department for use in an advertisement. Figure 16-3 features such a tag. After the layout (arrangement of the artwork, photographs, drawings, and copy—the written portion of the message—into a working design) has been created, the buyer should examine it to make certain that all the relevant information has been properly incorporated into the ad. This certainly includes very close inspection of proper terminology and price. How troublesome the wrong selling price can be!

Having verified all pertinent information, the satisfied buyer returns the layout to the advertising department for transmittal to the newspaper, magazine, or other medium that has been designated.

## Proof Examination

In addition to those on the advertising staff who are responsible for the advertisement in production, the buyer should meticulously examine the proof, a sample of the advertisement that has been prepared by the medium and is ready for publication. To the inexperienced buyer it might seem repetitious to examine carefully the proof if the advertising department's layout was studied. But mistakes may occur when an ad is translated from the original layout to the actual plate that has been prepared by the medium. When buyers forgo their right to proof examination because of lack of time, errors often slip through. Commonly they involve price, department number (necessary for

A&S

A.I.S. NUMBER

**MERCHANDISE TO BE ADVERTISED**

**ATTACH SEPARATE TAG TO EACH PIECE OF MERCHANDISE**

☐ NWSP ☐ INSERT ☐ CATALOG ☐ TV ☐ SPEC PRO

DESCRIPTION OF MERCHANDISE

DEPARTMENT NO. | CLASS | RETAIL

EVENT

DATE OR WEEK OF PUBLICATION | LOAN/SAMPLE NO.

SPECIAL INSTRUCTIONS TO ARTIST/PHOTOGRAPHER

RECEIVED IN ADVERTISING BY | DATE

THIS MUST BE SIGNED BY BUYER OR ASSISTANT

AUTHORIZED SIGNATURE | DATE | TEL. EXT.

**MULTIPLE COPY FORM PLEASE USE BALL POINT PEN**

THIS STUB MUST BE PRESENTED TO PICK UP MDS. ALL MERCHANDISE MUST BE PICKED UP NO LATER THAN 10 DAYS AFTER NOTICE OF RETURN FROM STUDIO.

A&S

A.I.S. NUMBER

DESCRIPTION OF MERCHANDISE

DEPARTMENT NO. | CLASS | RETAIL

EVENT | LOAN/SAMPLE NO.

DATE OR WEEK OF PUBLICATION | RECEIVED IN ADVERTISING BY | DATE

AUTHORIZED SIGNATURE | DATE | TEL. EXT.

DEPARTMENT MERCHANDISE RECEIPT

2/84

**FIGURE 16-3.** Department merchandise receipt *Courtesy:* Abraham & Strauss.

phone orders), department location, sizes, and so forth. The results of such mistakes are quite obvious.

After having examined the proof and indicated its correctness or necessary changes, the buyer waits for a tear sheet, an actual copy of the ad taken from the publication.

### Use of Tear Sheets

The tear sheet is used as a record by the advertising department that the ad has been published and must be paid for. A more important use of tear sheets is that undertaken by the experienced buyer. The buyer knows that the appearance of an advertisement in the newspaper is just the beginning of a sound promotional plan. It should motivate customers to come to the store to purchase merchandise (or to buy through mail order or phone order, if applicable). To make certain that customers who have seen the ad can find the merchandise easily, the tear sheet might be placed at the buyer's request, at the store's entrances. This also brings the ad to the attention of customers who have not seen it before. Figure 16-4, features a Neiman-Marcus tear sheet.

Similarly, tear sheets are strategically placed at appropriate places such as elevators and escalators. Their proper usage can enormously increase the effectiveness of the advertisement.

### Notification of Appropriate Staff

Since the buyer is usually the individual responsible for the merchandise that has been selected for an advertisement, it is his or her duty to make certain that greater sales will result. Whether the store is a self-selection unit or is service oriented, the proper notification of particular staff members is essential to the success of the advertisement. In the store where the buyer has an office, this is accomplished by simply calling a meeting of concerned managers, salespeople, and stock people (the goods can sell only of the merchandise is on the selling floor). Even elevator operators should be reminded so that they can direct customers to the right place. In companies that have branches or units away from the buyer's headquarters, notification is done through a directive, complete with tear sheets, to the appropriate manager. It is often the branch store that does the least to make an advertisement work. This can easily be corrected by an alert buyer.

### Evaluation of the Advertisement

Responsibility for evaluation usually belongs to the buyer. It can be a simple comparison of two sales periods for the advertised item—a period in which the item was sold without advertising assistance and the days on which the ad was run. Of course, more involved evaluative techniques may be employed to measure effectiveness. With the assistance of the research department

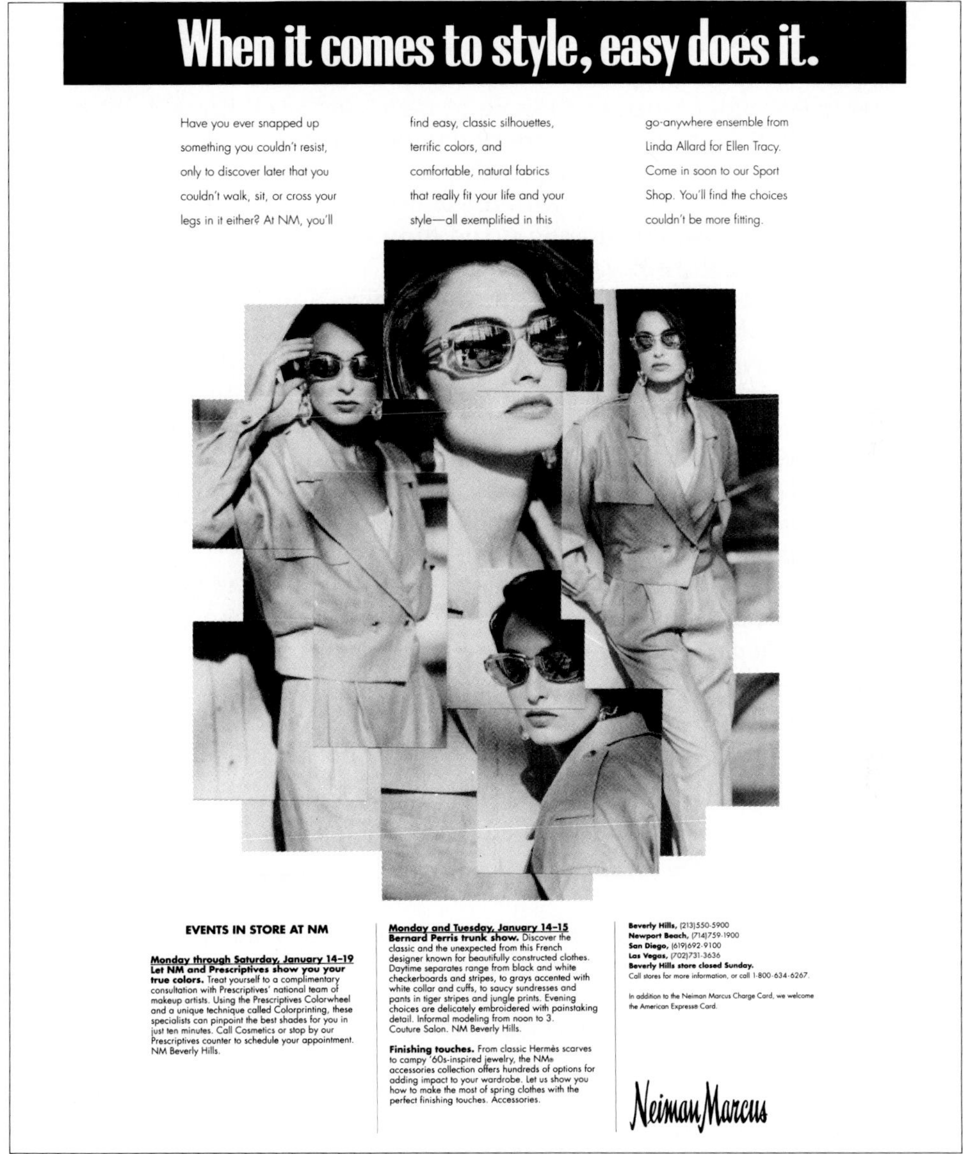


**FIGURE 16-4.** A newspaper tear sheet. *Courtesy:* Neiman-Marcus.

or management personnel, more sophisticated studies can be undertaken that might involve interviews, questionnaires, or traffic counts.

Whether the evaluation is simple or complex, it is the buyer who must decide exactly what information is being sought. Future promotional expenditures are usually based on past experience, and the buyer likes to know if the department's advertising is resulting in desired sales.

## VISUAL MERCHANDISING

*Visual merchandising,* the technical term used to describe the display of goods, is of major significance in the sale of merchandise. With more stores relying on self-selection than ever before, the importance of display continues to grow.

Visual merchandising, in this discussion, includes both the window and the store interior. In fact, with the enormous growth of "windowless" stores in shopping malls, the attention paid to interior display is probably equal to that given window display.

Unlike advertising, in which the buyer's role is limited to selecting merchandise and giving information, display often requires more active participation by the buyer. While windows are generally "dressed" by professional display people even in the smallest stores, interior changes often require the services of the buyer. Whether it is changing a mannequin, rearranging a few pieces of furniture in a room setting, or organizing a counter display of jewelry, the buyer should be able to accomplish the task. Seasoned retailers know that simply moving a piece of merchandise to another location and displaying it in another manner could motivate customers to buy.

Buyers of both soft and hard goods soon come to know the importance of display and their need for the appropriate display knowledge. Waiting for the display department (if a store has one) could result in very long delays. How many sales could have been made if the buyer had had the expertise necessary to make the change!

Figures 16-5 through 16-7 feature window and interior displays that typify the fashion-oriented retailing.

## SPECIAL EVENTS

One aspect of promotion that underscores the retailer's creative ability is the presentation of a special event. These events are termed *special* because they are not part of the everyday merchandising undertaken by the store. They run the gamut from such spectacular productions as Thanksgiving Day parades to informal fashion shows.

Major events such as holiday parades are the work of an enormous number of regular employees as well as specialists who are hired specially for the event. By contrast, the store buyer often plays the major role in a special event that centers on the offerings of his or her department. Such events as cooking demonstrations usually come as a result of the buyer's initiative and creative thinking.

One might question the value of a special event in terms of its cost and resulting customer purchases. While the success of some events is rather difficult to measure exactly, others can be evaulated easily. For example, the home furnishings buyer in a store might, as a special attraction, invite famous interior designers to create a number of model rooms in the store. Incorporated in the

**FIGURE 16-5.** A high-fashion window display. *Courtesy:* Neiman-Marcus.

layouts would be merchandise from the store such as draperies, rugs, lamps, and tables. Once the event has been carefully publicized, careful records of sales of the merchandise in the event can be made and analyzed. Comparisons can then be made between the period preceding the event and the event itself. Perhaps a better example of simple measurement is associated with fashion shows that feature high-fashion designer merchandise from abroad. After the show, which is attended by individually invited guests as well as those notified through newspaper advertisements, racks of merchandise featured in the show are made available to the spectators. A mere glance at the racks and the amount of customer activity can quickly measure the success or failure of the special event. An anxious store buyer is usually on the scene to see if the right merchandise was offered for sale.

Of course it is not always easy to see the exact impact of an event on sales. Take the Macy's Thanksgiving Day parade as an example. It is very difficult to measure its effect on a specific piece of merchandise. Will the lucite clock in the clock department sell better because of the parade? No one can provide an accurate answer. It is, however, an event that has been presented for almost half a century as the signal of the opening of the Christmas selling season, and retailers generally agree that without it sales would be much lower.

Buyers attempt to publicize their departments and stores through special promotional events for two fundamental reasons. First, they attempt to increase their sales immediately; second, they believe that the excitement and curiosity

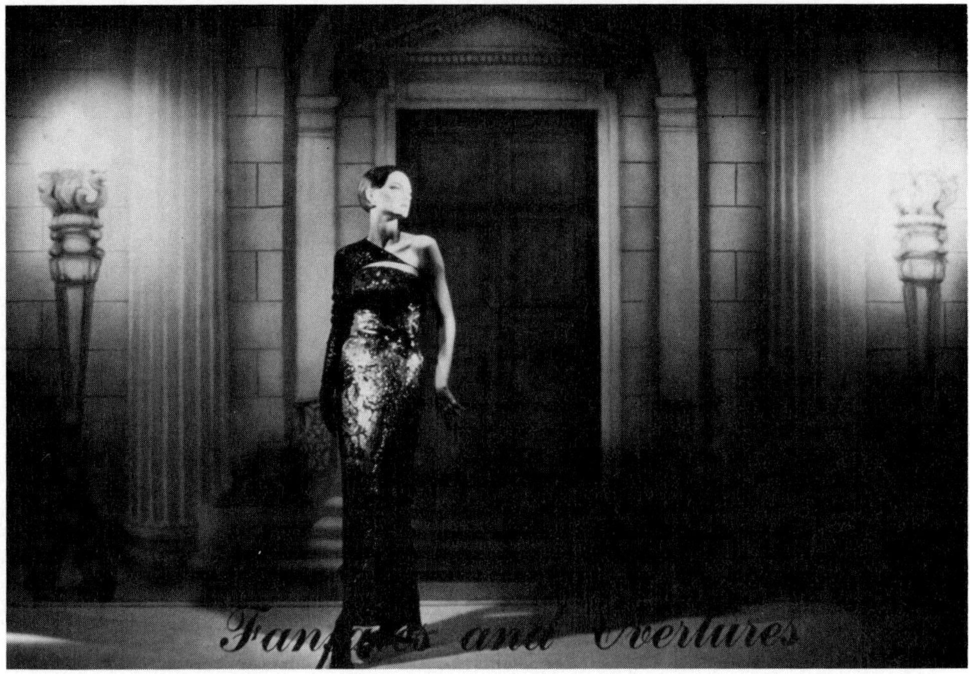

**FIGURE 16-6.** The Fanfares and Overtures promotion at Neiman-Marcus. *Courtesy:* Neiman-Marcus

generated by many of the promotions will eventually translate into increased customer purchases.

Bloomingdale's has regularly presented special events that concentrate on a particular country. For a specific period, the store is visually merchandised with that country in mind. Figure 16-8 features such an event.

Early in the chapter we focused on the buyer's budget for advertisement and promotion. We learned that skillful store buyers increase their advertising dollars through cooperative advertising allowances. Similarly, buyers often incorporate the services and dollars of manufacturers and wholesalers in joint promotions. The experienced buyer, through intelligent negotiation, might convince the manufacturer or wholesaler to participate in a special event at the store that would be beneficial to both parties. Increased sales would obviously improve the department's position and would result in reorders from the vendor.

While these joint ventures are visible in stores throughout the country, it is generally at the buyer's insistence that they become a reality. The buyer, as the direct link between the store and the vendor, is in the best position to motivate manufacturers and wholesalers to participate. Arrangements for such events are not automatic and require considerable negotiation.

The promotions take one of two forms. They are either institutional or geared to specific merchandise.

**FIGURE 16-7.** An interior shoe department visual presentation at Maison Blanche. *Courtesy:* Space Design International.

## Institutional Promotions

If a department or a store plans a promotion to project a particular image or good will rather than specific merchandise, it is called in institutional promotion. Lord & Taylor's Fifth Avenue, New York, store prepares Christmas window displays that feature magnificently attired animated characters rather than merchandise that is sold by the store. So successful has the promotion been that it is repeated annually for the pleasure of the thousands who come to see it. Although the throngs of people are initially drawn to this institutional promotion, their presence is often translated into sales once they have entered the store.

Another institutional promotion that some buyers arrange for is the appearance of famous personalities in their departments. Figure 16-9 shows a public appearance by Catherine Deneuve. Visits to sporting goods departments by noted athletes have steadily produced customer purchases. In fact, Macy's Thanksgiving Day parade is considered an institutional promotion in that it doesn't feature particular merchandise, but rather is supposed to build customer goodwill. Buyers benefit from this kind of promotion in the long run. While it is impossible to measure immediate results in terms of specific items, the institutional approach does eventually bring the department buyer a steady customer rather than the one-time or infrequent prospect.

**FIGURE 16-8.** Bloomingdale's America promotion. *Courtesy:* Bloomingdales.

**FIGURE 16-9.** Institutional Promotion—public appearance by Catherine Deneuve. *Courtesy:* Bloomingdale's.

## Merchandise Promotions

Advertisements in the various media often speak of such spectaculars as the January white sale, furniture warehouse sales, customer opportunity days. August fur sales, assistant buyers' day sales, and so forth. Many of these events are featured on an annual basis, with others being promoted as one-time affairs. In any event, the purpose of these promotions is to sell particular merchandise during a specific period. The promotions might be storewide or confined to a particular department. Whichever is the case, it is the buyers who play the most important part in guaranteeing the success of the event through proper merchandise planning. Carefully planned promotions permit the buyer to dispose of greater quantities of merchandise than normal. The merchandise offered for sale during these periods may include goods already on hand, special purchases that make available merchandise at prices lower than usual, and brand new, exciting items.

The merchandise promotions usually deliver the "punch" buyers need to increase sales. Some of the typical promotions deserve special attention to point out some of the problems that might arise.

### *One-Day Sales*

In an attempt to minimize the cost of a promotional sale, some buyers attempt to squeeze the selling period into one business day. While it might persuade customers to shop that day, the time limit could prove to be disastrous. Perhaps a snowstorm or an excessively heavy rain occurs on the day of the promotion. This could completely wipe out any possibility for a successful sale. To dispose of the merchandise planned for the event (some might have been specifically purchased to bolster current inventories), another day might be necessary. This would require additional advertising, thus increasing the costs of the promotion to a level that could be disproportionate with sales. Buyers should remember that the cost of promotion must be in line with the expected results.

Such abbreviated promotions could also cause traffic jams, intolerable parking conditions, an insufficient number of sales personnel to handle the crowds, abuse of merchandise, and the like. All this could cause customer unhappiness and second thoughts on one-day sales. Figure 16-10 features an advertisement of a one-day sale.

### *Two- and Three-Day Sales*

Special sales that last for two or three days usually avoid the pitfalls of one-day events. They allow customers to shop at more convenient times and with a minimum of discomfort.

Stretching the event longer, to perhaps a week, could result only in spreading out three days' traffic for a longer period, thus incurring unnecessary additional expense. It might also cause a curtailment of regular purchasing.

# 1 DAY SALE

## WED. MARCH 2 9 A.M.-11 P.M.

**Every Serta on sale, including Perfect Sleeper®**

**Every Sealy on sale, including Posturepedic®**

**Every Stearns & Foster on sale, including Correct Comfort®**

**Every Simmons on sale, including Beautyrest®**

**Bonus frame with every sale set**

### 50% OFF

| Twin, ea.pc. | reg. | sale |
|---|---|---|
| Sealy Alton | $90 | $39 |
| Simmons Maxipedic | $180 | $89 |
| Stearns & Foster Comfort Built | $200 | $99 |
| Serta Imperial | $240 | $119 |
| Sealy Hawthorne Posturepedic | $280 | $139 |

### 50% OFF

| Full, ea. pc. | reg. | sale |
|---|---|---|
| Sealy Alton | $180 | $89 |
| Simmons Maxipedic | $240 | $119 |
| Stearns & Foster Comfort Built | $280 | $139 |
| Serta Imperial | $340 | $169 |
| Sealy Hawthorne Posturepedic | $380 | $189 |

### 50% OFF

| Queen set | reg. | sale |
|---|---|---|
| Sealy Alton | $480 | $239 |
| Simmons Maxipedic | $640 | $319 |
| Stearns & Foster Comfort Built | $660 | $329 |
| Serta Imperial | $860 | $429 |
| Sealy Hawthorne Posturepedic | $960 | $479 |

**EXTRA 10% OFF**

ticketed prices on every Serta Perfect Sleeper®, Sealy Posturepedic®, Simmons, Beautyrest® & Stearns & Foster Correct Comfort® with this coupon

(dept. 603) Not at Garden City, Simmons also not at Sunrise, Serta not at Smith Haven. Add $15 delivery.

A&S®

**FIGURE 16-10.** One-day sale. *Courtesy:* Abraham & Strauss.

**FIGURE 16-11.** Two-day sale. *Courtesy:* Abraham & Strauss.

Some customers do not shop during special sales, and lengthy events could result in a loss of their business. An advertisement for a two-day sale is shown in Figure 16-11.

### *Warehouse Sales*

In recent years buyers of some high-ticket items such as furniture and major appliances have organized special warehouse promotions. Customers are invited to the store's warehouse to purchase certain merchandise at reduced prices. In a great number of cases, the promotions have been successful.

Caution must be exercised in the presentation of such an event. First, the hours of the promotion must be arranged so as not to interfere with the normal warehouse operations so the merchandise can continue to flow to the store as needed. Second, merchandise that is not included in the warehouse sale (rarely is everything earmarked for disposal at a reduced price) should be removed from the sale area so that customers will not be confused. Finally, the promotion shouldn't compete with the merchandise at regular price that is available for sale at the store. While these promotions do attract large numbers of customers, they should in no way be detrimental to regular store business.

### *Vendor-Sponsored Events*

Realizing that the lifeblood of the manufacturer is the retailer's ability to sell merchandise, many vendors sponsor or participate actively in a store's promotions. Manufacturers of all types participate occasionally in store events. This might take the form of sending a representative to demonstrate a household item such as a stain remover or a makeup expert to show the virtues of the company's products. Sometimes the promotion involves considerable cost and cooperation and involves many people from the vendor as well as the retailer. For example, a few years ago a major department store jointly sponsored a special event with Corning Glass in the promotion of Corningware. Cooks were used to prepare meals in the Corningware, demonstrations were presented to show the product's ability to resist extreme heat and cold, and so forth. This joint effort proved highly successful for both parties.

The types and levels of involvement for special events are practically limitless. It is the buyer, with the best knowledge of the product area, who is best equipped to come up with good promotional plans.

## COORDINATION OF PROMOTIONAL ACTIVITIES

In order to ensure the success of any promotion or special event, proper coordination of all promotional devices used by the store is necessary. That is, advertising, visual merchandising, store signs, and so forth should be coordinated to ensure maximum exposure to the prospective customer.

Buyers cannot rely on other managerial personnel for properly executed promotional presentations. While each promotion department will do its job expertly, only the buyer can make certain that the promotion presents a complete package. In other words, advertising must be used to bring the customer to the store, coordinated window displays should further motivate the customer to enter the store and find the appropriate department, and within the department the merchandise must be displayed appealingly to invite purchasing.

Too many promotions have failed because customers couldn't find the advertised event. The result is misuse of valuable promotional dollars and loss of sales.

## ACTION FOR THE SMALL STORE BUYER

Advertising, to be effective, must be planned by professionals. Large stores have advertising departments that plan their ads, usually with buyer input. Small stores not only don't have advertising experts in house but usually have little, if any, money set aside for advertising. Anyone who is knowledgeable in retailing, however, knows the value of advertising, no matter how small the store.

All is not lost for the small store. The buyers for such companies should seek out vendors who participate in cooperative advertising. Many suppliers are eager to get the company's name in print and are willing to pay for it. Through this method, the small store buyer would only have to pay half the cost of the ad.

Advertising isn't the only promotional avenue for small stores. Buyers may organize such special events as fashion shows at little or no cost. By contacting a social or charitable organization, a buyer could use the group's premises and members as models. This event shows off the store's merchandise to a preselected audience at virtually no expense to the store. Participation in the sponsoring of local contests, athletic teams, offering of discounts for a one-day sale with a percentage going to charity, and so forth are some other low-cost events that any store could organize.

If the buyer is creative, there is no limit to the amount of promotional activity in which its store could participate.

## SUMMARY OF KEY POINTS

1. Buyers are not called upon to create advertisements or visual presentations but are expected to initiate promotions, select appropriate merchandise for advertising and displays, and provide the necessary information for the experts to use in promotional preparations.
2. Promotional budgets are determined in a number of ways. Most commonly, buyers receive amounts that are commensurate with their expected volume; they may receive amounts disproportionate to their volume if the store wants to build up the particular department.
3. Cooperative advertising allowances bring vendor dollars to the store and increase the amount the buyer has to spend for promotional purposes. While this is generally desirable, the buyer shouldn't be influenced to purchase solely because of the cooperative allowance. The merchandise is the most important factor to be considered.
4. Buyers should select "proved" merchandise to be promoted. Experts agree that the promotion of unwanted merchandise will not increase its salability and will only result in misuse of the promotional budget.
5. The planning of an advertisement is initiated by the buyer in most retail organizations. The buyer must have money available in the budget,

carefully complete the necessary request forms, work closely with the advertising staff, and alert all staff to ensure the success of the advertisement.

6. Most large stores have professional visual merchandisers who execute window displays, while smaller retailers generally resort to free-lancers. The buyer, however, must have some knowledge of visual presentation to make the everyday changes required in the department.
7. Special events and promotions are activities that bring larger than usual crowds to the buyer's department. Knowledgeable buyers often originate the themes of special events and persuade vendors to participate with money as well as expert personnel.
8. If a promotion is to be successful, it is important for the buyer to make certain that all promotional activities such as advertising and display are properly coordinated to bring the customer right to the point of purchase.

## REVIEW QUESTIONS

1. Must the buyer be an advertising expert to play a satisfactory role in the promotion of goods?
2. On what general basis is the decision made as to how large a promotional budget a department is to receive?
3. How does a buyer increase his or her promotional dollars without having the store spend more money?
4. Are there any pitfalls in cooperative advertising for the store buyer?
5. Why do vendors participate in cooperative advertising?
6. Describe indirect advertising and its advantages for retailers.
7. If you were a store buyer, what would you consider in the selection of the merchandise to be advertised?
8. Who initiates the creation of an advertisement in most store organizations?
9. Of the media available, which do retailers use most extensively? Why?
10. Which sources of market information are available to buyers to use in determining the most appropriate advertising media for their promotion?
11. Compare the terms *regularly* and *originally* as they relate to advertising.
12. How do the advertising terms *comparable value* and *value* differ?
13. Is it sufficient for an advertisement proof to be examined by the layout people, or must a buyer be involved?
14. In what way may a tear sheet be used to carry out an advertising campaign?
15. Aside from sales personnel, whom should the buyer notify of an impending advertisement?
16. When might it be necessary for the buyer to have visual merchandising proficiency?
17. In your own words, describe the term *special event*.

18. Differentiate between institutional and merchandise promotions, and give an example of each.
19. Is the institutional form of promotion worthwhile? Defend your answer.
20. Discuss the importance of the coordination of advertising, window display, and interior display in a promotion.

## CASE PROBLEM 1

Taft's Department Store, a five-unit organization located in New England, has been in business for 35 years. It is considered to be one of the most successful operations of its kind in that region. Throughout its many years of operation, it has continuously provided its clientele with the finest, most unique merchandise available. Some of its merchandise, in fact, is available to no other organization within a 300-mile radius. Customers seeking the unusual in soft and hard goods have come from great distances to avail themselves of Taft's offerings.

For the past year the company has witnessed a considerable increase in its costs of operation. Management has held several high-level meetings to develop strategies to combat the higher cost of doing business. Many suggestions were made, including consolidation of the business day, which would decrease the payroll; fewer customer services; a campaign to discourage charge purchases; and a substantial decrease in the promotional budget.

Each senior manager was asked to digest the recommendations that had come forth at the meetings and suggest the most appropriate course of action. At the final decision-making meeting, it was management's consensus that a reduction in the promotional budget was the best plan. Against heavy opposition from the buyers, management argued that promotional dollars were available from many vendors and would make up for the deficiency in the budget.

The buyers were asked to organize their thoughts concerning their opposition to management's decision and be prepared to present their reasons at a future meeting.

### Questions

1. Are cooperatively sponsored promotions advisable in retailing?
2. Can Taft's possibly become as involved in this type of cooperation as other retailers?
3. Describe the disadvantages that might result from too much emphasis in cooperative promotion.

## CASE PROBLEM 2

Jane Camden has been appointed as the new furniture buyer for the Bliss Department Stores on the West Coast. Unlike most department stores, which emphasize soft goods, Bliss does the majority of its business in furniture. It carries a full assortment of traditional as well as contemporary upholstered furniture, case goods, and home accessories.

Although sales have kept pace with projections, management believes the company has never realized its full potential in furniture sales. Hence the decision to hire Ms. Camden, who has a reputation for excellent purchasing ability and a keen knowledge of merchandise production.

For her first special furniture event, Ms. Camden has decided on a warehouse sale so that she can quickly reduce the inventory developed by her predecessor. Understanding some of the drawbacks of warehouse sales, she nonetheless feels that this is the best technique to employ without radically altering the company's regular selling floors in the various stores.

Being a meticulous planner, Ms. Camden always carefully prepares each aspect of the promotion.

## Questions

1. In her preliminary outline, which areas should Ms. Camden consider?
2. Which media would you suggest she use to advertise the event?
3. For what duration should the event be presented? Why?
4. Can you suggest a better first event than the warehouse sale?

# GLOSSARY

**ADVERTISING.** Any paid form of nonpersonal presentation and promotion of ideas, goods, or services by an identified sponsor.

**ADVERTISING AGENCY.** A company that completely specializes in all aspects of advertising, beginning with creation of an ad and ending with its placement. For these services agencies are paid commissions by the media.

**ADVERTISING MANAGER.** The person responsible for all types of advertising that the buyer needs to prospect for customers.

**AGENT.** A business unit which negotiates purchases or sales or both but does not take title to the goods in which it deals.

**AIR EXPRESS.** Express service on regularly scheduled airlines.

**AIRFREIGHT.** Shipment by airfreighter planes. Quick and less expensive than air express.

**ANTICIPATION.** A special form of cash discount.

**ASSISTANT BUYER.** An individual who assists the buyer by taking over his or her less responsible tasks.

**BRANCH STORE.** A subsidiary retailing business owned and operated at a separate location by an established store.

**BRAND.** A name, term, sign, symbol, design, or a combination of them, intended to identify the goods or services of one seller or group of sellers and to differentiate them from those of competitors.

**BRAND NAME.** A brand or part of a brand consisting of a word, letter, or group of words or letters comprising a name that is intended to identify the goods or services of a seller or a group of sellers and to differentiate them from those of competitors.

**BROKER.** An agent who does not have direct physical control of the goods but represents the buyer or seller.

**BUYER.** The individual responsible for purchasing merchandise for a retailer operation.

**BUYING MIX.** The elements of buying: what to buy, how much to buy, and from whom to buy.

**CALIFORNIA APPAREL NEWS.** This is a regional trade paper that brings information concerning new merchandise, market weeks, and so on to retailers and other industrial participants on the West Coast.

**CASH DISCOUNT.** A reduction in price for prompt payment.

**CENTRALIZATION.** An arrangement under which one group of centralized managers controls all of the units in the organization.

**CHAIN STORE SYSTEM.** A group of retail stores of essentially the same type, centrally owned and with some degree of centralized control of operation. The term *chain* store may also refer to a single store as a unit of such a group.

**CHAMBRE SYNDICALE DE LA PARISIENNE.** The organization that regulates the fashion industry in Paris.

**CHANNEL OF DISTRIBUTION.** The structure of intracompany organization units and extra company agents and dealers, wholesale and retail, through which a commodity, product, or service is marketed.

**COLLEGE BOARD.** A consumer panel composed of college students.

**COMMISSIONAIRE.** A foreign resident buyer.

**COMPARISON SHOPPER.** An individual who provides comparative information on other retailers in the areas of price, display, promotions, and merchandise.

**COMPUTER HARDWARE.** The physical machinery of a computer installation.

**COMPUTER PROGRAM.** A set of computer instructions for solving a particular data-processing problem.

**COMPUTER SOFTWARE.** Programs, routines, and documents associated with the computer.

**COMPUTER TIME SHARING.** The renting of computer time at a commercial computer center.

**CONSIGNMENT BUYING.** An arrangement under which title to goods does not pass until the buyer resells the merchandise.

**CONSUMER PANEL.** A group of consumers used by stores for information on merchandise, pricing, and so forth.

**CONSUMER'S REPORT.** The periodical published by Consumer's Union.

**CONSUMER'S UNION.** A nonprofit organization that supplies accurate product information.

**CONTRACT.** An agreement between two or more competent parties that is legally enforceable.

**CONVENIENCE GOODS.** Those consumers' goods which the customer usually purchases frequently, immediately, and with the minimum of effort in comparison and buying. Examples of merchandise customarily bought as convenience goods are tobacco products, soap, newspapers, magazines, chewing gum, small packaged confections, and many food products.

**COOPERATIVE ADVERTISING.** Advertising that is paid for by both the manufacturer and retailer.

**COOPERATIVE BUYING.** An arrangement by which individual orders are pooled to qualify for discounts.

**COOPERATIVE CHAIN.** A grouping of independent retail stores organized for the purpose of competition with chains.

**COOPERATIVE RESIDENT OFFICE.** A buying office that is owned and operated by a group of stores.

**CREDIT AGENCY.** An institution that provides credit information.

**CREDIT LINE.** The amount of credit an organization is willing to extend to its customers.

**CREDIT MANAGER.** The person responsible for the extension of customer credit and supervision of collections of customer accounts.

**CUMULATIVE MARKUP.** Markup on goods on hand divided by retail price of goods on hand.

**DECENTRALIZATION.** An arrangement in chain store organizations that allows individual store managers to make decisions in such areas as merchandise selection, promotion, and markdowns.

**DEPARTMENT STORE.** A large retailing business unit that handles a wide variety of shopping and specialty goods, including women's ready-to-wear and accessories, men's and boy's wear, piece goods, small wares, and home furnishings, and that is organized into separate departments for purposes of promotion, service, and control. Examples of very large department stores are Macy's, New York; J. L. Hudson Co., Detroit; Marshall Field's & Co., Chicago; and Famous-Barr, St. Louis.

**DIRECT MAIL ADVERTISEMENT.** Advertisements that reach their markets exclusively through mail.

**DIRECT RETAILING.** Selling to consumers in their homes through such means as catalogs and cable television.

**DISCOUNT HOUSE.** A retailing business unit, featuring consumer durable items, competing on a basis of price appeal, and operating on a relatively low markup and with a minimum of customer service.

**DISPLAY MANAGER.** The person responsible for interior and window display.

**DOLLAR MERCHANDISE PLAN.** A budgetary system of merchandising based upon dollar amounts.

**DUN & BRADSTREET.** A credit checking agency.

**ELECTRONIC DATA PROCESSING.** An electronic system for processing masses of information.

**EOM.** End of month.

**FASHION COORDINATOR.** A specialist in fashion show production, style, and color forecasting who works closely with the store buyer.

**FISHY-BACK.** A transportation system in which a trailer truck is loaded directly onto a barge.

**F.O.B.** Free on board.

**F.O.B. DESTINATION.** Title to goods passes when it arrives at its destination. Since the vendor owns the goods until then, he pays freight.

**F.O.B. FACTORY.** Title passes at the point of shipment.

**FOCUS GROUP.** A small group of individuals who are questioned in terms of preferences. Their responses are analyzed to help make changes in product marketing and selling.

**FRANCHISING.** An exclusive arrangement whereby an individual and an operating company do business together in a specified way.

**HAND-TO-MOUTH PURCHASING.** Buying when the need arises.

**HARD GOODS.** Merchandise such as appliances and furniture.

**HAUTE COUTURE.** High fashion.

**HUMAN RESOURCES MANAGER.** The individual responsible for staffing the store and overseeing the various employee programs.

**IMPULSE GOODS.** Goods purchased without prior planning.

**INCOME STATEMENT.** A summary of revenues and expenses for a period of time.

**INDEPENDENT RESIDENT OFFICE.** A resident buying office that offers services to independent stores for a fee.

**INDEPENDENT STORE.** A retailing business unit controlled by its own individual ownership or management rather than from without, except insofar as its management is limited by voluntary group arrangements.

**INDIRECT ADVERTISEMENT.** A manufacturer's advertisement that mentions a store's name.

**LANDED COST.** The total cost of imported goods to the retailer.

**L.C.L.** Less than a full freight carload.

**LEASED DEPARTMENT.** An independently operated department within a department store.

**LINE ORGANIZATION.** A form of organization in which authority flows (in a straight line) from top management to lower levels.

**LOSS LEADER.** A product of known or accepted quality priced at a loss or no profit for the purpose of attracting patronage to a store.

**MAIL-ORDER HOUSE (RETAIL).** A retailing business that receives its orders primarily by mail or telephone and generally offers its goods and services for its sale from a catalog or other printed material.

**MANUFACTURER'S AGENT.** An agent representing a number of noncompeting lines of merchandise.

**MANUFACTURER'S BRAND.** Merchandise that has a manufacturer's brand attached. Frequently such goods have a following that is more important than the store's image.

**MANUFACTURER'S STORE.** A retail store owned and operated by a manufacturer, sometimes as outlets for his goods, sometimes primarily for experimental or publicity purposes.

**MARKDOWN.** Reduction in selling price.

**MARKET.** (1) The aggregate of forces or conditions within which buyers and sellers make decisions that result in the transfer of goods and services. (2) The aggregate demand of the potential buyers of a commodity or service.

**MARKET ANALYSIS.** A subdivision of marketing research that involves the measurement of the extent of a market and the determination of its characteristics.

**MARKETING.** The performance of business activities that direct the flow of goods and services from producer to consumer or user.

**MARKETING RESEARCH.** The systematic gathering, recording, and analyzing of data about problems relating to the marketing of goods and services. Such research may be undertaken by impartial agencies or by business firms or their agents for the solution of their marketing problems.

**MARKUP.** Difference between cost and retail price.

**MARKET WEEK.** A periodic event at which buyers from all over the country attend to preview manufacturer's new lines.

**MAZUR PLAN.** A four-function (merchandising, control, advertising and publicity, store management) organization plan.

**MERCHANDISE INVENTORY.** The value of goods being offered for sale.

**MERCHANDISE INVENTORY TURNOVER.** Cost of goods sold divided by average inventory.

**MERCHANDISE MANAGER.** The buyer's immediate supervisor whose responsibilities include overall merchandise decision making.

**MERCHANDISING PLANNING.** Supervision involved in marketing the particular merchandise at the places, times, prices, and quantities that will best serve the marketing objectives of the firm.

**MERCHANT.** A business unit that buys, takes title to, and resells merchandise.

**MIDDLEMAN.** A business concern that specializes in performing operations or rendering services directly involved in the purchase and/or sale of goods in the process of their flow from producer to consumer. Middlemen are of two types: merchants and agents.

**MINICOMPUTER.** A small computer designed for small- and medium-sized businesses.

**MODEL STOCK.** The assortment that a department offers.

**NATIONAL BRAND.** A manufacturer's or producer's brand, usually enjoying wide territorial distribution.

**NET PROFIT.** The profit after deducting cost of goods sold and operating expenses.

**NRF.** National Retail Federation the largest and most important retail trade association.

**OFF-PRICE RETAILER.** A merchant who buys merchandise at lower prices and sells it for less to the consumer. Buying later in the season gives the merchant a price advantage.

**OPEN-TO-BUY.** The difference between the merchandise available and the merchandise needed for a particular period.

**OPERATING EXPENSES.** All expenses of doing business other than the cost of merchandise sold.

**OPTICAL SCANNER.** A device used for converting hand-printed data into EDP machine language.

**PERSONNEL MANAGER.** See Human Resources Manager.

**POINT-OF-SALE TERMINAL.** A cash register that inputs directly into the computer.

**POSTDATING.** A means of extending the credit period.

**PRICE AGREEMENT PLAN.** A system of central merchandising for chain organizations in which the individual store has the greatest amount of independence.

**PRICE CUTTING.** Offering merchandise or a service for sale at a price below that recognized as usual or appropriate by its buyers and sellers.

**PRICE LEADER.** A firm whose pricing behavior is followed by other companies in the same industry.

**PRIVATE LABELS.** Clothing lines sponsored by merchants or agents as distinguished from those sponsored by manufacturers or producers.

**PRIVATE RESIDENT OFFICE.** A buying office that is maintained specifically for and owned by one company.

**PRODUCT LINE.** A group of products that are closely related either because they satisfy a class of needs, are used together, are sold to the same customer groups, are marketed through the same type of outlets, or fall within given price ranges, for example, carpenters' tools.

**PUBLICITY.** Nonpersonal stimulation of demand for a product, service, or business unit by planting commercially significant news about it in a published medium or obtaining favorable presentation of it on radio, television, or stage that is not paid for by the sponsor.

**RACK JOBBER.** A wholesaling business unit that markets specialized lines of merchandise to certain types of retail stores and provides the special services of selective brand and item merchandising and arrangement, maintenance, and stocking of display racks.

**RESIDENT BUYER.** An agent who specializes in buying on a fee or commission basis, chiefly for retailers.

**RESOURCE DIARY.** A detailed alphabetical listing of resource characteristics.

**RETAILER.** A merchant, or occasionally an agent, whose main business is selling directly to the ultimate consumer.

**RETAIL NEWS BUREAU.** A fashion reporting service.

**ROBINSON–PATMAN ACT.** An act that forbids price discrimination.

**R.O.G. (RECEIPT OF GOODS).** Dating does not begin until the goods are in the hands of the buyer.

**SALES ANALYSIS.** A subdivision of marketing research that involves the systematic study and comparison of sales data.

**SALES FORECAST.** An estimate of sales in dollars or physical units for a specified future period under a proposed marketing plan or program and under an assumed set of economic and other forces outside the unit for which the forecast is made. The forecast may be for a specified item of merchandise or for an entire line.

**SALES PROMOTION.** (1) In a specific sense, those marketing activities, other than personal selling, advertising, and publicity, that stimulate consumer purchasing and dealer effectiveness, such as visual merchandising, shows, and exhibitions, demonstrations, and various nonrecurrent selling efforts not in the ordinary routine. (2) In retailing, all methods of stimulating customer purchasing, including personal selling, advertising, and publicity.

**SCANNER.** The part of a point-of-sales terminal that automatically records the information on the merchandise tag.

**SELF-SERVICE.** The method used in retailing whereby the customer selected his own merchandise, removes it from the shelves or bulk containers, carries it to a check-out stand to complete the transaction, and transports it to the point of use.

**SHOPPING GOODS.** Those consumer's goods that the customer in the process of selection and purchase characteristically compares on such bases as suitability, quality, price, and style.

**SOFTWARE.** Computer instruction packages.

**SPECIALIZED DEPARTMENT STORE.** Companies such as Neiman-Marcus and Saks Fifth Avenue that restrict their merchandise offerings to one major classification.

**SPECIALTY GOODS.** Those consumers' goods with unique characteristics and/or brand identification for which a significant group of buyers are habitually willing to make a special purchasing effort. Examples of articles that are usually bought as specialty goods are specific brands and types of fancy foods, hi-fi components, certain types of sporting equipment, photographic equipment, and men's suits.

**SPECIALTY STORE.** A retail store that makes its appeal on the basis of a restricted class of shopping goods.

**STAFF RELATIONSHIP.** An organizational relationship that provides advisory services to line positions.

**STANDARDIZATION.** The determination of basic limits or grade ranges in the form of uniform specifications to which particular manufactured goods may conform and of uniform classes into which the products of agriculture and the extractive industries may or must be sorted or assigned.

**STORE MANAGER.** The person with full responsibility for the operation of the store. This includes security, housekeeping, and so forth.

**TEAR SHEET.** A copy of an advertisement.

**TERMINALS.** Devices that are connected to a computer for input or output purposes, for example, typewriters or visual display units.

**TRADE ASSOCIATION.** An organization of businesses with like characteristics.

**TRADE DISCOUNT.** A deduction from list price used to differentiate between buyers.

**TRADEMARK.** A brand or part of a brand that is given legal protection because it is capable of exclusive appropriation; because it is used in a manner sufficiently fanciful, distinctive, and arbitrary; because it is affixed to the product when sold, or because it otherwise satisfies the requirements set up by law.

**TRADING AREA.** A district whose size is usually determined by the boundaries within which it is economical in terms of volume and cost for a marketing unit or group to sell and/or deliver a good or service.

**VARIETY STORE.** A retailing business unit that handles a wide assortment of goods, usually in the low or popular segment of the price range.

**VISUAL MERCHANDISING.** The practice of presenting merchandise in window settings and interiors that enhances their sales.

**VOLUNTARY CHAIN.** A group of retail stores organized by a wholesaler from whom purchases are made.

**WANT SLIP.** A form used by retailers to record customers requests that are not in stock.

**WAREHOUSE AND REQUISITION PLAN.** A central merchandising system where the central buyer determines the assortment but relies upon the store manager to control inventory levels.

**WHOLESALER.** A business unit which buys and resells merchandise to retailers and other merchants and/or to industrial, institutional, and commercial users but which does not sell in significant amounts to ultimate consumers.

**WOMENS' WEAR DAILY.** A trade publication specializing in women's clothing and accessories.

# INDEX

## R



## S



## T